D0893760

MANUAL OF LEXICOGRAPHY

JANUA LINGUARUM

STUDIA MEMORIAE
NICOLAI VAN WIJK DEDICATA

edenda curat

C. H. VAN SCHOONEVELD

INDIANA UNIVERSITY

SERIES MAIOR

39

MANUAL

OF

LEXICOGRAPHY

LADISLAV ZGUSTA

in cooperation with

V. ČERNÝ, Z. HEŘMANOVÁ-NOVOTNÁ, D. HEROLDOVÁ, L. HŘEBÍČEK,
J. KALOUSKOVÁ, V. MILTNER, MINN LATT Y., L. MOTALOVÁ,
K. PETRÁČEK, K. F. RŮŽIČKA, I. VASILJEV, P. ZIMA, K. ZVELEBIL

1971

ACADEMIA
PUBLISHING HOUSE OF THE
CZECHOSLOVAK ACADEMY
OF SCIENCES
PRAGUE

MOUTON
THE HAGUE · PARIS

Scientific Editor:

Dr. Josef Filipec

Scientific Adviser:

Prof. Dr. Vladimír Skalička

CORRESPONDING MEMBER OF THE
CZECHOSLOVAK ACADEMY OF SCIENCES

Published with a support granted, on the recommendation of the CIPSH, by UNESCO

TABLE OF CONTENTS

Chapter II: Formal Variation of Words

Chapter III: Combinations of Words

Chapter IV: Variation in Language

CHAPTER V: THE TYPES OF DICTIONARIES

CHAPTER VI: THE MONOLINGUAL DICTIONARY

Chapter VII: The Bilingual Dictionary

Chapter VIII: Planning and Organization of Lexicographic Work

FOREWORD

In 1960, the United Nations Education, Science, and Culture Organization (UNESCO) offered a contract to the International Council for Philosophy and Humanistic Sciences (document 866717) to inquire into the situation in the domain of lexicography; the latter body offered the contract, in its turn, to the Union Académique Internationale. The Inquiry was undertaken and the final report was written by Professor C. C. Berg (Leiden).[1]

Acting on the recommendation of the report, UNESCO and CIPSH (Conseil International de la philosophie et des sciences humaines) partly co-sponsored, in 1962, a special international colloquium, organized by the Oriental Institute of the Czechoslovak Academy of Sciences, to discuss the problems of lexicography, mainly in the field of the languages of Africa and Asia. The final resolution of this colloquium mentioned also the desire that a Manual of Lexicography be prepared.

In consequence of this resolution, and in consequence of the continued interest in lexicography, evidenced in the sittings of UNESCO and some of its commissions, this Organization offered a contract to CIPSH for the purpose that the present book be written. On the recommendation of CIPSH (suggested by the resolution of the Prague colloquium mentioned above), the Oriental Institute of the Czechoslovak Academy of Sciences accepted the task of preparing the book. The contract having been concluded, UNESCO has not failed to aid the work on the book's preparation, as provided by the terms of the contract. This help has meant very much for the elaboration of the manuscript and for the necessary studies to be made on a really international scale, and we take great pleasure in stating our appreciation of the support. We also appreciate very much the help of the CIPSH: without this help it would probably have been impossible to surmount the different intricate problems and recurrent difficulties connected with some aspects of the work.

---

[1] The report was published by CIPSH as a booklet with the title "Report on the Need for Publishing Dictionaries which do not to-date exist, prepared by the International Academic Union", sine loco, sine anno.

The present book intends to discuss lexicography in its broad aspects, but with a concentration on monolingual and bilingual dictionaries; the hope is that the book will be useful to those who work on lexicographic projects or plan such undertakings. On the other hand, we also hope that a coherent statement and discussion of lexicographic problems will help to clarify them, and to demonstrate the importance of their being conceived in the framework of the linguistic theory more effectively. In spite of this general character of the book, we have in mind above all those lexicographers who work with languages which do not enjoy a long philological or even lexicographic tradition, as is frequently the case of the languages of Africa and Asia. The Amerindian languages do not enjoy a long tradition either, but their extralinguistic situation is different. Therefore, considerable space is given, in the present book, to the discussion of problems and examples taken from some of these languages. The respective examples and their linguistic interpretation are supplied by the co-authors. The respective passages for which the co-authors are basically responsible are usually preceded or—only exceptionally— followed by their respective names. For the rest of the book including its whole conception, the main author who has signed this foreword is responsible; the same applies to the occasional pronouns "I", or "we" unavoidably interspersed throughout the text. Exceptions to this general rule are duly marked in the footnotes.

One of the strangest features of lexicography is the fact that lexicographers have only rarely exchanged methodical experience: it was not until 1965 that B. Quemada started to publish reports about lexicographic projects on which work is in progress, discussions of the methods used and procedures applied. These reports are being published under the heading *Travaux lexicographiques en cours*; the first of them was published in Quemada's *Cahiers de lexicologie* 6, 1965, 105ff. But coherent discussions of lexicographic theory and practice are also very rare. If we omit papers which discuss different particular problems (they will be mentioned at the relevant places of the present book), we can find above all the following publications of a broader theoretical interest:

(1) L. V. Ščerba, *Opyt obščej teorii leksikografii* ("Attempt at a general theory of lexicography"), I, published in *Izvestija Akademii Nauk* SSSR 1940, Nr. 3, 89—117. (An English summary of the paper can be found in the English review of it by P. L. Garvin, Word 3, 1947, 129—130.)

(2) G. Devoto, *Dizionari di ieri e di domani*, Firenze 1946. (A volume of papers and reviews of different Italian descriptive dictionaries and etymological dictionaries. There are many ideas of general validity interspersed among the discussions of concrete problems.)

(3) R. W. Chapman, *Lexicography*, London 1948.

(4) J. Casares, *Introducción a la lexicografía moderna*, published in *Revista de filología española* 52, 1950. (There is also a Russian translation

of the paper, published in the form of a book: Ch. Kasares, *Vvedenie v sovremennuju leksikografiju*, transl. by N. D. Arutjunova, edit. by G. V. Stepanova, Moskva 1958.)

(5) B. Migliorini, *Che cos' è un vocabolario*, Firenze 1951 (2nd edition).[2]

(6) *Lexikografický sborník bratislavský* (The Bratislava Volume on Lexicography, a volume of reports read and discussed at a lexicographic conference in Bratislava, 1951), published by Vydavateľstvo Slovenskej Akadémie vied, Bratislava 1953.

(7) *Leksikografyčnyj bjuleten'* (Lexicographic bulletin; a series of volumes containing papers on lexicography, the first of them published:) Kiiv 1951.[3]

(8) W. Doroszewski, *Z zaganień leksykografii polskiej*, Warszawa 1954.

(9) J. Hulbert, *Dictionaries British and American*, London 1955. (Rich experience collected during a life-long lexicographical activity.)

(10) P. L. Garvin, *Problems in American Indian Lexicography and Text Edition* (published in: *Anais do XXXI Congr. International de Americanistas*, p. 1013ff.), Sao Paolo 1955.

(11) F. Hiorth, *On the Subject Matter of Lexicography* (published in: *Studia linguistica* vol. 9, 1955, p. 577), and *On the Foundations of Lexicography* (published in: *Studia linguistica* vol. 11, p. 8ff), 1957.

(12) *Leksikografičeskij sbornik* (a series of volumes containing papers on lexicography, six volumes to date, the first of them published:), Moskva 1957.

(13) I. J. Gelb, *Lexicography, Lexicology, and the Akkadian Dictionary* (in: *Miscelánea homenaje a André Martinet "Estracturalismo e historia"*, ed D. Catalán, vol. II, Canarias 1958) p. 63ff.

(14) *Problems in Lexicography*, report on the conference on lexicography held at Indiana University November 11—12, 1960, edited by Fred W. Householder and Sol Saporta, Bloomington 1962 (Indiana University Research Center in Anthropology, Folklore, and Linguistics, publication 21, also Part IV of the International Journal of American Linguistics, 28, 1962, Nr. 2).[4]

(15) L. Országh, *A szótáríras elmélete és gyarkorlate a Magyar nyelv ertelmezo szótárában*. (The Lexicographic Theory and Praxis in the Magyar explaining dictionary. Nyelvtudományi értekezések 36.) Budapest 1962. (I was unable to use this Magyar book extensively; a Russian paper containing a summary of L. Országh's experience is published in Leksikografičeskij sbornik 5, 1962. Cf. also his paper "Problems and Principles of the New Dictionary of the Hungarian Language", *Acta Linguistica* 10, 1960, 211ff.)

(16) S. Urbańczyk, *Słowniki, ich rodzaje i użyteczność*, Wrocław 1964.

---

[2] Prof. I. J. Gelb's suggestion; the date of the first edition is unknown to me.
[3] I owe my knowledge of this item to O. Leška.
[4] Cf. also the detailed review of K. D. Uitti, *Romance Philology* 16, 1962—3, 416ff.

(17) A. Rey, *Les dictionnaires: forme et contenu* (published in *Cahiers de lexicologie* 7, 1965, p. 65ff.).

(18) M. Mathiot, *The Place of the Dictionary in Linguistic Description: Problems and Implications*, Language 43, 1967, 703ff.

(19) G. Wahrig, *Neue Wege in der Wörterbucharbeit.* (Berichte des Instituts für Buchmarktforschung, Sondernummer.) Hamburg 1967.

(20) The *Cahiers de lexicologie* edited by B. Quemada; though not devoted exclusively to lexicography, they contain many papers concerned with it and belong to the most important publications in the field. (First volume published in 1959.)

These publications represent the most extensive efforts to date which discuss coherently the experience of lexicographers and the theoretical problems underlying their work. It is to be hoped, and it is very probable, that the publication of all these works is a symptom of a growing interest in the problems of lexicography. It goes without saying that we are greatly indebted to the single works mentioned above; we have naturally tried to express our obligation everywhere in the present book where it has seemed necessary, but it is probably impossible to acknowledge every mental stimulation.

At present, when the experience gained in work on lexicographic projects is not generally accessible, at least not on international scale, one of the main sources of information concerning the methods of lexicography is a careful study of the good dictionaries at present available. As far as this source of information is concerned, I have certainly tried to base my work on a general study of various dictionaries of different languages.[5] There are, however, some dictionaries to which I am more indebted than to others, because I draw very much from the experience accumulated in them; it is quite natural, I think, that it is in the first place certain Czech dictionaries to which I owe much in this way: after all, it is one's own native language of whose intricacies one has the easiest, quickest, and most comprehensive understanding. In this respect, I was fortunate enough to make use of the outstanding monolingual Czech dictionary published by the Institute of the Czech language of the Czechoslovak Academy of Sciences: an excellent work such as the *Slovník spisovného jazyka českého* (vol. I, Prague 1960, etc.) is such a mine of accumulated knowledge and experience that I can state my indebtedness to it only generally, without quoting it in every instance. In the field of bilingual

---

[5] But it should be stressed that the present book does give neither a survey nor a bibliography, nor an evaluation of existing dictionaries. (Cf. Pulgram, *Word* 3, 1947, 222, with good remarks in a similar respect.) For obvious reasons, we had to use some existing dictionaries of different languages to get some of the necessary material; though we, naturally, preferred to use good dictionaries, this does not imply that we regard the dictionaries quoted for this purpose as absolutely good or the only good ones, nor does it imply that we regard dictionaries of different particular languages that are not quoted here as being necessarily bad.

dictionaries, the same applies to the English-Czech and Czech-English Dictionaries of I. Poldauf (mainly I. Poldauf, *Česko-anglický slovník*, Praha 1959): again, I can state my obligation to them only generally. Third, I have had the good fortune of being involved in not a small number of lexicographic projects, in different capacities ranging from the immediate direction of the undertaking, through the status of a consultant, to the position of an interested colleague with whom things are discussed. The principal foci of this activity were mainly the *Oriental Institute* in Prague, the *Institut für Orientforschung der Deutschen Akademie der Wissenschaften* zu Berlin, and the *Xussar Irystony zonad-irtasság institut* in Tsxinvali (Southern Ossetia, USSR). I have gained from the discussion of various problems with different lexicographer colleagues more than I can state, but my gratitude is not less warm. Finally, the present book has the advantage that I was able to discuss large parts of it in such lexicographic centers as those at the University of Chicago, University of Texas (Austin), University of California (Berkeley), and Stanford University, and that the manuscript or parts of it were read by V. Abaev (Moscow), O. S. Akhmanova (Moscow), B. Fraser (Cambridge, Mass.), E. Hamp (Chicago), J. Filipec (Prague), I. J. Gelb (Chicago), P. Garvin (Los Angeles), D. J. Georgacas (Grand Forks), O. Leška (Prague), M. Mathiot (Los Angeles), I. Poldauf (Prague), and by the late U. Weinreich (New York). I wish to state my profound gratitude to these scholars for all their valuable remarks and observations. Some are duly mentioned in the respective places, but it was impossible to acknowledge every detail. Different colleagues were also kind enough to help with my English version. But the final responsibility, and above all the responsibility for the selection and interpretation of the English examples[6] (as, for that, the responsibility for all other examples not specifically acknowledged) rests with myself.

Prague, May 1968

L. Zgusta

---

[6] The analyses and presentations of the multiple meaning of English lexical units are taken from or inspired by Hornby, *Concise Oxford Dictionary*, and *Webster's Third*. All important and the majority of unimportant cases are specifically acknowledged. (To Hornby we owe also many examples of definitions and other techniques used for illustration. (It may happen that some readers will not agree with some of these analyses and presentations. This is inevitable, at least to some extent, because of the differences between the single speakers (cf. the remark on my Czech examples). On the other hand, the situation is considerably easier in respect to the English examples, owing to the now vastly current practice of testing the acceptability of sentences and expressions indiscriminately with one speaker from, say, Oshkosh, another from Laredo, and yet another from Boston, for that: after all, the authors of the dictionaries just mentioned are or were native speakers of English themselves, so why not accept them as well.

INTRODUCTION

0. There can be no doubt that lexicography is a very difficult sphere of linguistic activity. Many lexicographers have given vent to their feelings in this respect. Perhaps the most colourful of these opinions based on a lexicographer's long experience is that of J. J. Scaliger (16th—17th cent.) who says in fine Latin verses that the worst criminals should neither be executed nor sentenced to forced labour, but should be condemned to compile dictionaries, because all the tortures are included in this work.

H. A. Gleason,[1] a scholar of our epoch, states more succinctly but not less to the point: "Dictionary making is tedious in the extreme. It is exacting. It is an incredibly large job."

0.1 What are the reasons for these difficulties? It would serve no real purpose to try to enumerate them in isolation at this juncture, as they will become apparent from the whole book. It will, however, be useful to mention at least the following circumstances.

First, one could say in a very simple and naive way that "the lexicographer should know everything". Though he concentrates upon those properties of the lexical units (usually words) which stand at the focus of his attention (above all, the lexical meaning in its different aspects, but also the grammatical properties of the lexical units, we shall see that in order to do his work well, the lexicographer must take into consideration not only the whole structure of the language in question, but also the culture of the respective linguistic community in all its aspects, to mention only two outstanding fields of his immediate interest. "The theory of lexicography is connected with all the disciplines which study the lexical system) semantics, lexicology, grammar, stylistics ...", states the editorial paper in the first issue of the *Leksikografičeskij sbornik*[2] and this statement is echoed from the other side of the Atlantic by the equally correct dictum that "the dictionary is ... the meeting place of all the systems linguistic and non-linguistic which bear relevantly on speech

[1] PL 88.
[2] LS 1, 1957, 3.

behavior".[3] And let us not forget that the lexicographer is working with open classes of phenomena, because the number of words is generally not limited: if there is a need, a new word is created, or an existing one gets a new sense, etc. Therefore, the lexicographer can never know whether his collections of data are complete (which they practically never are) or at least sufficient, quite apart from the practical limits of his work set usually by financial considerations and considerations of time. Furthermore, the lexicographer cannot eliminate the element of linguistic change which may soon render antiquated even those indications he worked out with the greatest possible care and which were correct at the time of his work.

Second, the fact that it is precisely the meaning of the lexical units upon which the lexicographer concentrates his attention, presents very special difficulties of its own. We shall see in the chapter dealing with lexical meaning on what slippery ground we are. But not only this. In the last decades, the desire of a great number of linguists to make only what are usually called objectively verifiable statements, to avoid any introspection, and similar reasons have caused a certain neglect of semiasological problems or even an a version against the suspect notion of meaning. It would be true, at least to a very great extent, to state that the descriptive methods and procedures concentrate very much upon the form, meaning being generally taken into consideration only when it is necessary to find out what is linguistically relevant and how it is relevant. This attitude is not necessarily a mistake in itself: we shall see in the following discussion that the linguistic meaning is carried by the linguistic form. Without form, there is no meaning: only this makes language interpersonal. But Gleason[4] is certainly right when he says that "as now practised [the] operations [of dictionary making] are quite different from those in which the descriptive linguist feels thoroughly at home". It must be said, however, that it would be absolutely false to give the impression that the difficulties of lexicography are somehow caused by certain features of some descriptivist "schools". It can be observed that those difficulties are also felt in different countries in which the influence of descriptivism has been (or, in some cases, was) rather limited.

Thirdly, we must not forget that the lexicographer is doing scientific work, but that he publishes it for users whose pursuits are always more practical, at least as regarded from his own point of view. It would seem that this remark is true only in the case of the more or less commercial dictionaries for the general public. But on the contrary, the statement has a general validity. Let us consider a case like the *Thesaurus linguae Latinae*, or an Assyrian dictionary. Naturally dictionaries like these will never be used by a "general public" but only

[3] Gleason PL 101.
[4] PL 88.

by scholars. But even in these and in similar cases, the lexicographer must never forget that the scholars who will consult his dictionary will not usually be lexicographers by profession; they will have no or no great lexicographic sophistication, and will know neither his full intentions on how to deal with all the intricacies of the material nor the motives that underline his solutions and presentations. Therefore, even such highly specialized lexicographic works are written for a public for which the information sought in the dictionary is the main concern; the purely lexicographic specificities receive much less attenion. Usually, one does not read dictionaries from the first page to the last; one consults the single entries. Therefore, each entry must be, so to say, self-contained; and one must not suppose that the user, before reading the entry, will ponder too much about general lexicographic problems. The basis of a sound and efficient lexicographic work is a good theory, but on the other hand, the dictionary is written for a user who will not be primarily seeking to much of lexicographic theory nor a wide array of lexicographic problems presented in it; the user will be interested in finding quite different information, viz. indications concerning the facts of the respective language itself. In other words, the user of a dictionary does not wish, at least usually, to have the purely lexicographic problems presented, but to have them solved. As far as the majority of dictionaries goes, one cannot only say with full right that the general user must always be taken into consideration,[5] but also that a dictionary is good "if the theory which is inherent in it is so unobtrusive that it is no obstacle to the general user".[6] It would seem that this dual aspect of the lexicographer's work can be regarded as an additional difficulty.

0.3 The more astonishing is "the indifference which lexicography displays towards its own methodology".[7] Indeed, with some exceptions, the most important ones of which have been mentioned in the foreword, discussions of purely lexicographic problems are very rare. What we find at the utmost are analyses of isolated problems, reports on lexicographic projects in progress- or planned, and reviews of dictionaries published. But "the theory of lexicography is more than a generalized editorial instruction or than the technical rules of compilation".[8]

One of the primary purposes of the present book is to be of some use in this situation. We believe that a coherent discussion of the problems of lexicography, or at least of the more important ones of them, will be useful if not for their solution, so at least for a better understanding of them and for finding

---

[5] Ďurovič LSB 65.
[6] Havránek, Poznani 189.
[7] Weinreich PL 26.
[8] Editorial paper in the first issue of LS 1, 1957, 3.

ways to handle them more efficiently. We also believe that such a coherent discussion is useful because we suppose that lexicography (along with other adjacent branches of linguistics) will be given much more attention in the near future than has been the case hitherto. On the practical side, we have the fact that education, knowledge of different languages, and contacts between different communities are spreading. On the theoretical side, semantics has been relatively so very much neglected that it observably begins to come more into the focus of attention, if for no other reasons, then simply because of the pressure of the unsolved problems. And then, let us not forget that not only for many theoretical approaches such as the generative grammar, but also for undertakings such as machine translation it is precisely the mutual dependence (or interdependence) of "lexicon" and "grammar" which is of first-class importance.

0.3 Besides this general purpose, the present book intends to be particularly useful to the development of lexicography in Africa and Asia, above all in respect to the modern standard national languages of the area.

0.4 The present book tries to analyze the theoretical issues implied in lexicography, or at least to outline the more important ones. In connection with this, different topics of general linguistics must be discussed, though linguistic sophistication is not what the book necessarily seeks or presupposes.[9] Two remarks should be made:

First, we do not say that the theoretical approaches preferred in this book or suggested in it are the only possible ones, but we try to suggest those approaches and points of view which are, on the strength of our experience, the most useful, or let us say, practical ones, for the lexicographer's purposes. Second, some of the linguistic approaches suggested here are observably rather conservative. This is not only a matter of preference. Lexicography is an activity in which tradition plays a great role. Nobody is suprised when it takes half a century or so to compile a really big academic dictionary of a language. To plan at least a decade for a medium lexicographic undertaking or project is a matter of course. Once published, a good dictionary is used for many years, and new editions usually do not and cannot change the very conceptual basis of it. Consequently, Sledd[10] is absolutely right in his opinion that "the lexicographer cannot shift with every word that flutters the leaves of Word".[10a] But

---

[9] This is why we do not give detailed or even exhaustive bibliographical indications. It is our policy to indicate, if possible, only those publications which deal especially with lexicography and which are primarily connected with the lexicographer's theory and practice.

[10] PL 147.

[10a] It seems that this dictum will have to be modernized: "the lexicographer cannot shift with every inquiry published in *Linguistic Inquiry*".

it is not only the lexicographer's responsibility to tradition which is the cause of this, but also the sheer impossibility to change things, methods, and procedures once settled and decided upon, when work is in a progressed stage. Lexicography is traditional and will remain so, at least to some extent, within the near future. Of course, things may change slightly if more interest is given to lexicographic theory and if new work procedures or ways of presentation are developed, tried out, and used. But a more radical change is conceivable only in connection with some possible future developments in lexicography and related branches of linguistics, discussed in § 8.5.

Thus Gleason[11] is right when he says that "the current practice (of lexicography) is largely a result of a slowly accreting tradition". Therefore, what we are also trying to do is to sketch this tradition, or, to put it differently, to collect the experience of our profession. Of course it is out of the question to expect that we could achieve complete success in this task. As far as methods are concerned, it is very seldom that they are discussed or explained;[12] sometimes, they are not even described.[13] And as for practical experience, sometimes gained by bitter and costly trial-and-error, we can observe, precisely from lexicographic practice, the phenomenon that it is not collected and analyzed with the same attention as in other sciences. This is hard to believe, because lexicographic projects use to be rather costly, both in terms of time and money. I know, however, from my own observation how often it happens that problems already solved in a satisfactory way by a group working on a lexicographic project are again discussed and experimented upon in another group. Perhaps most lexicographic problems seem to be brought about primarily by the specifities of the concrete language with which the respective lexicographic project is concerned, and one does not always imagine that one could and should seek information in the experience of a lexicographic group concerned with a different language with absolutely different specifities of its own. Yet some of the problems of lexicographic analysis and presentation are surprisingly general, irrespective of the language in question. In any case, should this book succeed only in one single thing, namely in stimulating authors of lexicographic projects and of dictionaries to publish descriptions or discussions of their methods and approaches to their specific problems, as well as their solutions, to discuss all this within the more general framework of the linguistic theory, and not only to incorporate their theoretical results "as unobtrusively as possible" in their dictionaries of the most different languages of the world, we shall consider it a sufficient success.

[11] Gleason PL 90.

[12] Weinreich PL 26: "Lexicography uses many methods, none of which have been fully explained."

[13] Inquiries into the fundamental concepts of lexicography (like the studies of F. Hiorth, quoted in the Foreword) are exceedingly rare.

2*

0.5 The present book will also give some practical advice to lexicographers, above all to those colleagues who plan different projects of (linguistic) dictionaries, monolingual or bilingual. It would, however, be preposterous to expect that such advice should be very detailed and concrete. In spite of the lexicographic generalities mentioned in the above paragraphs, and many others as well, every language has enough specificities of its own. And not only that; every lexicographic project has also many specificities of its own, caused by its purpose, by its cultural background and tradition, by its expected public, and by the personal abilities and preferences of its authors. The lexicographer's work is always creative, in a greater or a lesser degree, because he must always try to find new solutions to problems as yet unsolved.[14] The lexicographer's work cannot be reduced, up to the last detail, to the application of a set of fixed rules and procedures. Apart from the real generalities of lexicography, probably the best universal advice the lexicographer can be given is that he should know the relevant properties of his lexical units as well as possible, and on the background of the whole system of language at that;[15] and that he should have a very clear picture of his future dictionary's disposition and of its purpose in his mind, and preferably on paper, before he begins the concrete work. The best procedures to choose are much influenced by fundamental facts, solutions, and decisions in both these respects.

[14] Cf. Havránek LSB 210.

[15] If the lexicographer knows the history of the language, so much the better. A knowledge of the cultural context is a matter of course.

CHAPTER I

LEXICAL MEANING

1.0 Lexical meaning stands in the center of the lexicographer's attention It is necessary to discuss it at the very beginning of the book, because practically all decisions of the lexicographer are in a direct or indirect relation to the way in which he deals with lexical meaning, in his dictionary.

To explain the motion of lexical meaning, it will be useful to interpret some simple examples in a rather impressionistic and oversimplifying way.

Even somebody who knows nothing about linguistics but has a reasonable command of English will understand the meaning of a sentence like

"Please give me the big book!"

He will understand that the situation involves at least two persons, a certain object, a command or desire that this object be transferred to, or put at the disposal of the person who uttered the sentence, and an expression of the politeness of the speaker (*please*). If this sentence is heard or read without any context (either the verbal context — supplied by something heard or read before and afterwards, as when one reads a sentence in book, or the *situational context* — supplied by what the people involved in the situation are doing, if one directly observes the respective situation itself,[1] by somebody to whom it is not addressed some points remain unclear, e.g., who the persons are, what book should be given, whether the giving of it implies only a movement in space or also the possession of it, and many others. On the other hand, it will be clear that the sentence pertains to a concrete situation, either actual in life, or fictive in fiction.[2]

The same linguistically unsophisticated but English speaking person will also understand that the meaning of the single words in the sentence is something different. The sentence was said to pertain to a concrete situation. A

---

[1] Note that there is some overlapping between the two types of context. For instance, when we read a novel, verbal descriptions supply what would be the immediate situational context in real life.

[2] It cannot be our intention to discuss here the problem of the sentence in all its intricacies. We attempt only to convey a general idea in order to have some basic concepts understood.

word like *book* can be, on the contrary, used in reference to any concrete object which belongs to this class of objects, or even in reference to similar objects. In the same way, the English speaking person will have no difficulty to in understanding that the word *big* refers to a quality of the object "book", but can be attributed to or predicated about a variety of other objects. The word *give* would probably cause a slightly greater difficulty to our supposed unsophisticated speaker of English, but he will surely understand that it is intended to describe an action of one of the persons involved in the situation, and that it can be used whenever such an action is to be referred to again.

On the other hand, the unsophisticated observer of the language would not fail to have the impression that forms like *book*:*books* and *give*:*gave* differ somehow in their meaning but that the respective basic notion remains the same: the object or the class of objects remains identical but there is a difference in their number; the action remains identical but there is a difference of the time in which it took place.

If asked, the mythical English speaker of ours would have no difficulty in pointing, in the extralinguistic world, to different objects which can be called *book*, to different objects which have the quality of being *big*; and he could either point to or imitate by his own behaviour the action of *giving*, at least as concerns the physical action of giving an object to somebody, outside of the more abstract or even legal sphere of the application of the verb: in this latter sphere, a real understanding of the word is not possible without the introduction and understanding of some concepts connected with the possession of things and possible changes of the possessor.

Even a very unsophisticated observer of the language would hardly fail to notice that the same speaker can, for example, characterize the same object once as big and at the same time as small, in relation to other objects; this discovery would lead him to see that the speaker's evaluations and categorizations (carried and expressed themselves in great measure by linguistic means again) are also important.

And even the most unsophisticated speaker of English (provided he absorbed the English manners with the English language) would have a good, if not quite clear, idea of what is conveyed by the word *please*; and this would show him, on reflection, that a clear-cut counterpart in the physical world is not necessary for a word's meaning.

And above all, the speaker of English (as well as of any other language) will have no difficulty in knowing that he can use the same words, as they are stocked in his memory, in different actual situations, in reference to different concrete objects, i.e., to use them in building different sentences.

We can comprehend the notion of lexical meaning on the background of this example: *Words* can be conceived as interpersonal units of language, as signs of the system of a language which are used by the speakers of that language above all to construct sentences. In the sentences, words are used to refer to parts of the extralinguistic (not necesarily material or physically really existing) world, as understood by the respective speakers, to indicate the sentence's constructional patterns, and to perform other similar functions which will be discussed later (§ 1.3.1.1).

Our further discussion will show that this is only a very rough model, in any respect. Notwithstanding its sketchiness, we assume that the reader will understand the notion of "lexical meaning", at least intuitively; we hope, however, to refine the notion in the following paragraphs. We shall see, for example, that it is not only single words which carry lexical meaning and are constituent elements of sentences, but also much more complex units (see § 3.3.4), so that we should rather speak about *lexical units* in order to cover both the simple and the more complex ones. It is only for the sake of simplification that we speak about words; as already stated, what has been said is meant only as a starting point for the discussion, to give the first general idea. And this is also the reason why we begin our whole discussion with the concept of lexical meaning, and not with the form of the words (lexical units); we shall see (§ 3.3.4) that their form is rather irrelevant: they are constitute more by the lexical meaning they carry than by anything else.[3]

SEMANTICS

1.1 The science, or the branch of linguistics, which studies lexical meaning is usually called s e m a n t i c s, or, less frequently in English, s e m a s i o l o g y. Let us say at once that it is one of the most difficult fields. There are many difficulties in this sphere of research, only some of which we shall mention.

There is no agreement among linguists, or at least no impressively strong concord of opinion, about the very nature of lexical meaning. Some are inclined to interpret it in more or less psychological terms, assuming that there are mental processes involved in the situation. Some linguists conceive of meaning rather as a property of the linguistic forms themselves, as their ability to refer to something, or their capability of standing for something

---

[3] Though the matter is probably sufficiently clear, we wish to prevent any misunderstanding by the statement that we put into contradistinction the lexical meaning of the particular, individual lexical units which constitute the sentence against the meaning of the sentence constituted by them. The contradistinction *lexical meaning* : : *grammatical meaning*, important in some terminologies and approaches, is apparently not too successfully established, at least not from the point of view of the present approach: one could maintain that it confuses, on the one hand, the designative and other functions of lexical units (cf. § 1.8), and the syntactic patterns and the morphological variation on the other.

else; other linguists see in lexical meaning only the regularity with which words are used; still other linguists think that words themselves have no meaning apart from the contexts in which they are used, etc.

The lexicographer will do well to give great attention to all researches in the field of semantics: the more he knows about the semantic properties of the words, the better he will do his job.[4] But on the other hand, the lexicographer will be well advised not to be too much impressed by the basic uncertainty concerning the nature of the lexical meaning. The problem of the nature of meaning is certainly broader than the lexicographer's tasks; it is probably even broader than the purely linguistic investigation, since it requires a combination of linguistic, psychological, philosophical, and other approaches. The lexicographer's activity, however, can be conceived as a rather pragmatic one, at least in this respect. It is no agnosticism when F. Hiorth[5] states his opinion: "... it is by no means certain that a clarification of the nature of meaning beyond what is known today is desirable for the purpose of present-day lexicographical research. Perhaps, an increased clarification of meaning would not change a bit in the actual research habits of the lexicographers." The present book is not a book on semantics, but on lexicography. Therefore, it takes no stand in this question. It may be that my personal preference (which is a rather psychological one) will nevertheless influence the text of some paragraphs; but we hope that this will do no harm, should it happen. Anyhow, what we put forward in the following text is not a complete semantic theory and it claims neither exhaustiveness nor exclusive correctness. What we put forward are such modes of understanding the problems of meaning and such approaches to work in this field as have been found most useful in the lexicographer's practice.[6]

THE SYSTEM AND THE APPLICATIONS

1.2 Another difficulty connected with the study of lexical meaning is more serious. It is caused by the circumstance that we try to obtain knowledge of the lexical meaning of a word as a part of the system of language, but our main source of direct information are collections of concrete utterances.[7] Let

---

[4] But some lexicographers doubt this, e.g. I. J. Gelb (private communication).

[5] Studia linguistica 9, 1955, 57.

[6] Cf. Weinreich PL 28 sq.: "Several ... semantic theories ... seem to be excluded as the bases of lexicography."

[7] As the only exception to this can be regarded the lexicographer's ability to derive from his own knowledge of the language in question, or preferably from his native speaker's competence, a direct descriptive or rule-like statement concerning the use of the respective lexical unit; and, similarly, the descriptive or rule-like statements of the informants, derived usually from their

us discuss this with the help of a simple example; and as it is both useful and by now traditional to employ a simpler system of signs than language for such an explanation, let us discuss the problem on the model of the traffic signs.[8]

Any person who possesses the driver's licence will know not only that there are traffic signs, but also that there is a finite number of them, and that they form a well balanced system (in many countries of Europe, all prohibitions are usually of circular, all warnings of triangular, and all informative signs of rectangular shape). And not only this: the driver is in the happy situation that he knows not only the types and classes of the signs, but even also the precisely defined meanings of all the single traffic signs before he begins to drive. This means: he can learn and know the whole system of the traffic signs and the meaning of its individual parts, i.e. of the individual sings, as laid down by the highway code. He can know the interpersonal, generally valid and obligatory code before he meets the actual manifestations of it. When he begins to drive, he identifies the individual, actual traffic sings he meets with the single traffic signs — members of the system, i.e. of the code he knows, and he has no difficulty in understanding their meaning. Let us now imagine the situation of a person who drives a car without a previous knowledge of the code of the traffic signs. Such a person would meet the posts with the traffic signs and would have to try to find out a significant, repeated co-occurrences of different circumstances with the individual signs; e.g., he would very soon observe that when he sees a red, yellow, or green light, there is a crossroad there, and that the other drivers display an observably uniform behaviour when seeing those lights. By observing the actual situations, namely the co-occurrence of different lights and differences in the drivers' behaviour, he would no doubt be able to reach the generalizing conclusion about what rule governs the lights and the drivers' movements. In this way, he would recognize particular lights as distinct units of the system of traffic signs and would recognize their meaning; and he would apply this knowledge when meeting another occurrence of them.

But even in this very simple and unambiguous system of traffic sings, there would be signs whose meaning would be hard to establish exclusively by

own knowledge of their native language. This exception, however, covers only a small part of the lexicographer's tasks. If he works with informants, the lexicographer usually tests their statements by the construction of contexts or whole sentences (sec § 6.3.2.1). And even if he works in the sphere of his native language, the lexicographer knows only a part of it: the unknown or less known part of his native language (which is always much larger than anybody without a direct experience in the field would suspect) is studied in a similar way as any non-native language, perhaps more easily but without great methodical differences. More than that: even within the range of his knowledge, the lexicographer will be keenly interested in borderline cases and will study them by testing the acceptability of pertinent contextual examples. Cf. below, p.

[8] Even this model is not original; its choice has some tradition. Cf. Garvin, *Natural Language and the Computer*, New York 1963, p. 9, as an example of this "tradition".

direct observation of the actual occurrences. It would probably be very difficult to get at the meaning, at least under normal circumstances, of a sign like the great capital *H* on a rectangular shield (which means, in many countries, that there is a hospital not far away), by the simple observation ot its occurrences only: the posts with this sign stand in very different surroundings and, furthermore, a uniform effect on the behaviour of the other drivers is hardly observable.

It goes without saying that the comparison implies a very strong simplification, because no artificial code reaches the complexity, richness, and creativity of natural language, but up to a degree, the lexicographer's situation is frequently comparable to that of the man who tries to get at the meaning of the traffic signs while driving rather than to that of the man who has a perfect knowledge of the abstract system before he begins to drive. Of course there is a vast difference between the work on a dictionary of an extinct language, where the meaning of the word can be established only by philological interpretations of their actual occurrences in the relevant passages and between work on a dictionary of one's own native language. In this case, the lexicographer has the necessary knowledge of the system, as manifested by his ability to generate sentences. But his knowledge of the system is never complete, the meanings and the rules of the application of the single signs of this system are not so clear-out as it would seem, and the system itself changes constantly. Interpretations of the actual occurrences of signs, in this case of the lexical units (words) and conclusions concerning their value in the system are, therefore, a constant component of the lexicographer's work, even if he compiles a monolingual dictionary of his own native language. If the lexicographer intends to compile a monolingual dictionary, his data, his material consists chiefly of many contextual quotations of the individual words, i.e., of examples of their actual occurrences in different aurroundings. From these different applications, the lexicographer must derive the generalized description, or formulation, of the lexical meaning of which these applications (and eventually also the future ones) are actual manifestations.[9]

This is the real difficulty in lexicography; the data consist exclusively of concrete, different applications of words (lexical units), but the goal of the lexicographer's work is their abstract value in the system.[10]

---

[9] In the field of bilingual lexicography the difficulties are even more severe and the situation is even more complicated, but the basic contradistinction *words as parts of the system* : : *words in actual utterances* (or *lexical units as parts of the system* : : *lexical units in actual utterances*) is the same.

[10] The fact that the lexicographer, especially when he studies his own native language, must and should use his own knowledge of it and not rely only on the excerpted slips does not change this situation. Cf. § 6.3.2.

This problem will be discussed in greater detail § 1.4. For the moment, it is necessary to remember that when we speak about lexical meaning, we generally have in mind the meaning of words (lexical units), as parts of the system of language.

THE COMPONENTS OF LEXICAL MEANING

1.3 The lexical meaning comprises a great number of different components and there are many pertinent phenomena and relations which must be studied completely, but preferably as dictinct, interdependent factors, if the whole lexical meaning of a word (lexical unit) is to be analyzed, understood, and described. It will be useful to discern the following main components of lexical meaning:

(1) the *designation*,[11]
(2) the *connotation*, and (possibly)
(3) the *range of application*.

1.3.1 By the term designation we mean above all the relations existing between the single words and the single parts of the extralinguistic world, as conceived by the speakers of a language.

It will be easy to understand that such a word as *book* has a relation to a type of material objects of the extralinguistic world. The thing itself, or, more precisely, the class of things to which the word has this type of relation is often called the denotatum.[12] The denotata will, then, be the classes of things in the extralinguistic world we speak about. It should be understood that not only things of the material, physically existing world are denotata of words. Any speaker of English will feel that a real, really existing quality of an object is the denotatum of the word *big*. In the same way, he will feel that a really existing action of a subject is the denotatum of the verb *to run*.[13]

[11] What we term *designation* is frequently called *denotation*. We choose the first term (after a discussion with U. Weinreich (precisely because in the majority of cases, the lexicographer is more concerned with the designata than with the denotata. — Cf. Horálek, *Filosofie jazyka* (Acta Universitatis Carolinae philologica, monographia XV, Praha 1967), p. 79 for a good discussion of the pertinent concepts and terms, broader than the present one; I do not mention the single points of agreement, nor those of disagreement.

[12] Semantic terminology shows the same lack of unification as linguistic terminology generally. Different scholars use different terms. Very often, the student will meet the terms *thing-meant*, *referent*, *referend* and others, used approximatively in the value of *denotatum*. It should be said, however, that the concepts of those scholars who use these different terms are not identical by far, so that it is not possible to feel free to use any of these terms as stylistic variants.

[13] Cf. Havránek LSB 15.

It would be, however, absolutely wrong to think that there is a direct relation between the "word" and the "thing";[14] on the contrary, one of the most important things in semantics is the fact that the relation between the word and the denotatum is not a direct one: there is the designatum between the word (lexical unit) and the denotatum.[15]

The designatum is a very elusive element of the lexical meaning. It can be described as the notion[16] of the respective "thing", of the denotatum, as conceived by the speakers of a language.[17] We can illustrate this by some simplifying examples.

Any speaker of English will use in his conversations the word *table* (piece of furniture) and there is usually no difficulty with the denotatum in the material, physical world in such a case. The point is that if the speaker of English sees a concrete piece of furniture the first time in his life, he is able to decide (in the majority of normal cases) whether he should call it a table or not. Obviously, the human mind is capable of abstracting from many individual and different occurrences of a "thing" a general notion also new occurrences of the members of the class. Such a notion is, then the designatum,[18] a component of the lexical meaning of a word.

We can imagine that this operates about as follows. If we remain in the sphere of our example (*table*), we can say that each piece of furniture has a vast number of qualities and properties. But when we are deciding whether we shall call a concrete piece of furniture a table, we find that it is irrelevant whether the piece is of wood or of metal; it is irrelevant whether it is brown or white; it is irrelevant whether it is beautiful or ugly, expensive or cheap, antique or modern, big or small; etc., etc.: all these and many other qualities and properties are irrelevant. There are, however, a few qualities or properties

---

[14] We must not forget that to speak about "things" in this respect is highly figurative, loose language. All formulations that try to be more precise tend to be cumbrous. Another good possibility is to speak about "segments of the extralinguistic world".

[15] Again, different scholars use different terms.

[16] Words like *notion, concept*, etc., are used here with their general meaning, not as terms defined by any school of psychology or philosophy.

[17] The plural "speakers" is vitally important there: though the creative power of the original new conceptualization of a single speaker is one of the forces in the development of language, it is primarily the interpersonally stabilized notions of the speakers as expressed in their language which are of importance. Cf. § 4.1, p. 164 on individual differences.

[18] Whether what is rather psychologistically called *notion* really is what is called *designatum* in linguistics, or whether there is only a correlation of the two, must remain unclear or undecided for the moment.

[19] All this is very unclear and difficult, above all because this is an area not yet sufficiently explored, and largely belonging to other sciences or at least overlapping with them. Though all this could be discussed also in other terminologies and different conceptual frame-works, we hope that what has been stated will suffice to give the lexicographer at least an intuitive understanding.

which really are relevant: the respective piece of furniture must form a flat, roughly horizontal surface on which other things can be put and which is supported by one or more legs. Any piece of furniture which can be thus described can be called a table in English; we can say that these qualities are criterial for our decision. The designatum can be visualized as consisting of the criterial features corresponding to these criterial qualities,[20] both if it pertains to a part of the material world and if it does not.

A good part of the lexicographer's research is concerned with establishing criteriality, with the task to find what is criterial and what is not, with the necessity to discover the criterial features as precisely as possible.[21] There is no universal repertory or inventory of criterial features valid generally in all the languages; some criterial features seem to be universal (but it will need yet much investigation to state them with some precision), but what seems to be an endless number[22] of them varies from one language to another. What is irrelevant, non-criterial in one language, can be relevant, criterial in another. For instance, the criterial features of Eng. *table* are identical with those of Czech *stůl* (roughly = "table"). But for the designatum of Czech *stůl*, the purpose of the furniture is not criterial: whether it is used for eating, or work, or games, or writing is irrelevant. For the designatum of Engl. *table*, however, the purpose of the piece of furniture is criterial: if a similar piece of furniture is used primarily not for eating but for writing and generally for work, this is criterial for the constitution of the designatum of Eng. *desk*, in contrast to *table*, which is generally not used in this case (negative criteriality).[23]

English *morning* (just as French *matin*) can be used in reference to any part of the day between dawn and noon (or the mid-day meal: Hornby); no other circumstance is criterial. In Czech, German and Swedish, a further temporal specification is criterial: Czech *ráno*, German *Morgen* can be used only in reference to a part of the day up to, say, 9 or 10 a.m., Swedish *morgon* only up

---

[20] There is a vast area of overlapping between what we have discussed here and the *defining qualities* and *accompanying qualities* of logic, etc. It is preferable, however, to remain in the sphere of linguistics proper, as far as it is possible. — Some authors prefer to use the term *criterial attributes*.

[21] We shall return to this in § 1.7.3.

[22] "endless" is not to be understood in the mathematically precise sense of "infinite". If all languages of the world were semantically analyzed to the last detail, the number of criterial features might be found to be finite, at one point of the development. All such speculation is pure theory, however; in any case, any semantic change could add to them or reduce their number.

[23] There will be also differences beetween the two designata, but for the purpose of this discussion, it is not necessary to mention them. — In any case, it is interesting to see (as reported by Zima) that the Eng. word *table* was borrowed in Hausa in the form *teebùr* with the meaning of "table"; it seems, however, that it is sometimes used also in reference to a desk (for which Hausa gadon rùbùutin verbatim "pad for writing", was recently coined), so that the English criteriality (originally introduced with the objects and expressions) seems to be disappearing.

to 6 a. m.[24] Those parts of the day which are not covered by *ráno, Morgen, morgon* can be referred to by Czech *dopoledne*, German *Vormittag*, Swedish *förmiddag*, respectively: these latter words have designata for which the criterial temporal boundaries are *"morning"* and *"afternoon"* (as constituted in the respective languages. We see in this example that a factual circumstance of the extralinguistic, in this case material, world can be irrelevant in one language (Eng. *morning*), negatively criterial for the designatum of a word and positively criterial for another word in another language (*ráno* : : *dopoledne, Morgen* : : *Vormittag*, etc.).

A rich ramification of such a temporal criteriality can be seen in the following Hausa terms (reported by Zima):

àlfijìr — the early time of half-darkness and half-light
jijjifii — the protracted period of brighter light preceding sunrise
'àsùbaà — "just before sunrise"
saafee — "between sunrise and about 8 a.m."
hàntsii — "between 8 a.m. and 11 a.m."
raanaa tsakà or *tsakàr raanaa* — "noon" (verbatim "mid-day")
àzahàr — "between 2 and 3 p.m."
yàmma — "between 2,30 and sunset", which is further
    là'asàr — "between 4 and sunset"
    làruurii — "immediately before sunset"
    màgàribà or *àlmùruù* — beetween sunset and *lìishaa*
    mareecee — "late evening"
lìishaa — "from nightfall to midnight"
daree — "night" (any time between *àlmuurù* a *àsùbaà*)
tsakàd daree — "midnight".

The extralinguistic reality (material or not) is organized into designata that consist of the criterial features. Just as there is no universal repertory or inventory of the criterial features valid for each single language and for all of them, there is no such universal repertory or inventory of designata which would be identical, only expressed or labelled by different words (lexical units) in different languages. Just as languages differ in selecting some qualities as criterial, they differ also in forming different designata that pertain to the same extralinguistic reality.

It will be clear that, for example, the upper limbs or the lower limbs of the human species are basically identical in all the members of the species, irrespective of details, irrelevant (uncriterial) in this connection, such as colour of the skin, size, prettiness etc. These basically identical physical realities are

[24] Cf. B. Malmberg, *Structural Analysis and Human Communication*, Berlin 1963, p. 157, by whom this example is partly inspired.

not, however, conceived in the same way the speakers of different languages, and the difference in conception finds its expression in the respective words. In English, the whole upper limb is called *arm*, in French *bras*, in German *Arm*, in Chinese *ke-pei* (Heroldová); its outmost part with the fingers is called in Eng. *hand*, in French *main*, in German *Hand*, in Chinese *shou* (Heroldová); a similar difference is also found in Eng. *leg*, French *jambe*, German *Bein*, Chin. *t'ui* (the whole lower limb) and Eng. *foot*, French *pied*, German *Fuß*, Chin. *chiao* (Heroldová; the lowest part of it). This way of conceiving the human limbs is identical with the conceptions established in many other languages, but it is not general. For example, in the Slavonic languages, at least in their colloquial forms, the limbs are conceived as a whole; if we take Czech as the representative, the upper limb is called *ruka*, and the lower limb *noha* without any further distinction. In Tamil (as reported by Zvelebil) *kāl* "leg" and *aṭi* "foot" are distingueshed but not "arm" and "hand" which are both designated by the word *kai*. This shows the difference of the designata in the language: native speakers of English are accustomed to conceive the same physical reality in a different way from native speakers of languages like Czech.[25]

The fact that the same part of physical reality is differently organized and segmented into different designata in different languages can be observed without difficulty. One of the most discussed cases of the semantic differences resulting from different conceptions of the same physical reality in the case of the colours. Gleason[26] has a very illustrative diagram which shows the relation of the physically existing spectrum to the colour terms in three different languages: English, Shona (a language of Rhodesia), and Bassa (a language of Liberia). The diagram shows what part of the spectrum is covered by the single words.[27]

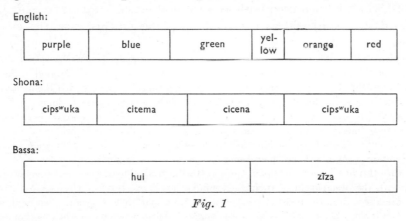

English:

| purple | blue | green | yel-low | orange | red |

Shona:

| cips^wuka | citema | cicena | cips^wuka |

Bassa:

| hui | zĩza |

Fig. 1

[25] Akhmanova, *Očerki po obščej i russkoj leksikologii*, Moskva 1957, p. 45ff.

[26] *Introduction* 4.

[27] "The Shona speaker divides the spectrum into three major portions. *cipa^wuke* occurs twice, but only because the red and the purple end, which he classifies as similar, are separated in the diagram." Gleason, loc. cit. — Futher indications in Nida, *Towards a Science of Trans-*

This juxtaposition is very instructive, because it shows that an absolutely identical physical reality can be conceived in different ways. What we called designatum is just this conception which stands between the reality and the word. The whole extralinguistic world known to them, either material or not, is organized, for the speakers of a language, into designata.[28] Differences in this respect are extremely frequent, in any pair of languages. Just these differences are one of the main obstacles one has got to cope with when learning a foreign language and one of the main problems of a bilingual dictionary.

It must be especially noted that we have used, to make the discussion as clear as possible, only examples from the physical extralinguistic world. The same situation can be met, however, in other cases as well. The differences in the constitution and the organization of the designata between different language are observable in all sorts and categories of lexical units.[29]

A notion very similar to that of the designatum is the (scientific) concept. It would seem at first sight that the two are identical. Their fundamental difference lies, however, in that the concept is the result of exact scientific work or at least of precise logical thinking, and usually is exactly defined and rigorously used, whereas the designatum generally does not have these qualities. Of course, the concept can be quite justly regarded, from one point of view, as a special case of the designatum. This can be observed in the majority of scientific and other terms. The designatum of a word like *polyvinylchloride* coincides with the precise scientific concept of this chemical compound.

There is no absolutely sharp line between the broader notion of designatum and that of concept, which is a special case of designatum. It very often happens that a precise concept is worked out by a science on the basis of a designatum of a word which is then used both as a word of general use (expressing in this case the designatum) and as a term (expressing in this case the concept).

---

lating, Leiden 1964, p. 35: three colour distinction in some languages of Africa, four in Northern Brazil, five in Northern Mexico, etc. — These are only a few examples, easy to find in the bibliography of the subject. The differences in colour designations are a very rich theme and many examples and interpretations could be quoted, almost from any language we know.

[28] According to some scholars (such as, e.g., H u m b o l d t, W h o r f, and W e i s g e r b e r), the designata are so important that the understanding of the extralinguistic world depends on them and, consequently, varies from one language to the other. For the lexicographer, such — undoubtedly exorbitant — opinions and their discussion are of minor importance.

[29] On the other hand, German *Handschuh* and Ossetic *ärmxud* both have the same designatum, identical with the designatum of their Eng. equivalent, *glove*. But the German word consists (at least when seen from the point of view of its origin) of parts which mean, when used in isolation, *hand* and *shoe*, whereas the Ossetic word consists of parts which mean when used in isolation *hand* and *cap*. These and similar phenomena are just the reverse of what we have discussed above: instead of different designata, here we have to deal with different ways of expressing identical designata. (Cf. A k h m a n o v a, *Očerki* 44.) The lexicographer will sometimes meet the term *inner form* referring to this: Germ. *Handschuh* and Oss. *ärmxud* are said to have an identical meaning, or, to be more precise, an identical designatum, but a different inner form.

Thus, there is a difference between the word *animal* and the term *animal*, because the concept of the latter covers also entities which would never be conceived as animals by the unsophisticated man: they are not covered by the designatum of the general word.[30] This is a circumstance of great importance mainly for the bilingual lexicographer who is sometimes forced to seek and indicate a different equivalent for a word which is used also as a term expressing the concept, besides its general use as a word expressing the designatum.

It would be wrong, however, to convey the idea that precise terms and concepts are used in the scientific sphere only. On the contrary, it would be hard to enumerate all the fields in which concepts are worked out: not only must the legislator work out what is *robbery* and what is *theft*, the athletic union what is *running* and what is *walking*, but a similar trend to an always greater preciseness pervades, in varying degrees, practically all the spheres of the languages spoken in the complicated world of modern civilisation. Indeed, in the case of languages that have a long tradition of philological, philosophical, and generally cultural work one can say that a great part of the designata tend to approach the status of precise concepts, at least as used in the literary language. We can also state in advance that it is one of the most important tasks of the lexicographer to help to foster (if only indirectly) this conceptual and terminological clarification.[31]

In the field of designation, the relation of the words to the segments of the extralinguistic world, there are, thus, three main elements: the (form of the) word as the expression capable of being communicated to the hearer (or reader etc.), the designatum (or the concept) as the respective mental, conceptual content expressed in it, and the denotatum as the respective segment of the extralinguistic world. The relation of these three components can be roughly illustrated by the famous triangle of Ogden and Richards.[32]

---

[30] No need to stress that the variety of differences between the word used as a term and the same word used as a general expression in the general language is very rich. What we mention above is only a sample of the richness.

[31] L. B. Salomon, *Semantics and Common Sense*, New York 1966, p. 41 and 91 describes very instructively how the legal decisions are important or the conceptual clarification: for instance, when a judge has to decide whether a series of actions is to be regarded as a strike or not, he not only tries to discover what has really happened, but he also analyzes the criteriality of strike to see whether the concept can be applied or not. ... "a large part of the tremendous accumulation of legal decisions consits in establishing borderlines of meaning for such terms as strike, labor, obscenity, commerce, freedom of speech ...". Compare with this the experience of the distinguished linguist and lexicographer A. Sommerfelt (Proceedings of the 8th Congress of Linguists, Oslo 1958, p. 98): "Definitions from the dictionary [viz. Norsk Riksmålsordbok] have often figured in lawsuits." We bring this example from the legal sphere, but the validity of the observation made above is more general, it pertains to any sphere of man's activity.

[32] *The Meaning of Meaning*, London 1923(4th ed. 1936). Ogden and Richards use another terminology and their approach is observably different.

The only reason why we show this triangle in the present book is that it illustrates what is stated above: There is a direct relation between the word and the designatum on the one side, and between the designatum and the denotatum on the other side, but the relation between the word and the denotatum is only an indirect one. Indeed, as far as the word — denotatum line

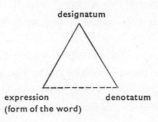

Fig. 2

goes, it is mostly only the onomatopoetic words that show a more direct relation to their denotata, the form of words like *cuckoo* being doubtlessly inspired by the sound typical for the bird.[33]

There is an interplay between the three elements of designation. The situation which we shall consider typical is that a word is used to express its designatum and together with it denote the respective denotatum. There are, however, other situation, as well.

Very often, a new thing, or animal, or process, or set of qualities, or set of events, etc., is found in the extralinguistic world and it strikes the observer as sufficiently coherent and/or as sufficiently contrasted from other similar things, animals, etc., to be conceived as a unified designatum (or concept) with a respective expression in a word (eventually a term). In our age, this happens very frequently in the science: the discovery of new animals, minerals, the invention of new machines, etc., all these and similar cases belong here. A new denotatum (either newly discovered or invented, etc.) results, then, in a new designatum (or they come into existence step by step together), and the new designatum finds expression in a new word, a new lexical unit, or in a change of the meaning of a word.

Sometimes, however, the process goes the other way round. For instance without the discovery of new data, or the invention of new facts, but chiefly

---

[33] In this discussion, we do not mention the deeper layers of the symbolism of sounds, the synaethesy, and similar topics, because they are relatively unimportant for the lexicographer. — Polymorphemic words whose meaning is derivable from the meaning of their constituent parts (they are sometimes calles *motivated words*) do not belong here. The circumstance that a polymorphemic word such as Eng. *homesickness* can be "understood" by analysis into its constituent parts, i.e. that the meaning of the whole word ist derivable from that of its parts, which is another way of stating that the word can be conceived as "motivated" by the meaning of its constituent morphemes, does not alter the fact that as far as these constituent morphemes themselves are concerned (in our example mainly *home*, *sick*), they have no direct relation to their denotata.

by observing and connecting events regarded up to his time as disconnected, N. Weiner was able to conceive a new designatum, or rather concept, for which he coined the term *cybernetics*. (It is not necessary to lose time by discussions which could be endless, as to whether he established a new denotatum or not.) A good number of philological, sociological and similar terms has been established in a similar way.[34]

But though there is an intimate interplay between the three factors of designation, it would be wrong to suppose that they are always present with identical clarity.

Let us mention above all those words which clearly do have as clear a designative character as words like *book*, *dog*, etc., but which either have no denotata, or only unclear or fictive ones. The easiest way how to understand the mutual situation of these three factors of designation in the (by now famous) case of the word *unicorn* (the fabulous animal), is to my mind the assumption that it has no denotatum at all, that is has only a designatum, or that the denotatum is only a fictive one. The latter assumption may have the disadvantage of being unnecessarily complicated, but one could possibly maintain, on the other hand, that the assumption of a fictive denotatum makes it easier to deal with these words on the model of those which have real denotata.

In the case of some very broad notions, the designatum (though frequently hard to define itself) is sometimes more clear, at least impressionistically, than the denotatum: in the case of word like *justice*, *love*, it would probably prove impossible to state exactly and exhaustively which area or group of events of the extralinguistic worlds constitutes the denotatum, though the words obviously and undoubtedly can refer to some complex segments of the extralinguistic world. All this shows that the in the lexical meaning the designatum is a hierarchically higher element than the denotatum.

The importance of the designative function cannot be overestimated. Indeed, the point of view can be well argued that the ability of the human species to conceptualize and understand the world is in a very intimate relation to the designative function of the lexical units and of language generally. And some scholars, both linguists and philosophers, even hold that not only the power to conceptualize, but also (at least the more basic) designata (or concepts, or whichever approach and terminology is chosen) are inborn. (Cf. on this the critical survey and deep own discussion of R. I. Aaron, *The Theory of Universals*, 2nd ed., Oxford 1967.)

The designative component of the lexical meaning is sometimes called the intellectual or notional component or the intellectual or notional

---

[34] The other possible case, the invention of a meaningless word which gradually acquires meaning by being used, most frequently for the sake of a joke or of a play, in recurring, similar context (e.g. *abracadabra*) ist a peripheral phenomenon for lexicography. — Cf. § 4.5 on the neologisms and the different methods of their coinage.

core of it. But sometimes this term is taken in a broader sense, so that it covers also the other functions of the lexical units which we shall discuss now.

1.3.1.1 Not all lexical units have precisely the same type of lexical meaning as the preceding category of what can be called purely designative words (lexical units). We shall mention in the following discussion some of the more outstanding differences. It is important, however, to say at once that the lexicographer (and usually the semantician as well) can deal with different types of these lexical meanings on the background of the basic model of the designative function.

If we take an attitudinal symptom like any interjection (Eng. *hello, hullo, aha*), it would be hard to show an immediate denotatum. Opinions may differ as far as their eventual designatum is concerned; to my mind, they either do not have it at all or it is a very different designatum from that described above; they do not designate a segment of the world but they inform the hearer about an attitude taken by the speaker, or about his "feelings" (in the broadest sense of the word), etc. But that does not matter: the information they carry in a sentence about the attitude of the speaker is comparable to that carried by the purely designative words. Therefore, the lexicographer considers this ability to convey this information as something directly comparable to the designation of designative words, and deals with the former on the model of the latter, the more so since these attitudinal symptoms are usually as conventionalized in their form and meaning as any other words.[35] In short, though there is a difference between the basic semantic functions of the designative words and of the attitudinal symptoms, the lexicographer tends to dealing with them in a basically identical way. In the case of the designative words, he tries to describe the designatum; in the case of the attitudinal symptoms, he tries to describe the attitudes and "feeling" of the speaker of which they are the expression.

The same can be said about the pragmatic operators (like Engl. *please*[36] one of the main functions of which is to exert influence upon the hearer: their function is comparable to the designatum of a designative word and they

[35] This conventionalized form (e.g., they consist, in the majority of cases, of the normal phonemes of the language in question) is the feature which separates them from individual symptoms of a vocal but at the best only semi-linguistic character: e.g., a man prickled with a needle in a fleshy part of his body may use an attitudinal symptom of a linguistic, conventionalized (phonemic) character, like "*oh!*", or "*hell!*", but he may emit a vocal yet not linguistic (not phonemic, i.e. what is frequently called an "unarticulated") sound. Lexicography, as linguistics, is usually concerned only with the former category, though the study of the latter category commands a considerable interest, too.

[36] As used, for example, in the sentence quoted above. In this discussion, we consider the semantic content of the word from the point of view of the general speaker who does not know anything about the original ellipsis from *if you please* or *if it please you*.

can be dealt with on its model by the lexicographer. Again, the lexicographer does not describe their designatum, but instead of it, their function: how and in what respect they try to influence the hearer.[37]

Other groups that belong here are: the deictic words (e.g. Eng. *this*, *that*): they are usually used for direct reference to parts of the extralinguistic world:[38] the way they are used and what information they give, for example, about the mutual relation of the speaker, the hearer, and of the object of reference is comparable to the designation of the designative words. Another group is the quantifiers (usually numerals, e.g. Eng. *one*, *three*): what they convey about one single quality of any part of the extralinguistic world (i.e. about its quantity) is comparable to the designatum.

Yet other groups that belong here are the propositional operators[39] (like Eng. *not*, *or*) and grammatical, or relational lexical units (like Eng. *to*, *the*, or Hindi — as reported by Miltner — *ki* "that", *aur* "and", *par* "but", or Armenian — as reported by Motalová — *oč* "not", *kam* "or", *isk* "but", etc.). Just as in the case of the preceding groups, it could be maintained (and some scholars do maintain it, with different emphasis and using different arguments) that the meaning of these words is embedded in the facts of the extralinguistic world, as conceived by the speakers of a language. However this may be, the most important thing for the lexicographer is to find out what information they carry, how they are used in a meaningfully relevant way, and to conceive and present this on the model of the designatum of the designative words.[40]

[37] The more sophisticated reader will have recognized that these three functions we have mentioned up to now correspond closely to the three categories of K. Bühler (*Sprachtheorie*, Jena 1934). This scholar established the following three (semantic, or semiotic) functions of words: (1) Darstellungsfunktion: words are symbols of the extralinguistic world (i.e. the designative function); (2) Ausdrucksfunktion, words are symptoms of the speaker's attitudes (i.e. attitudinal symptoms); (3) Appellfunktion: words are signals by which the hearer's attitude is to be affected (i.e. pragmatic operators). This trichotomy is in itself good and distinguishes well the different functions. It is, however, not sufficient, because there are words which have none of those three functions, such as the pragmatic or grammatical operators. (Cf. the following discussion). Bühler's theory was considerably enriched and modified by subsequent research. In the present discussion, we follow closely the terminology of Uriel Weinreich. — The branch of science which studies these most general questions is frequently called *semiotics*.

[38] Note the difference between *designation* (i.e., stated primitively, the conceptualization, in a designatum, of a denotatum, of a class of objects) and *reference*, which is the pointing to one concrete object of the extralinguistic world, referred to in an actual sentence.

[39] In mentioning this category separately from the subsequent one, I follow (as in other points of this enumeration) U. Weinreich, *Universals* 120. For practical lexicography, no harm is done if the two are conceived as one group.

[40] This discussion represents only one of the possible approaches to these problems. Other scholars have other views: for example, some of them posit a designatum also for numerals, for pronouns, etc. Lexicography is fully entitled to handle the pertinent problems in a practical way, as suggested here.

The lexicographer's basis is undoubtedly the designative words (lexical units). But he is obliged to present, in his dictionary, all lexical units and deal with all the functions they are able to perform, as individual units in a sentence, irrespective of whether these functions are designative, attitudinal (emotional), pragmatic, operative, or grammatical: they are units of the system of language which perform different but comparable functions in the construction of a sentence.

This point of view is based not only on theoretical considerations, but also on practical ones. In this respect, one must not forget that lexical units which must be considered identical may have different functions (e.g. Eng. *devil* as a designative word and as an attitudinal symptom in an exclamation like *the devil!;* or Eng. *upon* in its locally — designative function, as in *to put something upon the table* (in contradistinction to *under* etc.), and in its grammatically-relational function as in *to declare war upon the enemy.* Consequently, the only reasonable thing is to present all of these functions in a dictionary, not only because of the theory, but also because it is frequently impossible to find a sharp boundary between them. In any case, any semantically relevant function of a lexical item is to be presented in the dictionary, even the purely grammatical one, though this is probably the one which is the most removed from the basic model of the designative funtion.[41] More on this below, § 1.8.

1.3.2 All the other components of lexical meaning (with the exception of the range of application) that do not belong to the designation (and the other functions dealt with on its model), can be covered by the general term of connotation. In a more positive way, we can describe connotation as consisting of all components of the lexical meaning that add some contrastive value to the basic, usually designative function. We shall mention the most important categories of connotation.

It will be useful to begin with a very simple example. If we consider the two following statements:

(1) *He died,* and

(2) *He pegged out,*

we see that their meaning is precisely the same, as far as the the sad factual information goes, and so is the meaning of the two crucial verbs, up to a

---

[41] It is worth while to mention that some scholars conceive as much sharper the contrast between words with the designative function on one side and those with the grammatical-relational one on the other. Some of them would even term it as the contrast between the lexical meaning and the grammatical meaning. This is to some extent only a question of terminology; the fundamental thing is that the lexicographer has to present all the functions, and also all the grammatical functions performed by lexical means (i.e. by the lexical units). Whether the latter, i.e. the lexical

degree. This is the consequence of the fact that the two verbs *to die* and *to peg out* have the same designation, in this respect. Their only difference is that whereas *to die* is so to say colourless because it conveys only the factual information, *to peg out* has the additional value of being vulgar. The verb *to die* has no connotation, *to peg out* has the connotation of vulgarity or so. In this way, we can conceive connotation as a very broad category comprising all further semantically relevant properties of the word, besides the central area of designation (or an analogous function of the word) itself.

The lexicographer will be well advised to study the words which have some connotations always in contrast to their connotatively colourless counterparts. The usual situation is that there are such pairs or groups of words (lexical units). Whether we, then, say that a word like *to die* has, in comparison with *to peg out* and *to decease,* no connotation or whether we say that it has a neutral one, is, considered from the point of view of lexicography, irrelevant. In any case, a good many of words will have no connotation as understood in this approach, and they will be a useful background for the study of those words which do have one.

Stated very generally, probably the broadest category of words that have a strong connotation are the expressive words, among which those with an emotive connotation will be the most numerous; at least this seems to be the situation in the languages which are well described. It will, however, be wrong to think that only the emotive words carry expressive connotation. The concrete reasons why somebody speaks not about the nose but about the pecker may be various, but they can be conceived as expressivity, as the desire to use a "stronger", more colourful word instead of the "usual", colourless one.

From the point of view of the lexicographer, the whole field of different styles and of the whole variation of language (see chapter IV) belongs or may belong in its lexical results to the category of connotation.

If we consider the variants *to decease — to die — to peg out,* we see that there are connotative variants not only on the "lower" part of the scale, but also on the "higher" part of it: *to decease* is not as colourless and purely factual as *to die*; it has the connotation of belonging to the high, or frozen, style. A similar distribution of connotations can be found in Armenian (as reported by Motalová) *vačxanvel* "to decease" — *mernel* "to die" — *satkel* "to peg out).

---

units performing grammatical functions, are conceived as belonging to the sphere of the lexical meaning or as something apart, is irrelevant for the lexicographer's practice. But as far as theoretical considerations go, I thing, that it is better to conceive the lexical meaning as a very broad category with the designative function as the central one and other different functions more or less remote from it, in different dimensions, the grammatical-relational function expressed by lexical means being on the utmost periphery of it. Therefore, all these things are discussed in this chapter, with the designation serving as the model for the conceptualization of the other categories.

But let us compare the following rich series of Chinese expressions (reported by Heroldová):

(1) *t'a szu le* "he died": neutral connotation;

(2) *t'a ch'ü-shih le* "he died": used about ordinary people, but more respectful than (1) (e.g. used in reference to a friend; a mother can say this about her child etc.);

(3) *t'a ku-ch'ü le* ("he died": same connotation as (2);

(4) *t'a shi-shi le* "he deceased": about famous people, very deferential;

(5) *t'a ch'ang-mien le* "he deceased": poetical (verbatim: "he fell asleep for ever");

(6) *t'a yü shi ch'ang-tz'u le* "he passed away": literary cliché (verbatim "he bid the world farewell");

(7) *t'a hui lao chia le* "he joined the big army": a common expression, sometimes used jocosely (verbatim "he came back to the old house");

(8) *t'a wan'r wan le* "he pegged out": more jocose than (7);

(9) *t'a ken'r le* "he pegged out": as (8);

(10) *t'a yen-ch'i le* "he expired": neutral;

(11) *t'a ken'r p'i le* "he pegged out": very vulgar.

Any stylistic property of a word, the fact that a word belongs to a certain style of the respective language, to a certain slang or a social dialect, or even to a geographical dialect (if the word is used in a non-dialectal context), or that it is either recently coined (a neologism) or on the contrary, obsolete carries additional semantic relevance, additional "information" about the speaker, about his attitude to or evaluation of the subject, gives "colour" to the subject, conveys the information more powerfully, humorously, emotionally, ironically, is in consequence more expressive, and is, therefore, connotative.

But not all words of, say, dialectal origin are necessarily connotative. The historical development may cause that they stop being felt as "alien" elements in the general language and that they lose any connotative value.

For instance, Motalová reports the following pairs of words from Armenia:

(a)	*ačk'alusank'*	(b)	*avetik'* "who brings good tidings"
	avelçuk		*mnaçord* "rest, surplus"
	viz		*paranoç* "neck"

All words listed under (a) came originally from the dialects, those under (b) from classical Armenian (Grabar). But as both series are equally used in Modern Armenian, they do not carry any such connotations as those mentioned in the preceding paragraph.

It is probably worth-while to mention that it is not only the designative words that can be observably connotative. For example, the difference between

(1) *Though he failed, he is a great man* and
(2) *Albeit he failed, he is a great man*

can be conceived as purely connotative: *albeit* having the connotation of being archaic and belonging to the frozen, high style only.

As far as connotation goes, it is necessary to note that this component of lexical meaning frequently causes even greater difficulties than designation. This is so because there are few rigorous criteria for classification and because the respective words, probably with the main exception of the dialectal ones, frequently change their status rather rapidly. What was a neologism yesterday may be a normal expression today and may be bookish or obsolete tomorrow, etc.[42] The lexicographer will have to be very prudent as far as statements about the connotation and the connotative status of words are concerned. It is impossible to rely exclusively on one's knowledge, in this respect more than in other fields, even if one is dealing with one's own native language, because the connotative values show greater variations from one speaker to another than does the designative function of the word. On the other hand, the lexicographer should try to do his best in this respect, not only when he prepares a monolingual dictionary (which usually has the basic purpose of describing the lexicon, the lexical stock of a language), but also when he prepares a bilingual one. If such a bilingual dictionary is intended as a tool for expressing oneself in a foreign language, it is certainly the lexicographer's duty not to allow the user of his dictionary unwittingly to use vulgar, or absolute, or other similarly displaced words and thus to put himself into a ridiculous position or even into a misunderstanding or conflict.

It is not always easy to distinguish connotation from the power of a word to evoke individual feelings; see on this § 4.1.

1.3.3 As the third basic component of lexical meaning we may, perhaps, conceive the range of application of the word.[43] For example, the words

---

[42] Janský LSB 139ff. — Some authors apply the term *expressivity* in such a way that it overlaps vastly with what we call *connotation*. Anyhow, expressivity (even if understood in the broadest way) is necessarily a narrower notion that connotation: the former is one of the possible causes of the latter. We can conceive expressivity as a function of the speaker's wish not only to communicate, but to communicate in a more-than-usually forceful, or impressive, way. J. Zima (*Expresivita slova v současné češtině*, Rozpravy Československé akademie věd 71, 1961, Nr 16) discerns three types of lexical expressivity: (a) inherent expressivity (the respective word is in all its senses and in all possible contexts expressive); (b) adherent expressivity (one of the senses of a polysemous word is expressive, in all its possible contexts); (c) contextual expressivity (the word gets an expressive value only in a certain concrete context). Cf. also § 1.5.7 on the role of context and on contextual nuances.

stipend and *salary* have a designatum which can be regarded as practically identical. Broadly spoken, it is the financial remuneration people regularly receive for doing some work. There is hardly any conceivable difference of connotation between them. It is basically only the range of application which makes them different: *stipend* is mostly used in connection with a teacher, clergyman or priest, whereas *salary* is used in connection with an official, etc.[44] In Chinese (as reported by Heroldová), *kung-tzu* (wages, pay, salary) can be used in reference to any workers, but *hsin-shui* which has the same meaning, only in reference to the brainworkers.

The meaning of the prepositions *between* and *among* is practically identical. The range of application of the first word is, however, severaly restricted to those cases where only two subjects form the environment referred to by the preposition.[45]

The restrictions of the range of application are sometimes very severe. It may even happen that a word's range of application is limited to one possible combination. For example, Eng. corned has probably a very strictly limited range of application; the only really usual way to apply it is when speaking about *beef* (corned). Chinese *pai-ai-ai* "white, dazzling white" can also be used only in reference to snow (*pai-ai-ai ti hsüeh* "white snow": Heroldová). Armenian *ašxet* "brown" can be used only in reference to a horse (Motalová). The usual situation is, however, that the range of the application of a word is broader.

In a certain sense, every word's applicability is limited by some of its properties, beginning with its stylistic value, through its semantic connections, to its grammatical category.[46] But the lexicographer is primarily interested in the more specific restrictions of the range of application which can be conceived as individual properties of the word in question and which frequently seem to overlap with the criterial features of the designatum.

These restrictions are connected with factors which are so different that they cannot be enumerated. For example, Turkish *yarem* "half" (as reported by Hřebíček) is used only without any other numeral. In combination with another numeral, *buçuk* must be used: e.g. *bit buçuk* " one and a half".

---

[43] Other terminologies use the term *selective* or *selectional restrictions*. This latter term is usual in the transformational grammar; the concept of the selective restrictions is more comprehensive; for instance, it is usual to consider expressions like *a hungry rock* non acceptable in transformational grammar, just because *hungry* is conceived as having a selectional restriction which limits its application to living organisms only. (On selectional restrictions, see e.g. J. D. MacCawley, *The Role of Semantics in a Grammar*, in: Universals in Linguistic Theory, ed. E. Bach and R. T. Harms, New York 1958, p. 134).

[44] Cf. *Webster's Third* s. vv.

[45] This is a purely grammatical-lexical restriction today. The etymological fact that between comes from by twain is synchronically irrelevant.

[46] Feldmann LS 2, 1957, 84. Cf. footnote 43 on the selectional restrictions.

In Czech, the adjectives *červený* and *rudý* are very close near-synonyms, meaning "red" (the latter word perhaps with a weak connotation of being slightly elevated), and their respective ranges of application overlap to a considerable degree; but in things political, only the adjective *rudý* and never the adjective *červený* can be applied, so that *rudá hvězda* is either any "red star", or the "red star, which is the symbol of the Communist movement", but *červená hvězda* cannot be applied in reference to the latter.

The Czech situation has a parallel in a similar phenomenon in Chinese (as reported by Novotná). The Chinese designations of colours usually have two forms, one monosyllabic and one disyllabic. The first syllable of the latter is the same morpheme as that occurring in the monosyllabic form, the second syllable is in all these cases the bound morpheme *se* (meaning "colour" when occurring alone). In the direct sense, both the monosyllabic and the disyllabic forms can be used; but in the transferred (usually political) sense, only the disyllabic form can be used. In this way, we have:

I. (a) *hung i-fu* "red dress"
   hung-se ti[47] *i-fu* "red dress"
   (b) *hung-se ch'eng-ch'üan* "red power"

II. (a) *pai ch'ün-tzu* "white skirt"
   pai-se ti[47] *ch'ün-tzu* "white skirt"
   (b) *pai se k'ung-pu* "white terror"

III. (a) *huang hu tieh* "yellow butterfly"
   huang-se ti[47] *hu-tieh* "yellow butterfly"
   (b) *huang-se kung-hui* "yellow trade unions"

It is only in the last few years that we can observe that this restriction is discontinued, but only in the case of *hung* "red": this monosyllabic form can also be used with the transferred, political sense. For example, *yu hung, yu chuan* "to be red, and to be a good specialist", *hung wei-ping* "red guards".

There are similar phenomena in other languages, too. For instance, Zima reports in Hausa the word *fat* "completely" which has a restricted range of application, occurring above all only in combinations of the type *farii fat* "quite white (as snow)", in combination with verbs designating a completed action as *cinyee, shanyee* ("to eat, to drink completely") and in some other expressions (as, e.g., *yaa yankèe shi fat* "he cut it clean in two [parts]").

Petráček reports Arabic *razaqa* "to present a person with something" which is used only when the donor is Allah.

According to Černý, the Georgian verb *makvs* "to have" is applied in reference to things: *cigni makver* "I have a book". *Mqavs* "to have" is applied in reference to persons and animals: *dedmama mqavs* "I have parents", *mona*

---

[47] The particle *ti* has no influence on the lexical meaning.

mqavs "I have a slave", *cxeni mqavs* "I have a horse"; but motorcars are treated not as things but as animals, because one says *mankana mqavs* "I have a motor-car".

In a great number of cases, the unclear status of this category is quite palpable. Sometimes, it is not clear whether the respective difference rather belongs to what we call connotation; and in other cases, many scholars would rather speak about a difference in designation itself. So is it, e.g., in a case like the difference between Hindi *sīkhnā* "to learn" and *paṛhnā* "to learn (from a book only)".[48]

Very important also are those cases of restriction which constitute set combinations of words (§ 3.3), at least in a given situational context. In discussing a day, one can say that it was good, or that it was excellent, or one can use any other near-synonym. Should one, however, great another person by bidding him *"Excellent day"*, this odd greeting would miss its purpose, *good* being an obligatory restriction in this culturally set combination of words.

The range of application of different grammatical or propositional operators can be restricted, too. Petráček reports the following situation from Arabic: there are three verbal negative particles, *mā, lā, lam*. The application of *lam* is severely restricted, because it is used only in connection with the verbal form called "apocopate" (with past function). The application of the other two particles is restricted only broadly and preferentially; *lā* is generally used with the imperfect (with present or rather future function) and with the function of the negative imperative.

The knowledge of the applicability of the single words is extremely important for the real mastery of a language. As far as mere communication goes, a great many of these restrictions could be disregarded. But we know from everyday experience that we register every divergence from what is usual, in this respect, just as we note any other aberration from the system of language, grammatical or lexical. Therefore, it is the duty of the lexicographer to try to indicate the range of application especially in a monolingual dictionary or in a bilingual dictionary which is intended to help the active user of a foreign language. The lexicographer should discern, in this respect, what is an obligatory restriction and what is only a preferential one. As stated, the restrictions depend upon very different circumstances. It is the more regrettable that we have extensive data on these restrictions only in the case of the best described languages and that our knowledge is, even in these cases, far from complete. The situation is caused above all by the fact that statements concerning these restrictions require an enormous study of material and long work with the informants.

[48] Example from Barannikov, *Leksičeskaja sinonimija* 18f.

When the lexicographer collects and evaluates the material necessary to decide a problem of applicational restriction, i.e. a problem of the range of application, he must be aware of the fact that whereas his contexts yield only a positive evidence of how a word is used, his own conclusions must be and his statements will be taken as being not only positive, but also negative: to know how a word is used implies the knowledge of how a word is not (or even is not to be) used. Let us discuss en example.[49] In Hindi, the words (a) *prem*, (b) *lāṛ*, (c) *pyār*, (d) *sneh*, (e) *cāh*, and (f) *prīti* designate "love". There seem to be no differences in connotation, but considerable differences in the range of application: the correct statement (as given by Barannikov) is that *prem* is not used in relation to human beings and things; *lāṛ* usually in reference to the parents' love of their children; *pyār* and *sneh* are said to refer usually to "tender love, above all that of adults towards children"; *cāh* can refer to love of different things and *prīti* is the love of a man and a woman. Let us now imagine that the lexicographer has at hand only the following contexts:[49]

(1) *tumse merā prem kis prakār ho gayā, yah bhī mujhe ṭhīk prakār se yād nahī*
   I do not recollect exactly how my love to you was orn
(2) *unhẽ sigār se baṛā prem thā*
   he liked cigars very much
(3) *mã — bāp kā, lāṛ baccõ ko bigāṛ detā hai*
   "the parents' love spoils the children"
(4), (5) *donõ baccõ ko bahut bahut sneh (pyār)*
   "much, much love to both the children" (a lettre)
(6) *inhẽ nit- navīn āmod-pramod kī cāh rahtī thī*
   "they had a (strong) liking for always amusements"
(7) *unkī prīti unke mã-bāpõ ko nahī bhātī thī*
   "the parents did not like their love"

The lexicographer would be happy if his contextual passages were always as clear as these, because (1) and (2) show applicability of (a), (3), that of (b), (4) that of (c), etc. But there is obviously a vast difference between an observation that the contexts show a certain range of application of the word in question, and the statement that the word can be used only or predominantly only within that range and not in another. We have adduced here one contextual quotation for every applications; this is certainly not enough — but the lexicographer, unless he has the plan and the funds to prepare a big academic dictionary on the basis of an exhaustive or nearly exhaustive material, will very frequently find that he does not have a more extensive material at hand. But in any case, even the fact that the lexicographer has, say, twenty or thirty contexts with *lāṛ* as the parents' love is no absolute guarantee that the word is not also used

---

[49] Taken from Barannikov, *Leksičeskaja sinonimija* 17.

in another way: a negative conclusion is always difficult and an *argumentum e silentio* always fragile. Therefore, this is one of the fields where it is absolutely necessary to use the native speaker's competence, if it is a living language with which we deal. The lexicographer must use either his own knowledge (if he works in the field of his native language) or the knowledge of his informants to complete what he knows from the contextual quotations: only from an informant is it possible to elicit the statement "We do not say it this way", which is the necessary supplement of the positive evidence as to how it is said. But in any case, statements about the restrictions in the application of a lexical unit belong to the most delicate tasks of the lexicographer. If his work concerns a language not yet much studied and described or even not yet absolutely stabilized, he will be well advised to give much care to the study of the range of application, but not to be too authoritative and definite in his statements. And even after a very long and detailed study, the lexicographer cannot be sure that a word will not be applied in a new way, in a new range, because his material as a whole is only rarely entirely recent and because change in this sphere of language can occur rather rapidly.

For instance Minn Latt reports that he is not always sure about the range of application in Burmese. The Burmese have various words for "wash": to wash one's hair is *shó*, to wash one's hands or feet is *hsêi*. Minn Latt is, however, uncertain whether a hairdresser would not use the question *khâun hsêi mălâ* instead of the usual *khâun shó mălâ* will you wash your head (hair)?" It should also be noted that *khâun hsêi* is often found in reference to the hair-washing ceremonies.

Therefore, as already mentioned, statements concerning the range of application should be made cautiously and with due prudence. It is mainly the classification of a severe restriction as an obligatory and absolute one which requires great circumspection an extremely rich, or if possible exhaustive documentation and a thorough checking with many informants; and even then it is usually possible to indicate such restrictions in a definite way only in languages which are highly normalized and stabilized.[50]

It must be stated that not all linguists would accept the opinion that the range of application is a component of the lexical meaning of its own. For the lexicographer, however, it is of the very highest importance to take these and similar phenomena into consideration and not to neglect them, irrespective of their status. Even if the lexicographer is of the opinion that the range of application is not a component of the lexical meaning of its own, he will have

---

[50] This discussion takes into consideration above all the situation which seems to occur most frequently, viz. that the lexicographer starts with written sources and needs more additional information from the informants. If oral sources (informants) are used exclusively, only some change in the technique are implied, but not a change of the basic attitude.

to regard it as one of the individual (i.e. not categorial — general) rules on how to apply (or how not to apply) the word in question, or as a part of its designatum, and the result will be the same: the lexicographer will have to state the restriction in his dictionary.

THE ACTUAL SIGNIFICATION IN THE CONTEXT

1.4 Up to now, we have discussed the stabilized meaning of words as parts of the system of language. The problem of lexical meaning is, however, not exhausted by this approach. Words do not have an abstract existence of their own as some unalterably defined units of a system, but they are used.[51] The distinction is so very important that it is useful to discern even terminologically the meaning of a word as a part of the system (we shall mention later that it can consist of more senses than one and its s i g n i f i c a t i o n, or a c t u a l s i g n i f i c a t i o n when it occurs in a text.[52]

One of the outstanding properties of lexical meaning is its g e n e r a l i t y. This generality can be perceived in different dimensions. First, a designative lexical unit (if we use this category as the example) can be used in reference to any member of the class that belongs to the designatum and, eventually, the denotatum (i.e., one can use the word *flower* in reference to any flower). Second, the designata are usually broad (cf. how many different things can be referred to as *furniture*), frequently overlapping (cf. that it is possible to refer to the same quality of a great number of things both with the adjective *big* and *large*), and sometimes lacking clear boundaries (i.e., are not sufficiently criterial; cf. *honesty*, *justice*, etc.). Third, we shall hear later (§ 1.5) about polysemy which adds considerably to the generality of lexical meaning.

On the contrary, c o n c r e t i z a t i o n is the outstanding result of the application of a lexical unit (word) in an actual utterance (usually a sentence). Therefore, whereas lexical meaning is general, signification is concrete. This concretization results from the context (verbal or situational) which either connects the word used with the concrete "thing" referred to by it, or eliminates any other

---

[51] This statement is also valid in the case of a dead language, except that the application took place at some point of history, not now. In this connection, it is perhaps not without interest to mention that R. S t e p h a n u s characterizes his *Dictionarium seu Latinae linguae Thesaurus* (Parisiis 1531) as "opus ... de verborum Latinorum significatione atque usu multiplici" (see the foreword to the dictionary). It could, I think, be maintained that this "usus multiplex" refers just to the manifold actual application: lexicography is a highly traditional descipline. — The whole problem ist well discussed by W. S c h m i d t, *Lexikalische und aktuelle Bedeutung, ein Beitrag zur Theorie der Wortbedeutung* (Schriften zur Phonetik, Sprachwissenschaft und Kommunikationsforschung Nr 7), Berlin 1963.

[52] Cf. R. A. A l l e n, *Proceedings of the 9th Congress of Linguists*, p. 422.

possible senses of the word than that in which it is applied (we shall hear later that this mechanism is called disambiguation), or performs both operations.

Let us now discuss the consequences of the concretization of significations in actual sentences. Naturally, in the absolute majority of cases, words are used in a way which is conformable to the system as established by general use. If this were not the case, and if the absolute majority of applications and significations were not conformable to the system, i.e. to the interpersonal system, the communicative power of a language would decrease considerably. On the other hand, when we observe how the words are used in concrete utterances, we can see variations which we frequently feel forced to interpret as divergences from what we consider to be the norm inherent in the system.

The relation of the meaning of a word (lexical unit) as a part of the system of language and of the actual significations can be demonstrated by the following diagram:

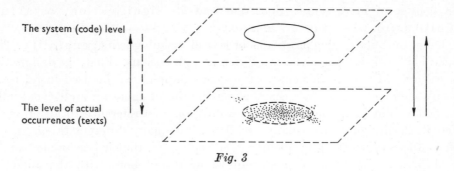

The system (code) level

The level of actual
occurrences (texts)

Fig. 3

On the system level, we see a circle which indicates the range of the meaning of a lexical unit as a continuum with boundaries.[53] This circle is supposed to cover all the possible significations of the lexical unit which are considered normal by other speakers of the language and are understood by them as such without any further complication.

On the level of actual occurrences, single actual significations are represented by single dots. Both the meaning on the system level and the set of the actual significations on the level of texts are represented by an area, because both the designata and the possible fields of reference in the extralinguistic world generally happen to be broad. One must imagine what a variety of vastly different qualities can be called *beautiful*, what different objects can be called a *vehicle*, supposing only that they have the criterial qualities of their designata and vary only in the non-criterial respects. It is only some of the very precisely defined terms for very specific concepts like, say *polyvinylpyrrolidone*, in the case of which the diagram would have the following form.

---

[53] We shall try to refine all these ideas in the following discussion.

When we return to Fig. 3, we see on the level of the actual occurrences that the majority of the dots is within the dashed circle: these are actual significations which correspond absolutely to the meaning of the respective lexical unit as

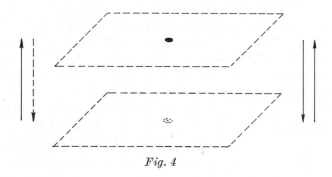

Fig. 4

part of the system; there are, however, some dots which are not withithin the area of the circle: these are significations which diverge from the systemic meaning of the lexical unit in question.[54]

This is a fact of really vital importance, mainly for the compilation of a monolingual dictionary. The lexicographer will heave many difficulties with this circumstance and must take it always into consideration, above all when he prepares a monolingual dictionary of a language the lexicon of which is as yet unstabilized or is rapidly developing.

1.4.1 These divergences of the actual signification from the meaning of the respective lexical unit (as a part of the system) could be classified in many ways and probably not one of them would be exhaustive and fully sufficient. We shall limit ourselves to some of the most crucial points. Sometimes, we hear or read utterances in which words are used in a way which is more or less different from what we know about their lexical meaning.

We can begin with those cases when words are used in an absolutely "impossible" way, say by someone who does not have a sufficient knowledge of the language and simply does not know what the word means.

In well-known languages, there occur for instance the so-called m a l a - p r o p i s m s; for example, Engl. *humility* and *desirous* as used in the sentences

"It is a humility to be kept waiting about"
"I thought it desirous that the test should be applied".[55]

[54] In some older terminologies (e.g. H. Paul, *Prinzipien der Sprachgeschichte*, 5th edition, Halle a. S. 1937, p. 75), the meaning of the level of the system is called *usual* (*usuelle Bedeutung*), whereas any actual signification is called "*occasional meaning*" (*okkasionelle Bedeutung*). As we shall see in our further discussion, the value of the term *occasional* as used in the present book is much narrower.

[55] Examples from A k h m a n o v a, *Slovar' lingvističeskich terminov*, Moskva 1966, p. 223.

In these cases, the speaker did not know the precise meaning of these and similar words foreign to his own idiolect. To the educated speaker, the mistake is obvious; yet constant use can change such an original mistake into a normal meaning.

For example, the Eng. word *premises* (plur.) is now known to have mainly two senses, viz (1) "what has been said above", and (2) "a building with its ground appurtenances". The second sense has its origin in the circumstance that legal instruments among which those dealing with immovable property belong to the most frequent ones, in the lives of ordinary citizens, always tended to be worded in a rather complicated way and to be full of *"premises"*, "as stated above". Now this was obviously misunderstood. The whole situation being focused on the immovable in question, the word was taken as if it referred to the building etc., by someone who did not know it but tried to understand it from the context. As this error often arose, and as the word began to be directly used in this sense in contexts which do not allow another interpretation, it has become stabilized and a part of the system, with this new sense.

The lexicographer, mainly when working in the field of yet unstabilized languages, must take into account even the possibility of similar "erroneous" and not yet stabilized applications of a lexical unit.[56]

But as already stated, cases like these are not too frequent. More frequent is a situation like the following one. If we read or hear the sentence

"His innocence throws such an aurora borealis *round him that he obviously must have done some mischief"*

in a pregnant situation, e.g., when parents are speaking about their son, it is clear that it is not the natural phenomenon which is referred to but that what is really meant is the *halo*, here used to characterize the sly little rascal's efforts to hide his depravity under an innocent face. The speaker can be imagined to use the expression *aurora borealis* instead of *halo*, because it is similar to it, but has the additional advantage of being far greater. (Quite apart from the fact that this expression is new and original, and therefore more expressive, which is the motive of its being used.) In the sentence quoted above, the expression *aurora borealis* ist not used in the meaning in which it is

---

[56] The fact that the originally erroneous application of Eng. *premises* "building etc." is perfectly normal today, is quite clear. Constant use can sanction any development and can establish as the norm what was originally a mistake or an error, but only after a considerable time. What we discussed above, however, was the situation of an isolated, single erroneous application, which must have been the situation of premisses at the beginning of the narrated development. Such situations pose hard problems of selection for inclusion in the dictionary. — An extreme case of an erroneous application for example, is, Armenian (reported by Motalová) *koyuǧi* "drainage, sewerage" which was used as a first (given) name for their child by parents who obviously had no idea about the real meaning of the word.

normally applied: it is used instead of the word *halo* and instead of this word's normal meaning; therefore, it is used in a figurative sense. This application of the lexical unit was meant as a joke, there is no other example of it (at least not to my knowledge, or to the knowledge of any English lexicographer); therefore, it is occasional, not usual, not systemic. Consequently, it would be wrong to assume, on the strength of this example, that the Eng. lexical unit *aurora borealis* has, as a part of the system of English, such a meaning.

The case just discussed is a rather extreme one, because the occasional application of such a rare lexical unit is really rather remote. There are, however, even stronger cases.

For instance, one of the persons in S. Lewis' Babbitt (XIII, 10) says to a waiter:

"... *just shoot me in that steak, with about two printer's-reams of French fried potatoes on the promenade deck ...*"

Unfortunately, we cannot dig out and discuss all the different layers of beauty hidden in this sentence. The interesting thing for us, at least at this juncture, is the expression *promenade deck*. Obviously, it is impossible to understand it in its normal meaning "an upper deck or an area on a deck of a passenger-ship where passengers promenade" (Webster); what is really meant here is that the fried potatoes should be put on the steak, or beside it, and should be served with it. But it would be wrong to assume, on the strength of this application, that the lexical unit *promenade deck* has, as a part of the system of English, a meaning like, say "upper part of a steak when served"; we have here only an occasional application before us again. The way in which the lexical unit is used, is, in this case, so remote from its usual, systemic meaning that it can hardly be understood at all.[57]

The lexicographer will register such applications probably only if he compiles a thesaurus or if he considers it his duty to be exhaustive at least-as far as some authors go. It will not be to difficult to see that such applications diverge from the usual, normal meaning, i.e. that they do not correspond to the meaning of the respective lexical unit as established in the sytem of the language. First, each of the two cases (*aurora borealis*, *promenade deck* as discussed above) is a co-called hapax, i.e. such applications occur in the corpus of texts only once (and the informants, in this case the native speakers of English, can corroborate this by the statement that they can under-

---

[57] The speaker who utters the sentence intends to be as "jocose" as possible in order to disturb the waiter. There are translations of Lewis' Babbitt in which the passage is really misunderstood and the "promenade deck" is taken as if it referred to the restaurant in which the scene takes place. I quote this very extreme example to show that the lexicographer must be prepared to meet the strangest things even when working in the field of a language that enjoys such a lexicographic tradition as English, primarily in colloquial, slang, and journalistic texts or passages, but not only in them.

stand the lexical unit in question as used in the respective passage, but that they would not use it in such a way, for normal communicative purposes). Second, the actual significations of the lexical units, as (figuratively) used in the above sentences, are quite remote from their normal meaning.

Not all cases of figurative application are as extreme as these, however. Sometimes it is even hard to decide whether we have at all a case of a figurative application before us. The meaning of Eng. *bondage* is "serfdom, slavery". What if the lexicographer finds a text in which a man who had lived in an unhappy marriage and then succeeded in getting his divorce refers to the years of his married life as *"the years of my bondage"*? The expression is quite easy to understand though it is (at least to my knowledge) only occasional. But is this a case of figurative use? The answer to this question depends on how we conceive the designatum of the word *bondage*: if we conceive it so that the subject's being a slave or serf or tenant is criterial to it, then we have here a case of the figurative use, because the unhappy husband was neither a slave, nor a serf, nor a tenant of his wife. If, on the other hand, we do not conceive this as criterial for the designatum, then the designatum necessarily becomes much broader and the actual signification of the expression quoted, occasional as it is in this application, can be conceived as corresponding to the normal meaning as established in the system; if we accept this position, we should probably classify this case as contextual nuance (cf. § 1.5.7).[58]

Sometimes, the occasionality of the signification is caused by the fact that the word in question is applied in a way which is not consistent with its usual range of application. Let us consider the following sentence (taken from Nestor [a bibliographical journal in the field of the Mycenaean studies, edited by E. L. Bennet in Madison, Wisc.] Nr. 107 of 1_{st} November 1966, p. 465, under the heading Communications):

"James Lees Sons Co., Bridgeport, Pennsylvania, has named one of its carpet patterns, one with a primitive personality, 'KNOSSOS', and advertised it in House Beautiful, *November 1966."*

The word *personality* seems to be used well within its sense, "the complex of characteristic that distinguishes a particular individual" (Webster); but whereas it is quite usual to apply it in reference to persons, it seems to be rather occasional to use it in reference to a carpet pattern.[59]

[58] About one half of the native speakers of (American) English whose reaction to this expression (plus the subsequent discussion) I was able to observe (which I had several occasions to do, in different places of the United States) took it as a case of figurative use; the other half found it as corresponding to the designatum without any further complication.

[59] The editors of the OED seem also to have seen a similar context, because they remark upon it (s. v., p. 727, sub 2), but against their usual policy, they do not quote it, probably just because of the occasionality of the application (and possibly also because of the low literary status of the source).

1.4.2 It may be clear that the occasional use of a lexical unit and its being used in a figurative sense are two categories which, in many cases, vastly overlap but are nevertheless distinct.[60] Both are of the greatest importance when we study the actual significations of a lexical unit.

For the lexicographer, it is absolutely necessary not only to understand an actual signification of a lexical unit as used in the text; the lexicographer must try to make up his mind about the lexical status of the signification. In this respect, there are basically three possibilities:

(1) The lexical unit occurs as a mere hapax, occasionally, as a "private" expression in a (figurative) signification which is caused by the occasion and is not repeated. (E.g., *aurora borealis* above.)

(2) The lexical unit (*premises* "building etc.") is used so often in another sense, that it is generally understood and is normally used, with this sense. It has thus become a part of the system of language, with the sense. If we wish to qualify such a sense from the historical point of view, we can call it trans-ferred.

(3) Between these two possibilities, there is a vast range of transitional cases. What if the joke about "*bondage*" is frequently repeated? The new application will tend to become a part of the system. What if there are many similar cases of such applications, say *bondage* in reference to the blind love to a woman, in reference to the fanatical subservience to an idea or so? We will tend, in that case, to conceive the designatum as broader, with less specific criterial features.

This whole complex of problems is a cause of constant trouble for the lexico-grapher. There are two main difficulties.

The first of them is of a rather gnoseological nature and can be stated as follows. Language is an interpersonal communicative system which must be stabilized to be interpersonally objective and effective; i.e., the different speakers of the same language cannot use formally identical lexical units with meanings varying vastly from one speaker to another, otherwise the communi-cative power is lost. The lexicographer is mainly interested in the lexical units as parts of this system, in their systemic value, in the lexical meaning they have as parts of the system, in the norm of their use. This system, however, cannot be perceived *per se*, but only when actually manifested in concrete utterances. In the case of a living language, the lexicographer's eventual own knowledge of how to apply the respective lexical unit of his own language is of great importance, and the informants' summary rule-like statements concerning their own knowledge (see below) are valuable as well; but they are based as it were on one idiolect, whereas the lexicographer aims at

---

[60] A similar distinction is established by Akhmanova IJAL 31, 1965, 1959. Cf. also Kovtun LS 1, 1957, 68.

the interpersonal system. — Therefore, the lexicographer (above all when he prepares a monolingual dictionary) must observe all the actual significations of a lexical unit he has at hand and abstract from them what he considers a correct description of the lexical meaning which the lexical unit seem to have as a part of the system of language and to which its actual significations correspond (at least the greatest part of them).

In Fig. 3, this work of the lexicographer is symbolized at the left side of the diagram by the arrow which points from the actual occurrences to the system. But there is also the other arrow which points in the reverse direction, from the system to the occurrences. This symbolizes the fact that the lexicographer's picture of what he considers to be the system exerts a certain influence upon the actual occurrences: we shall see (§ 4.6; 6.7) that the lexicographer's influence upon the usage is if not strong yet appreciable and in some respects important. But this is only a secondary task, both in the hierarchy and in the chronological order of tasks: the recognition of the system must come first; therefore, the second arrow in the above Fig. 3 is only dotted.

The first, basic task is the correct description of the abstract, interpersonal system. It is in connection with this task that the lexicographer meets his first main difficulty. For different reasons, the actual usage (the whole mass of utterances) always shows a degree of vacillation, also in respect to lexical meaning of the lexical units (different occasional uses tec.). The lexicographer must so to say make up his mind where to draw the dashed line of the lower circle (see fig. 3) which is intended to include only those significations that correspond to the system and to leave aside the occasional ones, i.e. he has to decide which signification will be regarded as systemic and which not. But as there is no direct knowledge of the interpersonal system of language and as the lexicographer is forced to derive it from the observation of different actual significations (and eventually from the comparison of the descriptive, rule-like statements of his informants and his own knowledge of the language), he can never be absolutely sure whether he draws the line correctly between what he considers systemic and what occasional.

The lexicographer will be well advised to have the contradistinction *systemic* : : *occasional* as sharply distinguished as possible, in his notional framework. On the other hand, the lexicographer would probably mishandle his data if he tried to treat them with a greater degree of distinctive precision than that which is inherent in the facts of language. It is a fact that the usage vacillates around a focus of what is most usual (and it is this focus which is considered the norm). This vacillation occurs for several reasons: One of them is that the designata are not scientific concepts (as stated above), they are necessarily less precise and broader; the designatum of a word like *beautiful* is necessarily very general, broad, and must allow a considerable vacillation in the concrete applications of it. Another reason of vacillation, which is at the same time the second main difficulty of the lexicographer, is the dynamism of language. It can be generally stated about language that, on the one hand, it must be interpersonally understandable, but that, on the other hand, there are always innovations in it, since it is always used by many people who like expressive innovations because of the vigour, colour, jocose, emotional or any other values of the "new" expression, and because innovations (among them also an originally divergent signification of a lexical unit) are necessary in order to find expressions for new designata etc.[61] There is also the other part of this picture; lexical units or their senses may become obsolete and their use may be discontinued. The lexicographer must constantly take this dynamic aspect of language into consideration.

The dynamic aspect is symbolized by the two arrows on the right side of Fig. 3. The first of these points from the system to the actual occurrences, because the latter emanate from the former and correspond to it. But there occur also the divergent significations; the occasional ones can be conceived as peripheral vacillations around the focus of the systemic use, but some of them become (by repeated, constant use) sanctioned as a part (or as parts) of the system: therefore, the second arrow points from the occurrences to the system. In this respect, a hapax is always more suspect of being merely occasional than those significations for which we have more numerous evidence. We could illustrate this by the following diagram:

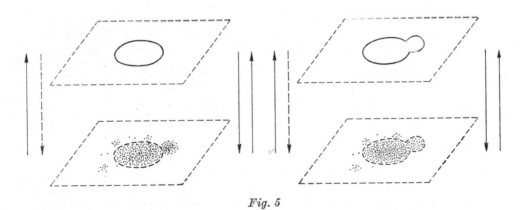

Fig. 5

The following question is, however, constantly present in the lexicographer's work: a great number of occurrences is the cardinal symptom that we have a systemic use before us; but is it only the number of occurrences that changes an occasional use into the norm — part of the system — and if this is so, how many occurrences should be required? It is really only the fact that a word is

---

[61] Cf. Berg, *Report*, p. 4, with a different terminology but a similar approach.

used in a certain way and with a certain meaning, antilogical and antihistorical as it may be (though usually it is not), which causes, in the last instance, the word to have its respective meaning as a part of the system.[62] But it is not sufficient to ask how many occurrences we have attested, unless their number is so overwhelming that it is self-evident that the use is systemic. Much depends on the value of the sources in which the new use occurs (for instance, matter-of-fact texts in written language tend to contain fewer unstabilized expressions — with the eventual exception of terminological innovations — than colloquial or poetic texts) on the eventually observable trend (the number of occurrences may be increasing or decreasing with time), and on other factors. Anyhow, in this respect the descriptive[63] lexicographer's situation is different from that of other descriptive linguist. For him, the factor of the vacillating and diverging applications is of the highest importance even if his interests are absolutely synchronic, because in borderline cases where it is difficult to decide whether a signification is systemic or occasional, his comparison of eventual other similar cases, his estimate of their productivity, or even his attempt at an anticipation of the development will be one of the most important and, if applied with knowledge and success, one of the best criteria.[64]

1.4.3 It is necessary to distinguish a contradistinction of the categories *occasional* : : *systemic*, on one side, and of the categories *figurative* and *transferred*, on the other. Both the contradistinction and the categories are concerned with the status of the respective lexical unit, but the contradistinction *occasional* : : *systemic* is more general. A word can be occasionally used with a strange, new designation (as *aurora borealis* in the sense of *halo* or *bondage* in the sense of "a kind of marital state") connotation, e.g. if somebody says

"*That awful cur of the old spinster deceased, at last*",[65]
or range of application, as if somebody says
"*our last maidservant abdicated*",[66]

[62] Notions like those of the system, of its single constituent parts, etc., are certainly important. On the other hand, it would be wrong to deify these concepts too much.

[63] "Descriptive" is to be taken here as meaning "whose main purpose is not the history of the development of a language".

[64] The point of view taken here is admittedly controversial (I. J. Gelb). The present author accepts a considerable dynamism even in a very stabilized state of language, studied purely synchronically. Cf. my paper *The Synchronic State of Language*, in: Actes du Xeme Congrés International des Linguistes, vol. I (forthcoming).

[65] The point ist that the verb *to decease* has the connotation of belonging to an elevated style. It is an occasional thing to use it in connection with the death of a dog, in order to ridicule the owner's veneration of the animal.

[66] The range of application of the verb is so restricted that it is usually used when a monarch declines to continue his function.

or refers to *two printer's reams of French fried spuds*, as in the sentence quoted above.[67] The fundamental things in these cases is that it is an application of the lexical unit which is coined on the spur of the moment on a certain occasion and is isolated and usually not repeated. Every eventual repetition of such an occasional application, even if it is independently coined at another point of time by another person, tends to stabilize the divergent signification, until it may finally become a part of the system.

The category of figurative senses is concerned primarily with designation. But since the basic components of the lexical meaning (designation, connotation, and the range of application) are very frequently complexly interwowen and determine one another so that they cannot be easily or unequivocally separated, the term *"figurative"* can be understood also in a broader way: e.g., the example of the occasional application of the verb *to abdicate* in an unusual range of application could be also regarded as an example of a figurative use of the word. The main difference between the terms *"figurative"* and *"occasional"* is, however, that the term *"figurative"* is concerned primarily with the semantic relation to the systemic meaning (irrespective of whether this relation is metaphoric, metonymic, etc.), whereas the term *"occasional"* is concerned with the status in the system. When an originally occasional and figurative signification begins to occur frequently and is, therefore, stabilized as a part of the system, it tends to become also what we call the transferred sense. Developing an excellent idea of Casares,[68] we can illustrate the difference between the terms *"figurative"* and *"transferred"* as follows:

The word *crane* has two main senses: (1) "a large wading bird with long legs, neck, and bill"; (2) "a machine for moving heavy weights". Obviously, the second sense came into existence by a metaphorical use of the word which originally possessed only the first sense.[69] This historical consideration, however, has no influence on the fact that today, there is no necessity to understand the connection between the two senses, or to realize it at all, in order to understand the second sense. A sentence like

"For the construction of the bridge, we shall need at least five high cranes"

can be understood even by a person who does not know that there is a bird called *crane* at all. This is, then, a transferred sense, stabilized as a part of the system. On the other hand, in a sentence like

After ten years of matrimonial bondage, he got his divorce,

[67] The lexical unit *printer's ream* has a severely restricted range of application, as a measure for paper only.

[68] See *Introduccion* § 26.

[69] A very old, natural metaphor; the first occurrence of it is to my knowledge in Greek: *géranos* (1) "crane" (bird), (2) "crane" (machine for hoisting). Cf. also, e.g., Armenian *k̆runk* "crane" with the same polysemy (Motalová).

the word *bondage* is necessarily interpreted on the background of its general meaning "slavery etc.". This is figurative use.

It follows that *"transferred"* is a historical category which is concerned with semantic relations that have brought into existence some new sense of a lexical unit but that are either not known or not perceived by the general speakers today. In contradistinction to this, *"figurative"*, is a synchronic category, because it is perceived and understood as such by the present speakers.

Figurative significations use to be occasional, or at least have their origin in an occasional application, because they are generally individual creations of a speaker. But it is not absolutely necessary that a figurative signification be occasional in the strictest sense of the word. As discussed above, there is a vast field between the occasional, isolated application or a *hapax* and the stabile meaning — part of the system: recurrent occurrences of an occasional, figurative signification, either by imitation of the usually famous or influential man who is the author of the innovation or by independent creation of different speakers. In such a case, what was originally occasional tends sometimes to become stabilized. But we call a signification *"figurative"* even if it is no *hapax* and even if there are more occurrences of it, when we can assume that it is understood on the background of the systemic meaning. In this way, we get, by the combined application of the terms discussed above, principally the following three categories; figurative, occasional signification; figurative signification or use which tends to be stabilized, or is at least recurrent; and transferred sense, part of the system.[70]

It is possible to posit a fourth category, namely that of the figurative senses completely stabilized, i.e. which have become part of the system. Zima reports a case in Hausa which seems to belong in this category: *kaafìrin dookìi* (word-for word translation: "pagan horse") has the meaning (1) "speedy horse", (2) "vicious horse": both senses would seem to be figurative, but stabilized. The example has the additional interest of showing the polysemy of figurative senses. *Kaafìrar taabà* = "strong tabacco", *kaafìrin baabaa* = "excellent indigo", so that it can be maintained that *kaafìrii* "pagan" is used figuratively to emphasize the respective good or bad quality.

---

[70] One could make the effort to classify the figurative significations according to the underlying metaphors, metonymies, etc. Such a laborious classification would be of no advantage to the lexicographer. Cf. Filipec SS 18, 1957, 138. — Some authors also use different terms for the concepts discussed above, but it is not necessary to enumerate or analyse them here: the fundamental thing is to understand the conceptual framework. Let us only mention that an element which we say to be stabilized (as a part of the system) is sometimes called a *lexicalized* element. *Lexicalization* is for some authors the process of becoming lexicalized (i.e. what we called stabilized), or its result: the fact that an element has become, i.e. is, a part of the system. Cg. also footnote 16 to chapter III for further terminological remarks concerning the term *lexicalization*.

The point is, however, that the stabilized figurative sense is a rather transitional category, because the respective cases tend to go over to the category of transferred senses: the semantic bridge that connects the two senses gets lost or becomes obscure, just by frequent use. It is, however, in the different styles and restricted languages that we can observe most of the cases which belong here. For example, in poetical language, or in journalistic language, there are some constantly recurring expressions, frequently called clichés, which clearly have a figurative sense, but which are so constantly used that they can be regarded as parts of the system,[71] with figurative senses, but, naturally, only in the system of the respective restricted language. For example, such an expression as *to be devoured by anxiety* can be classified as a stabilized figurative expression, stabilized in poetic language only.[72] In Hindi (as reported by Miltner), *mere rām* means "my Rama" (a God), but when used by a Hindu saint, this expression is used in a figurative sense instead of "I" (because "I", i.e. the individual referring to himself, is no individual but only part of the divinity). This figurative sense seems to be rather stabilized in the respective social dialect.

But in any case, this is only a transitional category. Just by being used (too) frequently, such expressions lose their poetic or expressive or any other colouring, with the result that they either stop being used, or stop being understood as figurative.

Words with figurative senses are frequently found also in different set combinations of words. The lexicographer must remember, however, that such petrified expressions are real wholes, used and understood as wholes, so that for this purposes, let us say twenty occurrences, in his corpus, of the German proverbial saying *das Hasenpannier ergreifen* "to clutch the hare's banner", i.e. "to bolt it" are not twenty occurrences in the figurative sense, of the word *Hasenpannier* "hare's banner", but only one.

1.4.4 The discussion of these categories and of the dynamic aspect of language requires one more remark — on semantic change, as observable in the history of language. It is not necessary to stress the fact that every language changes and develops constantly. Indeed, the fact that words change their meaning, to put in an oversimplifying way the whole difficult and complicated phenomenon of semantic change, is sufficiently well known, and has been so studied that there are very detailed schemes of classification of the various changes, and various theories of the causes of the change.[73] For the lexi-

---

[71] A similar discussion (with Czech examples) in Získal SS$_w$ 4, 1938, 156.

[72] So according to the *Concise Oxford Dictionary*.

[73] Mainly H. Kronasser, *Handbuch der Semasiologie*, Heidelberg 1952, S. Ullmann, *Principles of Sematics*, 2nd ed., Glasgow–Oxford 1957, V. Zvegintsev, *Semasiologija*, Moskva 1957, O. Ducháček, *Précis de sémantique français*, Brno 1967.

cographer, all these classifications of semantic changes are relatively unimportant.

The lexicographer has to indicate the history of the meaning and to classify the change if he is preparing a philological dictionary of a language with the special purpose of indicating the history of the words, an enterprise which is not in the center of interest of the present book; and he has to indicate (but not necessarily classify) the semantic change in the greatest possible detail if he is compiling a synchronic, descriptive dictionary of a language, but intends to deal with the multiple meaning of the single words exclusively on a purely historical principle. For the general purpose of compiling monolingual descriptive and bilingual dictionaries, it is not necessary to indicate in which category of semantic change the development *crane* "bird" > *crane* "machine" belongs; the main thing is to indicate that there are two senses, and what they are.[74] If it is known which of them is the original one, and we have a case of a metaphorical change before us, so much the better; if not, *tant pis*. What must, however, always be taken into consideration, as far as the dynamic aspect of language goes, is the lexical status of a lexical unit (occasional : : stabilized, etc.) and the so to say "contemporaneous history" of it: the fact that changes are going on, in front ot our eyes, by an accumulation of occasional applications that vacillate around the normal use which constitutes the system. Indeed, as already mentioned above, one of the best qualities of an accomplished lexicographer is reliable judgment in such problems as: what is really isolated, whether there is not a similar trend of occasional uses of other words which allows an opinion that the new nuance will be stabilized, whether there are reasons to believe that an accumulation of occasional significations is only ephemeral, etc. But for such a judgement, a mere excerption of words from texts does not suffice; for this purpose, it is necessary to have a really profound knowledge of all spheres of the total language, both literary and spoken, a fine feeling for the subtleties of every utterance, and a historical perspective, at least of the recent epoch of the language in question.

POLYSEMY

1.5 The fact has been mentioned that the Eng. word *crane* can be used in reference to birds of a species and to machines of a type. This phenomenon is usually called p o l y s e m y. As a general term, it designates the fact that a

[74] It goes without saying that we do not militate against the knowledge of the history of language. The lexicographer will certainly gain by it, in any case. The point is, however, that it is not necessary to indicate all those details, and that it is also possible to work ·in languages whose history is unknown.

single word can have different senses; polysemy is, then, a general linguistic category. The same term *polysemy* can be used, however, to refer to a single, concrete word (lexical unit) of a language: the "polysemy of a word" means, then, all the possible senses the word has. Because of possible terminological complications and misunderstandings, it is probably better to avoid the term in this case and to speak either about the *total*, or *polysemous*, or *multiple meaning* of a word, or about *all the senses of a polysemous word*, or to use similar terms.

It is probably not necessary to explain the notion of polysemy in great detail, because it is generally known. One can open any dictionary of any language and one will find examples of polysemy on every page. Indeed, polysemy is such a frequent phenomenon that it is generally only very specific words like *to outfly, to outfoe, to outfox, medallionist, ninox* and the terms that are not polysemous. But even the technical terms are polysemous more frequently then one would think (e.g. *carburettor* (1) in a combustion engine (2) in an apparatus for manufacturing carburetted water gas).

It is also necessary to stress the fact that polysemy is a phenomenon which is not restricted to the designative type of lexical meaning, cf. Eng. *but, yet*, etc. Zima reports the following Hausa example: *koo* (1) "or", (2) "whether", (3) "either — or", "whether or" (*koo-koo*), (4) "even, yet", (5) question-in-troducer. Heroldová reports Chinese *hai-shih* (1) "or", (2) "still", (3) "rather", Kalousková Chinese *ho* (1) "with", (2) "and", Novotná Chinese *yu* (1) "again", (2) "moreover", (3) "and", "both — and, neither — nor", Mota-lová reports Armenian *or* (1) (interrog. and relat.), (2) "that"; in the collo-quial language also (3) "in order to", (4) "when", (5) "if".

For the practice of the lexicographer it is necessary to discuss mainly the following points and, above all, the following terms (§ 1.5.1—1.5.5).

1.5.1 One of the simplest terms can be illustrated by the verb *to devour*. If we accept the analysis of the Concise Oxford Dictionary,[75] we can say that we find in the verb one direct sense, viz. "to eat". This *"direct sense"* is a term without which the lexicographer can hardly do, though it is not possible to define it in a rigorous way. Probably the easiest approach to it is the nega-tive one: the direct sense is the sense from which other senses can, in the semantic analysis, be derived by the assumption that they are characteri-zed by some added[76] connotation, or by the sense being figurative, or in a similar way: they are marked, whereas the direct sense is unmarked. Direct senses will usually be those which do not belong to a special restricted language,

---

[75] 4th edition, 1951; our presentation is reduced in length and unsubstantially changed.

[76] This term "added" must be taken only in the sense of the semantic analysis supposed here.

style etc. In this way, we can conceive the lexical meaning of the verb *to devour* as consisting of the direct sense "to eat" (of beasts), with an expressive connotation if used about men. To this sense, the various figurative senses in various degrees of stabilization — some of them perhaps nearly transferred — and belonging to various spheres of the language, can be joined: "waste, destroy" (property, or its owners), "kill, decimate" (of fire, plague etc.), "take in greedily with ears or eyes" (book, beauty), "absorb the attention of" (part.), *devour the way* etc. "go fast", esp. of horses.

1.5.2 In the same way, transferred senses can be conceived, in the semantic analysis, as being grouped around the direct sense. This is very often the case of a word that is used in general language with a general sense and in technical terminology with transferred, technical sense (which is frequently coined, at the origin, as a figurative one, but becomes absolutely stabilized). In this way, we can conceive, for instance, the relation of the senses of the Eng. word *nut* (1) "kernel of a hard fruit" (direct sense of a general nature), (2) "part of different machines" (transferred sense of a technical — terminological nature).

In languages the speakers of which only recently changed their cultural surroundings (usually, in our age, by accepting some elements of European and American civilization), there are semantic situations which can be understood in a similar way. Garvin[77] reports some Kutenai words which have both what can be called with him "*native senses*" and "*accultured senses*", as examples. Similar cases of multiple meaning are known in other languages. Petráček for example, reports the Arabic *barqun* (1) "lightning", (2) "telegraph"; *wisāmun* (1) "branded mark on a camel's skin", (2) "order, decoration". Miltner reports Hindi *bijlī* (1) "lightning", (2) "electricity"; *tār* (1) "wire, string", (2) "telegraph". Generally, such cases can be conceived as examples of the specialized sense (§ 1.5.3). Zvelebil reports Tamil kuntu (1) "anything globular and heavy, ball", (2) "bomb".

A more intricate, and in its outcome highly optimistic, example of this type of acculturation is reported by Zima from Hausa: *sìyaasà* (old loan-word from Arabic) has the senses (1) (a) "clemency", (b) "the reduction of price of an article", and recently also (2) "politics".

There will be, however, similar cases which one will be disinclined to conceive in this way. Let us take, for instance, the case of the word *crane* (1) "bird", (2) "machine". The metaphorical transfer of the second sense is here, from the point of view of the development, precisely analogous to that of the second sense of the word *nut*. What is the difference, then? *Crane* (1) "bird" does not seem to have such a clear status as a general — language word as *nut* (1).

[77] Anais 7.

Indeed, it would be interesting to know (among other criteria) whether the occurrences of *crane* (2) are not, statistically, more frequent than those of *crane* (1). In psychologistical terms, the sense of *crane* (1) is less likely to be thought of first by people faced with the word in isolation than *nut* (1). As far as synchrony goes, the word *crane* approaches (at least) the status of the word with two direct senses. Of course we know the historical development, in this case, and take it into consideration.[78] But in many cases, we do not know it; and in the languages for which the present book is primarily written, the number of cases in which the precise history will remain unknown, at least for the moment, is considerable. Nevertheless, the point is that what is historically a transferred sense can be, in synchronical semantic analysis, a direct one this is so above all when the word is very frequently used in the sense in question: ignorance of the real development may be an additional factor in the situation.

1.5.3 Another important notion for dealing with polysemy is the specialized sense. This term designates a sense of a word, that reveals itself in some specialized contexts, usually dealing with a unified subject matter, as, e.g., a branch of science, technology etc. It is most often the case that these specialized senses have a terminological value; that the word in question is used, in these contexts, as a term of the respective branch of knowledge. For example the word *table* has different senses in different broad ranges of contexts, but it has the sense of "flat, usually rectangular surface, horizontal moulding esp. cornice" only when used as an architectural term. In a similar way, Armenian (reported by Motalová) *vernahark* means generally "the highest floor"; in the sphere of apiculture, however, it has the specialized sense "the upper part of the bee-hive". Armenian *xonarhvel* means "to bow, to submit to"; but in grammatical terminology, "to be conjugated".

One word has sometimes more specialized senses, which belong to different terminological sets; sometimes, the processes of specialization can be proved to have taken place in different epochs, and sometimes even the texts an which the two senses occur come from different epochs; but this is not always necessarily the case. Petráček reports from Arabic: The act. partic. from *hatafa* "to cry, shout aloud" is *hātifun* "shouting aloud". In texts of the older mystics, this substantivized participle has the specialized sense "the unknown shouting voice, he who shouts, and is not seen". In contemporary Arabic, it is used in the sense "inner voice" (attested e.g. 1954); but it has also the other specialized sense "telephone".

Sometimes, the specialized sense has arisen in a multiword lexical unit which was later shortened by ellipsis (§ 3.3.1). For example Arabic (Petráček)

---

[78] That is, we take it into consideration in the lexicographic presentation and we know it as students of language. Clearly, this is a situation vastly different from that of the general speaker's understanding and constantly perceiving the relation of a direct and a figurative sense.

ǧāmiʿatun "league, society : : *ǧāmiʿatun* "storage battery" which is a stabilized ellipsis for the original *ǧāmiʿatu' l-kahrabā'*i; "apparatus for the storage of
electricity".

1.5.4 The meaning of many polysemous words can be conceived as consisting
of direct senses, transferred senses (if these are not yet so frequently and so
independently used that they should themselves be regarded as direct ones),
specialized senses, figurative senses, and occasional significations; and all this
in any combinations and any quantities. Some of the non-direct senses can be
grouped with the direct ones, but this is not always the case.

The lexicographer will see in his practice that the single senses (usually
with the exception of the terminological ones), overlap or that there are many
borderline cases. Indeed, we shall see later (p. § 1.6) that where the single
senses lose their connection, homonymy begins and the word and its meaning
can be split into two. But though it is an error if the lexicographer tries to
make the single senses more sharply distinguished from each other than is
indicated by the data, the establishment of the single senses and their organization are, on the other hand, among the lexicographer's cardinal tasks.

If we assume, for example, three direct senses of the word *table*, namely (1)
"article of furniture", (2) "slab of wood or stone", etc., and (3) "list of facts,
numbers, etc., systematically arranged esp. in columns", we can then posit
that the following senses (special, figurative, or transferred) are connected in
various and different ways with the direct senses: (a) "part of machine-tool
on which work is put to be operated on" — probably a specialized sense related
to (1); (b) "level area, plateau" — related to (1)?; (c) "company seated at
table" — to (1); (d) "food provided at table" — to (1); (e) "matter written on
a slab" — to (2); (f) "flat, usually rectangular surface, horizontal moulding
esp. cornice"; (g) "flat surface of gem, cut gem with two faces"; (h) "palm of
hand"; (i) "each of two bony layers of skull" — all these last senses are probably connected with (2).

1.5.5 In the case of some highly polysemous words, one of the senses,
usually one of the direct ones, can be called d o m i n a n t.[79] This is a purely
impressionistic notion, but very important for the lexicographer. In psychologistic terms, the dominant sense is the one which is the first to be thought
of by the majority of the speakers of a language if presented with the word in
isolation, without any context.[80] It is quite possible that if someone were to

---

[79] Cf. F e l d m a n LS 2, 1957, 86.

[80] The present psychologistic approach is inspired by H. P a u l. — K. L. P i k e, *Language in
Relation to a Unified Theory of the Structure of Human Behavior*, The Hague — Paris 1967, p. 600ff.,
uses the term *central meaning*. According to him, *central meaning* (i.e. *sense* in our terminology)
is "the one which was leaned early in life" (though "as the speaker grows older, ... the central

make an experiment in which the isolated word *table* were put before a number of average speakers of English, a mathematician would indicate the sense "list of numbers" as the one which occurred to him first; but it is most probable that the majority of the questioned persons would think of the piece of furniture first. If this is really so, then the sense "article of furniture" is the dominant one in the meaning of the word *table*.

Several remarks must be made in this connection. First, there are words which have several direct senses, but none of them is clearly dominant. This is very often the case when all of them are rarely used, (e.g. *escutcheon* (1) "shield with armorial bearings", (2) "middle of ship's stern where name is placed", (3) "pivoted keyhole-cover") or, on the contrary, when all of them have a very high rate of frequency (e.g. *work* (1) "application of effort to some purpose", (2) "task undertaken" and probably also (3) "thing done", (4) "employment, esp. the oppurtunity to earn money by labour, etc.").

Second, the notion of the dominant sense is purely a psychologistic one and is concerned only with the way language is spoken by the general, average speaker. There will be a connection between the psychologistically founded notion of the dominant sense and some other notions founded on the statistical frequency of the word with the sense in question. As this relation however is, practically unexplored, it will be better not to venture speculative opinions on its nature, but to wait until precise experiments and counts are done. The lexicographer will be well advised to rely more on the psychologistically founded notion of the dominant sense, because he will always be able to add some objective value to his own judgment by arranging a little inquiry among the members of his staff and among his informants; the relative numbers of different contexts collected in his files may give him also some orientation, but a really representative statistical count will usually be impossible.[81]

Third, the notion of the dominant sense is not dissimilar to that of the basic sense as used by some lexicographers and students of semantics. The latter, however, is usually connected either with logical or with historical considerations. If conceived as a historical notion, (*basic sense* = the most original one, from which all the other senses really developed) the term has

meaning becomes to some extent relative to the universe of discourse in which it is used"). For example, "the word *nose* ist learned in the context of the child's body rather than in that of projectiles". There will be a great area of overlapping between this notion of Pike's and our *dominant sense*.

[81] Let us not forget that for a decision over a question such as, say, whether some signification is absolutely occasional or not, five, ten, twenty or so contextual passages may be of some use, whereas for a question like that about the eventual dominant sense of Eng. *work*, there would be scores of thousands of occurrences. — The intention of this remark is not to dissuade or deter the lexicographer from using statistical counts where they are at his disposal; but experience shows that the lexicographer generally is not in a situation to make them himself, at least not on a really representative scale and with the full rigor of the statistical method.

some disadvantages. First of all, the historical aspect is sometimes at variance with the synchronic state of affairs. If the lexicographer puts too strong an emphasis on the notion of the basis sense in its historical acceptation, he will, seeing Latin *tabula* = "board", probably feel the inclination to conceive the meaning of the word, say, *table* as consisting of the basic sense "board, slab of wood or stone", and only then of the other senses; but this would probably be at variance with the situation in present-day English. This does not mean that the lexicographer should display a disregard of or even contempt for the historical aspect. For example, if there are no other factors to consider, why not indicate the sense of the word *crane* in their historical order, (1) "bird", (2) "machine". But if a lexicographer finds, to consider a fictive (or yet fictive) example, that the second sense as indicated here is the dominant one, say by a well founded test, then he should be permitted to indicate the sequence (1) "machine", (2) "bird", if it is a descriptive dictionary of the present day language that he is compiling and if he does not accept and consistently apply the purely historical principle in all other entries.

The logical interpretation of the term *basic sense* also causes some difficulties. Is it the sense from which the other senses can be derived, by a logical procedure, which should be regarded as the basic one? If so, it will be impossible to find it, in the majority of cases, or there will be several candidates to the title. Or is it a general sense that covers the single senses which should be regarded as the basic one? But there will most often be no such sense observable in the linguistic data. One must also take into consideration the circumstance that the logical approach, though it cannot be eliminated absolutely (as we shall see § 6.5.5.1), brings with it the danger that the logical, notional apparatus of logic and logical classifications will clash with the classifications of language. The psychologistic approach with the notion of the dominant sense has at least the advantage that it brings results observably based upon the way in which speakers themselves understand their own language — a factor certainly not irrelevant or foreign to the linguistic world.

1.5.6 The lexicographer will do well to reckon always with polysemy: this will cause him to undertake very deep analyses of the words' meanings. There are, however, two main dangers connected with the notion of polysemy which he should avoid.

The first of these dangers is that the lexicographer might try to put all his data into the pigeonholes of the categories which were discussed above, disliking the idea that there are always borderline cases. Worse than that, he might try to posit only a few patterns of polysemy and then try to arrange all his data in all his items *only* according to these few schemes. On the one hand, it can be contended that every word has some properties that are similar to those of some other words, as, for example, some grammatical or semantic properties, or that the word is archaic, or symptomatic of its user's being a learned and possibly a starchy man, or that it is without any connotation, etc. But every word (lexical unit) has also something that is individual, that makes it different from any other word. And it is just the lexical meaning which is the most outstanding individual property of the word. And more than that, the dictionary's purpose is to present the words (lexical units) as individual entities, with all their relevant properties (or at least the more important ones). Therefore, the lexicographer must study very carefully every lexical unit with all its combinatorial possibilities, and comparing it with all similar words, no doubt, but as a world of its own, though; in his presentation, he must not iron out the differences, really existing among the single lexical units, for the sake of an absolutely uniform treatment of polysemy.

By this remark, I do not intend to puncture the whole foregoing discussion.

Indeed, we do not deny by the preceding remark that, for example, connotation is an objectively observable component of lexical meaning and that many words show identical connotations. The lexicographer will have to study each of his words to see which, if any, connotation plays a role in its lexical meaning. But the lexicographer must not forget that there is for example a world of difference between the slightly bookish and elevated style connotation of the word *do devour* "to eat" (of beasts), and the strongly expressive and vulgar-style connotation of the nasty words. To take an example from another field, the lexicographer will know that he is able to state with sufficient conviction that the range of application of the verb to *miaow* (in the direct sense), is severely restricted to cats only, but that his eventual indication that *stipend* concerns mainly the clergyman's salary cannot be stated with a similar absolute validity. He will know that the terminological clarity of a word like *typhlitis* is vastly different from that of *reflex* "medicinal, psychological etc. term", as contrasted from but connected with the nonterminological senses (1) "reflected light or colour or glory", (2) "image in a mirror" etc., (3) "reproduction, secondary manifestation, correspondent result". He will know that the single direct and figurative senses of some words can be put into contradistinction with sufficient clarity, while they overlap in the case of other words. In short, the lexicographer will know that the variety of patterns in which the polysemous meaning of the lexical units can be organized is caused not only by the presence or absence of different properties and by their different combinations, but also by the fact that the same quality can be present in different words in widely differing degrees.

The other danger the lexicographer must be aware of is that he could regard some phenomena as symptoms of polysemy while they are not so. We shall discuss as an example the English verb *to take*. We can see that it occurs in a great number of various contexts,[82] e.g. *to take offence, to take a wicket, to take sides, to take someone's meaning*. One might think that these contexts show that the verb is highly polysemous. But to the contrary, these contexts show the so-called de pletion: the verb is semantically depleted. Weinreich[83] very aptly says that in expressions like these, the verb functions "as little more than a verbalizer, not entirely unlike *-ize* and other affixes".[84] That he is certainly right cannot be doubted; cf. the Amharic example reported by Petráček: *alä* "to say" is used as verbalizer when there is no verbal stem, e.g. *k'äs* "slowly, attentively" :: *k'äs alä* "he was attentive, he went slowly he made something slowly" etc. Other similar depleted "verbalizers" are reported from Armenian (Motalová), e.g., *anel* "to make; to give": *ban anel* "to do something, to work", *baç anel* "to open", *zoh anel* "to sacrifice", *vnas anel* "to do harm", *lvaçk' anel* "to wash", *vizit anel* "to pay a visit", *likvidacija anel* "to liquidate". Novotná reports Chinese *ta* "to beat" (as in *ta kou* "to beat a dog"); for the depleted sense of the verb, cf., e.g., *ta p'ir* "to remove the peel", *i-fu pei ch'ung ta le* "the dress was damaged by the moths", *ta yü* "to catch fish", *ta ch'e-piao* "to buy tickets" (for train or bus), *ta yao* "to buy a medicament", *ta san* "to hold the umbrella", *ta chi-tan* "to break eggs", *ta hsi-kua* "to cut (a fresh) melon", *ta ching* "to build a well", *ta ch'eng* "to buid a wall", *ta mao-i* "to knit a sweater", *ta lien-tao* "to make sickles", *ta la* "to wax", *ta p'u-k'e* "to play poker", *ta tien-pao* "to telegraph", *ta tien-hua* "to telephone", *ta chu-i* "to get an idea", *ta leng-chan* "to shiver from cold". Cf. also Ossetic *känyn*, § 3.3.1.

How shall we draw a line between polysemy and depletion?

If we take an extreme example, we can speculate about the meaning the verb *to take* may have in a sentence like

I think she will take well.

The most probable assumption seems to be that the whole sentence and the verb will convey no real information until one knows, either from the context of what was or will be said or written earlier or later, or from the context of the physical situation in which the sentence is said, that somebody is giving his opinion on the question of whether a girl is photogenic or not. If this is

---

[82] The following examples can be conceived as cases of set expressions; such a conception does not change the point of views on depletion adopted here.

[83] *Universals* 144 ff. (cf. also 162) and IJAL 30, 1964, 409; the following example is largely inspired by Weinreich and Poldauf, the notion of depletion mainly by Weinreich and Horálek LSB 13.

[84] Cf. that some of the cases discussed § 1.8.1 where a lexical unit either has a designative meaning or a functional one can be conceived as cases of depletion. Petráček reports a good example from Amharic: *allä* "to be" is used, in a shortened form *al*, as auxiliary verb to form the periphrastic imperfect conjugation.

true, then nearly all concrete information is supplied by the context; therefore, the verb as used in this expression is semantically depleted.[85]

If we consider the English expressions quoted above from this point of view, we see that the situation is practically the same; the information is conveyed almost entirely by the context, except that in the above cases the context is a verbal and close one (*offence, wicket, ship, sides* etc.).

In this way, the borderline between depletion and polysemy can be drawn. In a case of depletion, the context adds very substantially to the meaning of the word in question, or it is only the context which conveys the concrete information. In a case of polysemy, the context eliminates out of the whole meaning of the word those senses which do not apply. By such an elimination of those senses which do not apply the meaning of the polysemous word (lexical unit) can be said to be disambiguated.

Let us consider what we called the direct senses of the polysemous word *table*. If we hear a sentence like

"Don't put it into the cupboard, put it on the table here",

we do not hesitate a moment to assume that it is the piece of furniture which is meant, senses (2) and (3) being eliminated. If, on the other hand, we hear a sentence like

"I forgot the value of n for $12°$, look it up in the table!",

we do not hesitate about what is meant — senses (1) and (2) are eliminated and the meaning of the word *table* is thus disambiguated.

Another symptom of semantic depletion is that it is hard to formulate the designatum of such a word because of the lack of some concrete semantic features, and that the designatum, if formulated at all, is extremely vague.

---

[85] For the sake of simplicity, we discuss depletion as if it were an either-or phenomenon. But there are different degrees of depletion. Let us consider the following Burmese problem (reported by Minn Latt): The word *loup* carries besides the more common senses as "to do", "to make", "to word as a specific sense", "to act artificially or assume a rather improper, affected attitude", as found in expressions like

> *ethíj loup* "to play guest (instead of making oneself at home)"
> *hsăyá loup* "to assume the role of a great teacher or adviser"
> *thúhtei loup* "to behave like a millionaire"
> *lútat loup* "to act like a know-all"
> *mjekhná loup* "to fawn upon someone".

We can often hear an utterance *loup néi pyán pí* "(he's) doing it again!" groaned by someone, but this can be understood only when we have some knowledge about the particular weaknesses of the third person in question. Here we may say that *loup* is depleted, but certainly not so much as the verbs mentiond abouve; one could perhaps take this as a situation which shows the generality of meaning. Let us suppose that we raise the question *bhá loup néi thale* "what is (he) doing?" We do not necessarily have a case of depletion here. The answer may also be a prosaic one — *auyoup twéi loup néi té* "(he) ist making dolls".

Naturally it will not be always possible to decide with sufficient clarity and persuasion whether we have a case of depletion or of polysemy before us. A decision must, however, be sought and a solution tried if the lexicographer wishes to perform his duty satisfactorily: otherwise, the lexicographer may commit the error of indicating as different senses what are in reality only different applications of a depleted word.

It is also true that a word can be polysemous just because it can be used either as a semantically depleted word or with a full lexical meaning. This can be shown by a comparison of the expressions containing the verb *to take* quoted above with a sentence like

"I asked nobody for permission, but simply took it"

where the verb is not semantically depleted.

And let us not forget that quite apart from the depletion, the meaning of a word possesses in any case a certain generality, so that what we might consider single senses are characteristic peaks in the continuum of possible applications.

1.5.7 At this point, it will be necessary to examine in greater detail the role of context. Weinreich[86] is perfectly right when he says that the meanings of words grammatically combined (i.e. forming a context) interact. There are different degrees of this interaction or of this, if we wish to consider the matter from another angle, influence of context.[87]

First, we have words which are semantically autonomous, autosemantic; the context exercises only a weak influence on them.[88] It is mostly words which are not polysemous and most frequently, terms that belong to this category: e.g. *typhlitis* will be the same illness, irrespective of the context in which it may appear. But even terms frequently need disambiguation: the patient 's reflexes are not only different from the reflexes of public opinion; even within the former category, much depends upon whether it is the psychiatrist or the surgeon, or a behaviorist, for that, who tests the patient.

Second, the context determines the sense of a word which applies, and eliminates those which do not. It is the polysemous words (and the homonyms, see p. 74) that belong here. This disambiguation was mentioned above (§ 1.5.6) in connection with semantic depletion, but we shall mention it here

---

[86] LP 25.

[87] The classification is to some extent inspired by Filipec SS 18, 1957, 135.

[88] In other terminologies, *autosemantic* are termed lexical units of designative character, *synsemantic* those lexical units which perform expecially the grammatical functions, which function as substitutes (pronouns), etc.

again to complete the discussion of the context.[89] A good example is discussed by Amosova.[90] If we take a sentence from a newspaper, say

"The cutter moved a paradoxical solution of the issue",

we can see that it is only the word *paradoxical* which is not influenced by the context. That *moved* is to be taken here in the sense "propose in a deliberative assembly" is indicated by *solution*, which, in its turn, cannot mean "separation", or "chemical, mechanical dissolving" just because of the verb *moved*. The word *issue* cannot mean "progeny; result" or anything else, because of *solution*. What remains is the word *cutter*: that it is neither a boat nor a brick nor a thing that cuts is clear from the verb + object phrase *moved a solution*; but what sort of a cutter "person who cuts" we have here is indicated only by the context of the situation as narrated in this broader verbal context: the sentence is taken from a report on a miners' meeting.

Third, the context gives the word a meaning, or renders its meaning more concrete. This is the case of the synsemantic, semantically depleted words. Cf. Eng. *to take* as discussed above, p. 68.[91]

As already mentioned, the borderline between the second category and the third is neither absolute nor always clear.

There is yet another type of the word — context relation which, regrettably rather unexplored as it is, possibly deserves to be singled out as the fourth category. Sometimes, the context significantly adds to the meaning of a word which is not semantically depleted. In such a case, we can speak about a contextual nuance; we shall do so mostly when this modification of the sense is not absolutely occasional, but not (yet) stabilized, either. For example, the Ossetic verb *adargh wyn* means "to become more extended" and it is extension in space that is implied; if there is, however, an Ossetic sentence like

nyxas ägär adargh is "the talk was too extended",

then we can conceive the obvious temporal extension as a contextual nuance of the verb.

---

[89] Other terminologies use the term *determination*; so especially German and other rather philosophically oriented terminologies.

[90] N. N. Amosova LS 5, 1962, 44. The discussion is reduced here.

[91] Cf. footnote 88. — Another terminology calls such or similar words *syncategorematic*; for instance (to take a modern example), J. Katz, *Philosophy of Language*, New York 1966. This term, however, implies, at least in the way Katz applies it, rather the circumstance that a syncategorematic word needs context to have its signification concretized. Cf. contexts as the following ones: *a good doctor, a good man, a good knife, a good afternoon's walk*, in which *good* is syncategorematic, because the "goodness" implied is of different character. (In the approach of the present book, these cases belong to the generality of meaning.)

One of the senses of Eng. *to canonize* can be indicated as "to regard as sanctioned, rightly and securely established ..." (Webster). In Galsworthy's Forsyte Sage 3, Part III, Chap. 1, we read the following sentence:

"Jolyon had become an Eton boy, for old Jolyon's whim had been that he should be canonised at the greatest possible expense".

We can take this as a case of contextual nuance, as what is, in a rather unusual way, implied is the social position gained by the stay in a Public School, not an ecclesiastical dignity, fame, or reputation.

Contextual nuances are very elusive. If we compare the preceding paragraph with what has been said § 1.4.1, we see that there is an area of overlapping: undoubtedly, there will be many cases which will be considered by some scholars as examples of the figurative senses, by other scholars as examples of contextual nuances.

For example, we read in Galsworthy's Forsyte Saga 3, part II, chapter 7, the following sentence:

"The thing" [viz. a new, too luxurious car considered by a conservative man of non-ostentatious tastes] *"typified all that was fast, insecure, and subcutaneously oily in modern life".*

The word *oily* undoubtedly has the sense "unctually ingratiating or insinuating"; *subcutaneously* seems to be inspired by an expression like *subcutaneous fat*, but seems to suggest that the "ingratiating or insinuating" properties indicated by *oily* are covert, hidden, disguised. I incline to the opinion that we should classify this as a contextual nuance of the meaning of *subcutaneous(ly)* though the classification as a case of an occasional, figurative sense of this terminological word is not impossible, either. But also on the other side of the scale will be a great amount of overlapping: we know from § 1.4 that the application of a lexical unit makes its signification more concrete than its systemic meaning can be. Therefore, what are concretizations for one scholar can be regarded as contextual nuances by another. For instance, cf. the following two sentences:

"My fork is broken, give me a good one, please";

"I am rather wet after the walk, I would like to have a good fire in the bedroom to-day".

Though the concrete qualities of a good fork are vastly different from those of a good fire, my opinion would be that neither sentence shows a contextual nuance of the word *good*; it seems that we have to do with cases of concretization of general meaning by application in different contexts, by reference to different denotata. But opinions may differ on the matter.

The lexicographer should not be disgusted by all these possibilities of different conceptions and classifications; they are caused by the generality of lexical meaning the description and presentation of which is one of the lexico-grapher's tasks.

In all these four categories, it is the lexical meanings of the words which interact in the context; therefore, we can call it the lexical context and see in it a species of the verbal context.

1.5.8 Taken on the whole, polysemy will always prove a hard riddle for the lexicographer. He will be forced to study it not only from the point of view of "pure" semantics, by analyzing the lexical meaning of isolated words itself, basically in the categories suggested here, but also from the point of view of the grammatical and the semantic combinations and combinatorial possibilities of the words.

Because of polysemy, we will have to give our original diagram (fig. 3) a more complicated form:

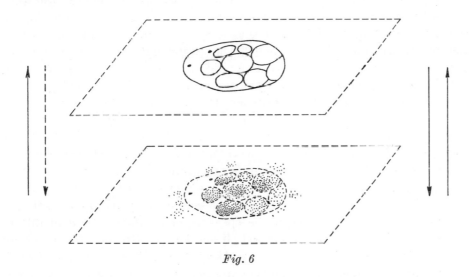

Fig. 6

On the level of the system, meaning is shown as having a certain extension and as consisting of discernably different senses: the direct, around the direct the transferred and figurative ones, with the small dots of the specialized senses; the whole area of meaning is not covered by the sub-areas of the senses.

On the level of occurrences, the dots represent actual significations; the majority of them corresponds to the meaning on the level of the system and is enclosed in the dashed circle. Within this circle areas of greater density of dots correspond to the single senses on the level of the system: they are enclosed in the dotted circles.

What has been stated about the difficulties connected with the establish-ment of the systemic meaning from and by the actual significations is equally valid as far as the senses go. The situation, its description and presentation is frequently even more difficult, because the applications form a continuum with observable peaks but unclear boundaries.

HOMONYMY

1.6 A notion very closely connected with that of polysemy is homonymy. If somebody who knows English hears three sentences, say

(1) *"In the class, there are 20 boys and 15 girls"*,
(2) *"John went out with his girl today, so he will come late, probably"*, and
(3) *Cook can't do all her work; we'll have to get a new girl to help her'*,

he will probably sum up his observations by the statement that the word *girl* has three different senses, namely (1) "young female child", (2) "sweetheart", and (3) "maidservant". If somebody who knows Ossetic hears four different sentences and finds in one the word *fyd* meaning "meat", in the other the word *fyd* meaning "millstone", in the third the word *fyd* meaning "father", and in the fourth the word *fyd* meaning "evil", he will probably sum up his observations by the statement that there are in Ossetic four words with the identical form *fyd* but each with a different meaning. In the case of English *girl*, polysemy is assumed, the three senses being regarded as belonging to one identical word. In Ossetic, homonymy is assumed, the four meanings[92] being regarded as belonging to four different words.

In this way, the category of homonymy is founded on the way the speakers understand and interpret the meaning or the senses[92] of identical forms. Homonymy begins at the point when the speakers of a language are unable to conceive different senses as connected: if speakers of Russian are unable to conceive *mir* "world" and *mir* "peace", or *blenda* "screen" and *blenda* "miner's" safety lamp[93] as connected[94], then they are not single words with polysemous meaning, and we have to regard both pairs of words as pairs of homonymous words, as pairs of homonyms.

It is on purpose that we speak about "unconnected senses" in a very general way. In Arabic (as reported by Petráček), there are rather numerous pairs of words with different meanings (*addād*) like:

---

[92] No need to draw the reader's attention to the fact that the difference between sense and meaning in this passage is caused by our terminology only.

[93] Examples and conception inspired by Ďurovič LSB 67; cf. Kutina LS 4, 1960, 43.

[94] This "connection" is a very broad term which includes any type of relation existing between a direct sense on the one side and a transferred or figurative sense on the other, or even between different direct senses.

ašǧā	"gay"	— "sad"
sadfatun	"darkness"	— "light"
ʿaǧūzun	"young girl"	— "old woman"
bāna	"he appeared"	— "he disappeared"
raǧā'un	"hope"	— "fear" etc.[95]

It these opposite meanings are conceived as "connected" by the speakers of Arabic, then we can conceive of these cases as of examples of polysemy, not of homonymy.

Of course it is a pity that we have to rely on the subjective interpretations of the speakers, but we have hardly anything else on hand. And after all, a language exists to be spoken and understood, and it exists by being spoken and understood, so that the intersubjective understanding of the speakers can be considered a criterion.

There is here a vast area of uncertainty and very much depends upon the speaker's knowledge of the language, upon the lexicographic tradition existing in the concrete case and upon the speaker's knowledge of it, and upon similar varying factors. But this is not necessarily a proof that the conception of homonymy submitted here is wrong. Why should such a variation be a negative proof? After all, it seems to be reasonable to assume that the status of *crane* "bird" and *crane* "machine" will differ, depending upon the speaker's knowledge of the language and his imagination; and also that there will be a tendency of development which may make the pair absolutely homonymous, in the end.[96]

Very much depends upon the speaker's education and other circumstances, too. For instance, the speaker's personal decision whether Eng. *minister*, standing for (1) "state dignitary" and (2) "clergyman," is one polysemous word or two homonyms will be highly influenced by his eventual knowledge of Latin. But such an influence of education on the interpretation of one's own language is a rather frequent phenomenon: for example the morphemic status of such everyday words as *telegraph*, *telephone* will vary vastly, the speaker's education being the free variable.[97]

---

[95] Quoted from V. Monteil, *L'arabe moderne*, Paris 1960, p. 211. — Zima reports similar pairs from Yoruba: *kú* "to die" : : *kù* "to remain"; *bó* "to strip off" : : *bò* "to cover". There certainly is a connection between the members of the pairs, but for the lexicographer (as for the linguist) they are sufficiently distinguished by the tones so that they are neither homonyms nor homophones; were the tones not expressed in the orthography, the members of the pairs would, however, be homographs (cf. § 1.6.2).

[96] On the tendency of specialized, technical and terminological senses of words with polysemous meaning to develop into independent homonyms (e.g. Czech *matka* "mother" : : *matka* "nut of a screw"), see Ďurovič LSB 72 and Horálek LSB 16.

[97] The point is doubted by L. J. Gelb (private communication). See, however, further on the different understanding of a word by different speakers, with different education.

As an example of variation on another dimension, Petráček reports (after D. Cohen) that the connection of Colloquial Arabic *şkhaṭ* "to afflict with God's wrath" and its form *məşkhūṭ* which has the meaning "beautiful" is realized only among female speakers, and not among the male ones.

These examples seem to show that it is not necessary to see in the variation of the single speaker's conception an argument against the conception of homonymy advocated here, because similar variation can be observed also in other categories. Generally, it can be remarked that there is more subjective variation in the understanding of language. What is an intolerably dirty word for one speaker is a normal expression for the other; what seems to be ridiculously archaic to one speaker is an everyday word to the other, etc. In spite of these differences, the lexicographer makes his decisions and classifications in these areas, too. His decisions are founded frequently not on a unanimous agreement of all the speakers, but only on a reasonably impressive agreement of a number of speakers he accepts (for reasons which will be discussed later) as representative. There is no reason why he should not be guided by the same principle in his dealing with the homonyms.

It is pleasant to have the intersubjective attitude of the speakers corroborated by the history of the two respective words. If we take Russian (I) *ikra* 'caviar' and (II) *ikra* "calf of the leg", we are not surprised to find that the intersubjective conception of the speakers of Russian classifies the two as a pair of homonyms; we are, however, happy to have this corroborated by the historical study which shows that the two words have different etymology and converged later in their form.[98] The same applies to Eng. (I) *calf* "young of cow" and (II) *calf* "hinder part of leg-shank" and to Arm. (I) *ket* "point" and (II) *ket* "whale" which have vastly different meanings and differ in their etymological origin.

Very frequently, one member of the pair has been borrowed from another language, as in the preceding Armenian example or as in French *pilotage* "pile driving, pile-work" (from French *pilot* "pile") and (II) *pilotage* "pilotage; piloting" (from Eng. *pilot*).

Zvelebil reports pertinent examples from Tamil (the first of them comes from the sixth, the other two from about the fifth cent. A. D.):

(I) *kalai* "he-goat" (Dravidian origin)
(II) *kalai* "part, portion" (Indo-Aryan origin)
(III) *kalai*   (borrowed from Malay *kalah*).

Sometimes both the homonyms are borrowed from another language, in which the original forms were different; such is the case (reported by

---

[98] Ďurovič LSB 67.

Zvelebil) of Tamil *kavi-* "poet" (Skr. *kavi-*) and Tamil *kavi-* "monkey" (Skr. *kapi-*).

We cannot, however, restrict the conception of homonymy to such cases where the etymology of the two members of the pair differs.

First, formal convergence of etymologically different words usually stops at establishing homonymy, but there are cases in which the development goes on until the status of polysemy is reached. In English, the words *ear* "organ of hearing" and *ear* "spike, head of corn" have remote, unconnected meanings and a different etymology. According to some specialists, however, "a link was a posteriori established between the two, as though the »ear« of corn were anthropomorphic metaphor of the »eye of the needle, mouth of a river, foot of a hill« type".[99] Another still better example is quoted by Migliorini.[100] Italian *serpe* (dele carrozze) "driver's box, seat" and *serpe* "snake" are frequently presented in Italian dictionaries as a polysemous word, the technical sense being conceived as a transferred one, though we have here the outcome of two different Latin words: *scirpea* "a wagon-body of basketwork" (< *scirpus* "rush") and *serpens* "snake".[101] In French, we find the following example: The verb *errer* can be conceived as having two senses: (1) "to err", (2) "to move to and fro". Historically, these are two homonymous verbs, namely I *errer* < Lat. *errare* "to err", and II *errer* < Lat. *itinerare* "to travel". Some dictionaries, above all the bilingual and the smaller monolingual ones, take this as a case of polysemy, other dictionaries present this as a case of homonymy.

Second, the eventual acceptance of the absolute historical principle, i.e. of etymology as the only decisive criterion, would not help in those cases where the etymology is unknown as, e.g., in Armenian *p'og* "stem, stalk"; "horn"; "money" (Motalová). Such cases will be numerous, especially in those languages whose history has not yet been studied in detail but whose dictionaries are to be compiled.

On the other hand, there are isolated voices defending the opinion that there are as many different words as different senses are ascertained.[102] This is obviously a point of view which cannot be accepted, at least not by lexicographers, both for practical and theoretical reasons. Practically, this would lead to an impossible number of homonyms with very similar meaning (*to fall* "to descend freely", *to fall* "to become detached, sink to a lower level",

---

[99] Ullmann, *Principles of Semantics* 128, quoting Bloomfield, *Language* 436.

[100] *Vocabolario* 50ff.

[101] But recent Italian lexicographic works indicate this as two homonyms; cf., for instance, Zangarelli, *Vocabolario della lingua italiana*, 8th ed., Bologna 1959, s. v.

[102] Probably the most important lexicographer who had this opinion was Ščerba, *Izvestija* 107. He stated, however, that this can be accepted only "in principle". In his lexicographic practice, he never followed such a principle.

to fall "to cease to stand" etc.) and it would be most difficult to keep them apart. As far as the theoretical points are concerned, many of these phenomena are much more correctly conceived as belonging to the generality of meaning.[103]

The preceding discussion must not unduly dispirit the lexicographer. After all, homonymy is a problem of the identity of the word; and problems of identity are frequently the most and difficult ones in any investigation, irrespective of the philosophical basis of the approach. The lexicographer will be well advised to steer a reasonable middle course, accepting as homonyms only pairs with vastly different unconnected meanings. He will do well to control his own opinions by testing the intersubjective opinions of speakers of the language who have a reasonably representative level of education and speak the language he describes well.[104] He will also do well to have some respect for the lexicographic tradition of the language in question, if there is any.

1.6.1 The problem of homonymy requires some further remarks. First, the lexicographer has to do, in the majority of cases, with languages which are reduced to writing.[105] To assume homonymy, it will, therefore, be necessary that both the written and the spoken form are identical. Eng. *knight* and *night* are not homonyms, though their pronunciation is identical. Nor are *right, rite, write, wright* homonymous, despite their identical pronunciation: they are h o m o p h o n e s only. The same applies to any other language. E.g. in French, we can find *sain* "healthy", *sein* "bosom", *seing* "signature", and *saint* "holy" which we would not consider homonyms, though they are pronounced in the same way.[106] As examples of Armenian homophones, M o t a - l o v á reports *ord* "worm" :: *ort'* "twig of vine" (both pronounced [vort]; *uġt* "camel" :: *uxt* "vow, promise" (both pronounced [uxt]). R ů ž i č k a reports the following example of homophony from Suahili: *bagala* "sail-ship" :: *baghala* "mule" (both pronounced [baga:la]).

Very important in the phenomenon of homophony as contrasted to homonymy in Chinese. N o v o t n á reports the following examples of homophony in Chinese: (I) 會 *hui*[4] "meeting; to be able", (II) 匯 *hui*[4] "to remit money", 燴 (III) *hui*[4] "to stew (meat)"; 坐 (I) *tso*[4] "to sit", 做 (II) *tso*[4] "to do". In these cases the homophony is absolute, because even the tones (indicated

---

[103] Cf. above, p.

[104] For example he will not regard as decisive the opinions of the speakers of dialects if he intends to compile a dictionary of the standard national language, etc.

[105] If this is not the case, then it is usually precisely the lexicographer who creates or helps to create the written form.

[106] Examples and discussion by H e l c l LSB 76, 79.

by the indexed numbers) are identical. Absolute homophony can be observed in disyllabic words, too, as e.g.

(I) 數目 *shu⁴-mu⁴* "number"

(II) 樹木 *shu⁴-mu⁴* "trees"

(I) 權利 *ch'üan²-li⁴* "right"

(II) 權力 *ch'üan²-li⁴* "power".

These examples of homophony, i.e. of coincidence of the spoken form, have
their written forms different.[107] But even in Chinese, there are cases of perfect
homonymy, with both the spoken and the written forms coinciding; e.g. (as
reported by Novotná again):

(I) 儀表 *i²-piao³* "appearance, outward form"

(II) 儀表 *i²-piao³* "measuring instrument".[108]

The situation is complicated by the Chinese script in yet another respect.
Existing characters have been used rather frequently to express homophones
so that, such an originally "transferred" application of the character having
been fixed by the use, both the spoken and the written form coincide. In this
way, perfect homonymy is produced; but sometimes, it is impossible to decide
what is a case of such a homonymy and what is a case of polysemy.

In Burmese we can find examples of homophony (reported by Minn Latt),
e.g.:

puleip [pălei?] "police" : : *păleip* [pălei?] "plague";
thăyéi [θăyéi] "leather, hide" : : *thwâaíɟ* [θăyéi] "saliva"
hsíncjéi [śíɲjéi] "argument" : : *hsíncyéi* [śíɲjéi] "leg of an elephant".
Perfect homonymy can be found in Burmese too, e.g.:

(I) *tú* [tú] "nephew"

(II) *tú* [tú] "hammer"

(III) *tú* [tú] "Libra (7th sign of the zodiac)"

(IV) *tú* [tú] "be alike".

1.6.2 It can happen, on the other hand, that the written forms are identical
but their pronuciation is different. In Czech, we have *panický* "virginal,

---

[107] It is the Chinese script in which the written forms are different. Vasiljev reports that
when Vietnamese and Korean were Romanized, many homphones of this type were changed
into homonyms.

[108] Tone differences sufficiently distinguish similar pairs; e.g. Chin. *hui¹* "dust" : : *hui²* "to
come back"; *li³-k'e¹* "natural sciences" : : *li⁴-k'e¹* "instantaneously" are not homophones. Cf.
footnote 95.

chaste" and *panický* "panic"; they differ only in the pronunciation, because the first member of the pair quoted is pronounced with palatal *n*: therefore, they are homographs only. In Eng. we have, e.g., *primate* ["praimit"] "arch-bishop" and *primate* [praimeit] "one of the highest orders of mammals". Sometimes, the mere accent suffices to distinguish the two homographs in the pronunciation; Petráček reports (after H. Rosén) Mod. Heb. *ᶜiróniy* "ironic" : : *ᶜironíy* "municipal" (derived from *ᶜir* "town, city").

Theoretically, this type stands on a par with the preceding one: pairs like these are not homonyms in the strictest sense of the term. It is, however, highly probable that the lexicographer will treat the two words of the pair as homonyms. By distinguishing the two words, say by numbers, he will help the user of his dictionary, because the two members of the pair will follow each other in the alphabetic sequence. But if the lexicographer, notwith-standing these practical consideration, decides, on the strength of the theoretical arguments discussed above, not to distinguish them and not to treat them as if they were homonyms, he will be quite within his rights.

Differences in the linguistic structure and differences in the linguistic tradition may cause various complications. For example, the situation is not too complex in Burmese where we have pairs of homographs like the following ones (reported by Minn Latt):

pêi sâ [pĕi sâ] "share food with someone" : : *pêi sâ* [pêizâ] "give someone in marriage with someone"
khâun [gâuŋ] "head : : *khâun* [kâuŋ] "coffin"
sá yêi [sá yêi] "write something" : : *sá yêi* [săyéi] "clerk"

But in Arabic (as reported by Petráček), the situation is more complicated: there are roots which are graphically identical in the canonical form (in which the vowels are not written); but in the actual full spoken form, they are different, because their vowels differ.

E.g. root *d̲kr*: *d̲ikrun* "mention, recollection"
                   d̲akarun "male, masculine; penis"

Real homonyms in Arabic are only those words in which all the phonemes coincide, as

 (I) *naqdun* "money, cash"
(II) *naqdun* "criticism".

1.6.3 Another circumstance the lexicographer must take into consideration is the fact that the words with which he is working very often have different forms, that they very frequently form a paradigm. (More on this subject

§ 2.1.) It is the lexicographer's duty to take the whole paradigm into consideration, not to consider one form only, because things often take on another aspect with more extended study.

For instance, the Eng. parallelity of *crane* (1) "bird", (2) "machine" is echoed by Czech *jeřáb* (1) "crane" (bird) and *jeřáb* (2) "crane" (machine). In Czech, however, *jeřáb* (1) bird has the paradigm proper to those masculine substantives which denote animate beings, whereas *jeřáb* (2) machine has the paradigm proper to masculine substantives that denote inanimate beings. Therefore, we have:

	jeřáb "crane" (bird)	*jeřáb* "crane" (machine)
Gen.	*jeřába*	*jeřábu*
Dat.	*jeřábovi*	*jeřábu*
Acc.	*jeřába*	*jeřáb* etc.

It is mainly in the nomin. sing. that the two words have identical forms. The two words are sufficiently distinguished in this way and cannot, therefore, be considered homonyms. The situation in Czech is even more interesting because there is yet another word *jeřáb* "a sort of tree, rowan". Etymologically, this word has very close ties with the word denoting the bird, but practically not direct connections with the word for the machine. But as this word *jeřáb* "rowan-tree" has the paradigm proper to masculine substantives that designate inaminate beings, i.e. a paradigm identical with that of *jeřáb* "crane" (machine), it must be considered a homonym of the latter. In this way, the historical connections of the words are broken and instead of the English crane (1) "bird", (2) "machine", where the identity of form allows one to interpret it even as one polysemous word, we have in Czech a situation vastly different from that suggested by the history of the words themselves, viz. *jeřáb, jeřába* "crane" (bird),[109] (I) *jeřáb, jeřábu* „rowan-tree", (II) *jeřáb, jeřábu* "crane" (machine).[110]

The case just discussed is important not only as an illustration of the interplay of various factors in the constitution of homonymy, but above all as an illustration of the important principle that the lexicographer must always take into consideration all the grammatical forms of the word which he studies. Czech substantives are usually quoted in dictionaries in the nominative singular. As we shall see, this is their canonical form (more on it § 2.1.1). When the canonical forms are identical but at least some of the other forms of the two paradigms differ, we can regard such a situation only as a case of partial homonymy. This means that (total) homonymy presupposes the identity of all the forms of the two words, whereas partial homonymy presupposes only the identity of some forms.

---

[109] A word of its own.
[110] A pair of homonyms.

Partial homonymy can extend over grater or smaller parts of the two paradigms. There are extreme cases of unimportance. For instance, the paradigm of the Russian word *bej* "a Turkish dignitary" has some ten different forms one of which is the nominative just quoted. The paradigm of the Russian verb *bit'* "to beat" has at least a score of different forms, one of which is the imperative 2nd sing. *bej*. The partial homonymy constituted by the identity of these two forms is so unimportant that the lexicographer will hardly take similar cases into consideration.[111]

Similar examples are reported by Miltner from Hindi: *pīle* "yellow" (masc. plur.) and *pīle* "drink" (imperative), by Zvelebil from Tamil, *ney* "butter" (nomin. sing.) ans *ney* "weave" (imper.) which coincide in these two forms only, by Petráček from Arabic: *yazīdu* "he gets augmented, multiplied" (3rd. sing. ind. impf.), *yazīdu*, name of persons (noun), and Zima from Hausa: *gaarukà* is plural either to *gàarè* "gown", or to *gàaruu* "wall".

At the beginning of this section, we mentioned the four homonymous Ossetic words, *fyd* "meat", *fyd* "millstone", *fyd* "father", *fyd* "evil". The case of *fyd* "father" is similar to that of Czech *jeřáb*; in the singular, the forms of the word are identical with those of the other word, but in the plural, there are forms that differ from the other word: instead of *fydtä*, the word with the meaning "father" has the plural form nomin. *fydaltä*, and in this way all other plural cases are formed. This is, consequently, a clear case of partial homonymy, as in Czech. This type deserves a special attention, however, because it is just the canonical forms that coincide, so that the entry words in the dictionary will be identical, and because the partial homonymy is more extended. But even in this case, i.e. in the case of the partial homonymy of the canonical forms, there are different degrees. If the Russian verb *znat'* "to know" has a score of different forms, the Russian substantive *znat'* "aristocracy" some seven forms with at least twelve different functions, and the adverb *znat'* "perhaps, probably" (colloq.) only one form, and if it is only these three canonical forms of the three words that are identical, all other forms differing vastly, then the area of coincidence of the forms is so small that there can be no trouble, within a reasonable understanding.

The same applies also to those cases where there are yet other important categorial differences between the two words. Such is, for example, the situation of German:

der See "lake"   *die See* "sea".

Not only are the two paradigms different, but the gender, obligatory in all German substantives, differs. As gender is always indicated in German dictionaries, along with the canonical form, the area of coincidence in the para-

---

[111] Ďurovič LSB 68, sf. Helcl, ibid. 76.

digms of the two words is so small that the partial homonymy is very weak and unimportant: the two different words are easy to discern.[112]. Cf. the identical situation in other languages, e.g. Hindi (Miltner) *or* m. "limit, end, beginning" :: *or* f. "side, direction"; Braj (Miltner) *sak* m. "doubt" :: *sak* f. "power, strength".

Similarly, there are categorial, paradigmatic differences between the following Tamil words (as reported by Zvelebil) *tel* (subst.) "flea" :: *tel* (adj.) "clear". The same can be said about the Hindi examples reported by Miltner: *magar* "crocodile" :: *magar* "but"; *par* "on, above" :: *par* "but" :: *par* "other, foreign, higher" :: *par* "feather, wing".

The area of concidence of the Ossetic words discussed above is greater, and they belong to the same category (subst.); but even in a case like that there can be no real confusion, because the two paradigms are clearly distinguished. In similar cases, it is not even necessary to indicate the partial homonymy in the entry word in the dictionary.

One can compare the clearly differentiated partial homonyms in Suahili (as reported by Růžička):

mpaka, plur. *wapaka* "plasterer, painter"
mpaka, plur. *mipaka* "boundary, limit, border"
mpaka, no flexion "up to, as far as, till"

There is, however, one type of partial homonymy which deserves greater attention. It is the case of two words one of which is used only with a part of the usual paradigm and it is just the canonical form, the form in which the word is quoted in the entry, which is lacking.

In Czech, there is the word *hodina* "hour; lesson" the paradigm of which is quite normal: the nomin. plur is *hodiny* "hours; lessons". Besides this word, there is *hodiny* "time-piece, clock" which has no singular (it is a plurale tantum), but has in the plural identical forms as the first word.[113] We have, thus

Sing. *hodina* "hour, lesson"
Plur. *hodiny* "hours, lessons" :: *hodiny* "time-piece, clock"

The situation is similar as in English.

damage "injury"
damages "injuries" :: *damages* "compensation for injury" (legal)

with the only difference that the English situation is usually regarded as a case of polysemy, whereas the Czech words are usually considered homo-

[112] Žirmunskij LS 4, 1960, 67.
[113] Ďurovič LSB 69.

6*

nyms. But as we know, polysemy and homonymy are very closely related notions.[114]

A particularly disagreeable case of this type can be illustrated by the following example. In Czech, there is a substantive *večer* "evening" which has its full paradigm. But the word *večer* can be used as a temporal adverb which has the meaning "in the evening" and has then no paradigm at all. The difference between the two is, consequently, that *večer* "evening" (subst.) has a full paradigm of its own in which večer "in the evening" ist not included. But even in this case, there is no absolute necessity to conceive of the two forms as a pair of homonyms. Similar situations arise also, for example, in Armenian. Motalová reports the following example: *tun* "house" (subst.); "home" (adverb).

I do not think that anybody could produce arguments sufficiently persuasive to induce all lexicographers to solve each and everyone of these and similar cases in the same way. For instance, I would see with Ďurovič[115] partial homonymy[116] in the Czech case just discussed, because the substantive and the adverbs are two clearly distinguished categories in Czech, and because cases like the one here considered, which one could eventually conceive as a substantive being used in the function of an adverb, and thus avoid any question of homonymy, are rather rare, in that language. On the other hand one can conceive the situation as a kind of polysemy. And in some similar cases, one can even suppose that it is only a contextual nuance one is dealing with.

Partial homonymy of this sort is very frequent in some languages and its treatment depends largely upon the whole structure of the language in question and probably not less on its lexicographic and grammatical tradition. In English, we are accustomed to regard the two forms (1) *plough* and (2) *plough* as a case of partial homonymy, i.e. as two canonical forms representing two words with different paradigms:

(1): *plough — ploughs*, i.e. a subs.;
(2): *plough — ploughs, ploughed* ..., etc. i.e. a verb.

---

[114] The tendency (observable in some languages) to construct some of such *pluralia tantum* with verbs in singular can result in their formal distinction or even in a complete loss of any homonomy. (Kind suggestion of I. J. Gelb.)

[115] LSB 65f.

[116] Partial because the adverb has no paradigm, so that there are no counterparts to the paradigmatic forms of the substantive. Their absence suffices to make the distinction. — Cf. also Isačenko, Cahiers F. de Saussure 7, 1948, 27; this scholar assumes that unproductive forms like German des Nachts 'during the night' have an adverbial status and do not belong to the paradigm. This is a very good observation and certainly correct in its own limits; it does not, on the other hand, prove (and does not even attempt to prove) that all productive forms do, a *contrarie*, belong to their paradigms.

A similar treatment may be made of all cases of so-called motion, i.e. of the "transition of the word from one grammatical category to another.[117] On the other hand, in the Chinese lexicographic tradition, it is usual to regard cases that can be called substantival and verbal applications of a word as cases of polysemy of a single word. E.g., Kalouskova reports

kung-tso (1) "to work" (2) "work";
yen-chiu (1) "to study", (2) "study";
sheng-huo (1) "to live", (2) "life".

This multiplicity of grammatical functions can be conceived as polysemy. In Archaic Chinese, this multiplicity of functions was a general phenomenon; in Modern Chinese, there is still a great number of pertinent cases, so that the lexicographical treatment as polysemy is caused not only by tradition but also by practical considerations.

The speaker's education plays an important role in the status of the partial homonyms again. Let us contrast the following two pairs of Armenian examples (as reported by Motalova):

(1) *ser*, gen. *siro(y)* "love" and *ser*, gen. *seri* "cream" have different declension in modern Armenian; obviously then, they are partial homonyms because only their canonical forms coincide, in any speakers usage.
(2) *ayr* "man" and *ayr* "cave" have an identical declension in modern Armenian, but a different one in the classical language (Grabar): *aṙn*, or *ayri*, respectively (gen.).

It would seem, then, that for a speaker of modern Armenian who does not know Grabar the two are total homonyms, whereas for the speaker who knows the classical form, the two tend to have a status of only partial homonyms also within the system of modern Armenian.

1.6.4 On the whole, homonymy is a category with which the lexicographer may be thoroughly dissatisfied. It has no clear boundaries against polysemy. For instance, the Tamil example as reported by Zvelebil:

  (I) *ma* "animal",
  (II) *ma* "mango",
 (III) *ma* "flour",
 (IV) *ma* "blackness",
  (V) *ma* 1/20 (fraction),

is certainly a case of homonymy, but how to treat for instance

pacai "viscosity, paste" and
pacai "love, adherence"?

---

[117] I quote here a paraphrase of the traditional grammar to show the relativity of the approach.

Homonymy is constituted more or less exclusively by an intersubjective interpretation and understandig which will, precisely in this case, probably offer less clear results that in other spheres. We have, however, shown above that etymology cannot be accepted as the fundamental criterion for the decision. Neither is it the difference in the denotata that could be regarded as the fundamental criterion of all cases of homonymy. If this were the case, how many scores of homonymous words with identical forms would we have to assume for example for the word *screw*?[118] After all, we know the importance of the designàtum in the lexical meaning. If speakers of a language are accustomed to conceive different things by a unified designatum (as in the case of *screw*), then this fact is decisive for the meaning for the respective word.

Some authors accept the point of view that differences in the derivational series are symptoms of homonymy, in contradistinction to polysemy. For instance, we have in Russian *klass* (1) "class" (group of people) and *klass* (2) "class" (group of students). Is this a case of polysemy or a case of homonymy? *Klass* (1) has the adjective *klassovyj*, *klass* (2) has the adjective *klassnyj*. Even a restrictive contradistinction should suffice to establish the difference; e.g., Arabic (as reported by Petráček) *naqdun* "money" has an adjectival derivation, *naqdun* "criticism" has not. Such differences in the derivation of adjectives are regarded by some authors as a proof of homonymy,[119] but other scholars reject this point of view.[120] Personally, I think that such a cleavage in the derivational series is strongly indicative of the fact that the bases of derivation, in this case *klass* (1) and *klass* (2) are getting polarized in their meaning and in their mutual status, so that we may assume that the process of transcending from polysemy to homonymy is here going on. But I would hesitate to accept this as the decisive criterion, because not all similar cases are as clear as the one discussed here.

R. Wells[121] points out that we can speak about polysemy if the relation of the two senses has other instances in the language in question, but otherwise we have to speak about homonymy. In this way, Eng. *crane* "bird" and "machine" would be a case of polysemy, as there are other instances like Eng. *cat* "animal" and "a strong tackle used to hoist an anchor..." Observations of this type should always be attempted; but their eventual results. do not always have a definitely decisive persuasiveness, either.

Deliberations concerning the differentiation of homonymy and polysemy can be very complex. As an example, we quote the following discussion of a

---

[118] Cf. a similar discussion by Kutina LS 4, 1960, 48.

[119] Kutina LS 4, 1960, 48. Cf. a similar line of reasoning by Ďurovič LSB 73.

[120] Filin LS 4, 1960, 59f.: cf. Weinreich, *Universals* 162.

[121] Proceedings of the 8th Congress, Oslo 1958, p. 662.

Burmese situation by Minn Latt. He himself terms it "a exercise in differentiating between polysemy and homonymy".[122]

> *tjek* 1a. "be cooked"; 1b. "be healed" (said of sores; 1d. "recognize";
> 2a. "study incessantly", to "memorize".

The Burman does feel the association of (1b) or (1d) with (1a), when he reminds himself of the existence of lexical units like *ănásêim* "an open (raw) sore" and *lúsêim* "a stranger; an unknown (raw) person". The trouble arises, however, when one ponders over utterances like *mjekhná tjek mi té* "(one) recognizes a face" and *ăthám tjek htâ té* "(one) keeps a voice committed to memory". A Burman can be undecisive over whether *tjek* in the two utterances belongs to (1d) or (2a) .Some scholars, for example A. Judson, would choose to state (1) and (2) as cases of polysemy. If one adopts historical criteria alone, both Judson and U Wún can be correct, as no doubt they are, in each historical range. We may however try to examine whether synchronic standards cannot be established.

To begin with there is the causative-effect pair, *cjek* "cook" ("someone cooks something") and *tjek* "be cooked" ("something is cooked") which is patterned like many others on the aspirated-nonaspirated contrasts — *cjôu* "break something": *tjôu* "something is broken"; *cjéi* "crush something": *tjéi* "something is crushed", etc. On this basis (1a) is isolated from the others. Further if we compare *aná tjek* "a sore is healed" (1b) with *sá tjek* "study" (2a) we find that the former unit as a whole cannot be preceded by a subject, whereas the second can; in other words the first verb is intransitive and the second is transitive. The difference between (1b) and (1c) can also be handled in a similar way. Finally, the difference between the remaining two, (1d) and (2a), lies in the fact that when one acquaints oneself with a voice (*tjek*) the resultant effect is acquaintance (*tjek*), but when one studies (*tjek*) the resultant effect is knowledge (*tat*, not *tjek*). With these considerations Minn Latt queries whether the four senses of *tjek* should not be classified as four homonyms on a synchronic plane.

On the whole, the lexicographer can rely really only on the intersubjective understanding of the speakers of the language and he must expect many unclear borderline cases and uncertainties. But there is no harm in this. From the theoretical point of view, the lexicographer cannot and should not try to offer more in his presentation of the data than what are the facts of language: if the language itself indicates no clean-cut distinctions and boundaries and even tolerates their absence, and if the speakers of the language have no clear

[122] To mention only those points which are pertinent to the discussion, Minn Latt has abridged the entry, omitting (1c) and (2b) (i.e. 1.3 and 3.1, in the original) and also by simplifying the translation into English. Homophony with *tyek* is also outside the range of the discussion.

understanding of the difference, then why should the lexicographer try to create something that seems not to exist? It is a fact of language that homonymy is closely related to polysemy. This can be shown not only from the point of view of semantics, but also by the observation that just as it is context, which eliminates various senses of a polysemous word, it is context again by which the elimination of an unapplied homonym is made. In the two sentences,

(1) *"There is some strange sound in the gear-box, I am afraid there is a new car in my future"* and
(2) *"We shall be able to sail to the sea, there is a sound behind that hill"*,

probably no confusion of (I) *sound* "auditory effect" and (II) *sound* "narrow passage of water" is possible. There are only exceptional cases where the context does not eliminate the ambiguity. This rather rare phenomenon is called by some linguists the pathology of language. Gilliéron, who coined the term, held the correct opinion that homonymy can cause difficulty only when both members of the pair can occur in the same context. In any case, the proximity of the two notions of homonymy and of polysemy is clear, because both have the same result, viz. ambiguity, which is eliminated, disambiguated by the same means namely, by the context.

1.6.5 From the point of view of the lexicographer's practice, the whole question of homonymy has a greater importance only if he is preparing a descriptive dictionary of a language the purpose of which is to give a true and precise statement about the entire status of the word (lexical units) of the language in question. In this case, the lexicographer will try to do his best, making intersubjective tests with reasonably educated speakers of the language, but also taking the lexicographic tradition of the language into consideration, lest there be unduly radical changes where they are not abolutely necessary.

In the more practical dictionaries which serve other purposes, e.g. in small bilingual dictionaries, it is really of quite minor importance whether the lexicographer presents his data basically in the form:

crane (1) "bird"; (2) "machine",

indicating thus that he considers it a case of polysemy, or in the form

(I) *crane* "bird"
(II) *crane* "machine",

indicating thus that he considers it a case of homonymy.[123] But the lexicographer will have to try to observe the same coherent policy, through the whole dictionary: for instance, if respect to history is a decisive factor in his solutions of other problems, the homonyms must also be handled with history being strongly taken into consideration.

SYNONYMY

1.7 As stated above, homonyms are words which have identical form but different meanings. The opposite can be said about synonyms: they are words which have different forms but identical meaning.[124]

Considered generally the identity of meaning required for the synonyms can be understood in two ways: either as an absolute identity or as a very great similarity. In the majority of cases, the term synonymy is used so that it covers both eventualities, identity and a great similarity of meaning. It is however, advantageous to reserve the term *synonymy*, *synonyms*, eventually specified by the attribute *"absolute"*, only for cases of absolute identity in meaning. For the "great similarity of meaning", we shall use the term *near-synonymy*, *near-synonyms*.[125] Both categories, synonyms and near-synonyms, can eventually be called "synonyms in the broader sense of the word".

1.7.1 The absolute identity of the lexical meaning requires the identity of all the three basic components of meaning.[126] It goes without saying that under such strict conditions, absolute synonyms are rather rare: it is mostly the defined terms which are neither polysemous nor connotative and offer, therefore, most examples, because there are fewer complications. Ullmann[127] has the splendid example of Eng. *caecitis* and *typhlitis*: both mean "inflammation of caecum and vermiform appendix" and belong to the specialized (medical) language, their only difference being that one is derived from a Latin and the other from a Greek word. There are, however, absolute synonyms among general words, too, and sometimes even they have some slightly polysemous

[123] Ďurovič LSB 65, 75.

[124] The present approach to synonyms is strongly inspired by J. Filipec, *Česká synonyma s hlediska stylistiky a lexikologie*, Praha 1961. For a recent attempt at a classification of synonyms, cf. O. Ducháček, Orbis 13, 1964, 35ff. ans *Précis de sémantique française*, Brno 1967, p. 55ff.

[125] We use this term after consultation with E. Hamp. Ullmann, *Principles* 109, uses the term *homoionyms*. Other terminologies speak about *quasi-synonyms*. The term *tautonyms* is sometimes used in reference to synonyms which are used by different groups of speakers. For instance, Brit. Eng. *trunk call* and Amer. Eng. *long-distance call* would be tautonyms.

[126] No need to say that when using the term *meaning*, we wish to stress that the two words must be indentical in all the senses they may eventually have.

[127] Passage quoted footnote 92.

meaning. In Czech, the word *hoch* and *chlapec* have both the meaning "boy" with the same senses: (1) "young person of male sex", (2) expressively, "man generally", (3) "a girl's lover". The two words have the same connotation (either neutral or slightly expressive — affectionate) and have the same range of application.

1.7.2 If there is a difference at least in one of the three basic components of meaning (designation, connotation, and range of application); the respective words are *near-synonyms* only.

Some examples of near-synonyms which have the same designation and connotation, but a different range of application were quoted above (*stipend, salary*, § 1.3). An instructive case of this type of near-synonymy is reported from Burmese by Minn Latt. In reference to some situations there are different words to be applied according to the standing of the person involved, depending on whether he is a common man, a monk, or a member of the royal family.[128] If a common man dies, the words or expressions *théi* or *hsôum* or *kwé lún*, or *ǎneissa yauk* are to be used; if a monk dies, *pjáṃ lún*, and if a king, *nat ywá sám* is to be said. If a common man eats, his action is called *sâ, thôum hsáun*, if a monk, *phôun pêi*, if a king, *pwêtó tíj*. If a common man sleeps, the proper word is *eip*, if a monk, *tjêin*, if a king, *sektó khó*.[129] It is basically by the range of application that Bailly[130] distinguishes the French words *an* and *année* "year" which have the same denotation and connotation (viz. a neutral one): "*an* exprime une durée indivisible, une simple unité de temps...; on l'emploie en général pour compter ou pour marquer une époque — et il admet rarement d'épithètes ... *année*, qui reçoit presque toujours un qualificatif, s'emploie quand on considère la période annuelle relativement à ses divisions ..."

---

[128] The connotation is also identical, mainly that of the words applied to monks and kings.

[129] But Weinreich's discussion of a similar case in Thai (*Universals* 124) results in the statement that "the honorific component of meaning ... can be considered on a par with any designational feature". To make the round complete, W. J. Gedney, *Special Vocabularies in Thai* (in: Report of the Twelfth Annual Round Table Meeting on Linguistics and Language Studies, Monograph Series on Languages and Linguistics, Georgetown 1961, Nr. 14, p. 109ff.) considers similar words as having a special connotation. On the other hand, J. D. McCawley (in: Universals in Linguistic Theory, ed. E. Bach — R. T. Harms, New York 1968, p. 136) thinks that the choice of similar honorific forms of pronouns etc. "is dependent on features attached to the whole discourse" (which is correct, because in normal situations, there will be other symptoms of respect present in the whole utterance, the whole discourse will be couched in a proper style, etc.) "rather than to individual lexical items" (but the chosen item must have, it would seem, an individual property which distinguishes it from the non chosen one and thus makes possible a purposeful choice). This example sufficiently shows the relative nature and vagueness of a good many of our semantic judgements and classifications and how far we still are from a *communis opinio* on some points.

[130] *Dictionnaire des synonymes de la langue française*, Paris 1947, p. 35.

(The basic difference seems to be in the range of application, though there seem also to be differences in the designation.

Near-synonyms that differ as far as their respective connotations are concerned are very frequent. Practically all cases of stylistic differences and of differences between general language and restricted specialized languages belong here. To exemplify this, let us quote the following near-synonyms: *prostitute* (no connotation, or a neutral one, educated language) — *loose woman* (no connotation, simple language)[131] — *harlot* (bookish) — *whore* — *tart* — *drab* — *bitch* — *bag* (different sorts of expressivity and slang).

Whole series of pairs of such near-synonyms are frequently found in languages with observable diglossia (see § 4.3), as e.g. Mod. Greek *spíti* "house" : : *oikía* "house" (obsolete, bookish); *neró* "water" : : *hýdor* "water"; *psári* "fish" : : *ichthýs* "fish", etc. The second members of the pairs occur only in the so-called Katharewusa, an archaic form of Modern Greek.

In a similar way, there are frequently pairs of terms one of which is of foreign the other of "native" origin (usually a terminological neologism); e.g. Arabic (reported by Petráček) *tilifūn* "telephone" : : *hātifun* "telephone". Sometimes, the members of such pairs are absolute synonyms, but usually one of the members has a connotation (e.g. formal style only etc.).

The third group of near-synonyms comprises those words whose lexical meaning slightly differs in the sphere of designation.[132] There is a practically endless number of at least impressionistically perceivable degrees of the difference obtaining between the respective near-synonyms.

First, there are those cases when two words have the same meaning, their designations being identical, but by a precise comparison we see that one of them has some additional characteristic feature in contrast to the other. As an example, we can quote the Hindi words (which will be discussed in greater detail in the following section) *bāriš* "rain" and *būridābaridē* "drizzle". They are identical in two respects, in their connotation and in their range of application absolutely; as far as the designation goes, one could regard them as identical, except for the component of the second word's designatum for which it is criterial that the raining drops be fine.

1.7.3 We have discussed above (§ 1.3.1) the designatum and the criterial features out of which it seems to consist. We can see now that it is not only the designatum which can be analyzed as consisting of such elements. The whole lexical meaning of words (lexical units), irrespective whether designative

---

[131] In this case, a two-word lexical unit is used as a member of a series whose other members consist of one word only; cf. § 3.3.1 on multiword lexical units.

[132] This category partly overlaps with the semantically related words, cf. § 1.7.7.

or not, can be analyzed as consisting of elements, or partial components, which we shall call criterial semantic features or simply semantic features.[133]

In the case of designative words, the criterial features of the designatum are at the same time also semantic features; but the latter concept is much broader, because it covers also those parts of lexical meaning that do not belong to the designatum.

It is highly instructive to observe how Bally[134] explains some of what he calls synonyms in French (i.e. near-synonyms or semantically related words (§ 1.7.7) in our terminology):

"amuser, c'est occuper l'esprit par de choses agréables ou simplement droles.

Distraire, c'est amuser dans l'intention de faire oublier les soucis de la vie quotidienne.

Recréer, c'est amuser surtout avec l'intention de reposer, de sélasser.

Dérider, c'est distraire un court instant quelqu'un qui, jusqu'alors, avait l'air sévere ou soucieux."

One begins with the definition of the meaning of a word (*amuser*), and the following near-synonyms are put into contrast to it by a statement of the respective semantic features.

For the lexicographer, the detection of criterial semantic features is of the very highest importance. They are sometimes very specific and their detection requires a very minute observation. Cf. the following group of Chinese near-synonyms (reported by Heroldová):

(1) *na* "to carry": something light in the hand (e.g. a book, a newspaper);
(2) *t'i* "to carry": something heavier in one's hand (e.g. a bucket, a bag);
(3) *t'ai* "to carry": about two people who carry something together (e.g. a stretcher);
(4) *tai* "to carry": on one's body, in the pocket;
(5) *t'iao* "to carry": something that hangs on a bar carried across the shoulders;
(6) *k'ang* "to carry": on one shoulder (e.g. a rifle, a bag of potatoes);
(7) *pei* "to carry": on one's back (e.g. a child);
(8) *k'ua* "to carry": across one's arm (e.g. a coat);
(9) *ting* "to carry": on one's head (e.g. a vessel with water);
(10) *t'uo* "to carry": on one's palm.

---

[133] There are terminological (and conceptual) differences among the linguists; very frequently, these features are called *semes* (*sèmes*), *semantic components*, *semantic factors*, *noemes* or *markers*.

[134] *Dictionnaire des synonymes de la langue francaise*, Paris 1947, s. v. — The way in which BALLY glosses the near-synonyms is superior by far to their mere juxtaposition (cf. Aleksandrov LS 6, 1963, 33), not only for the user of the dictionary, but also for the development of semantic studies. A similar English work is S. I. Hayakawa, *Funk & Wagnall's Modern Guide to Synonyms and Related Words*, New York 1968: BALLY's statements, however, are sharper and more pointed.

For the bilingual lexicographer, it is important to observe that there are very different groupings of semantic features, in different languages. One of the most obvious cases is the following one: in one language, there is a pair or a series of near-synonyms the lexical meanings of which differ in respect to some semantic feature(s): in another language, there is only one word the lexical meaning of which does not have those additional semantic features (i.e. it is more general) which, in their turn belong to the lexical meanings of other words.

E.g.:	Hindi	Eng.
	nazar	*glance*
	kankhī	*slanting glance*
	katākṣ	*casual glance*

Or there may be different possibilities:

	bāriš	*rain*
	būridābāridē	*drizzling rain, drizzle*
	pluhār	*nearly imperceptible drizzle, drizzling rain*[135]

Each of the last groups of examples had one member which was more general, i.e. in comparison to which the other members of the group had more semantic features. There are, however, endless possibilities of different constellations of the semantic features. One of them is that there is no "general word" within the group of near-synonyms. For example we have

Hindi	Eng.
vaidy	*doctor* (trained in the Brahman tradition)
kavirāj	*doctor* (trained in the Hindu tradition
hakīm	*doctor* (trained in the Islam tradition)
ḍākṭar	*doctor* (trained in the European tradition)[136]

And cf. a similar situation in Suahili (as reported by Růžička):

mwamuzi	"native judge"
jaji	"European judge"
kadhi	"judge of Mohammedan law".

If there is a "general word" within the group of near-synonyms, it can also be used in reference to, say, denotata for which there are more "specific words" at hand, if the respective criterial semantic features is considered irrelevant, at the moment. Is is a situation similar to that of the attributive specification of a general word by an adjective or adverb, in English: it may be that the rain we are walking in is a drizzling one; but if we consider this circumstance

---

[135] Examples from Barannikov, *Leksičeskaja sinonimija* 15.

[136] Example from Barannikov, ibid., who does not, however, understand it as a case of synonymy (near-synonymy).

as immaterial, we can use the word *rain*, without any specification. Similarly, it is possible to use, in Hindi, the word *bāriš*, even if the rain we are speaking about is a drizzling one.

1.7.4 If this is so, then the "general word" can be called the hyperonym and the more "specific words" its hyponyms.[137] Hindi *nazar* is, then the hyperonym, *kankhī* and *kāṭakṣ* are its hyponyms. Eng. *flower* is the hyperonym, *rose*, *tulip*, *daisy*, ... etc. are its hyponyms.

The lexicographer will frequently have considerable difficulties in detecting these relations in his excerpted contexts or in eliciting the necessary contexts, or information from his informants.

Sometimes, however, the lexicographer will find a much more difficult situation: a polysemous word is sometimes used, in one of its senses, as a "general word" (hyperonym) and in another of its senses as a synonym of a more "specific" word (hyponym). If we take a simple example: French *voiture* has, among different senses, these two most frequent ones: (1) "a vehicle of any sort" (hyperonyms), (2) "automobile, motor-car" (hyponym). In this case, it is relatively easy to prove the existence of sense (2), i.e. that *voiture* is, in this sense, the synonym of *auto(mobile)*, because no modern speaker of French who hears the question

"Comment allez-vous là?" and the reply
"En voiture"

will have any doubt concerning the type of the vehicle referred to, the reply would seem to him to be as specified as the other possible and equivalent answer

"En auto."

But not all pertinent cases will be as easy to discern as this one. Generally, more will be gained, in these cases, from the rule-like descriptive statements of the informants than from the excerpted contexts.

The example discussed in the preceding paragraph can be conceived as a case of the so-called pregnant use of a word. In a similar way, in a good part of contemporary English contexts, the *pill* is used in the pregnant sense: the word is used not generally, but in the specific sense of the one pill which has outpilled all other pills. This type of the pregnant use is, however, different from the preceding one, because this application can be conceived either as a case of the application of a hyperonym instead of a hyponym or as a case of the dropping of a part of the multiword lexical unit. (Cf. footnote 19 to Chapter III.)

[137] Cf. J. Lyons, *Structural Semantics* (Publications of the Philological Society 20), Oxford 1963, 69.

Generally, the fact that word are polysemous must always be taken into consideration when synonymy is studied. A polysemous word can have different synonyms and/or near-synonyms, according to its different senses. Hindi *ghar* has the senses (1) "house", (2) "family, kin", (3) "buttonhole". There are the following groups, or chains, of synonyms and/or near-synonyms:

ghar (1) — makān — imārat
ghar (2) — kul — vãš
ghar (3) — chēd — kāj[138]

1.7.5 There is no synonymy or near-synonymy between *makān* and *kul*, or *vãš*, or *chēd*, etc. But we can speak about partial synonymy or partial near-synonymy in a case like this, when only one sense, apart from the whole lexical meaning of a word, is concerned: (1) is a group of partial synonyms, (2) another, and (3) yet another.

1.7.6 In his practical work, the lexicographer will see an endless variety of types of near-synonymy. When comparing the near-synonyms, the most important thing is to analyze their respective lexical meanings into the single senses, to find the criterial semantic features, to establish the connotation (which may differ from one sense to another) and the respective ranges of application (which may also differ from one sense to another). Only by a comparison of all the observable components of the lexical meaning in the respective near-synonyms can we perceive how far and in what respect they are identical (similar) or not. Let us discuss some very simple examples (based on the Concise Oxford Dictionary).

The English words *forest* and *wood* are not absolute synonyms though they both mean "a large tract covered with trees", both have the same connotation (neutral, or none) and the same range of application; this is so because *forest* has the additional semantic feature of being usually larger than *wood*. Not only this; the word *wood* has also the sense (2) "fibrous substance between pith and bark of tree" (as the Concise Oxford Dictionary nicely puts it) and (3) different special senses as "firewood", "musical wind instrument(s), cask, barrel" etc.

If we compare the English words *boy* and *lad*, we find that whereas the former is mainly used in reference to (1) "a male child", but also in reference to (2) "a youth", in the case of *lad*, this proportion is reversed: it is primarily used in reference to (1) "a youth", but also in reference to (2) "a male child". Apart from this, both words can be used (3) with an expressive connotation in reference to or when addressing adults. And further *boy* has also the sense (4) "servant" in different spheres of English.[139]

---

[138] Example from Barannikov, op. cit. p. 6.
[139] Different archaic senses are not taken into consideration.

Let us now discuss a more complicated group of near-synonyms to show the interplay of the differences in all the components of the lexical meaning. In order to show how minute these differences are, we choose a group of Chinese near-synonyms, all of which can be translated as "white". (The example was worked out by D. Heroldová: it is based partly on the general sources, partly on the idiolect of Kuan Ming-che, born in Peking in 1936 and living for the last ten years in Prague.

The Chinese near-synonyms translatable by Eng. "white" can be classified into four groups according to whether the criterial semantic features which distinguish them from the other near-synonyms are concerned with the

(1) intensity: *pai-ai-ai, pai-teng-teng, pai-shua-shua, pai-sha-sha, pai-liu-liu, pai-ching-ching, pai-su-su, pai-szu-szu, pai-shen-shen, pai-mo-mo*

(2) brightness: *pai-kuang-kuang, pai-liang-liang, pai-shan-shan, pai-huang-huang, pai-hua-hua, pai-hsüeh-hsüeh*

(3) space: *pai-man-man, pai-mang-mang, pai-meng-meng, pai-yang-yang, pai-t'eng-t'eng*

(4) feelings of   (a) softness: *pai-jung-jung, pai-t'eng-t'eng*
              (b) fear: *pai-sen-sen*
              (c) vividness: *pai-sheng-sheng*

(1) The expressions *pai-ai-ai* and *pai-teng-teng* can be used in reference to snow; both can be used if what is referred to is a rather thick layer of a coherent snow surface. According to the informant, *pai-ai-ai* belongs to the litterary language, whereas *pai-teng-teng* is colloquial. The range of application of *pai-ai-ai* is severely restricted; it can be applied in reference to snow and to hoarfrost. *Pai-teng-teng* cannot be applied in reference to the latter, but in reference to silver objects and silver generally (as in *pai-teng-teng ti yin-tzu* "white silver evius").

Pai-ching-ching, pai-sha-sha, pai-shua-shua, and *pai-su-su* are used in reference to parts of the human body. But while *pai-ching-ching* is used if the impression is a pleasant one, the object referred to being white, alabaster-like, soft, the other three expressions are used if the impression is able to cause fear or disgust or if the object referred to has a sickish, cadaverous, pallor or generally pale appearance. *Pai-sha-sha* and *pai-su-su* are more restricted than *pai-shua-shua,* which can be used also in reference to a wall (as in *pai-shua-shua ti ch'iang* "white wall"). *Pai-su-su* is somehow weaker than pai-sha-sha; it tends to be used in reference to the unhealthy complexion, whereas *pai-sha-sha* can be used in reference both to a white complexion caused by sickness and to a white colours caused by strong fear.

Pai-liu-liu is an expression which occurs only rarely; it is used in reference to an object which is white, smooth, round, and long. According to the informant, this expression could be best used in reference to a rod whose rind is removed.

Pai-szu-szu is used in reference to objects which are not intensively white and which have the form of stripes; its range of application is restricted practically to hair only.

Pai-shen-shen is also "white" or "whitish" (i.e. not intensively white) but it describes the whole surface of a substance, usually a liquid one. E.g., *pai-shen-shen ti mi-t'ang* "white rice soupe", *pai-shen-shen ti nao-chiang* "whitish brain".

(2) *Pai-kuang-kuang* and *pai-liang-liang* are very close near-synonyms which describe a relatively strong source of light which does not move. The second expression is used more frequently if the light comes from within the object, whereas the first of them is used rather if the light comes from the surface of the source. Both expressions can be used, for example, in reference to the moon (*yüeh-liang*) or to money (*yang-ch'ien*); but in reference to a lamp (*teng*), it is better to use *pai-liang-liang*.

Pai-hua-hua describes the whiteness of light which makes a halo round the object and which dazzles. It can be used, for example, in reference to silver (*yin-tzu*), hoarfrost (*shuang-hua*), or a surface of water (*shui-mien*).

Pai-shan-shan describes the whiteness of a sharper, more shining light which comes from a surface which is not necessarily very big. In contradistinction to this, *pai-huang-huang* can be used also if the surface of the shiny object is bigger, but if the light is not so sharp.

(3) *Pai-mang-mang* and *pai-man-man* are very close near-synonyms used in description of objects that are white and vast, extended in great distance or practically endless. The former expression seems to be used in rather three-dimensional reference, the latter only in two-dimensional one; e.g. *pai-mang-mang ti ta hai* "white sea": in this expression, not only the vast, endless, white surface is included, but also what is above it, the sky with white clouds; but *pai-man-man ti hu-mien* "white lake"; only the vast surface of a big lake is included. *Pai-mang-mang* occurs more frequently and has a broader range of application; for example it can be used in reference to clouds (*pai-mang-mang ti yün-ts'eng*) and also (in a transferred sense) in reference to abstract notions as future (as in *pai-mang-mang ti wei-lai* "far, distant, unknown, endless future").

Pai-yang-yang can also be used in reference to a water surface, but only such as is quiet, or with small waves only. *Pai-man-man* is used if only the upper layers of the water surface are included, but *pai-yang-yang* can be also used if the whole bulk of the concrete mass of water is to be described as white.

Pai-meng-meng and *pai-t'eng-t'eng* are used in reference to smoke (*yen-ch'i*) and to fog (*wu-ch'i*). The former expression is used if the smoke or fog (etc.)

is lying without motion, whereas the latter expression is used if the substance is rising. *Pai-meng-meng* has a broader range of application; it can be used also in reference to the moonlight (*yüeh-kuang*).

(4) (a) *Pai-meng-meng* is used if the white object described as white is soft, light (as e.g. *i ts'eng pai-meng-meng shuang* "white down (on fruit)", *pai-jung-jung* rather if the object is soft, hairy (as e.g. *pai-jung-jung ti i chih-kou* "white, hairy, small dog"). *Pai-t'eng-t'eng* is used in the description of an object which is inflated, puffy, soft, without a compact substance; it is a rare expression whose range of application is practically restricted to the dumplings (as e.g. *pai-t'eng-t'eng ti man-t'ou* "white, puffy dumplings").

(b) *Pai-sen-sen* is used in reference to objects which cause fright, as for instance *pai-sen-sen ti ya-ch'ih* "white teeth" (in a suitable context) or *pai-sen-sen ti pao-tao* "white, cool dagger").

(c) *Pai-sheng-sheng* is used practically only in reference to living beings or to parts of the human body (e.g. *pai-sheng-sheng ti hsiao-hai-tzu* "a vivid little child with white skin").

The discussion of this example may suffice to show how complex the study near-synonyms can be. The example shows also how intervowen are the components of the lexical meaning; for instance, it would be difficult to make up one's mind, in each particular distinction, what to consider a part of the designatum and what a restriction of the range of application. (Cf. above.) When reading the preceding discussion, we also have a feeling that some parts of it are not detailed enough, that the picture gained is not rich enough, at least not equally in all its parts. This, however, will frequently be the situation with which the lexicographer will have to cope. And in order to prevent erroneous ideas, it is necessary to make the final remark that the complexity of the example discussed above is decidedly not connected with the circumstance that the language concerned is Chinese; though geographical and cultural distance has an observable influence upon the anisomorphism of languages (cf. § 7.1), a similarly complex group of near-synonyms could be found in any European language.

In any case, the study of the near-synonyms and the analysis of their differences is one of the most outstanding duties of the lexicographer. Indeed, the importance of this task cannot be stressed enough, because it could be maintained that one does not really know the meaning of a word in all its complexity if one does not study it in comparison with and in contrast to its near-synonyms.[140]

---

[140] Antonyms, i.e. the words of opposite meaning (e.g. Eng. *white* :: *black*, *good* :: *bad* etc.) are also of some importance for this study but not as much as the near-synonyms. On the antonyms, see O. Ducháček, *Sur quelques problèmes de l'antonymie*, Cahiers 6, 1965, 55ff. (with a bibliography and a classification of the different types of antonyms), and *Précis de sémantique française*, Brno 1967, p. 45ff. Antonyms are systematically indicated, e.g. in Hayakawa's Dictionary of synonyms, cf. footnote 134.

Obviously, the notion of near-synonyms can be understood in a narrow sense or a broad one. Consequently, it is also possible for some authors to regard as near-synonyms words which would not be regarded as such by other scholars. There are, at least for the moment, no quantitative criteria on hand by which one could "measure" the degree of the near-synonyms' similarity. It will, however, always be possible to ascertain, at least quite impressionistically, which basic components of meaning of the near-synonyms are identical and which are not; in which and how many senses the partial near-synonyms agree and in which and how many they do not; what and how many criterial semantic features cause the difference; it will also be possible to observe whether it is their most frequently occurring senses in which the near-synonyms agree, or, on the contrary, whether it is not some special, rarely occurring sense which rendess them related.

And it is also possible to put together chains of near-synonyms in which the adjacent words have a very close meaning, but the terms at the beginning and at the end of the chain have a rather distant meaning. Practically all dictionaries of so-called synonyms[141] work on this principle. If this is done prudently, there can certainly be no objection. The most important thing is that the lexicographer must study the respective meanings comparatively and that he must indicate not only the differences in the designation but also in the connotation and the range of application.[142]

It was in its time certainly correct when a dictionary of synonyms[143] indicated the following synonyms (which we could call near-synonyms) of the word *girl*: *girl, lass, lussie, wench, miss, colleen, flapper, bobbysoxer, damsel, maid, maiden, jeune fille*. It is one of the lexicographer's most important tasks to know near synonyms like these, to know which elements of their lexical meaning coincide and which differ — and this not only as far as the designation is concerned. It is necessary to know the differences in connotation and the range of application, and this not only in cases like the preceding one, but also when the lexicographer has to deal with words which invite emotion and expressivity less than the preceding example; e.g.: *clean, cleanly, pure, spotless, unspotted, immaculate, unstained, stainless, unsoiled, unsullied, taintless, untainted, sterile, aseptic, uninfected.*[144]

When collecting and comparing the near-synonyms, the lexicographer must not forget what has been said above about partial synonymy and near-syno-

[141] It is just in this branch of lexicography that the term "synonym" is usually taken in the broadest sense possible, including also what we call near-synonyms and semantically related words.

[142] Cf. Aleksandrov LS 6, 1963, 34f.

[143] Both this and the following example are taken from P. Roget — D. C. Browning, *Thesaurus of English Words and Phrases*, London–New York 1952, p. 40.

[144] Roget-Browning, op. cit. p. 202.

7*

nymy: the single chains that belong to the single senses of a word are different, and have different directions. In the last paragraph, we quoted the near-synonyms of *girl* (1) "female child";

for *girl* (2) "a young female" the near-synonyms were: *Damsel girl, lass, lassie, maid, maiden, demoiselle, flapper, miss, missie, nymph, wench, bint, floosy, popsy, fouster, jade, dona, grisette, colleen*;

for *girl* (3) "sweetheart", the near-synonyms were: *girl friend, lady-love, fiancée, sweetie, cutier mistress, inamorata, idol, daxy, dona, Dulcinea, goddess.*[145]

1.7.7 When we observe these and similar chains of near-synonyms, we see that their mutual differences can be visualized as being situated in different dimensions. This becomes still clearer if we do study not only the near-synonyms but also whole sets of semantically related words.

There is an extensive overlapping between what we call near-synonyms and semantically related words; in fact the first category can even be included in the second.[146] The difference between the two is not, however only one of degree: whereas we require at least some contexts in which either of the near-synonyms can be used, there is no such need in the case of the semantically related words. This latter notion is constituted rather externally: when observing the extralinguistic world, we can conceive some spheres of it as connected, as forming more or less homogenous areas which can be usefully understood and studied as coherent wholes, distinct from the rest of the extralinguistic world. Lexical units which designate the single segments of such an area of the extralinguistic world are, then, the semantically related words (lexical units): words that designate relationship and family connections, or the legal terms, or words that designate life in the sea, or words of friendship and love, or any other groups of words similarly constituted.[147] These words occur frequently but not necessarily in clusters (according to the topic of the respective text) and sometimes also combine or co-occur with another group of semantically related words. For example, it would seem that the group of words semantically related to deep-sea life combines with a different group

---

[145] Roget-Browning, op. cit. p. 111 and p. 288 — The reader can observe how quickly words of this type change their status: the dictionary from which we quoted this example was published in 1952 (which implies that the material is somewhat older), but there is more than one expression among the near-synonyms which is rather obsolete by now.

[146] But the two categories cannot be kept apart in each particular case; cf. Rey, Cahiers 7, 1965, 95.

[147] Semantically related words are sometimes called *paronyms* (cf. H. Kurath, *The Semantic Patterning of Words*, in: Georgetown University, Monograph Series on Languages and Linguistics 14, 1961, p. 91). The term in itself would be good; I do not, however, use it, because it is traditionally used in another meaning. Traditionally, paronyms are those words which have a similar form but a dissimilar meaning (e.g. Italian *traduttore* : : *traditore* "translator : : traitor").

50544

of, say, verbs than the words semantically related to eschatology. But the difference is not neat, there are always overlappings; in any case, research is badly needed in this whole field.

But it is not only the designative words among which one can find the semantically related ones.[148] In a similar way, we can find analogous groups also among words (lexical units) which perform other functions: thus, we can speak about group of semantically related words which express negation, conditionality of a sentence, or disgust of the speaker etc.[149]

A study or at least a comparison of a group of semantically related words shows those properties, which can be called the dimensions of differences existing within the group, usually more clearly than chains of near-synonyms. For instance, W. Schmid-Hidding studied the English words which belong to the sphere of humour.[150] According to him, the pertinent words are related in the following way (see fig. 7, p. 102).

When we compare this schematic representation with the merely linear chains of near-synonyms e.g.: *wit, humour, comicality, imagination, fancy, fun, drollery, whim, jocularity, jocosity, facetiousness, waggery, waggishness, silliness, sult, smartness, banter, chaff, persiflage, badinage, farce, espieglerie; jest, joke, jape, conceit, quip, quirk, quiddity, crank, wheeze, side-splitter, concetto, witticism, gag, wisecrack, repartee, retort, comeback, mot, bon mot, pleasantry, funniment, flash of wit, happy thought, sally, point, dry joke, idle conceit, epigram, quibble, play upon words, fun, conundrum,* etc.,[151] we see the single dimensions of the differences much better represented in the figure of the semantically related words.

Such schematic representations are of the greatest importance for the lexicographer. In the case which we used here as example, the figure we reproduced was based on very deep onomasiological studies. The lexicographer

---

[148] Consequently, it is not to advantage to speak about "designative" or "denotative fields" to which such groups of semantically related words belong.

[149] A closely related term is Halliday's (A. McIntosh — M. A. K. Halliday, *Patterns of Language*, London 1966, p. 20) *lexical set*. The lexical set is defined as "a grouping of words having approximately the same range of collocations", i.e. which occur in approximately identical combinations with other words. For example, *"trains, taxi, car* and so on frequently collocate with *take, drive, passenger, engine* and others". Halliday accepts also a point of view similar to that advocated in our discussion when he states that the set is a grouping of words having the same situation type. He also states with full right that the formal and the contextual (i.e. situational) criteria yield generally the same groupings but that they are "distinct from a methodological point of view, since they represent different ways of approaching the facts". The formal criterion (i.e. the discovery of combinatorial [collocational] groups) is very useful, but in my experience primarily in the sphere of designative words: grammatical and other non-designative words seem to have rather unlimited combinatorial possibilities, whether semantically related or unrelated.

[150] W. Schmid-Hidding, *Humor und Witz*, München 1963.

[151] Roget — Browning, op. cit. (footnote 134), p. 268.

will be well advised to know the publications that deal with these and similar problems. On the other hand, it would be illusory to think or even postulate that the lexicographer could or should produce studies like the quoted one

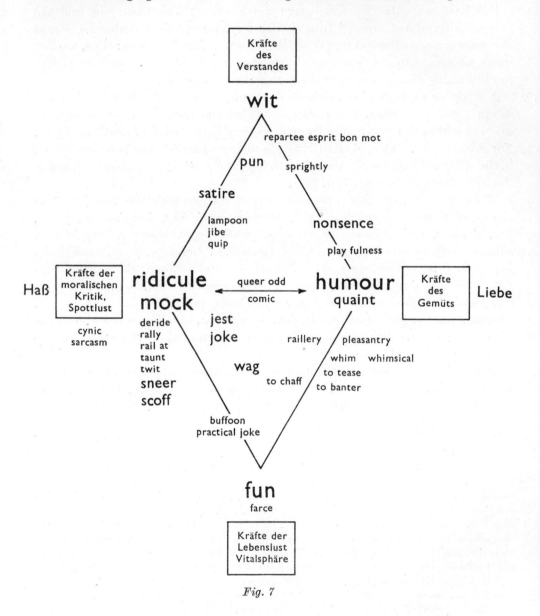

Fig. 7

as a by-product of his own, lexicographic work, or in the way of preparation for his work: he will never have time for that, at least not in the usual cases. What must be required from him, however, is that he should develop the ability to survey groups of semantically related words as wholes and to perceive the semantic dimensions (foggy as they may happen to be) which can be discovered.

There are two main methodological approaches which are concerned with these problems. The first of them is the so-called "Wortfeldforschung", i.e. the study of the word-field. This approach, founded by J. Trier, devotes its main attention to the question of the delimination of the meaning of semantically related words.[152] A representative of this type of studies is the just quoted work by Schmid-Hidding.[153]

The other methodological approach is called onomasiology. In this approach, we analyze a coherent part of the extralinguistic world and study how its single segments are designated.[154] For instance, we analyze agricultural techniques and study how the particular tools, apparatus, machines, activities, processes etc. are named. Onomasiology is largely based on the analysis or at least knowledge of the denotata; very generally speaking, it could be maintained that it takes the existence of denotata (and designata) for granted and studies their expression in the particular language.[155]

1.7.8 It is necessary to try to study whole groups of semantically related words to discover, at least in a general way, the broad semantic dimensions on which the lexical meanings seem to vary, just as it is necessary to study the closest near-synonyms in order to discover the semantic features which make the single lexical meanings different. There are approaches which go back, at least to a considerable degree, to Hjelmslev, in which these purposes

[152] There are many works which are written in terms of this "field theory" (*Feldtheorie*). All these works will be usefull, irrespective of whether the lexicographer is or is not ready to accept the ultimate claims of the theory.

[153] For a study of a French field of words, cf. O. Ducháček, *Le champ conceptuel de la beauté en français moderne*, Brno 1963.

[154] Cf. for instance the papers by E. Tappolet, *Die romanischen Verwandtschaftsnamen*, Strassburg 1895, and A. Zauner, Romanische Forschungen 14, 1903, 339ff. who can be regarded as the founders of onomasiology.

[155] Another related branch of study is *lexicology*. In this approach, both the meaning and the forms of words (expecially their derivations) are studied, as well as the different layers of lexicon, its recurrent patterns, the regulatities and discrepancies of the connection between meaning and form, etc.; lexicology is a systematic study of the lexicon, whereas lexicography ist more concerned with individual lexical units (cf. Weinreich PL 26; de Tollenaere, Beiträge zur Sprachkunde und Informationsverarbeitung 1, 1963, 33). But it is very useful if lexicographical practice is based on rich lexicological research (Babkin LS 4, 1960, 8). On lexicology, see O. S. Akhmanova, *Očerki po obščej i russkoj leksikologii*, Moskva 1957; U. Weinreich, *Lexicology*, in: Current Trends in Linguistics I, The Hague 1963, p. 60ff. (basically a report on pertinent new publications in Eastern Europe, but with good theoretical discussions and insights); J. Filipec, *Zur Theorie und Methode der lexikologischen Forschung* (in: Zeichen und System der Sprache III, Berlin 1966, p. 154ff.).

Le champ sémantique

Nom spécifique	Ane	Cheval	Mulet	Bœuf	Chèvre	Mouton	Porc/Cochon	Chien
Mâle	âne	*étalon*	mulet	*taureau*	bouc	*bélier*	*verrat*	chien
Mâle châtré		HONGRE		BŒUF		MOUTON		
Femelle	ânesse	*jument*	mule	*vache*	chèvre	*brebis*	*truie*	chienne
Jeune	ânon	*poulain*		*veau*	chevreau	*agneau*	porcelet cochonnet pourceau (*)	chiot
Nouveau-né						AGNELET		
Jeune mâle				TAURILLON BOUVILLON				
Jeune femelle		POULICHE		GÉNISSE		AGNELLE		
Portée (couvée)							cochonnée	*portée*
Parturition		*pouliner*		*vêler*	chevreter	*agneler*	cochonner	chienner
Local d'élevage	*écurie*	*écurie*	*écurie*	bouverie étable vacherie	*étable*	bergerie	*toit, soue* porcherie cochonnier (*)	chenil NICHE
Cri spécifique	braire	hennir		*mugir meugler beugler*	*bêler* chevroter	*bêler*	*grogner*	*aboyer*
Groupe d'animaux semblables	TROUPEAU OU TROUPE							MEUTE
Nom collectif I				bovins	CAPRINS	OVINS	porcins	
Nom collectif II	GROS BÉTAIL				MENU BETAIL			
Nom collectif III	CHEPTEL							

des animaux domestiques

Chat	Lapin	Canard	Dindon	Oie	Pigeon	Pintade	Poule
chat	lapin	canard	dindon	jars	pigeon		coq
CHAT COUPÉ	LAPIN { COUPÉ / TAILLÉ						chapon
chatte	lapine	cane	dinde	oie	pigeonne	pintade	poule
chaton	lapereau	caneton	dindonneau	oison	pigeon-neau	pintadeau pintadon	poulet
							POUSSIN
							COCHET COQUELET
		CANETTE					POULETTE POULARDE
portée	*portée* nichée	*couvée*	*couvée*	*couvée*	*couvée*	*couvée*	couvée
chaton-ner	lapiner						
	clapier lapinière				pigeon-nier colombier		poulailler
miauler	*clapir couiner*	*cancaner nasiller*	*glousser*	*jargonner cacarder*	*roucouler*	*criailler*	*glousser caqueter*
		TROUPEAU OU TROUPE			VOL VOLÉE	TROUPEAU TROUPE	
		VOLAILLE					
	BASSE-COUR						

Nom spécifique }	Ane	Cheval	Mulet	Bœuf	Chèvre	Mouton	Porc/Cochon	Chien
Dérivation adjectivale		chevalin	mulassier	bovin	CAPRIN	OVIN	porcin	CANIN
Gardien spécifique	ânier	*étalonnier*	muletier	bouvier	chevrier	*berger*	porcher	
Viande		DU CHEVAL		DU BŒUF DE VEAU	CHEVREAU	MOUTON AGNEAU DE LAIT AGNEAU GRIS BROUTARD	PORC, COCHON DE LAIT	

* Toutes les fois qu'une case comporte plusieurs termes, l'analyse en traits sémantiquement pertinents devrait être poussée au-delà du présent tableau, par exemple: *porcherie* (caractère industriel), *cochonnier* (méridionalisme), etc.

are usefully combined. As a typical example of a very good study of this sort, we can reproduce here the final table from G. Mounin's paper about the words designating domestic animals in French.[156]

We have here a group of semantically related words. The first horizontal line indicates the single animals. Of primary importance is the first vertical column, which indicates the single semantic features which modify the lexical meaning (male, castrated male, ... young female) and different categories to which the more distant words belong (specific cry, specific custodian, etc.).

Besides the immediate use of analyzing this concrete group of semantically fact, namely that a semantic feature may be recurrent, that it may be present in the lexical meaning of more words than one. As the study of semantic features is, for different reasons, one of the most important tasks of linguistics in our day, it is to be expected that many studies will be published in this field in the coming years. The lexicographer will do well to know these works, because they will help him to find out what is systemic in the lexicon, i.e. in the total stock of the words (lexical units) of a language. The greater the number of the identical, recurrent semantic features that are part of the lexical meanings of a group of semantically related words and the more regular their patterning, the more expressed is the systemic character of this part of the lexicon: in such a case, we speak about a subsystem, within the lexicon,

[156] G. Mounin, *Un champ sémantique: la dénomination des animaux domestiques*, La linguistique 1, 1965, 50ff.

Chat	Lapin	Canard	Dindon	Oie	Pigeon	Pintade	Poule
					COLOMBIN		
	DU LAPIN	DU CANARD	DE LA DINDE	DE L'OIE	DU PIGEON	DE LA PINTADE DU PINTADON	DU POULET

reserving the term s y s t e m for use in reference to the whole lexicon.[157] But the discovery of the semantic features has also some very practical purposes: in the first place, it is very useful for the lexicographer who is compiling a monolingual dictionary to be able to use the criterial semantic features in his definitions of the lexical meanings. The bilingual lexicographer will certainly be interested in checking whether the supposed equivalents in the two languages really do have identical semantic features. Therefore, the lexicographer will certainly try to find out, by comparison, what are the semantic features of a small subsystem, of a small group of semantically related words, even if there are no special studies in this field on hand. The lexicographer will not usually have the time necessary to undertake really large-scale analyses with rich material. But limited comparisons of a few near-synonyms or of a few semantically related words will always be useful (even if they are not published, but only jolted on paper in the form of a note, or done only mentally), because they will show at least the distinctively most important semantic features. But the lexicographer must be very prudent in this respect: above all, he must not try to find parallelism where there is none, or regularity in the patterns of semantic features where there is a real difference. For instance, it

[157] Some scholars find such a statement too optimistic. But without a systemic character, the lexicon could not be supposed to function. It should be granted as a matter of course, however, that the system of the lexicon is much less neat and incomparably more polydimensional than any other linguistic system. It is also quite imaginable that the only common property of all the lexical units of a language is just the fact that they function as lexical units. This would suffice, in the opinion of the present author, to establish the systemic character of the totality of lexical units; but other scholars may find it too limited a basis for a system. All the pertinent problems, even the most fundamental ones, still need much study. Cf. Horálek, *Filosofie jazyka*, Praha 1967, p. 86: a full discussion, with bibliography.

would be totally wrong if the lexicographer tried to establish the following two small subsystems, though everything seems to be very neat and correct:

BOS	EQUUS
ox	*horse*
bull	*stallion*
cow	*mare*

This analysis might seem to be correct, at least at the first glance. The trouble is, however, with the word *horse*: though a good part of its applications would allow the interpretation, a more careful analysis will show that the word is used in just these cases where the three criterial semantic features obtaining in this subsystem are irrelevant, i.e. as the hyperonym. Therefore, the scheme should have the following form:

	BOS	EQUUS
general	Φ	*horse*
male	*bull*	*stallion*
castr. male	*ox*	*gelding*
female	*cow*	*mare*

In this scheme, it is clear that the two subsystems are not parallel.[158]

Nevertheless, similar schemes and their analysis are of use to the lexicographer, who must, however, be aware of the limits to the usefulness of this approach.

Above all, the lexicographer will have to remember that words are frequently polysemous, so that usually only one of their senses is dealt with in one scheme. So, for example, the word *gelding* can be indicated in the preceding scheme only in one of its senses: in a more general sense, it can be applied to any castrated animal.

Another thing that must be taken into consideration is the fact that the semantic features gained by such comparisons usually pertain only to the designation, wheres differences may be found also in the connotation, etc.

Polysemy is analyzed with the help of what we called semantic features by Fodor and Katz;[159] their method, however, is different. They originally distinguished two different categories of what could be roughly called semantic features. To the first category, which they call "markers", belong those seman-

---

[158] The scheme is highly reduced. — In Armenian (Motalová), *tavar* is the hyperonym in the column of *bos*; there is, however, not term for "gelding".

[159] J. J. Katz — J. A. Fodor, *The Structure of Semantic Theory*, Language 39, 1963, 170 ff.

tic features which are present also in the lexical meanings of other words; to the second category, which they call "distinguishers", belong those semantic features which are individual, which do not recur in the lexical meanings of other words. Thus, the meaning of Eng. *bachelor* can be represented in the approach of the two scholars, as follows:

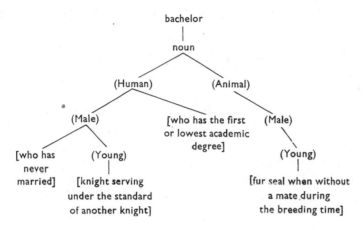

Fig. 8

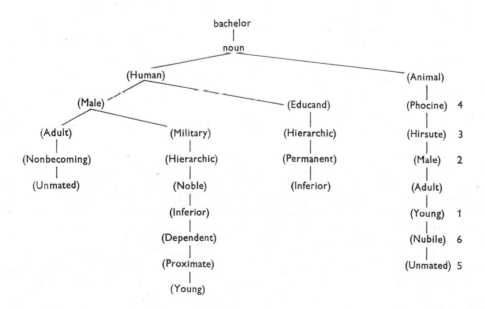

Fig. 9

It is not necessary to discuss in detail[160] that the greatest of semantic features is to be found among the distinguishers.[161]

This semantic approach was considerably improved by J. J. Katz.[162] In the new version, the semantic presentation of the dominant sense of Eng. *to chase* has the form:

> *chase* → Verb, Verb Transitive, ...;
>   (((Activity) (Nature: (Physical)) of x), ((Movement) (Rate: Fast)) (Character: Following)), (Intention of X: (Trying to catch ((Y) ((Movement) (Rate: Fast)))));
>   ⟨SR⟩.

It can be seen that the abandoning of the difference between the markers and the distinguishers led to a greater coherence of the treatment. A pleasant feature of the new versions is that it obviously does not try to treat meaning as something purely definitional but with due respect for the extralinguistic world.[163] The formula ⟨SR⟩ at the end of the presentation (or representation, as J. Katz himself calls it) refers to the *Selective Restrictions* (i.e., broadly speaking to what we call the *range of application*, or *applicational restrictions*). In this respect, we can observe the greatest progress of this semantic theory; we do not summarize the respective discussion here, but Katz' remarks (which follow the passage indicated) show that much has been done.

The semantic studies of Katz and Fodor and of Katz are closely connected with the transformational grammar.[164] Seeing the great and rising interest in this approach to linguistics and seeing the vast and increasing efforts to elaborate it and to apply it practically to different languages, it is to be expected that this school of linguistic thought will produce further semantic studies which will be of high interest.

[160] Katz-Fodor, op. cit. p. 190. The markers are included in square brackets, the distinguishers in parentheses.

[161] Cf. the criticism of Katz and Fodor by D. Bolinger, *The Atomization of Meaning*, Language 41, 1965, 555ff. Other important analyses of the approach of Katz an Fodor are: E. A. Nida, *Towards a Science of Translating*, Leiden 1964, U. Weinreich, *Explorations in Semantic Theory* (in: Current Trends in Linguistics, ed T. A. Sebeok, III, The Hague 1966), p. 395ff.; E. Coseriu, *Zur Vorgeschichte der strukturellen Semantik* (in: To Honor Roman Jakobson, The Hague — Paris, 1967), p. 493, footnote 3.

[162] J. J. Katz, *The Philosophy of Language*, New York 1966, p. 167ff.

[163] Cf. J. D. McCawley, *The Annotated* Respective; the *Respective Downfalls of Deep Structure and Autonomous Syntax* (privately circulated paper, p. 8): "For the purposes of natural language, the proposition *four is the square root of sixteen* must be regarded as following from the factual knowledge about *four* and *sixteen* rather than from their definitions".

[164] Which does not mean, however, that it could not be accepted or used by a scholar whose interests are not focused on the transformational grammar.

One of the important recent developments within the transformational grammar is sometimes called "generative semantics". Within this approach (represented mainly by J. D. McCawley, G. Lakoff, J. Ross, and others; mostly in preprints, but cf., e.g., McCawley's paper quoted in footnote 165), a sentence like "John killed Harry" is derived from "John caused Harry to die", and a sentence like "John murdered Harry" from "John caused-to-die-by-illegal-means-with-malice-aforethought Harry". Obviously, this trend of thought may develop (at least partly) into a study of the criterial semantic features of lexical units. And studies pertaining to other developments of the transformational approach, such as the abstract, or logical, syntax (as represented, e.g., by the scholars just mentioned, J. Gruber, E. Bach, and others) may lead, at least to some extent, to similar results.

Therefore, the lexicographer will be well advised to give some attention to developments and results in this field.[165]

It goes without saying that the lexicographer cannot himself make detailed studies of semantic features. It could be impossible to make them, if there is no preparatory work available, even for the more important lexical units, and it is out of the question for the lexicographer himself to do the entire work for all the words he will include in his dictionary. But where such studies have been done, the lexicographer is well advised to know them of as background for his own analyses and presentations in single entries. In any case, a systematic description of the whole lexicon in terms of semantic features and their recurrence must be regarded as a major goal of future linguistic studies.[166]

1.7.9 It follows from the preceding discussion that the lexicographer must steer a difficult middle way. On the one hand, he must, in any case and without any exception study in detail and in mutual contradistinctions the near-synonyms of the word with which he is at the moment dealing and have a broad survey of the semantic dimensions found in the groups of semantically

---

[165] Cf., e.g., J. D. McCawley, *The Role of Semantics in a Grammar*, and E. Bach, *Nouns and Noun Phrases*, both in: *Universals in Linguistic Theory*, New York 1968. Some developments taking place within the transformational theory are very radical. For example, R. Binnick, *On the Nature of the "Lexical Item"* (in: Papers from the Fourth Regional Meeting, Chicago Linguistic Society, Chicago 1968, p. 1ff.) maintains that "... given the proper transformational apparatus, the lexicon will need only a handful of basic, non-derived verbs, probably *be*, *go*, and *come* [but possibly even *can* may be derived from *go*, and *go*, in its turn, from *be*]. All other locative and motive verbs, ... like *run* and *climb*, ... *surround* and *enter*, ... can be derived by transformations." This trend of thought would probably lead to transformations which would add what we call semantic features to the basic verbs.

[166] Cf. e.g. E. H. Bendix, *Componental Analysis of General Vocabulary: the Semantic Structure of a Set of Verbs in English, Hindi, and Japanese* (IJAL 32, 1966, Nr. 2, Part III, published as *Publication* 40, Indiana University Research center in Anthropology, Folklore, and Linguistics). — J. Apresjan, *O ponjatijach i metodach strukturnoj leksikologii* (in: Problemy strukturnoj ling-

related words; on the other hand, he cannot usually undertake detailed onomasiological and similar studies himself, at least not to a great extent. There are, however, parts of the lexicon which he will have to study in an onomasiological way, even if he is forced to do the necessary preliminary work himself: this applies above all to the more coherent subsystems of the lexicon.

Generally, one can say that the more clearly related are the words in a group, the greater number of semantic features they have in common; the more coherent a lexical subsystem is, the greater is the necessity to study the pertinent lexical units not in isolation, but in their relations within the group.

Above, we discussed the different ways in which the same physical spectrum of colours is segmented and the single segments named in different languages. It may be clear that a lexicographer who compiles a monolingual or a bilingual dictionary of a language like Shona will explain the pertinent words for colours much better if he takes the whole spectrum and all the words under consideration as a coherent group.[167] The same observation applies to those cases where the extralinguistic and in particular the physical world as seen by the man in the street is clearly articulated and a part of it forms a coherent whole. For example, it is a generally perceivable fact of the extra-linguistic world that some people are genetically related, and that genetical relations are the same in the whole world and in all ages, with only minor differences: basically, everybody must have a father and a mother (even if they may remain unknown for different reasons); the same parents (in identical pairs, or with different partners) frequently have more children than one, so that there are brothers and sisters; sometimes, the man in question will have children of his own, and so on. But these identical relations are conceived in quite different ways in different languages. A good example of this is given by Conklin.[168] Let us suppose that there are six people related in the following way (see fig. 10):

(a is a man, b his sister, c her husband,
d the son of b and c, f the son of the son of e)

vistiki, Moskva 1962, p. 141ff.); S. Lamb, *The Sememic Approach to Structural Semantics,* Berkeley 1963; B. Pottier, *Vers une sémantique moderne* (in: Travaux de linguistique et de littérature II, Strasbourg 1964, p. 107ff.); A. J. Greimas, *Sémantique structurale,* Paris 1966; G. F. Meier, *Noematische Analyse als Voraussetzung für die Ausschaltung der Polysemie* (in: Zeichen und System der Sprache III, Berlin 1966; p. 117ff.). All these and similar studies (for instance Coseriu, Ivanov) belong to different trends of thought. It is impossible to discuss here all details; we have chosen here, for the purpose of illustration, the transformational approach as that which seems to be most rapidly developing, — A good survey of the whole field and of the different approaches is T. Todorov, *Recherches sémantiques* (in: Langages 1, mars 1966), p. 5ff. — For the study of non-designative words, cf. e.g. R. Austerlitz, *Semantic Components of Pronoun Systems: Gilyak,* Word 15, 1959, 102ff.

[167] Cf. Gleason PL 100.

[168] PL 126.

By a speaker of English, a will be regarded, together with c, as f's grandfather. By a speaker of Tagalog, the same person would be regarded, together with d, as f's cousin. The different conception of the same reality is clear.

That there are groups of plants and animals which are related is a fact obvious even without scientific study. Consequently, the lexicographer will do well to study such groups as wholes, not only the single words with their near-synonyms. He must, however, not forget that the folk classification of plants and similar subsystems of the extralinguistic world is often different from the scientific one.[169] Good examples are given by Migliorini:[170] e.g. Italian

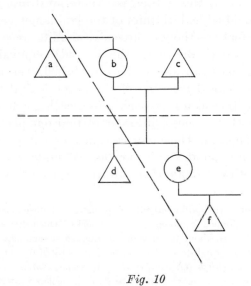

Fig. 10

porcospino is scientifically two animals (*Erinaeus europeus* and *hystrix crystatus*). Therefore, the lexicographer will need the scientific classification in order to identify the denotata of the words, but he will have to base his study of the word's meaning on the conception expressed in the respective language.[171]

[169] Migliorini, *Vocabolario* 35; Conklin PL 129.

[170] Op. cit.

[171] These studies must be done with due care and circumspection. It is very dangerous to base the interpretation on the analysis of an isolated word only. For instance, no English speaker will take a *guinea-pig* for a *pig*, though this is what the lexical unit would suggest if English were a language correlated with some exotic culture. But it is hard to say whether *Rosetti* (*Linguistica*, The Hague 1965, p. 31) is right when he states: "Unie écrévisse est donc ≪une espèce de petit poisson qui marche à reculons≫, car la définition du dictionnaire (≪genre de cruastacés décapodes qui vivent dans l'eau≫) n'est juste que du point de vue biologique". It seems to me to be difficult to say or even to prove about an average speaker of French today that he would

If we compare corresponding lexical subsystems in different languages, we see the differences in the way the same extralinguistic reality is segmented and organized into different designata more clearly than if we compare only isolated words. The semantic boundaries are practically always different: the same extralinguistic reality is segmented in another way. These differences between single languages are, of course, of the greatest importance, particularly for the lexicographer who is preparing a bilingual dictionary. On the other hand, the lexicographer should not be unduly discouraged by this diversity nor by these differences. The experience of the profession is that it is possible to translate from one language to another with a remarkable degree of precision and accuracy. If this is the case, there must also be some lexical equivalence of the individual lexical units of the two languages, or at least of some of their semantic features though these lexical units are certainly not in a one-to-one equivalence. With due care, the semantic equivalence of lexical units of different languages can always be established. The most important thing is to analyze the lexical meaning of the single lexical units in the respective languages and then compare each sense, each connotation and each semantic feature in both languages in order to find out partial coincidence, differences, and overlappings. The main conspicuous exceptions to this rule are the so-called culture-bound words, i.e. lexical units whose denotata or designate simply do not exist in another culture. More on this § 7.1.

class a crayfish as a little fish — though historically, it is just the English word *crayfish* (adapted from *crevice*, the older form of French *écrevisse*) the second part of which shows by its assimilation to *fish* that this could be supposed about the speakers of English at some point of time. Historically, this interpretation of the English word could be corroborated by the analogous cases of Eng. *crawfish*, *cuttle-fish*, and *shellfish* (cf. Jespersen, *Mankind, Nation and Individual*, Oslo 1925, p. 111). This situation inspires more confidence than the isolated interpretation or classification of *écrevisse*, because we have here a series of parallel phenomena and because the interpretation is founded on some facts of language. But generally, the best and safest thing that can be done in this respect is to establish the taxonomic classes as revealed by whole series and groups of pertinent words. Generally, it is better to do this not by means of etymology (which is fragile and which brings us back to different points of time and possibly, therefore, to different cultural settings), but by the finding out of the hyperonyms and their respective hyponyms. As representative of this type of study can be quoted M. Mathiot, *Noun Classes and Folk Taxonomy in Papago*, American Anthropologist 64, 1962, 340ff. (reprinted in Hymes, *Language in Culture and Society*, p. 154ff.). — Very instructive is J. A. Frisch, *Maricopa Foods: a Native Taxonomic System* (in: IJAL 34, 1968, Nr 1, part I, p. 16ff.); the advantage of the paper is that it establishes the taxonomic classes not only by the discovery of the hyperonyms and hyponyms, but also by observing how the respective terms for food combine with different verbs equivalent to Eng. "to eat". Another danger connected with this type of studies is caused by the possible ignorance of the informants. Petráček reports that when he asked different uneducated urban inhabitants of Cairo to give him the terms for different trees, the answer was invariably *šagara* "tree", i.e. only the general hyperonym.

DESIGNATIVE AND NON-DESIGNATIVE WORDS

1.8 Up to this point, it has been mainly the lexical meaning of the designative word that we have discussed. We have seen that there are three basic components of lexical meaning: the designation, the connotation, and the range of application. We have also seen that the largest group of words which carry lexical meaning are the designative words — words which refer to segments of the extralinguistic world as conceived by the speakers of the respective language. Words which perform other functions than the designative one, as we discussed them above, § 1.3.1.1, are treated by the lexicographer on the model of designative words.

1.8.1 It is important to state this above all about the words which perform grammatical functions. For the lexicographer, these grammatical words, or function words (or whatever he chooses to call them) are just a part of the total lexicon of the language, as any other words. It is his duty to register them and to indicate their meaning, in this case roughly speaking, to indicate with what grammatical function, when and how they are used. The lexicographer's indications will, at least in the majority if cases, be less copious and detailed than those of the grammarian, but nevertheless they will have to be sufficient for the user's information.

The point of view advocated here, that the function of so-called grammatical words should be described in a dictionary, does not depend upon any theoretical consideration as far as the structure of language goes. Whatever opinion the lexicographer may have on the relation of lexicality and grammaticality (and on grammaticality expressed by lexical means), even if he is inclined to put the two into a rather sharp contradistinction, he will be forced to indicate the grammatical words with their function, in his dictionary, if for no another reason than that many words can perform both designative and grammatical functions. This is the case, for example, with the different auxiliary verbs and similar semi-lexical, semi-grammatical elements well known in all languages. For instance, the sentences

"I shall buy the book" and
"I will buy the book"

sufficiently show the combination of grammaticality and lexicality in *shall* and *will*. French expressions like *je viens de finir* "I have just finished", *je vais vous dire* "I am going to tell you" show the verbs *venir, aller* performing rather grammatical functions; but it would hardly be possible not to mention them apart from their designative lexical meaning, in a lexicographic presentation. There are cases when the difference between the designative and the grammatical function of a word is accompanied by a difference in form: the

Eng. verb *to have* has the negation with the auxiliary verb *to do* if it is a verb with a fully designative function ("*I do not have a penny*"), but without it when it is an (auxiliary) verb performing a grammatical function ("*I have not seen him for ages*").

Cases of this type are very frequent in Chinese (as reported by Kalousková), e.g. *hui* "can, to be able" — future auxiliary (*pu hui hsia yu* "it will not rain"); *kei* "to give" — prepos. of dative; and in Burmese (as reported by Minn Latt), e.g. *sî* "to ride" — numerative, formal word used when animals or things ridden are counted; *tyî* "to be big" — augmentative element; *kălêi* "to be petty" — diminutive element; *mjâ* "to be much" — plural marker. Similar phenomena can be observed in other languages; however, it is not always just the canonical form, but another form of the paradigm which is used in such a formal function. Zima reports Haussa *baayaa* "the back" — but *baayan* gaysuuwaa "after the greeting", *sunàa baayansà* "they are behind him". Zvelebil reports Tamil *en* "to say so-and-so" — formal marker of direct speech (*nan pokiren enru connan* "I go thus-having-said said-he"). Miltner reports Braj *kāran* "cause" which has no paradigm; but only the isolated form *kāran* "because" when used as a propositional-grammatical operator.

Not infrequently, the lexicographer will observe that among the differences of a polysemous word, there are different senses some of which are more designative, but some rather grammatical and frequently without any formal distinction. For example, a preposition like Eng. *on* has rather a designative meaning in a phrase like *on the table*, where it expresses the situation of an object and can be replaced by another preposition with an observable effect on the meaning (*behind the table, under the table*), but in a sentence like "During her history, Korania declared war on many states" it has hardly any other function than a purely relational, grammatical one.

Zvelebil reports the following example of highly developed polysemy:

Tam. *mēl* (1) s. "the surface; the sky; the west"; (2) adj. "upper; western; best; first; great; previous"; (3) postposition,
    (a) local: 1. with dative "over", 2. with. gen. "upon",
    (b) temporal 1. "henceforth", 2. "after", adverb. postp.: "more, more, than"; (4) adverb "against".

In different languages, there is a great variety of such gradations, or combinations of grammaticality and lexicality. Uncertainties of this kind are sometimes accompanied by uncertainties or difficulties concerning the morphological boundary of the word. Very difficult are the cases of elements which somehow stand between a word and an affix.

Vasiljev reports examples of Vietnamese auxiliary words which are used in substantive predicative expressions, e.g. *việc* "thing, matter", *sự* "thing, matter" *cuộc* "situation", which cannot be used in isolation, but usually only in more or less set expressions e.g. *cho'i một cuộc* (verbatim "play-one-situation, game") "to play cards". But they are, on the other hand, autonomous, particularly *việc* which can also be used fully independently with the meaning "work". The best policy of the lexicographer is probably to list them as entities of their own. In the case used here for illustration the decision is relatively easy. A similar policy, however, should be advocated in all such borderline cases.

In particular cases, the lexicographer must be aware that it is not always true that the lexical somehow merges with the morphological-grammatical. Sometimes, we observe just the reverse. A clear example is supplied by a Northern dialect of Altaic in which the usual plural ending of substantives *-lar/-ler* is also used as an independent word with the meaning "they". But inversely, Yoruba *àwon* "they" is used (as reported by Zima) as a pure pluralizer in e.g. *àwon ẹṣín* "horses" (sing. *ẹṣín* "horse").

1.8.2 On the whole, it is the lexical meaning of the designative words (lexical units) which serves the lexicographer as basis and model for his treatment of all words (lexical units). It is interesting to observe that the category of words lexical units) which is most different from this model is that of proper names. It is not necessary here to discuss proper names in detail. Nor shall we discuss the opinions of some scholars who classify them (not without some reason) among the designative words. We regard here as proper names, in a highly simplifying way, those words (lexical units) which are customarily or at least habitually used in reference to single individual entities in order to distinguish them from other members of their own class of entities. Considered from this point of view, it is quite logical that the unique objects of reference of these words are so preponderant that if the lexicographer indicates proper names in his dictionary at all, they usually bring a strong encyclopedic element with them. If the lexicographer decides to avoid any encyclopedic elements, it is possible to treat proper names in a more general way: in that case, it suffices to indicate only their function (e.g. *mens' given name*; *family name*; *place name*; etc.). But short explanatory (encyclopedic) glosses are usually expected by the user of the dictionary (such as the situation of the place etc.).

The bilingual lexicographer should not overlook the fact that some proper names have different versions in different languages. Few personal names show such a variation: but cf., for example, Eng. *Charlemagne* :: Germ. *Karl der Große*. But not a small number of the traditional Christian (given) names belong here: for instance, Eng. *Charles*, French *Charles*, Germ. *Karl*, Italian *Carlo*. Most important are the place names which belong here (for example

French *Paris*, Italian *Parigi*).[172] The bilingual lexicographer should indicate these versions, at least in the more important cases.

Proper names can change their status and become appellatives. For instance, *W. C. Roentgen* was a German physicist (1845—1923) who discovered the so-called X-rays or Roentgen-rays. His name is used as an appellative to designate the apparatus and the procedure by which these rays are used for diagnostic purposes, particularly in medicine. In the selection of entries, such a word should be taken into consideration simply as an appellative. Sometimes, such an appellative is adapted in its form (spoken or written, or in both of them); for example, the apparatus and the procedure just mentioned are called in Czech by now *rentgen*.[173] Such words are, then, simple appellatives and we would not mention them in this connection but for the many irritating borderline cases which may cause trouble.[174]

---

[172] The written form is sometimes identical, but the pronunciation is different; cf. for instance French *Paris*, Eng. *Paris*, Germ. *Paris*, pronounced [pa'ri:], ['phæris], and [pa'ri:s], respectively.

[173] The example was kindly suggested by J. Filipec.

[174] Trouble caused by an appellative which has changed or is changing status into a proper name is less frequent, but nevertheless observable. For example, Eng. *god* :: (Christian) *God*; cf. M. Kohl, Ought God *be in Webster's Third?* (in: Names, Journal of the American Name Society 16, 1968, 134ff.).

CHAPTER II

FORMAL VARIATION OF WORDS

THE PARADIGM

2.1 One of the bases of the lexicographer's work is the fundamental assumption that such series of words as *book* : : *books*, or *work* : : *works* : : *worked* belong together. In other words, the usual working model of the lexicographer is the so-called word-and-paradigm model. When using this model (and for the lexicographer, it is really the best one), the lexicographer assumes that the lexical meaning of every single series of forms such as those quoted above remains the same, while only the different grammatical categories are expressed by different forms. There is no need to go into details: *book* and *books* both have the same lexical meaning "literary composition of considerable length (etc.)"; the first form belongs to the grammatical category "singular", the second to that of "plural". Mutatis mutandis the same can be said about the other series which are normally called paradigms.[1]

2.1.1 In English, paradigms are rather limited. In many languages, however, a word's paradigm can comprise tens or scores of forms. In the Slavonic languages, the usual paradigm of a substantive has some twelve or fourteen forms. In Greek, the paradigm of a verb has more than 200 forms. In Sanskrit, the total paradigm of a verb has about 1350 forms. It is only natural that the lexicographer cannot indicate all these forms in his dictionary. For every paradigm, i.e. for every inflected word and for the totality of its forms, he indicates only one form that is considered basis; this is the so-called c a n o n i c a l f o r m of a word.[2] The canonical form represents the whole paradigm.

---

[1] The whole paradigm, the whole range of forms that belong to one word is sometimes called the *lexeme*. In other terminologies, the *lexeme* is that part of the word which seem to carry the lexical-meaning in contradistinction to the grammatical morphemes. Thus, there would be the lexeme *work* — and the morphemes *-s*, *-ed*, (and eventually, zero), in the Eng. forms *works*, *worked*, *work* (in this sequence). In yet other terminologies, all the forms which belong to one word are called the *formal dispersion of the word*. Note that the term *paradigm*, *paradigmatic* is used here in its classical (i.e. morphological) sense. In other terminologies, *paradigmatic* are called the relations obtaining within the system, as apposed to the *syntagmatic* relations, observable in a concrete text.

[2] Considered from the point of view of the composition of the entry, the canonical form is the form in which the entry-word is quoted. In other terminologies, it is called the *basic form*, or *entry-form*.

The canonical forms of different paradigms are usually established by tradition, at least in those languages that enjoy it. It is for instance quite traditional in many languages to use the nomin. sing. as the canonical form of the substantives, or the nomin. sing. of the masculine gender in the positive degree as the canonical form of the adjectives; and either the first person sing. ind. praes. act. or the active infinitive pres. as the canonical form of the verbs. This does not, however, mean that this is or should be the rule in all the languages that have similar inflections. On the contrary, different forms are used as canonical forms. In some languages, one uses even canonical forms which are abstract, which cannot be used themselves in any sentence. To the former category belongs Magyar, where the canonical form of the verbs is the third person sing. indic. act. To the latter category belongs Greek, where the first pers. ind. act. is used as the canonical form of the verb; but instead of the so-called contracted forms as *filô* "I love", *timô* "I esteem" which really exist, uncontracted forms as *filéō* are used, forms which one does not find in Attic Greek (i.e. in the dialect most frequently used in literary works). In Sanskrit, substantives and adjectives are quoted in no case but in the stem (e.g. *mitra-* "friend"), and verbs in no person or any other form, but in the root (e.g. *pat-* "to fall", *kar-* or *kṛ-* "to do"): both the stem and the root are mere abstractional constructs which cannot be directly used as such. In Tamil (as reported by Zvelebil), the canonical form of the substantives is the nomin. sing., that of the adjectives the stem, and that of the verbs the 2nd pers. imper. which is equal to the stem. In Arabic (as reported by Petráček), the canonical form of the verb is the 3rd person sing. of the perfect tense (*katab-a* "he has written), because it is the simplest verbal form. The canonical form of the Arabic nouns is the nomin. sing., which is indicated with the indeterminate article.

The guiding principle for the choice of the canonical form is that it should be as good a starting point for the construction of the other forms of the paradigm as possible. In the majority of languages, the canonical forms are by now fixed by tradition and the lexicographer will do well not to abandon the tradition unless the reasons for a change are really imperative and the lexicographer is preparing a dictionary which will really command an authoritative influence.[3] If it is, on the other hand, the lexicographer's task to found a tradition for a certain language, i.e. to choose the canonical forms, he will probably do best if, as already stated, he chooses those forms from which the rest of the paradigm is easily derivable. If this requirement is compatible with the desire to have the chosen canonical forms as similar to those which are best known in other languages (e.g. nomin. sing. for the substantives etc.), the better for the lexicographer.

---

[3] Both conditions are important.

2.1.2 The lexicographer must never forget that the canonical form he indicates is only the representative of the word's whole paradigm. Two precautions are necessary in this respect.

2.1.2.1 First, there should be no ambiguity about the word's whole paradigm. In an English dictionary, it is usually not necessary to indicate any further form of the substantives: their paradigm is so simple and regular, and the morphophonemic variants (*book* :: *books*, but *box* :: *boxes*, etc.) so easily taken care of in an eventual grammatical appendix to the dictionary that only a simple indication of the canonical form, plus the fact that the word belongs to the category of substantives, is usually sufficient.[4] The same statement can be made about French substantives. But all "irregularities" (such as for instance Eng. *goose* :: *geese*, *sheep* :: *sheep*, French *oeil* :: *yeux* "eye") should be indicated together with the canonical form.

A radically different situation arises if the canonical form itself could belong to different paradigms. For instance, Latin substantives that end in nomin. sing. (which is the canonical form) in *-us* can belong to different paradigms: *dominus* "master" has the genit. *domini*, dat. *domino*, *vulnus* "wound" has the genit. *vulneris*, dat. *vulneri*, *manus* "hand" has the genit. *manus*, dat. *manui*, etc. In such a situation, the lexicographer has to indicate not only the canonical form, but also such information as makes the rest of the paradigm clear and unambiguous. And it goes without saying that if a good number of the canonical forms of a language requires further specifications and indications in order to yield the paradigm unambiguously, the lexicographer will do well to supply these indications everywhere.

The usual procedure is as follows. Either the regular paradigms of the language in question are known, or the lexicographer must establish them himself. In any case, they are either supposed to be known from the grammar of the language, or they are printed in an appendix to the dictionary. Each canonical form (or at least those about whose paradigm one could be uncertain, which could be supposed to belong to different paradigms) is referred to this model paradigms. This reference can be done in different ways, for instance by numbers if the model paradigms are numbered. Or by the so-called cardinal forms and indications: if we indicate, in Latin, not only the canonical form *dominus*, but also the gen. *domini* and the gender, viz. masc., the word's paradigm is unambiguously indicated by implication.[5] Besides this, every form which belongs to a specific paradigm, and which is different from the form of the model paradigm (i.e. every form which is usually called "irregular"), should

---

[4] But in a dictionary for beginner's use, even the indication of morphophonemic variants will be welcome.

[5] Cf. Gleason, PL 90.

be indicated in the entry of the dictionary.[6] Let us remark in this connection that the lexicographer should indicate not only the eventual irregular forms of individual words, but also the irregular absence of forms. If the Eng. substantive *evidence* has, contrary to the model paradigm, no plural (at least not in modern English), this should also be mentioned in the dictionary.[7]

It will hardly escape the lexicographer's notice if the paradigm of a word is restricted in such a way that it is just the normal canonical form which is lacking. In such a case, the lexicographer will be forced to use another form as canonical *ad hoc*. This is very frequently the case of the *pluralia tantum*, i.e. substantives which have only the plural, not the singular, as Eng. *scissors*, *trousers*, Russ. *vorota* "gate". In these examples, the nomin. plur. will serve as the canonical form (instead of the normal nomin. sing.). But an indication that the word is a plurale tantum is very important, above all in a bilingual dictionary where the other language discerns singular and plural, in the equivalent word; e.g. Russ. *vorota* "gate" is, precisely taken, equivalent both to Eng. *gate* and *gates*.[8] In contrast to this, Burmese *kattjêi* and *bhâunbhí*, in the singular, are equivalent to Eng. "a pair of scissors" and "a pair of trousers", respectively (as Minn Latt reports). Consequently, what is "a pair of scissors" in Burmese will have to be translated into English as "two (or more) pairs of scissors".

The paradigm may be incomplete for quite different reasons (known or unknown), and it may lack different forms. Petráček reports, for example, that the imperative of Arab. *ra'ā* "to see" is never used. Theoretically, one could form the imperative *ra*; but this form is so short that it is dissimilar to the usual structure of Arabic words; therefore, the imperative *unẓur* (from the verb naẓara) is always used.

It must be mentioned, too, that words sometimes have parallel, different forms without any observable difference in meaning. For instance, the paradigm of the Eng. verb *to lean* (canonical form) has the parallel forms *leant* and *leaned*. In Armenian (as reported by Motalová), for example *aryun* "blood" has both the regular genit. *aryuni*, and an irregular genit. *aryan*; the verb *t'oġnel* "to leave" has both the regular past tense *t'ogeci* and the irregular *t'ogi*, without any difference in the meaning.

In a descriptive dictionary, the lexicographer will have to indicate such facts as well.

The strongest case of such a "variation of the paradigm" unaccompanied by a variation in meaning is suppletivism: absolutely different forms (or at least stems)[9] combine to form one paradigm with one lexical meaning. If we

---

[6] More on this, and on the exceptions to this rule, chapter VI.

[7] Cf. Hoenigswald PL 109.

[8] Cf. Majtinskaja LS 1, L 957, 167.

[9] I.e. those parts of words in inflected languages that seem to carry the lexical meaning; cf., approximately, the "lexemes" as explained in the second sentence of footnote 1.

begin by the contrast, then for instance Eng. *work* — *worked* is a case of a regular, Eng. *do* — *did* a case of an irregular, but Eng. *go* — *went* a case of a suppletive formation of the same grammatical category. An example of a suppletive paradigm in French is *je vais* "I go" — *je suis allé* "I went" — *j'irai* "I shall go". The Greek verb *paideúō* "to educate" has the future *paideúsō*, the aorist *epaídeusa*, which is the regular formation. The Greek verb *horáō* "to see" is, on the other hand, suppletive, because it has the future *ópsomai*, aorist *eîdon*, without any change in the lexical meaning. In Arabic, *imra'atun* is "woman", but the plural is *nisā'un* "women" (Petráček). In Hausa (Zima), there is, e.g., *bàbbaa*, plur. *manyaa* "big" infortant.

The lexicographer will list these forms in the lemma; but it will be good to list the different forms as separate entries in their alphabetic order, with a cross-reference to the canonical form (i.e., to the main entry).

2.1.2.2 Second, the lexicographer must always ascertain whether the whole paradigm of a word really has, as he assumes, the same lexical meaning. It cannot be stressed enough that in different languages, any members of any paradigm, whether "regular" or "irregular", can have a lexical meaning more or less different from the rest of the paradigm. Two categories should be distinguished in this connection. To the first of them belong polysemous words whose different senses are partially distinguished by differences in their paradigm. For instance: The German word *Aas* has two senses: (1) "carcass", (2) "adulator". In the singular, all forms (gen. *Aases*, dat. *Aas*, acc. *Aas*) are polysemous in the same way. In the plural, on the other hand, we have either the forms nom. *Aase*, gen. *Aase*, dat. *Aasen*, acc. *Aase* which can mean only "carcasses", or we have the forms *Äser*, gen. *Äser*, dat. *Äsern*, acc. *Äser* which mean only "adulators". Well known cases like Eng. *genius*, pl. *geniuses* "person having an exceptional capacity of mind", plur. *genii* "demon, supernatural being" belong to the same category.

This phenomenon is rather frequent in languages with morphologically rich paradigms. Petráček reports the following examples from Arabic:

baytun "house; verse", plur. *buyūtun* "houses"
        plur. *abyātun* "verses"
ʿaynun "eye; important person", plur. *ʿuyūnun* "eyes"
        plur. *ʿayānun* "important persons".

Motalová reports from Classical Armenian:

akn "eye; water spring; jewel", plur. *ačk'* "eyes"
        plur. *akunk'* "water springs"
        plur. *akank'* "jewels".

Miltner reports from Sanskrit: *pati-* "master, lord" has a regular paradigm;
when used in the sense "husband", it has the same regular paradigm, with the
exception of two forms, viz. dat. sing. *patye* (not the regular form *pataye*)
and ablat. + gen. sing. *patyus* (not the regular form *pates*). In Hindi (as
reported by Miltner again), *moṭar* is masculine when meaning "motor", but
feminine when "automobile".

Sometimes a certain regularity of such parallel forms and their corresponding meanings can be observed; such a phenomenon can then be conceived
as being on the borderline between lexicon and grammar, but it is certainly
worth while to mention it in the dictionary, too, supposing that it is not a
purely grammatical phenomenon observable in any respective item. Růžička
reports from Swahili:

rafiki "friend", plus. *rafiki* "friends"
          plur. *marafiki* "a circle of acquaintances"
baba "father", plur. *baba* "fathers"
          plur. *mababa* "forefathers"
simba "lion",   plur. *simba* "lions"
          plur. *masimba* "pack of lions".

It must be noted, however, that the existence of parallel forms in the paradigm does not always imply such an either — or distribution of the different
senses of a polysemous word. Sometimes, the parallel forms are used without
any observable distribution of meaning. For instance, Petráček reports that
in Arabic, the perf. tense of one root can be either *qašifa* or *qašufa* "to lieve
in dirt and poverty", without any difference in meaning.

And in yet other cases of polysemous words it also happens that one of the
parallel forms tends to be used indiscriminately as far as the lexical meaning
goes, i.e. with different senses, but the other form is restricted to one sense
only. For instance, Czech *koleno* means above all (1) "knee" (joint in the leg)
and (2) "knee" (of a pipe). The word has a completely regular paradigm all
forms of which can be used in both senses; but besides the regular locative
plural *kolenech*, there is also a parallel form *kolenou* which is, however, restricted
only the first sense (joint in the leg), usually when the reference is to the human
body.[10] All cases similar to those discussed here should be carefully observed
and indicated by the lexicographer.

---

[10] It is worth while to mention that this form belongs historically to the dual number, so that
the restriction to the (human) body can easily be understood. But it is only our understanding
of the development which is fostered by this knowledge. For the presentation of the facts of
language, as they are today, this is irrelevant: though the dual forms are historically older and
the plural forms more recent (and, when used in sense (1) joint in the (human) leg", "not correct"
at an early stage of the development), in the description of today's language it is the plural forms
which must be considered the basic ones.

The other category which belongs here comprises those cases where one form of the paradigm, irrespective of whether regular or irregular, shows a peculiarity in its lexical meaning that is not observable in the lexical meaning of the other forms. For instance, the negative paradigm of the Armenian verb "to be" begins (as reported by Motalová) with the forms *čem, čes, čē* ...; the form *čē* "he is not", however, functions also as the negative operator "not" (in sentences with a finite verb). In such a situation, it is not difficult to conceive *čē* as a lexical unit of its own. But not all pertinent cases are as clear as that. As an example, we shall quote the Russian word *šag* "step". All its forms (cases) have the lexical meaning as indicated; but the instrumental sing. has not only the same meaning ("by the step"), but can also mean "slowly" when used as an adverb. Phenomena as the one just described are very important for the lexicographer, and sometimes also rather awkward because it will not always be easy to decide how the data are to be conceived and how they are to be presented in the dictionary. They could be conceived as constituting a partial homonymy between *šag* "step" (this canonical form representing also all the forms of the paradigm, incl. genit. *šagu,* ... instr. *šagom*) and *šagom* "slowly"; which solution would imply a separate entry for *šagom* "slowly". This possible solution will occur mainly when it is the canonical form itself about which the lexicographer is uneasy (cf. above, § 1.6.3). But the conception that this is only a case of "restricted polysemy" (i.e. restricted only as to the form in question) is obviously not impossible; such a solution would imply only one entry, *šag*, with due presentation of the restricted polysemy. Much will depend on the semantic ties of the two forms and on the intersubjective understanding of native speakers. (Cf. the discussion of homonymy, § 1.6.3.)

As far as unclear cases go, Borovkov[11] is probably right when stating that a monolingual dictionary can well afford to have cases like the one shown above (*šag*) under one entry but that for a bilingual dictionary, the indication of two entries will be more useful.

A similar situation can be seen in Ossetic. Formally, the paradigm of the substantive *lag* "man, human being" is absolutely regular; the comparative case *lagaw* is, however, usually itemized in different dictionaries, i.e. it is regarded as the canonical form of an entry of its own, because it means only "as a man", but usually not "as a human being". The absence of a sense suffices to put form into contradistinction.

The decision is easier if both the grammatical status and the meaning of the member of the paradigm lexicalized in this way are very different from the rest of the paradigm. Zvelebil reports an example from Tamil: the verbal stem *aku* means "to become, to be"; the instrumental case of the verbal noun

---

[11] LS 1, 1957, 137.

akaiyal functions as the conjunction "therefore", though its "paradigmatic" meaning is "by the being, by the becoming".

Generally, there is an endless number of possible cases. For example, nobody will hesitate to take Ossetic *käm* "where" as an entry, as a canonical form of its own, though it is, basically, one of the cases of the pronoun *či* "who" and could, at least theoretically, be conceived as a part of its paradigm. The same applies to Arabic *fī* "in" which is considered a lexical unit of its own, though it is originally a declensional form of the word *fū* "mouth" (Petráček). But a decision as to whether Eng. *to be born* is still a part of the paradigm of to bear is incomparably more difficult; such "united" a presentation is prescribed by the whole tradition and by the analogy of the other verbs, but it is contradicted by the absence of the mechanical mediopassive : : active opposition of the two forms.[12]

In any case, the lexicographer should always count on the possibility that a form — any form — of a paradigm can show a peculiarity in respect to its lexical meaning when compared with the other forms of the paradigm.

2.1.3 Because it is not always easy to decide what is one paradigm and what not, opinions may differ in this respect. As far as European and other languages with a long lexicographic tradition go, the paradigms are fixed, to some extent, by the facts of the languages themselves, and by tradition in those cases where the facts can be interpreted in different ways. In these languages, the lexicographer will hardly be inclined to break with tradition in a general way. But he should feel free to induce minor changes in those cases where he feels that his data warrant it and where his new presentation makes the indications of his dictionary more clear.[13]

In languages whose lexicographic tradition has just begun, the lexicographer should try to use to the greatest possible extent the grammatical description of the language which is available and reliable. Yet in any case, he will have to check it carefully and change it when necessary. If there is as yet no description of the language which could be used, the lexicographer will have to work out a grammatical sketch of his language himself: without a grammatical analysis, there is no possibility of dealing with the lexicon.[14]

[12] Cf. W. Winter, Language 41, 1965, 488 ff. A similar reasoning, with a similar example (Eng. *to bear, bearing*) in *Garvin*, Anais 3.

[13] But there are some difficulties with the decision as to which forms are to be considered members of one, single paradigm and which not (i.e. which should have their own entry) even in such a language as French: cf. Rey, Cahiers 7, 1965, 77 ff. In contemporary Armenian, the establishing of paradigms is a very disputed problem (Motalová).

[14] Private communications from I. J. Gelb and Minn Latt induced me to re-word this passage in stronger terms than it originally was.

The real difficulty with paradigms is that sometimes we observe a sudden break in the series of forms accompanied by a change in the meaning, but the break is not impressive enough to convince us that there are two different paradigms.

DERIVATION

2.2 The main line of distinction which should be drawn (or sought) is that regarding what are considered derivative categories. It is necessary to distinguish, on the one hand, those cases where a change in the form of the word signals, or carries, a change in the grammatical category but leaves the word's lexical meaning unchanged (Eng. *book* :: *books*, Russ. *znaju* "I know" :: *znaješ* "you know", etc.) and, on the other hand, those cases where a change in the form of a word implies a change in the lexical meaning itself. The first type of morphological change is called (morphological) inflection, the other type is called **word derivation**, or (morphological) **word formation**.

As examples of the latter can be quoted Eng. *bad* :: *badly, mad* :: *madly, swift* :: *swiftly*; *girl* :: *girlish*; *Turk* :: *Turkish*; *child* :: *childish*; *waiter* :: *waitress, count* :: *countess, Jew* :: *Jewess*; French *acteur* :: *actrice*; *éventuel* :: *éventuellement*, and endless other cases. The different types of word formation in the Indo-European languages are well discussed, in relation to the lexicographer's work, by Swanson.[15] They differ from one language to another.[16]

The basic difference between grammatical morphology, inflection on the one side, and morphological word formation, or derivation on the other is that the former is more abstract.[17] The difficulty is, however, that derivation is in many respects similar to inflection. The basic similarity is in the fact that derivation is frequently almost as regular as inflection. For instance, let us consider the open series of German pairs as

Kind "child"	*Kindlein* "little child"
Haus "house"	*Häuslein* "small house"
Buch "book"	*Büchlein* "small book" etc.

or as Arabic (Petráček)

kalbun "dog"	*kalaybun* "little dog"
kitābun "book"	*kutaybun* "small book" etc.

---

[15] PL 66.

[16] In the following discussion, only cases of derivation by means of suffices are used as examples. It should be understood, however, that prefixes and infixes can also be used for the purpose.

[17] M. Dokulil, *Tvoření slov v češtině I*, Praha 1962, p. 17.

or as Eng.

frequent	*frequently*
mad	*madly*
silent	*silently*
swift	*swiftly* etc.

or as Japanese (Heroldová)

hayai "to be quick"	*hayaku* "quickly"
osoi "to be late"	*osoku* "late"
yoi "to be good"	*yoku* "well" etc.

Obviously, cases like these are very similar, in their formal regularity, in their uniform effect on the lexical meaning, and in the openness of the series or at least in the great number of their members, to the grammatical inflection. Indeed, many dictionaries do not list all words which are formed in this way.

One must not, however, forget that word formation is not as regular and as uniform in all cases. For instance, let us consider Eng. pairs like:

jail "place of confinement"   :: *jailer* "person keeping people there"
prison "place of confinement" :: *prisoner* "person hept there".[18]

The difference between pairs as the one just quoted is so great that it is unlikely to be overlooked by the lexicographer. From his point of view, more dangerous are those cases where the difference of meaning is not so great but still observable, as e.g.:

red :: *reddish* "similar to the red colour"
girl :: *girlish* "typical for a girl".

Cases of derivation must, therefore, be studied by the lexicographer with even greater care than the purely grammatical categories. Let us suppose that an English dictionary does not list all adverbs derived by *-ly*. In such a case, e.g., *brusquely* can be omitted even if *brusque* is listed, because both the form and the meaning of the adverb are regular, predictable. On the other hand, an adverb like *badly* must be listed, though its form is regular, because it has some senses the adjective does not have (*to need something badly*). That an adverb like *well* must be listed is clear: the meaning is regular, predictable from the meaning of the adjective good, but the form is suppletive.

Obviously, not all cases of word derivation are as regular and as similar to grammatical inflections as the preceding ones.[19] In very general terms, one can

---

[18] Example inspired by Jespersen.
[19] Cf. Isačenko LSB 46f. who discerns "semantic derivation" and derivation with prevailing grammatical elements.

state the following observation: the greater the number of words in which the same derivational morpheme causes the same change of the lexical meaning, the smaller will be the inclination of the lexicographer to list all these words. Put in another way, the more frequently a derivational morpheme can be used, and the more uniform its effect on the lexical meaning, the more does its function resemble a grammatical function. On the contrary, if a derivational morpheme is not frequent and/or if its modifying effect on the lexical meaning is far from uniform, the similarity to a grammatical function will be incomparably smaller and the lexicographer will be more inclined to indicate the respective words as separate items. There is no absolutely sharp boundary between derivation and grammatical inflection; and the classification of single phenomena is often a matter of tradition and linguistic convention which is not always in complete accord with the facts of the language in question.[20]

Differences in derivation sometimes imply no difference in meaning. For instance, the two Eng. adjective *lexicographic* and *lexicographical* are synonymic. The members of such synonymic pairs are frequently called d o u b l e t s.

The lexicographer will be well advised to respect the eventual tradition of his language, because he will have to take into consideration the fact that the users of his dictionary will be trained in school to conceive these phenomena precisely in the traditional way. In the absence of a tradition, the lexicographer must himself decide what he will regard as rather grammatical and what as a rather derivational. But in any case, it will be useful to the present necessary information on the derivative categories in the eventual grammatical sketch, if such an appendix is added to the dictionary.

Derivation is a morphological process (or can be conceived as such) which gives origin to units, usually words, that are morphologically delimited. This morphological clarity and the impression that one has to deal with well-delimited units should not, however, be accepted as a proof of the stabilization of the lexical unit in question, without any further inquiry. On the contrary, we have to deal, in the field of lexical derivation, with forms, with occasionality, as in any other field.

For instance, no English dictionary in general use indicates the existence of an English word *girlless*. In the Supplement to the OED, we find it, however, with the following quotation from the Daily Chronical, 1903:

"If »Harper's Weekly« may be trusted, the girlless telephone will soon be as familar as the horseless carriage or the boneless sardine".

The quotation shows how the derivation has its origin partly in the changes of the extralinguistic world of that time (telephones without operators, motorcars), partly in the jocose tone of the discourse. The author coined the deri-

[20] Dokulil (footnote 17) with good Czech examples. Cf. E. Stankiewicz, *The Interpendence of Paradigmatic and Derivational Patterns*, Word 18, 1962, 1ff.

vation which can be perfectly understood, though it is quite occasional.[21] This is because the suffix -*less* is very productive and the effects of its application semantically very uniform. Therefore, it is always possible to form, *ad hoc* with the suffix, new derivations which may remain occasional nonces, or which may become stabilized. The result of this is that in the case of very productive derivational morphemes, whether they are suffixes, prefixes, or infixes, it is impossible to say how many and which words do really exist that are formed by their means, because there is a field of always new, ephemeral nonces and/or semi-stabilized forms around the stabilized formations.

Let us discuss the following example. The 1835 edition of the *Dictionnaire de l'Académie* (which French dictionary is, in all its editions, consciously normative and enjoys an incomparable authority) lists many verbs with the prefix *dé-*, but does not list *déconstruire*. In the foreword to that very edition of the "Dictionnaire", its author, Villemain, tries to show that language changes also for internal reasons, without any external impulse, and says:

"... *dans une contrée de l'immobile Orient où nulle invasion n'a pénétré, où nulle barbarie n'a prévalu, une langue parvenue à sa perfection s'est déconstruite et altérée d'elle-même* ..."

Nobody who knows French will misunderstand the verb *déconstruire* as used here, so derivable is its meaning from its components, so well does it suit into the context, and so well does it express the idea of that time, viz. that linguistic change is decomposition and decay. The point, nevertheless, is that the Preface to a big normative dictionary uses a word not listed in the dictionary itself (nor in the subsequent editions of the *Dictionnaire de l'Académie*): the prefix *dé-* is so productive and the verb so well formed (i.e. in harmony with other derivations) that the moment it is used, it gives the impression of a stabilized expression, though it is only occasional, and the impression that it may be used or rather coined again in the future should the occasion aries. One can say that around the stabilized verbs with *dé-*, used over and over again, there is an area of a potential, ad hoc creation of further verbs with this prefix, of which *déconstruire* is an example.[22]

---

[21] The *Supplement* to OED has yet another quotation, from 1929 (Masefield); as discussed above, identical occasional coinages can arise several times independently.

[22] The example is taken from A. Darmester, *La vie des mots* (19th ed. Paris 1937), p. 116 (whose interpretation is, however, slightly different: he considers the verb as an ephemeral neologism without any further ado). — *Déconstruire* does not occur in the newer editions of the *Dictionnaire de l'Académie*; it is listed in Littré (*Dictionnaire de la langue française*, tome II, Paris 1885, p. 992), labelled by an obelisc (warning that the word is not accepted in the *Dictionnaire de l'Académie*). Littré indicates two technical senses of the verb (one mechanical and one grammatical) but only one sense of the reflexive *se déconstruire* and that only with the very sentence of Villemaine as the sole example. The verb as treated in Littré seems to have the same status in all three senses. Contemporary dictionaries, at least to my knowledge, do not list the verb. — More on the area of potentiality surrounding the stabilized productive formations can

Up to now, we have described the variation of words in which either the lexical meaning remains generally unchanged (grammatical inflection) or is changed in a more or less regular pattern (derivation, word formation). It is clear that it is only the grammatical inflection which can be called "formal variation of the word" in the strict sense, because the lexicographer regards all members of one paradigm as different, variant forms of one word; according to this conception, he indicates only one entry of the word, as represented by the canonical form. Derivation differs from this (according to the usual conception) in the important respect that it is the lexical meaning itself which is modified, so that the lexicographer, just like everybody else, will regard for example *mad — madly, bad — badly* as pairs of different words. Since there is however, a certain area of overlapping between the two categories, mainly because some cases of the derivation are so very regular and uniform that the lexicographer, if he does not intend to compile a fully exhaustive dictionary of the language in question, will tend not to indicate all derived words as separate entries (cf. on this § 6.5.4), we thought it useful to discuss the two categories in connection.

COMPOSITION

2.3 There is still a third category which is even more remote from grammatical inflection, namely so-called word composition. Without going into the details of morphological theory, we can broadly describe a compound word as such a word the single parts of which have a lexical meaning of their own, if used alone. Let us consider the following examples.

In German, the word *Holz* has the meaning "wood timber" and the word *Bau* the meaning "building construction; structure, edifice". The compound word *Holzbau* has the meaning "wooden structure". In English, a *gold-smith* is a smith who works in gold; in French, *wagon-restaurant* is a car (*wagon*) used as a restaurant, etc.

There are three important categories of phenomena which can be observed when we study compound words.

2.3.1 First, we can observe different phenomena in the *dimension of form*. Sometimes, the form of an element which carries a certain lexical meaning is fully or nearly identical both if it is used as a part of a compound word and if it is used alone, as a non-compound word. This is the case of German *Holzbau*

be found in my paper *The Synchronic State of Language* (in: Proceedings of the 10th Congress of Linguists, Bucharest 1967, vol. I; forthcoming) where different examples (more recent, if less dignified) are discussed.

where the only difference between -*bau* and *Bau*, apart form the orthography, consists in the fact that the latter has an accent of its own. Similarly, the difference between French *wagon-restaurant* and *wagon, restaurant*, again apart from the orthography, consists in the accentual reduction of the first part; and the same can be observed in Eng. *blackbird* as compared with *black, bird*, except that it is the second part of the compound whose accent is reduced.[23] But there are also compound words whose accentuation does not differ from that of the single parts.[24] Texts written in some scripts (such as the Roman alphabet of our days) indicate the individual words by spaces between them. Compound words are, then, indicated by the absence of space, the hyphen, or a similar device, even if there is no other difference in the form of the compound in contrast to its single parts.

On the other hand, the single parts of a compound word have sometimes a different form from that used in isolation. To quote a very simple example, the single parts of French *franco-tchèque* "French-Czech" would have the form *français, tchèque*, when used alone, not in the compound. Sometimes, the traditional spelling still suggests the single parts of the compound but the pronunciation does not, as e.g. in Eng. *cupboard*, only the spelling of which suggests the composition. In Burmese, Minn Latt reports, the normal criterion of a compound word can, in specific environments, be found in sandhi change. The element *sá* "letter; writing", used as a non-compound word in *sá yêi* "write" is phoneticall [sá], but used in a compound word, e.g. *sáyêi* "clerk", it is [zǎ-]. The same applies to *sâ* "eat" in *htâmin sâ*, [sâ] "to eat rice" and *htǎmînsâ*, [-zǎ] "lunch; dinner". Sometimes, the single parts of a compound word are so changed either in the pronunciation, or in the spelling, or in both, that the fact that we have a compound before us is obscured. "There are different degrees of obscuration" states Jespersen[25] with full right; a word like Eng. *lord* is by now not a compound one, in Modern English, though it goes back to Old Eng. *hlāford* < *hlāf-weard* "loaf-ward". This is the extreme case of obscuration: loss of the compound character.

The lexicographer, unless his aim is historical, is not too much concerned with these differences; they belong to the domain of historical and historical-descpritive morphology and lexicology. It must be noted, however, that it is better, though not indispensable, if the lexicographer understands these things, even if he does not discuss them in his dictionary. He should also take into

---

[23] The value of stress as a criterion of composition is rather small according to Jespersen, *A Modern English Grammar* VI (Copenhage 1942), p. 135, with a good discussion of Bloomfield's opposite view. The opposite point of view is now strongly and elaborately advocated by N. Chomsky and M. Halle, *The Sound Pattern of English*, New York–London 1968; these authors develop a whole theory of English wordformation in which the stress patterns have a crucial importance.

[24] Cf., for instance, Jespersen, op. cit.

[25] Op. cit.

consideration, without prejudice to other selective criteria, that the user will need more help to understand the obscured compounds than those whose meaning is derivable from that of their clearly distinguishable single parts; therefore, (partial), obscuration is of some consequence during the selection of entries.

2.3.2 The second type of phenomena connected with composition can be observed in the dimension of the *difference of meaning*. Sometimes there is no observable difference of the lexical meaning of the element in question when used in a compound word and when used in a non-compound one. Such is, for instance, the case of the example quoted above: Germ *Holz, Bau*; *Holzbau*. Let us, however, not forget that we must always anticipate the eventually polysemous meaning of the single elements: generally, it is the rule that the eventually polysemous meaning of single elements is simplified by the elimination of senses which do not apply in the compound word.

This is the disambiguation of meaning in composition; see § 1.56 on disambiguation in the context.

Sometimes, an element of a compound word is semantically depleted. For instance, Germ. *Hand* means "hand" and *Schuh* means "shoe"; but Germ. *Handschuh* means "glove". In some cases, the semantic depletion is only partial. Such is, for example, the case with Eng. *blackboard*: in our days, this pedagogical instrument very often has a green colour but is called *blackboard* notwithstanding this change in the denotatum.

So far we have been dealing with cases where the meanings of the component parts even if they are eventually depleted, are more or less known to average speakers. There are, however, cases where an unknown or extremely vague morpheme can serve as a component part of a compound word; e.g. Eng. *huckleberry*. Minn Latt reports three types of constructions with such component morpheme in Burmese: (1) The first type is where the known morpheme in the word can suggest the meaning of the whole, or where this component when used elsewhere as a monomorphemic word can be a substitute for the compound word in question. For example, in place of the compound words *sôuyéim* "to be anxious, concerned", *pyéipyis* "to be smooth", *cjômô* "to be beautiful", *kutha* "cure" the monomorphemic words *sôu*, *pyéi*, *cjô*, *ku* can be substituted. (2) The second type is where the known component cannot give the meaning of the compound word. For example, *mwêisâ* "to adopt a child", *pânpu* "sculpture"; cf. *mwêi* "to give birth to; to nurture; to grow"; *pân* "flower". (3) The third type is where none of the morphemes of which the words is composed carries a meaning well known to the average speaker of the language, e.g. *sókâ* "insult", *juja* "to be tender to". Naturally, the members of the last type may be considered monomorphemic words; but depending on one's educational background and also on one's concept of the structure of the language, the matter may be assessed differently.

It is frequently impossible to understand the meaning of a compound word simply by the combination of the meanings of its single elements, quite apart from the phenomena discussed in the preceding paragraphs. Usually, there is no formal indication of the difference in meaning. Let us consider the following examples:

Germ. *Raub* means primarily   "robbing, robbery; pray, booty"
Germ. *Vogel* means primarily   "bird"
Germ. *Raubvogel* means   "bird of prey"

so that the meaning of the compound word can be derived from or predicted on the basis of the meaning of the single parts, at least to some extent. On the other hand, let us consider

Germ. *Pech* means primarily   "pitch; bad luck"
Germ. *Vogel* means primarily   "bird"
Germ. *Pechvogel* means   "unlucky fellow, one who has always bad luck"

so that we see that the degree to which we can predict the meaning of the compound word is much lower than in the preceding case.

Minn Latt supplies the following list of Burmese compound words to illustrate the various degrees of predictability and nonpredictability of the overall meaning of compounds:

lúthis (elements: "man" + "new"): "a newcomer; a new hand; a new person"

sisthâ ("war" + "son"): "soldier"
póumtú ("picture" + "to be alike"): "portrait"
sápéi ("writing" + "palm leaf"): "literature"
dhátmî ("element" + "light"): "electric light"
dhátsek ("element" + "machine"): "gramophone"
dhátsá ("element" + "food"): "diet"
sheinéi ("front" + "to stay"): "lawyer; pleader"
cyauklôumpyû ("six" + "round things" + "to combine"): "revolver"
hsíncyéiphôum̥ ("elephant" + "foot" + "to cover"): "suburbs".

Theoretically, these differences in the predictability of the meaning of the compound word on the basis of its single parts is of an only secondary importance for the lexicographer; both types of compound words are equally eligible for selection for inclusion in his dictionary, those with the unpredictable meaning and those with the predictable one as well. This basic point of view should be fully respected by the lexicographer, mainly if he is working on a big monolingual dictionary the primary aim of which is to give a full description of the lexicon of a language. If, however, the lexicographer has only a limited space at his disposal, and especially if he is writing a bilingual dictionary the primary aim of which is to help to understand texts in the source language, practical considerations will lead him to omit rather those compounds the meaning of which can be understood from the meaning of their constituent parts than the other type. But if he is compelled by mere lack of space to omit many compound words he would otherwise accept, and if composition is a frequent phenomenon in the language in question, he will be well advised to discuss the composition and show the types of compound words in the eventual grammatical sketch appended to the dictionary.

2.3.3 The third type of phenomena to be observed in connection with compound words is the symptoms of their *stability*. In languages where composition is a frequent phenomenon, one can always, at least within some broad limits, construct new compound words according to what one whishes to say, just as one combines the necessary words in a sentence. When I heard on April 19th, 1966, in a discussion with a professor in Berlin, the compound *Textkonstitu-ierungsgrundstruktur*, it was certainly as unstabilized and as much formed only for the actual communicative need at that moment and in the context of that discussion as its Eng. translation "the basic (fundamental) structure of the constitution of a text" would be. In a similar way, if we read in S. Lewis' Babbitt:

"*... you better start a rapidwhiz system to keep tabs as to how fast you'll buzz...*", we can see that the compound *rapidwhiz* is certainly rather occasional.

Sentences like:

"*Much space is given to expounding a transformational creed of a palaeo-chomskian kind...*"[26]

or

"*As for number, the singular-plural dichotomy seems to satisfy ... but Sanskrit and Classical Greek had a three-number system inescapably calling attention to unity, duality, and more-than-twoness*"[27]

are perfectly understandable, though both *palaeochomskian* and *more-than-twoness* are to my knowledge occasional nonce-forms, hapax. Language is creative since it allows the speaker to coin new expressions which the hearer understands because the "rules of coinage" are not unfamiliar to him.

[26] N. E. Collinge, Archivum linguisticum 17, 1965, 54.
[27] L. Salomon, *Semantics and Common Sense*, New York 1966, p. 134.

Therefore, it would be a mistake to think that what is morphologically and orthographically characterized as a compound word[28] is necessarily more stabilized than a mere combination of single words. A compound word can have the character of a nonce-form, created for the occasion of the actual utterance, precisely as a free group of words.

On the other hand, there are also compound words which are stabilized as such, in the system of the language; they have, then, the same status as any other stabilized word irrespective of its morphological structure. The lexicographer will certainly prefer to list this second type of compound words, the stabilized ones, in any type of dictionary.

Stabilized compounds can be recognized mainly by the frequency of their recurrence and by the unity of their designative meaning. Very frequently, these compounds are either terms or words which approach the status of terms.

As in all other cases, these three types of phenomena (§ 2.3.1—3) are not mutually exclusive; on the contrary, they can be conceived as being placed in different dimensions, so that one can often find their different combinations in a single compound word. Some of the combinations are typical, as, for example, when obscuration of form is combined with stabilization.

2.3.4 Besides this type of composition discussed in the preceding paragraphs, which we could perhaps call organic composition, there is also a phenomenon which we may call unorganic composition. In the compounds which belong here, unorganic, mutilated parts of words or morphemes are put together to form a new word; most frequently, the first syllables or the first phonemes of the respective words are used. For instance, Russ. *kolkhoz* is an unorganic compound of the first syllables of Russ. *kollektivnoe khozjajstvo* "collective farm"; Eng. *radar* is an unorganic compound of the first phonemes of *radio detecting and ranging*. Unorganic compounds of this type (sometimes called acronyms) are also called abbreviated, or telescoped, or portmanteau words, in different terminologies. It is not always easy to discern them from real abbreviations of the type e.g. *U.S.A.* For instance, an abbreviation such as (Am.) Eng. *G.I.* is capable of forming a plural (*G.I'*.s) and it is not generally known what the letters represent (*government issued*). From an abbreviation such as (Amer.) Eng. *O.K.*, derivations can be formed, at least in the colloquial language: e.g.

"The boss okayed it".

[28] It is immaterial for the present discussion whether we regard *palaeo* — as a case of composition, or as a case of prefixation, or as anything else.

All that has been stated about the composition and about derivation (§ 2.2) are merely some general remarks which are only intended to draw the lexicographer's attention to these phenomena and to their importance for lexicography. In reality, there is a huge number of categories and sub-categories, many of them overlapping, by which these phenomena can be classified. These categories and classifications differ vastly from one language to another, so that one cannot attempt to summarize or even to survey them here.

CHAPTER III

COMBINATIONS OF WORDS

3.0 The lexicographer presents words in the entries of his dictionary as individual linguistic units. In the preceding chapters, only individual, single words have been considered. The lexicographer will, however, have to give special consideration to those cases where words are meaningfully combined.[1] This statement should be taken in a very broad sense, because after all, words are meaningfully combined in whole sentences. But the lexicographer is not primarily interested in whole sentence-patterns, the study of which belongs rather to syntax. Difficult as it is to draw the line, the lexicographer studies sentences from the point of view of the lexical meaning of the parts, of which they consist, and from the point of view of the individual properties of the units by which the lexical meaning is carried.

RECTIONS

3.1 Even with the restriction mentioned in the preceding paragraph, there is an area of overlapping, or a possibility of the same phenomenon being classified differently by different scholars. The direct object of the Latin verb *video* "to see" must be in the accusative case: *video aliquid* "to see something"; the direct object of the Latin verb *utor* "to use" must be in the ablative case: *utor aliqua re* "to use something". Opinions may differ on whether this is a syntactic phenomenon in the proper sense of the term. In any case, it is the lexicographer's duty to give the necessary indications to this effect. He must supply the user of his dictionary with information about the most important grammatical properties of the lexical units. Just as the lexicographer indicates, for example, the gender of the substantives, it is likewise his duty to indicate the rection of verbs, the cases governed by prepositions etc. These indications

---

[1] Mere sequences of words which are not meaningful (as, for instance, *grandmother he* in a sentence "*Having killed the grandmother he tried to fly with the money*") are of no practical importance to the lexicographer.

are necessary if the lexicographer compiles a descriptive dictionary of a language because he considers the rection of a verb one of its grammatical properties. But indications of this type are even more important if the lexicographer is trying to compile a dictionary which is to be used as help for producing sentences in the target language.

As stated, these indications are always necessary and important, even if the word in question is not polysemous. Very frequently it happens, however, that the word is polysemous and that its single senses require (or, seen from the other side, are indicated by) different rections, etc. In this case, these distinctive grammatical properties must be indicated in detail. It makes a great difference for instance whether the Russian verb *izmenit'* has the object in the accusative case or in the dative, because it means either "to change" or "to betray", respectively.[2] In giving these indications, the lexicographer must sharply observe all the relevant variables. For instance, it is not only the case of the object that matters in verbal rections: very often it is relevant whether the object is a person or a thing. So, for example, the Czech verb *sváděti* has, among other senses, the senses "to lead down" or "to bring together" or "to drain" according to the cases governed and according to whether the objects are persons or things.[3]

The phenomenon is reported by Petráček as very frequent in Arabic, e.g. *fahima* with direct accus. "he comprehended", with *ᶜan* "he understood him", with *min* "he learned, heard". Miltner reports from Hindi: *kisī se milnā* (postpositional instrumental) "to meet someone on purpose"; *kisī ko milnā* (postpositional accusative in the dative form) "to meet someone by chance"; *kisī mē milnā* (postpositional locative) "to mix with something". In Tamil (Zvelebil), e.g., *col* | acc. "to say", + dative "to invite".

On the other hand, the lexicographer must not expect that there will always be a one-to-one correlation between the differences in the lexical meaning and in the rections. Consider, for example, Eng. *to present somebody to somebody* is different from *to present something to somebody*; but the latter is equivalent to *to present somebody with something*, without any observable change in the lexical meaning.

Very frequently, considerable difference in the lexical meaning has no counterpart in the form, which remains identical. Cf. Eng. *to drop a handkerchief* :: *to drop one's bad habits* :: *to drop a hint*: the rection is identical, *to drop something*, but the single senses of the verb vary considerably.[4]

It must also be mentioned that rection is expressed not only by morphology (cases etc.) but by functional words; cf. Eng. *to mention* (something), *to remark*

[2] Example from Ďurovič LSB 68 who, however, seems to be inclined to understand it as a case of homonymy.

[3] Example from Filipec SS 18, 1957, 138 (with a good discussion of the principle).

[4] Example from Amosova LS 5, 1962, 39.

upon (something), *to speak about* (something). Naturally, both means, morphology and functional words, are used in various combinations in different
languages.

As already stated, these indications are a proper part of the lexicographer's
task, notwithstanding the circumstance that these facts of language can be
viewed as at least partly belonging to the sphere of grammar. There are, however, combinations of words which are important primarily from the point of
view of lexical meaning.

FREE COMBINATIONS

3.2 In the majority of cases, words are combined in a meaningful way in
sentences according to the communicative intention of the speaker; these
combinations may vary from one sentence to another, just as the speaker's
communicative intentions varies, too.

Very often, these free combinations are either attributive or completive.
Examples of both types of combinations are so extremely frequent (we find
them in practically every sentence) that it is not necessary to quote them
extensiveley; it will suffice to adduce only a few of them as illustrations. In
one sentence, we may see the word combination *wet sand*. In different other
sentences, we can see the word combinations *wet wood, wet feet, wet forest,* and
so on; and there will be other combinations as *dry sand, yellow sand,* etc. One
can *speak agreeably,* or *quietly* or *in a loud voice,* etc.: and one can *smile agreeably,
live agreeably,* and so on. A huge number of completive combinations could be
easily quoted, too: one can *carry wood,* or *carry a burden,* generally, or *stones,*
or *the bride over the threshold,* etc.; and one can *burn wood,* or *pick up wood,*
or *sell wood,* and so on. In short, we can call word combinations of this type
(irrespective of whether attributive, completive, or any other) free combinations.[5] They are created by the speaker *ad hoc,* on the spur of the moment,
for the purpose of the statement he just intends to utter. Their meaning is
absolutely derivable from the meaning of the single combined words.[6] They
cannot be considered to be wholes (or units), or to be members of the system
of language as wholes[7] (i.e. as complex units), because they are elicited only
by the concrete necessity of what the speaker intends actually to say.

For the lexicographer, these free combinations are highly interesting because
they show the different possibilities of combining the single words. To a very
high degree, they overlap with what we called the range of application of the

---

[5] In another terminology, they are called *free syntagmata.*
[6] Cf. Conklin PL 120.
[7] Dokulil LSB 20f.

word; who can eat — only man or also animals? In English, the verb can have as subject substantives which denote either. In Czech, what is expressed in English by the same verb must be expressed by two different verbs, viz. *jísti* and *žráti*, depending whether it is a human being or an animal who is the agent of the action.[8] What can one break? In English, almost everything: a stick, a string, an eff, etc. In Shilluk, one can break wood, but strings are "pulled in two", glass or eggs "are killed" etc.[9] A similar case can be seen in Burmese, Minn Latt reports. The proper words in the respective cases are *tjôu*, *pyat* and *kwê*, respectively. One cannot use the verb *pyat* when a saucer is broken.

The lexicographer should have a good command of the different potentialities of every word to combine freely with others.

First, because he can then see what are the most typical ways to use a word, and can give some examples to illustrate this, if he is compiling a bigger dictionary.[10]

Second, because he may see that there are restrictions in the combinatorial power of the single words.[11] These restrictions are a relatively unexplored field; it is no wonder, because their study requires a registration of huge quantities of contexts. But it is a very important study for the description of a language. These restrictions are sometimes rather severe; for instance, Eng. *to neigh* will frequently have a horse as subject.[12] But an expression as *the horse neighs* is a free combination of words, because no criterion of set combinations (cf. § 3.3) seems to apply here.[13]

---

[8] Of course, it is possible to disregard this, but the expression then takes on a rather strong connotation.

[9] Example from Nida, *Translating* 51.

[10] In another terminology, the (typical) *free combinations* are termed (*free*) *collocations*. — The lexicographer should be aware that some styles and some authors frequently use unusual combinations, or even such as are thought incompatible (cf. Weinreich, *Universals* 134 his term for this, namely *hypersemanticized discourse*, is, however, not quite successful: I should prefer rather something as *self-aware form*; O. Leška suggests a term as *transcontextualization*). Observations of this type have, then, some validity for the respective restricted language (e.g. that of poetry) only.

[11] B. A. Larin (apud Filipec SS 18, 1957, 136) shows that there are no really absolutely free combinations of words. He is probably right; and the latest developments in the field of transformation grammar go in the same direction. But even if we take this point of view, there is no harm in calling the least restricted ones free, for the sake of brevity.

[12] Example from Weinreich, *Universals* 144.

[13] There is a very deep and complicated interrelation between the organisation of the designatum and its criterial semantic features on the one side, and the range of application and the combinatory power on the other side; ontological properties of the denotata may also exercise an influence. (This is, incidentally, why combinatory relations are called, in a German terminology, *"wesenhafte Bedeutungsbeziehungen"*.) To a large extent, it could be maintained that all these are only glimpses of the same factual substratum seen from different viewpoints; one could also develop a more unified theory as a framework for this discussion. I prefer, however, to discuss these

And third, if the lexicographer is compiling a bilingual dictionary, the combinatory powers of the two respective words in the two languages are frequently different though the two words are close equivalents as far as lexical meaning goes; cf. the example of Eng. *to eat*, Czech *jísti*, *žráti*, mentioned above.

Another reason why these free combinations are useful to the lexicographer is that they may help him to perceive and to classify the multiple meaning of a word. If we take, for instance, the word *table* as discussed above, then it is probably clear that free combinations like *kitchen table* or *table of the values n* help very much to clarify the particular senses of the word.[14]

This does not, however, mean that each and every combinatorial difference should be taken as evidence that we have to deal with different senses. For instance, it seems that it would not be correct to accept different senses of the verb *to break* just because of the different combinations as to break a stick, a string, an egg etc. (as discussed above). Here it seems that we have a more general designatum before us, which is tantamount to saying that it has fewer criterial semantic features.

SET COMBINATIONS

3.3 In his study of the combinations of words, the lexicographer will soon observe that some of them recur very frequently. And more than that: he will observe that it is not possible to exchange their constituent elements, or substitute another for one of them, or sometimes even to add something. As already stated, the study of what we call the combinatory power of words is to a large extent overlapping or partly identical with what we earlier called the range of application of a word. Let us, therefore, discuss one of the cases mentioned above. The Eng. word *good* is free in the sense described above: an endless number of things can be described as good. In the same sense the word *day* is also free, because it can have an endless number of different attributes (leaving aside other possible combinations). In a sentence like

"*It was a good day*",

matters in this way, just because the lexicographer will most probably perceive the situation in these different aspects which are closely connected with (or eventually even caused by) the traditional method of lexicographic presentation.

[14] The matter is well discussed by Amosova LS 5, 1962, 36ff. Her examples, however (*black banner, black thoughts, black ingratitude*), have the disadvantage that one could contest whether they are free in the full sense of the term (cf. below, on *light*).

the combination is absolutely free because it would be equally possible to say

"It was a very good day", or

"It was a bad day", or

"a long day of work",

or many other things, according to the actual communicative intention. But as mentioned above, in the greeting

"Good day!",

it is not possible to say something else, e.g.

"Excellent day!",

nor to add something, e.g.

"Very good day!"

without basically changing the meaning of the expression, without affecting its acceptability as a greeting. The combination of the words *Good day* has, then, a lexical meaning as a whole, though it is ,,in this case" derivable from the single parts.[15] It is a s e t c o m b i n a t i o n o f w o r d s; in this case, it is a m u l t i w o r d l e x i c a l u n i t.[16]

[15] Dokulil LSB 117 who does not, however, state explicitly that he regards combinations like this one as multiword lexical units.

[16] Cf. Garvin, Anais 3. The basic difference is in Garvin's definition: in my opinion, only some of the multiword lexical units show the semantic property postulated by Garvin for them all. — What we call *multiword lexical units* are sometimes called *lexemes* or *complex lexemes*, *lexeme clusters* or *conjuncts*, *synthèmes*, *locutions*, or, in yet other terminologies, *bound syntagmas* etc. W. A. Coates (Proceedings of the 9th Congress of Linguists, Cambridge 1962, The Hague 1964 p. 1064) uses the term *compound lexical units*; Halliday (in: A. McIntosh — M. K. Halliday, *Patterns of Languages*, London 1966, p. 22) uses the term *compound lexical item*; I find these terms very good and would use one of them but for the collision with "*compound words*". Traditionally, the terms *composition*, *compound* belong to the rather morphological sphere. Our "multiword lexical units" try to avoid these associations but do have — I wish myself to be the first critic to put it on record — the disadvantage that they do not necessarily consist of words only (see below, and, on the other hand, that they may consist of only two of them. — The study of the subject got a strong impulse form Ch. Bally, *Traité de stylistique française*, 2nd ed., Heidelberg 1921, vol. I, where the preponderance of the function is established. The whole problem is discussed (with bibliographical indications omitted here) in my paper *Multiword Lexical Units* (in the Martinet volume, Word 23, 1967 (published 1969) p. 578ff.). Cf. also Halliday (op. cit., p. 21ff.); Machač SS 28, 1967, 137ff. — In a broader conception, what are called *multiword lexical units* here, plus some other set combinations of words, are frequently called *phrases* or *lexicalized phrases*, *fixed* (or *set*) *collocations*, *idioms*, etc. in other terminologies. Cf. M. Shaki, *Principles of Persian Bound Phraseology* (in: Dissertationes Orientales, vol. 10), Prague 1967, with a very good survey and analysis of the bibliography of the subject (p. 10ff.) and a classificatory table. — The transformationalist approach can be exemplified by B. Fraser, *Idioms within a Transformational Grammar* (preprint).

3.3.1 Multiword lexical units are very frequent. They carry lexical meaning as wholes (units); in this respect, they function in the sentence in the same way as those lexical units which consists of one word only. And in the same way as we have earlier constituted designative words as a subgroup of words generally taken, we can now say that there are numerous multiword lexical units with the designative function. They designate segments of the extra-linguistic world in a way which is precisely analogous to that of designative words. Enormous numbers of terms belong here: e.g., Eng. *sea acorn, sea anemone, sea angel, sea arrow, sea asparagus*, etc., but also designative units which do not have a strictly terminological character, like Eng. *guinea pig*, French *chemin de fer, salle à manger, salle de travail, bateau à vapeur* etc. A single, unified designatum is expressed in a multiword lexical unit of designative character in the same way as if it were expressed by a single-wordlexical unit.[17]

How are we to detect a multiword lexical unit? There are the following criteria which should be taken into consideration.

(1) *Substitution* is impossible in a multiword lexical unit, and in a set combination of words generally.[18] It is not possible to say *"Excellent day!"* instead of *"Good day!"* when we make a greeting. It is possible to speak about a *fat pig*, or about a *dirty pig* etc. and its is always a pig we are speaking about, with different qualifications: these are, therefore, free combinations. But if we change anything in *guinea pig*, we necessarily change the subject of the conversation. This "commutation test" is probably the most important criterion of a multiword lexical unit.[19]

Sometimes, a free combination of words has the same form as the multiword lexical unit. This is easy to demonstrate by the contradistinction of the free combination *cold feet* (where it is possible to make any substitution as *wet feet, hurt feet ...*) and the multiword lexical unit *cold feet* in a sentence as

"He will not do it, he's got cold feet"

---

[17] On the morphemic status of the constituent parts of the multiword lexical units, cf. below.

[18] Cf. Man LSB 105 and 107f. Explicitely stated and discussed in detail by M. Mathiot, Language 43, 1967, 703ff.

[19] It is only an illusory contradiction if Phal, Cahiers 4, 1964, 51 shows that *théorie du conditionnement, théorie pavlovienne,* and *théorie de Pavlov* are equivalent, that there is, therefore, the possibility of substitution, and that, consequently, these are no multiword lexical units. These expressions are probably to be taken as synonyms. The thing is that they can be used alternatively, but only as wholes: if we try to substitute something in each of them, the substitution test will show that they are set, because it is impossible to substitute in *théorie du ..., théorie...*, *théorie de ...* anything without changing the meaning. — The only possible change in a multiword lexical unit seems to be the dropping of one of the constituent elements (suggestion of I. J. Gelb); such cases however, seem to be possible only in situations where the context strongly disambiguates the meaning and seems to be elliptical, e.g. "... *day*" (as the greeting). Such an ellipsis can become stabilized by frequent use; e.g. Eng. *underground* (for *underground railway*), Arabic (Petrá-ček) *ǧamicatun* "storage battery" (cf. § 1.5.3 and 1.7.4).

where it is impossible to substitute anything without changing the overall meaning of the expression which makes it near-synonymous with "to be afraid".

The example used above, viz *"Good day!"*, shows us another important thing, namely that multiword lexical units are not only of designative character. They are used not only to designate segments of the extralinguistic world, but they also perform other functions, e.g. those of purely communicative or relational or other character: grammatical-relational operators like Eng. *so as to, inasmuch as* stand on a par with one-word lexical units as *when*; French *ne … pas* is not functionally different from a one-word lexical unit like Eng. *not*, Germ. *nicht*; Eng. *old girl* performs the same function of a symptom of affection as the one-word near-synonym (or at least semantically related word *darling*) though the application of the former is restricted to person and animals of female sex only).[20] In these cases, it is again the impossibility to substitute a part without a total change in the over-all meaning which seems to be the basic criterion.

When applying the substitution test, one must take into consideration that some words occur as constituent parts of whole series of expressions, e.g. Eng. *give away* :: *give off* :: *give over* (etc.) :: *turn away* :: *turn off* :: *turn over* (etc.). If and inasfar as the single expressions comply with the criteria of multiword lexical units, we should not be distressed by such concatenations, or series. After all, the productivity of a type of combination of words has basically not a different status from the productivity of, say, derivation by suffix, at least not in the trend of thought we are following here, in the formation of fixed clusters of morphemes. But it will not always be easy to differentiate such multiword lexical units from the set expressions on the one hand and from the free combinations of words on the other. And if such a type is very productive, it can, by its regularity, verge on the quasi-grammatical. E.g. French

être en branle :: *entrer en branle* :: *se mettre en branle* :: *mettre en branle*;

entre en colère :: *entrer en colère* :: *se mettre en colère* :: *mettre en colère*;

être en mouvement :: *entrer en mouvement* :: *se mettre en mouvement* :: *mettre en mouvement* (etc.).[21]

The following criteria do not seem to apply to all the pertinent cases and are, therefore, not of such a basic character as the preceding one.[22]

---

[20] It is worth while to mention that the "homonymy" of the free combinations versus the multiword lexical units can be observed in this example, too. Cf. *darling — old girl* :: *old girl — young girl — pretty girl* etc.

[21] Example from J. Šabršula, Travaux ling. de Prague 2, 1966, 183ff.

[22] A similar point is well taken by Blanár LSB 117; the main contradistinction is *free combination* :: *set combination*.

(2) Sometimes, it is impossible to *add* something to the set combination. For instance, the multiword lexical unit *black market* can be considered the set counterpart of the free combination *illegal market*. Now, although it is possible to say *illegal steel market*, the only way to express this with the set combination would be *black market in steel*.[23]

This principle may gain clarity when discussed on the basis of a seemingly contradictory example. In English, there is a set combination of words *red-handed* "in the act of committing a crime". When we read (The Times, February 4th, 1968) the caption

"The thief was caught infra-red handed",

it would seem, if only the form were considered, that *infra-* belongs to *red* and this impression would be strengthened by the frequent term *infra-red* (as in *infra-red* rays: the point is that the thief was caught by the use of a camera having infra-red rays). But it is just the impossibility of having *red*, as a constituent part of the set combination *red-handed*, modified per se on which the jocose effect is based. The whole is an absolutely occasional combination of two different, incompatible set combinatios one of the constituent parts of both of which is red.

(3) Very frequently, different *semantic phenomena* are criterial or at least indicative; so, above all, the eventual fact that the meaning of the whole combination is not fully derivable from that of the single parts. French *pomme de terre* "potato" is, in a word-for-word translation, "apple of earth", but it is not an apple. The meaning of Eng. *to give up* (in the sense "to stop trying") is less derivable from the single parts than the meaning of *to go in* (= "to enter"): therefore, we shall be more inclined to accept the former as a multi-word lexical unit than the latter.[24]

This phenomenon, the fact that the meaning of the whole is not derivable from the meaning of the single constituent parts, is extremely frequent.[25] Indeed, practically all of what can be called idiomatic expressions[26] in any language belong here: e.g. expressions like Eng. *to drop a brick*, French *revenir à ses moutons* "to come back to the main topic" (verbatim: "to return to one's sheep"). Such idiomatic expressions frequently have different connotations. For instance, Heroldová reports Chinese *tun li—pa—tzu* "to be in

[23] Coates, Proceedings of the 9th Congress of linguists (cf. footnote 16).

[24] Cf. Coates, Proceedings (footnote 16), p. 1051; his attitude is, however, much more decided, as far as these either — or decisions go, and this is for him the main criterion.

[25] In some terminologies, lexical units whose meaning is not derivable from that of their constituent parts are said to be *lexicalized*. In such an approach, *lexicalization* is a semantic process which can take place either in a word (whose meaning is, then, not derivable from that of its constituent morphemes) or in a multiword lexical unit.

[26] In some terminologies, only these idiomatic expressions are called *phrases* (germ. *Phrasen*, *Redewendungen*, French *idiotismes*, etc.).

quod (jug)" (verbatim: "to squat at a fence"), *ch'ih hei—tsao—erh* "to get shot, to get the brains blown out" (verbatim: "to eat black dates"), which are strongly expressive.

It is, however, important to stress that this semantic phenomenon is not the basic criterion of a set combination or even of a multiword lexical unit. Let us discuss an example. In Italian, we have the following three set combinations: *treno accelerato, treno direttissimo, treno rapido*. They have a terminological status and are multiword lexical units of designative character. Their word for-word meaning is, respectively, "accelerated train, most direct train, rapid train"; they designate different types of trains out of which *accelerato* is the slowest, *direttissimo* usually is not direct, but *rapido* usually really is rapid. But though *treno rapido* is the only one of the three set groups the meaning of which is largely derivable from that of its parts, it has the same status as the other two.

Indeed, it seems that idiomatic expressions like *to drop a brick*, or at least some of them, do not stand on a par with multiword lexical units, or rather that they are a subcategory of its own. They certainly do comply with the criteria, but the difference seems to be that whereas the (other) multiword lexical units have direct meanings (i.e. they simply designate a denotatum etc.), the real idiomatic expressions seem always to have figurative meanings: when we say about somebody that he dropped a brick, we understand the overall meaning of the set expression, but the expressive, or jocose, effect is produced by the fact that we simultaneously understand what would be the meaning of it if it were a free combination of words. Because of this, we shall use in reference to such expressions the term i d i o m a t i c, or simply s e t e x p r e s s i o n s. It is a category which will still need much study and which may one day be shown as consisting of phenomena which do not really belong together. At least it would seem that some of these set expressions verge on multiword lexical units with a direct meaning (above all those which begin to make no sense as free combinations of words), but other set expressions seem to verge on the set groups of words.

Sometimes a constituent part of a multiword lexical unit is s e m a n t i c a l l y d e p l e t e d. For instance, French *jeune fille* is not necessarily "young girl", as suggested by the meaning of the single words, but "girl" (of any age, an unmarried woman), as shown by the possibility to say

"*Elle est déjà assez agée, elle va rester jeune fille*".[27]

Such a depleted element can become rather productive in a series of paralell multiword lexical units. In Arabic (as reported by Petráček), *dū* "master,

---

[27] This and similar sentences seem to occur frequently, since prescriptive manuals list them among their prohibitions; cf. J. Hause, *Dictionnaire des difficultés grammaticales et lexicologiques* (Amiens 1949), p. 392: "*Ne dites pas d'une vieille demoiselle qu'elle est restée jeune fille.*"

possessor" is depleted (in modern language) in a series of units like *dū mālin* "rich" (verbatim "master of property"), *ḏū ša'nin* "important" (verbatim "master of thing") etc. With this, cf. above, point 1, last but one paragraph.

(4) A constituent part of a set combination of words may be severely or exclusively restricted to it, as e.g. Eng. *maid* "virgin, unmarried (young) woman" in *old maid*: at least in Mod. Eng., the word does not have the same sense, outside this multiword lexical unit. Eng. *fro* "back" seems to be absolutely restricted to the set combination *to and fro*, again, at least, in Mod. Eng. In other cases, single forms are preserved in set combinations which do not exist elsewhere; e.g. Miltner reports from Romani (Gipsy) that the participles in *-ando* or *-ndo* do not exist by now, but *urňando* "flying" is still preserved in the multiword lexical unit *urňando mišos* "bat" (verbatim: "flying mouse").

(5) The multiword lexical unit may have a *synonym* or a close near-synonym which consists *of one word* only. For instance, Eng. *loose woman* :: *prostitute*, *guinea pig* :: *cavy*.

(6) A small group of semantically related expressions may show analogous or *identical status* among the multiword lexical units and single words. For instance Amer. Eng: *elementary school* :: *high school* :: *college* :: *university*; French *pomme de terre* "potato" :: *radis* "radish" :: *betterave* "sugar-beet".[28]

(7) A *one-word equivalent* in a foreign language can suggest that we might have a multiword lexical unit before us. For instance, Russ. *koza* = Eng. "goat", Russ. *dikij* = Eng. "wild", but Russ. *dikaja koza* = Eng. "roe".[29]

(8) Multiword lexical units do sometimes have special *formal and grammatical properties*.[30] For example, there is no article in English set combinations like *at hand*, *by heart*,[31] nor is it present in French *apprendre par coeur*. When we read a sentence like

"*The college students get later in life usually better salaries than the non college students*",

we may safely assume from the position of the negative prefix *non* that the combination *college student* is a multiword lexical unit, at least in the idiolect of the man who wrote the sentence.[32]

---

[28] Example from Greimas, Cahiers 2, 1960, 52, who stresses mainly the commutability of these lexical units in a sentence.

[29] This criterion is very fragile. For instance, the English multiword lexical unit *guinea pig* has now French equivalents, viz. *cobay* (one-word) and *cochon d'Inde* (multiword).

[30] In some languages, there are also accentual characteristics of the multiword lexical units; cf. below. Cf. also, generally, Akhmanova IJAL 31, 1965, 164.

[31] Weinreich, Universals 146.

[32] Frank H. Bowles, *How to get into college*, New York 1960.

Similarly, the fact that such set combinations form wholes can be recognized by transformational techniques. If a sentence like

John looked at Mary and Mary looked at John

can be reduced into

John looked at Mary and Mary at John,

where the secont *at* cannot be dropped, we have before us a (free) combination of a verb (*look*) + preposition (*at*). But if a sentence like

Bill thought up this idea, and Tom thought up that one

can be reduced into

Bill thought up this idea, and Tom that one

where the second *at* must be dropped, we have before us a set combination (*think up*), a lexical whole (usually called prepositional phrase in English grammar). (Examples and idea suggested by a lecture of J. Ross.) And in the same way, the difference between the status of *to run up* in the two sentences

John ran up the bill (i.e. made it big; set)
John ran up the street (free)

or of *to roll up* in the three setences

John rolled up the carpet (i.e. made a convolute of it; set)
John rolled up the carpet (i.e. rolled his own body; free, up preposition)
John rolled up the carpet (i.e. rolled the carpet; free, up adverb)

is shown not only by the meaning, but also by the transformational counterparts of the single sentences. (Examples and idea suggested by a lecture of B. Fraser.)

But the importance of the formal criterion must not be overrated. Contrary to what one might expect, it is not always valid. To prove the secondary nature of the formal criterion, let us discuss the Ossetic "combined verbs".

In Ossetic, it is possible to combine almost any nominal element with the verb *känyn* "to make, to do". Very frequently, these combinations are made on the spur of the moment, for the purpose of the actual communication only, but many seem to be set, stabilized according to at least some of the criteria discussed above. All these combined verbs are divided into two big categories: in one of them, different grammatical and similar elements are put before the nominal element, in the other, they are put before the verb *känyn*; it goes without saying that combined verbs belonging to the first category would seem thus to be quite clearly characterized as wholes, in this way. Let us consider the following verbs:

iw "one" : : *iw känyn* "to unite" : : *nä iw käny* "he does not unite"

mästy "angry" : : *mästy känyn* "to anger" : : *nä mästy käny* "he does not anger"

art "fire" : : *art känyn* "to light fire" : : *nä art käny* "he does not etc."

We see that these verbs are characterized as set combinations, as wholes. In contrast, let us consider the following verbs:

dix "part" : : *dix känyn* "to divide" : : *dix nä käny* "he does not divide"

kärdzyn "bread" : : *kärdzyn känyn* "to prepare bread" : : *kärdzyn nä käny* "he does not etc."

dwar "door" : : *dwar känyn* "to open the door" : : *dwar nä käny* "he does not etc."

We see that these combination seem to be free, as far as the form goes.[33] If we analyze their meaning, however, we find that by criterion (3), only the meaning of *kärdzyn känyn* is derivable from that of its single parts, but hardly more than, say, that of *mästy känyn* from the first group. As far as *dix känyn* goes, its meaning is, to some extent at least, derivable from that of its single parts, but it has other polysemous senses of its own as a whole, viz. "to break into splinters, pieces, to splinter, split; to demolish, wreck", which are not derivable from the meaning of the single parts. And as far as *dwar känyn* "to open the door" of the second group is concerned, its meaning is certainly less derivable from that of its single parts than is the case of, e.g., *art känyn* of the first category. Consequently, it will be a correct conclusion to say that pending further study, the combined verbs of the second category (which has no formal characteristics to show that we have wholes before us) seem to form as set combinations, that they are as stabilized multiword lexical units like those combined verbs that belong to the first category (which can be regarded as characterized by the form).

Another remark must be made in connection with the formal criterion. It would be a mistake to assume that the set combinations must be continuous. On the contrary, some are discontinuous, as e.g. Eng. to *look* (something)*up*.[34]

(9) There are set combinations of words which should not be considered multiword units, though the first criterion and lexical at least some of the other criteria listed above seem to apply to them. In a set combination of words as *my house my castle*, it is not possible to substitute a constituent part of it; and other criteria will also apply to it. But though it is a set combination of words,

---

[33] V. I. Abaev, *Grammatical Sketch of Ossetic*, The Hague 1964, p. 68.

[34] J. J. Katz — P. M. Postal, *An Integrated Theory of Linguistic Descriptions*, Cambridge 1964, p. 40.

it is certainly not a multiword lexical unit, because it does not comply with the most fundamental requiremet, viz. that a multiword lexical unit must perform, in a sentence (syntagmatically) and in the lexicon, in the lexical stock of language (paradigmatically) the same *syntactic and onomasiological function* as a morphologically more simple unit which frequently coincides with the word, e.g. in the Indo-European languages. This fundamental requirement is the criterion by means of which set combinations of words like proverbs, sayings, dicta, quotations, and similar fossile, petrified expressions (which we generally call set groups of words) are distinguished from the multiword lexical units.[35] At least some of the idiomatic, set expressions (cf. point 3) will also belong here.[36]

The ninth criterion is as basic and as general as the first: it seems to be these two criteria, the first and the ninth, which are the fundamentum divisionis by which the multiword lexical units are singled out, whereas criteria (2)—(8) seem to be of a rather additional character, at least provisionally. One can perhaps also expect that the semantic depletion of constituent parts of multiword lexical units will gain importance when our semantic judgments are refined.

These are in my opinion the nine criteria which are necessary for the discovery of set combinations of words and for their rough classification. The frequency of co-occurrence of the respective words is sometimes also said to be indicative of their forming a set combination.[37] I do not know whether this is as useful a criterion as it would seem in our statistical age. I do not know of any conclusive count which could give us some undubitable examples. Anyhow, the lexicographer working in such a situation as we envisage in this book will not usually have the possibility of making the necessary statistical observations on a really big scale. And I strongly suspect that the frequency of the co-occurrence of two words may be even greater if we have to do with a fully free combination of words which have themselves a high frequency of occurrences; e.g., a statistical count would probably show that the combination *to drink beer* has an immensely higher frequency of occurrence than *to swallow stones*, but both are free combinations anyhow.

One case of frequent co-occurrence should, however, be kept apart, — the so-called stereotyped expressions or clichés. They are, at least originally,

---

[35] Set groups will be discussed in greater detail below, § 3.3.3.

[36] An either-or decision is sometimes difficult not only on the borderline between set groups and idiomatic expressions, but also on the borderline between the set groups and multiword lexical units. For instance, we quoted above the greeting *good day*! among the multiword lexical units, because it seems to function in a way similar to other attitudinal symptoms like *hello*!. But we are not quite sure about some other greetings and similar expressions, whether they should not rather be considered set groups.

[37] Greimas, Cahiers 2, 1960, 52: An imperfect but indispensable criterion.

free combinations of words, and very often even uncommon combinations as Eng. *divine beauty, dramatic development* etc. It is just this uncommonness which gave them a certain connotative value. Because of this, they came to be used so frequently that they are or tend to become semantically depleted. Such a depletion can be observed in the Arabic example reported by Petrá-ček: The cliché *alqā khiṭāban* "he delivered a speech, he discoursed" (verbatim: "he threw a discourse, speech" (is depleted and used in newspapers in the broader cliché *alqā khiṭāban wa qāla* "he delivered a speech and stated".[38]

These clichés are typically overused in literary works which are generally classified by the subjective but probably indispensable term "bad", and above all in newspapers of the same order. In my opinion they are frequently co-occurring free combinations; but there seems to be a large area of overlapping with idiomatic expressions. The important thing is that they are not multiword lexical units, because they do not comply with criterion (1).

3.3.2 It may be useful to discuss set groups of words in greater detail. As we have seen, it is primarily the quotations and dicta which belong here. If somebody uses in his conversation the set group of words *"to be or not to be"*, it is, whether he knows it or not, a quotation from Shakespeare's Hamlet. When somebody inserts in his conversation the advice *"cherchez la femme"*, it is a quotation from A. Dumas, Les Mohicans de Paris (1864) 2, 16 who, in his turn, coined it as a dictum of one of his characters, of a police agent. These and similar expressions are set combinations of words, but they certainly are not multiword lexical units. The basic criterion of a quotation (which usually can be precisely located (or a dictum (which usually can be located as the saying of a person, real or fictive) is that it is used to convey some meaning indirectly, by reference to the original meaning, original intention, and original experience of the original speaker. Sometimes these quotations and dicta have the character of a generalized experience expressed in pointed words. The authors of such dicta as *noblesse oblige* to be noble is to have duties", or *my home is my castle* are known (they are Pierre Max Gaston duc de Lévis, 1764 —1830, Maximes et réflexions sur différents sujets de morale et de politique, and Sir Edward Coke, 1551—1633, Institutes, respectively), but the erudition of a Büchmann[39] is necessary to find them out.

A similar category of set groups of words is proverbs. They are very close to the last examples. Their main characteristic is that they convey some accu-

---

[38] An extreme semantic phenomenon is the difference or opposition of the sense of the word when used freely and when used in a set combination. Petráček reports (after D. Cohen) from spoken Arabic as used by the Jews in Tunesia: *məkhūṭ* "beautiful", but in the cliché *məkhūṭ mən ʿan əlla* "cursed by God".

[39] G. Büchmann, *Geflügelte Worte* (28th edition, Berlin 1937), s. v.

mulated experience or generalized observation or that they give advice; they convey this meaning usually in a metaphorical way, and their situation in the text is usually that of a quotation. In the majority of cases, their author is unknown. As examples, we may quote Eng. *A bird in the hand is worth two in the bush*; *First come, first served*; *The proof of the pudding is its eating*; *Less said, sooner mended*; French *Qui veut tuer le chien, l'accuse de rage* "who wishes to kill the dog, accuses him of rage"; *après la pluie, le beau temps* "after the rain, good weather"; *le mieux est l'ennemi du bon* "better is the foe of good"; *aide-toi, le Ciel t'aidera* "help yourself, Heaven will help you". The lexicographer's interest in these quotations, dicta and proverbs is rather negative. They certainly are set combinations of words, they must be understood as wholes, but they are not multiword lexical units. Knowledge of them undubitably belongs to the knowledge of the language (and even more to knowledge of the respective culture), so that really big dictionaries may register them; but it should never be forgotten that though they are set groups of words, though they are understood as wholes and are frequently presented in the texts as wholes (intonation; quotation marks etc.), they are not single lexical units: they are built up of several of these lexical units in each case. The important thing in this connection is that apart from other formal characteristics,[40] we very frequently find as their constituent parts obsolete words and expressions which are not used elsewhere; this fact cannot surprise us when we remember that proverbs have basically the character of repeated quotations.[41] The lexicographer cannot use the lexical material gained from such quotations, etc., in the same way as he uses the other data, but must always take into consideration that these are expressions *sui generis*.

On the other hand, as there are borderline cases and cases of transition between all categories, the lexicographer must anticipate similar complications here, too. *We shall meet at Philippi* is originally a quotation ultimately from Plutarch, Caesar 60, and immediately from Shakespeare, Julius Caesar 4, 3 (in a modified form)[42] and it approaches the status of an idiomatic expression. But the original quotation *fin de siècle* (originally the title of a comedy by F. de Jouvenot and H. Micard, 1888)[43] became a lexical unit with designative meaning, even in English.

3.3.3 In this way, we try to distinguish the set combinations of words from the free ones (among which, the stereotyped expressions or clichés are those in

---

[40] Cf. Greimas (op. cit. footnote 37), p. 57ff.: in French, absence of the article and other features.

[41] Similar discussions in Greimas (op. cit.), p. 59.

[42] Büchmann, op. cit. (footnote 39), s. v.

[43] Büchmann, op. cit. s. v.

which the single elements frequently co-occur). Set combinations can be conceived as consisting of set groups of words (quotations etc.) and multi-word lexical units (to which the idiomatic, set expressions seem to belong).

As already stated, multiword lexical units are the most important category of set combinations of words.

For the lexicographer, the detection and correct presentation of multiword lexical units is one of his most important tasks. If he is compiling a monolingual dictionary, it is his duty to find out and describe the lexical units of the language. And there is every reason to believe that multiword lexical units really function as wholes, as units of language, not as free combinations, not as mere agglomerations of words. If the lexicographer compiles a bilingual dictionary, multiword lexical units are important because they can cause some additional trouble to the user. It is not enough to know the equivalents of their single constituents in the target language, because multiword lexical units frequently have other equivalents; cf. above, the examples sub (5). Without a knowledge of the special equivalents of the multiword lexical unit Russ. *dikaja kozá*: Eng. *roe*, the user of the dictionary would probably use only the equivalents of the single constituents and translate the Russ. expression as "wild goat". The knowledge of the single French and Eng. words *gaz* :: *gas, marais* :: *marsh, tonner* :: *explode* does suffice to predict that French *gaz de marais* is, no doubt, Eng. *marsh gas*, but not that French *gaz tonnant* is Eng. *explosive mixture*.[44] Everybody whos has some experience with teaching or learning a non-native language knows that such mistakes are extremely frequent.

Multiword lexical units carry lexical meaning in the same way as do single words. And just as in the case of single words, their lexical meaning can be of different types. Multiword lexical meaning like *sea anemone* or *guinea pig* has designative meaning; a multiword lexical unit as *good day!* is a pragmatic operator like (colloq.) *bye!*; a multiword lexical unit like *good heavens!* is an attitudinal symptom like *Oho!*; a multiword lexical unit like *as to, inasmuch as* is a grammatical or relational operator like *if* etc. The parallelism of the multiword lexical units and the single words is absolute and the lexicographer must take it into consideration.

Important as multiword lexical units are, the lexicographer must be prepared to meet considerable difficulties in dealing with them, just as in dealing with set combinations generally. It will suffice to mention only two of these difficulties.

(1) It is impossible to establish a sharp boundary between free combinations and set ones. It can be shown that there are different degrees of "setness", or

---

[44] Example from Phal, Cahiers 4, 1964, 56.

different degrees of restrictions.[45] If we compare expressions like *light burden*, *light bag* with combinations like *light supper*, *light food*, we see that in the latter ones, the combinatorial possiblities are more restricted. In combinations as *light infantry*, the restriction is more severe and the combinations seems to approach the status of a multiword lexical unit, if it has not reached it already. And in light hand, we have undoubtedly a set combination before us. The lexicographer should be aware of this and should try to evaluate the degree of "setness" of the combinations. The smaller the dictionary, the more severe will be his choice of examples in favour of the most stabilized set combinations; the bigger the dictionary, the greater the opportunity to begin with less setnes.

(2) The conceptual foundations of the whole field of pertinent problems need much further clarification. Some of the most evident problems are:

Is it a legitimate method to compare the equivalent expression in a foreign language to evaluate the status of an expression.

For the moment, there seems to exist no independent, objective method for deciding which of the two possible solutions is the more correct one: are French *salle à manger* and *salle de travail* to be considered two units which are in simple contradistinction, or do we have before us two different qualifications of the more general term *salle*? Considerations such as that *salle de travail* is, after all, a hall, whereas a *guinea pig* is not a pig at all will always tend to obfuscate the issue but what if we find a set combination like *guinea pig* in an exotic language and draw a conclusion that in the folk taxonomy of the speakers of X, a guinea pig is a pig? In all these questions, one should never forget at least that languages are different and that what is the correct solution for one of them is not necessarily true for another. If we compare the following series of Hindi words with their English translations

nazar	*glance*
kankhī	*slanting glance*
kaṭākṣ	*casual glance*[46]

or the following Tamil words (Zvelebil) with their English translations

paḻam		*fruit*
kaṇi	*ripe*	*fruit*
kāy	*unripe*	*fruit*

we see that what is expressed by one word with a unified designatum in one language must be expressed by a free combination in the other language.

---

[45] Cf. Man LSB 103 with excellent Czech examples; used here as background. — It should be remarked that the relation of the "setness" to the "restrictions" will need much further research; do these two notions overlap and to what extent? Or are their respective differences placed in different dimensions?

[46] Example from Barannikov, *Leksičeskaja sinonimija* 15.

The same trouble must be expected when the lexicographer works with the terminology of different sciences. To use an extreme example, specialists in different fields of science will insist that expressions like *bacille de Koch*, *bacille d'Eberth*, *bacille de Hansen* are multiword lexical units, that they are terms with a unified designatum and even denotatum, but the lexicographer will probably be disinclined to accept this position and will rather maintain that we have different specifications of *bacille* before us.[47] I would be prepared to accept the position that the status of such groups varies: in the specialized, restricted languages of the different sciences (and scientists) they may be multiword lexical units (of a designative, terminological nature), but in the general language, they may be more or less free combinations which specify the lexical unit *bacille* and are probably understood (in the general language, I emphasize) only in a general, vague way.

Such a variation in the status of a combination may also have other causes. For instance, Motalová reports from Armenian: in Western Armenian, "grandmother" is designated by the multiword lexical unit *mec mayr* (verbatim: "big mother"). In Eastern Armenian, "grandmother" is designated by the word *tat*, and *mec mayr* can occour only as a free combination, naturally with the verbatim meaning of the two constituent parts ("big mother").

Important as further research in these directions is, the lexicographer is able to do good work even before these questions are answered. In a monolingual dictionary, he is most concerned with the combinatorial possibilities and their restrictions. He can indicate either the free or the set combinations (or both); if necessary, with an explanation of the meaning of the set combination or with a gloss on the status of it. And he will itemize the stabilized lexical multiword units as entries or at least as subentries of their own.[48] In a bilingual dictionary, the lexicographer is most concerned with the equivalence of expressions in the two languages: does the set combination as a whole have an equivalent which is identical with, or predictable form, the equivalents of its single constituents, or not?

3.3.4 The problems of set combinations of words and above all of the multiword lexical units deserve the closest attention of the lexicographer. Their constituents can have different status. If we compare Eng. *sea anemone* with French *bateau à vapeur*, we see that the structure of French requires the presence of a functional element (*à*), whereas the structure of English does not. For the lexicographer, differences of this type, even if they can be observed within one language, are relatively unimportant. Within the limits of one language, it can also be observed that the constituents of multiword lexical

---

[47] Phal, Cahiers 4, 1964, 49 and 52.
[48] E.g. "*good day*" glossed as a conventional greeting.

units sometimes tend to develop formal differences in contrast to their counter-parts used in free combinations of words. For instance, in several areas of American English, there is an observable difference in the pronunciation of the combination *high school* in a sentence as

"*This is a big, high school*" (meaning that the building is big and high: free combination)

and in a sentence as

"*This is the local high school*" (the type of school is meant: set combination, viz. a multiword lexical unit).

In the second case, the pronunciation (primarily, only one main accent on *high* (differs from the pronunciation of the free combination *high school* in a similar way as the pronunciation of the compound word *blackboard* differs from the free combination *black board*. Therefore, we can establish the following proportion:

black board (free; a board :: *blackboard* (compound; physical
       that is physically   colour is irrelevant)
       black)

high school (free; a school :: *high school* (set; physical height
       that is physically   is irrelevant)
       high)

This observation has very important consequences.

First, as in all cases, the lexicographer will respect the tradition prevailing in his language. He will be aware that it may seem strange to write *blackboard* without, but *high school* with, an intervening space (not to mention the hyphen-ated forms). He will, however, not try to "amend" this, unless it is a special task of his dictionary to introduce or enforce a new orthography.

And second: though the term for a dictionary is derived, in various languages, from the term designating the word (Ital. *vocabolario*, German *Wörterbuch*), it is not words as such which the lexicographer is primarily concerned with and interested in, and which are the foundation of his work.

The lexicographer is concerned primarily with lexical units, i.e. with those units of language that are constituents of the most natural unit of the utterance (which is usually the sentence), and that have unified and distinctive lexical meanings of their own, irrespective of their formal structure or of the number or nature of their own constituent parts.

If we simplify things to the extreme, we may conceive language as con-sisting basically of units of two sorts, distinctive and meaningful. The distinc-tive units are the phonemes; they do not interest the lexicographer too much *per se.* The minimal meaningful units are the morphemes.[49] Morphemes, however, are not directly constituent parts of the sentence: this function is performed by the lexical units, a very frequent morphological category of which are the words.

There are clearly monomorphemic words like Eng. *black, if;*

there are clearly polymorphemic words as Eng. *blackbird* all of whose morphemes can be used alone carrying a lexical meaning;

there are words the morphemic status of which varies with the speaker's education, like Eng. *tele + phone, tele + graph, albeit;*

there are words whose morphemic status is more or less unclear, like Eng. *re + ceive, de + ceive, radar, contraption;*

there are polymorphemic words some morphemes of which perform a grammatical or derivational function only, like Eng. *fool + ish + ness, work+er, book + s.*

There are also, for example, bimorphemic lexical units, like Eng. *man-servant*, which are characterized both as one word (accent, no space) and as two words (plural *menservants*).

For the lexicographer, the insights into the structure of the words are of great interest, because they tell him much about the productive processes in the lexicon; basically, however, the lexicographer deals with all these lexical units, in this case specifically words, in the same way, irrespective of what internal structures they have and irrespective of whether he knows these structures and is able to classify them neatly (as very often happens).

Similarly, a lexical unit like Eng. *college* consists clearly of one word;

a lexical unit like Eng. *elementary school* consists clearly of the words;

a lexical unit like Eng. *high school* consists of two words and is treated as such in the written language, but tends to become a bimorphemic compound word in the spoken language;[50]

a lexical unit like French *pomme de terre* consists of three words, the second of which is capable of performing a grammatical function only and the first of which seems to be accentuated, in the spoken language, in a way similar to the accentuation of the first part of compound words.

In the case of single words, the lexicographer may have a legitimate interest in their structure, but must handle them all, irrespective of the differences in the structure. In the case of multiword lexical units, the situation is parallel:

---

[49] Though we do not use the term *moneme*, the Martinetian inspiration of this point of view is obvious. (In the Martinetian terminology, *morphèmes* are morphemes which perform grammatical functions, whereas *lexèmes* are the morphemes which carry the lexical meaning (cf. the lexeme as explained in footnote 1 to Chapter II); *monèmes* are, then, both the morphemes and the lexemes).

[50] Here the element of time is inevitably present in the lexicographer's work again. For example, even very traditional orthographies like the English one show changes e.g., *to pro rate > to prorate* etc.

the lexicographer is interested in their structure and in the nature of their constituent parts, but, basically, they all have the same status for him. The only difference is that he is much more bound by the tradition of his language.

In the Indo-European languages, and in many other languages, morphemes are so clearly organized in words (as the most frequent lexical units, constituents of sentences), that lexicography has usually been able to operate only with words. Only occasionally what seems to be sub-word units like the Greek enclitics have caused some trouble. The morphological category is so clear that all dictionaries of these languages generally itemize only words as their entries. And it is a relatively recent development of lexicography to go more frequently above the level of the word: only few Eng. dictionaries indicate lexical units like *no one*,[51] only few French dictionaries indicate lexical units like *jeune fille* "girl". This has been a disadvantage of lexicography even in those languages. But there are languages like Chinese or Vietnamese in which the morphological concept of the word lacks the Indo-European clarity. In these languages, as a logical consequence of this fact, it would not be adequate to base the lexicographer's work on the morphological concept of the word as known in the Indo-European languages: but even in my own limited experience I do know that quite a few lexicographic projects have been seriously hampered by such a concern.

Lexical units are the basis of the lexicographer's approach. He sees the great number of their formal types, ranging from monomorphemic single words to multiword units of complicated structure (and without sharp boundaries between the single types at that) but his main concern is their lexical meaning and their functioning in a sentence. He will not block his way and add to his difficulties by trying to find more in his data than what is in the facts of his language, and he will not deteriorate his results by limiting his attention only to some types of lexical units which have been traditionally preferred. On the other hand, the lexicographer will be disinclined to break absolutely with the eventual tradition of his language, if not for other reasons then certainly for the sake of his readers. Therefore, the words will have to play an important role in the dictionaries of Indo-European languages, and the strange concretion of morphemic value carried by a graphic character of traditional writing will have an important role in Chinese dictionaries (at least as long as Chinese is written in traditional script). Indeed, a successful compromise between his own approach and findings on the one hand and the prevailing tradition on the other must belong frequently to the lexicographer's art; but this compromise concernes only the presentation of things in the dictionary, not the methods of the lexicographer's work.

---

[51] Cf. Swanson PL 65. — For French examples, cf. Rey, Cahiers 4, 1965, 72ff. (*trait-d'-union* and sim.).

APPENDIX

3.4 For comparative examinations, we shall provide here two reports from different languages.

Petráček presents the situation in Arabic:

The most frequent lexical unit is the (free) word. This is quite evident in the case of the noun and the verb, but even in the case of prepositions and particles. Among the latter, there are some exceptions which are formally marked by being written together with the following word: *bi-*, *li-*, the article *al-*; in the case of the conjunction *wa* it is impossible to decide whether it is written together with the following word or whether it is separated. The particle *sa-* which expresses future is also written together with the following word.

The majority of the words can be said to consist at least of two morphemes, that is if we consider the so-called root (the consonants) as the morpheme carrying mainly the general lexical meaning and the vowels as another, derivational or grammatical morpheme (as it is usually understood). These two morphemes, the root and the vowels, form together the so-called stem. The stems are usually enlarg edfurther by other morphemes, usually prefixes, suffixes, and infixes.

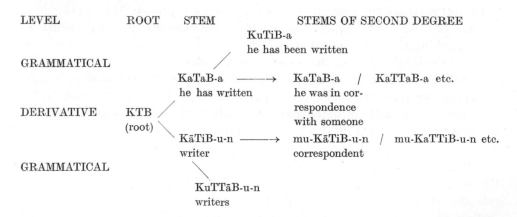

LEVEL	ROOT	STEM	STEMS OF SECOND DEGREE
		KuTiB-a	
		he has been written	
GRAMMATICAL			
		KaTaB-a ⟶	KaTaB-a / KaTTaB-a etc.
		he has written	he was in correspondence with someone
DERIVATIVE	KTB (root)		
		KāTiB-u-n ⟶	mu-KāTiB-u-n / mu-KaTTiB-u-n etc.
		writer	correspondent
GRAMMATICAL			
		KuTTāB-u-n	
		writers	

Such a regularity can be perceived only in the verbal forms (incl. the participles etc.); in the sphere of the underived noun, the system is less closed or only minimally realized.

There are some monomorphemic words which do not have the structure described; they are mostly functional words and pronouns, e.g. *huwa* "he", *anta* "you".

Compound words are very rare in Modern Arabic. There are some compound words used in scientific terminology, as, for example, *kim-fīzīyun* "chemical-physical", *ǧaw-mā 'īyatun* "amphibious plane".

Set combinations (multiword lexical units) of the most varied types are extremely frequent. A few examples show the different types:

ġayru insānīyin "inhuman" (verbatim "other than human")
ġayru mašrū͑in "illegal" (verbatim "other then legal")

͑adamu ʾal-ḥaddi "indetermination" (statistical; verbatim "lacking deter-
                                                                                  mination")

Similar types of what we would call "negative adjectives" are frequent above all in scientific terminology. Similar productive types are:

šibhu ġazīratin "peninsula" (verbatim "similar to island")
šibhu l-ma͑danīyi "metalloid" (verbatim "similar to metallic")
ḍidda ġāsūsīyatin "counter-intelligence" (verbatim "against the intelli-
                                                                            gence": preposition *ḍidda*)
huǧūmun mu͑ākisun "counter -offensive" (verbatim "attack going against":
participle *mu͑akas* as congruent attribute).

In scientific terminology, one can observe the equivalence of different members of set combinations to different members of compound words in European terminology. For instance:

auto-:	*naqdun ḏātīyun* "self criticism"
	ḥukmun ḏātīyun "autonomy"
	(*ḏātīyun* is a congruent attribute, "self")
hyper-:	*farṭu l-ḥussāsīyati* "hypersensibility"
	(*farṭun* "abundance, excess")
infra-:	*taḥta ʾl-aḥmari, dūna ʾl-aḥmari* "infra-red"
	(*taḥta, dūna*: prepositions "under")
meta-:	*mā warāʾa ʾṭ-ṭabī͑ati* "metaphysics" (verbatim "that which is
	behind nature")
	(*mā warāʾa* "that which is behind")
micro-:	*iqlīmun ṣaġīrun* "micro-climate"
	(*ṣaġīrun* "small, little")

It must be remarked, however, that these and similar terms are still rather artificial; in practice, foreign expressions are frequently used.

Multiword lexical units of designative character are, however, very frequent also in general language. For instance:

ākhḏun wa ͑aṭaʾun "commerce" (verbatim "taking and giving")
ibnu ādama "man, human being" (verbatim "son of Adam")
banū māʾi ʾs-samāʾi "Arabs" (verbatim "sons of heavenly water")
al-mawtu ʾl-abyaḍu "natural death" (verbatim "white death")
sikkatu ʾl-ḥadīdi "railway" (verbatim "way of iron")
muqābilun li-ʾs-suknā "habitable" (verbatim "fit to live in").

Minn Latt presents the situation in Burmese (but requests the reader to take into consideration that "statements like the following one are too brief to be watertight or to mention all the finesse that may be desired"):[52]

The paradigm model does not answer Burmese structure, or rather it is not necessary for it, as there are no series of inflected forms. The combinations of lexical and grammatical morphemes, other than those mentioned below, do not constitute items for lexicographic entries or forms of lexical units. Grammatical words, which are always monomorphemic, may be included, if that is the lexicographer's policy, as separate entries in the dictionary.

Structural studies reveal words, highwords and lexical expressions. A polymorphemic word does not, as a rule, include any grammatical morpheme and its component parts are combined by close juncture (with corresponding assimilations or sandhi change in all relevant instances).

The most important lexicographic items are independent (free) lexical words, monomorphemic or polymorphemic. The latter are mostly bimorphemic but words can also contain 3, 4 or 5 morphemes. Among morphemes that constitute larger composed units, dependent (bound) morphemes require special attention: some of them, namely those archaic units with obscure or unknown meanings, are best treated as components of words, but some, namely those elements that some would like to call "derivational" enclitics, for instance -săyá in sâscyá "food"; -yêi in lut lapyêi "independence", may perhaps deserve individual attention in separate entries, especially because of their high frequency.

Highwords are also treated as lexical items: they differ from polymorphemic words in that they contain grammatical morphemes. For instance, in lekwâ-tyîoup "monopoly", tyî is a grammatical component, in pyîjtwînsis "civil war", twîn is grammatical. They are formally different from free lexicogrammatical structures; in the samples presented, a grammatical unit is followed in close juncture by a lexical one, a structure that does not appear in free combinations.

The lexical expressions or multiword lexical units are combinations of lexical words and/or highwords. Examples are ăsíyin khám "give a report", tâin pyíj "country", jín tjéihmu "culture", náinngámkû lekhmat "passport".

In a dictionary where certain limitations of space must be made, polymorphemic words, highwords and lexical expressions need not figure as separate entries where their components help to predict the overall meaning: to further clarify, there may also be a brief grammatical survey attached to

[52] In this report, Minn Latt uses his own terminology, which he has coined in his analytical works on the structure of Burmese. We preserve the terminology here because the terms are sufficiently explained in the text and because the lexicographer must be in any case prepared to cope with vastly varying terminological sets.

the volume. Thus lexical items like *ăthis* (strength + be new) "new strength", *myánmyán* (be quick + be quick) "quickly", *meitatthú* (forget + be in the habit of + person) "a forgetful person", *kâun tâun tâun* (be good + rhyming elements) "rather good", *sînsîn sâsâ* (from *sînsâ* "think") "thoughtfully", *bămá pyíj* (Burmese + country) "Burma", need not be entered separately. The more complicated units whose components do not offer the required meanings should, however, receive individual mention.

It pays, however, to be prudent in our decisions. For instance, *sêimsêim* "greenish") cf. *sêim* "to be green") is a word comparable to many other regularly constructed words on the same principle of reduplication. But *sêimsêim* also means "unintimate, strangerlike etc." *Lúkâun* is not only "a good person", but also "a healthy person". In such cases reliance on some brief grammatical sketches cannot suffice; special entries in the dictionary are required.

It should also be mentioned that Burmese writing graphically distinguishes syllables but not words or larger units. Thus the word as a concept is rather loose. All types of lexical units mentioned above are often recorded without graphical distinctions but especially in bilingual dictionaries attention should be directed to these formal differences. The single word *săkâkâun* "a good piece of news" is not only different from the lexical expression *săkâ kâun* to be engrossed in conversation" in meaning, they are also phonetically distinguished — [zăgâgauŋ] and [zăgâ kâuŋ], respectively.

Words of foreign origin that have not become fully domiciled show special types of behaviour. For instance, a monomorphemic foreign, alien word may have between its components syllables open juncture, instead of the close juncture usual inside the domiciled words: e.g. *hóté* [hó té]. It is also problematic in some cases whether a word that is polymorphemic in the original language will have to be conceived in Burmese as polymorphemic or rather as a monomorphemic unit. Besides, Burmese is undergoing a period of rapid terminological expansion and many foreign borrowings are as yet unstabilized in the language. In these cases it is often impossible for the lexicographer to be precise in cases where obscurity is the rule in real life.[53]

[53] Cf. the recent symposium in Lingua 17, 1966, 1—216, where different scholars study the word classes in different languages.

CHAPTER IV

VARIATION IN LANGUAGE

4.0 Up to now, we have been speaking about language as if it were absolutely homogeneous. But to the contrary: there is variation in language, a variation that also concerns the lexical units, a fact which the lexicographer must always take into consideration. The concrete situation varies widely from one language to the other. We shall discuss only quite generally those aspects of the pertinent problems which are most important for the lexicographer's work, to provide the broadest conceptual and terminological framework. In any case, the lexicographer must begin his work with an analysis of the language whose dictionary he is about to compile in order to see how the language is stratified and what differences there are.

DIALECTS

4.1 If we observe language very minutely, we shall see that no two persons, even if they are speakers of the same language, speak it in an absolutely identical way. There may be only trifling differences, but they are observable. They concern pronunciation, preferences in sentence construction, knowledge of lexical units, their use etc. In this sense, the linguistic system of a single speaker of a language is called his idiolect.[1]

The notion of an idiolect must not be taken two sharply, as if it were a homogenous body of speech habits, dearly distinguished from all other idiolects. Neither assumption would be true. The idiolect is not absolutely homogeneous: there is variation in it in all dimensions which we shall discuss in this chapter. The idiolect changes with time (when one is old, one has slightly different speech habits and above all a considerably different lexicon from when one is young); the idiolect comprises differences which are particular to

---

[1] The notion of the idiolect is similar to the Chomskian notion of the speaker's competence, but not identical with it, by far.

the written and spoken form of language, to the different styles etc. The most important (at least for our purpose) heterogeneity inside the idiolect consists in the fact that the speaker knows and understands more words than he really uses. This heterogeneity is frequently meant when one speaks about the active and the passive lexicon. The active lexicon comprises those lexical units which are really used in new sentences. The passive lexicon comprises, then, those lexical units which one understands but does not use. Again, the whole variation of language as we shall discuss it in this chapter is involved: one understands words that belong to other dialects, jargons, that are obsolete, etc. The notion of active and of passive lexicon can be conceived as pertaining to an idiolect only, but one can also have a broader conception of it. For example one can discern the active and the passive vocabulary of the educated urban population etc. The difference between the active and the passive lexicon is of particular importance in work with informants (cf. § 6.3.2.1): the fact that the informant is able to understand and interpret a word in a context does not guarantee that he would use it himself in a new sentence.

There are still other differences between the single idiolects which are more difficult to grasp, but which are not less important. Let us quote here a passage from the poet Mallarmé:[2]

«Je dis: une fleur! et, hors de l'oubli où ma voix relègue aucun contour, en tant que quelque chose d'autre que les calices sus, musicalement se lève, idée même et suave, l'absent de tous les bouquets.»

No doubt, the poet's description is not couched in precisely linguistic terms, but what is so beautifully described is the fact that the word used in a sentence evokes all the speaker's and hearer's accumulated experience and all his knowledge of the word, of the denotatum, and of then single things ever referred to by it if they left a trace in his memory, irrespective whether they have been pleasant, unpleasant, etc. But it stands to reason that different speakers of the same language may have different experience, different feelings, attitudes, etc. There are some important consequences of this.

When a speaker uses a word in a sentence, the word does not carry to the hearer so to say "a piece of the speaker's mind": it evokes in the hearer's mind his (the hearer's) counterpart of the speaker's idea.[3] If the evocation does

---

[2] *Avant-dire au Traité du Verba de R. Ghil*, 1885, Quoted from H. Weinrich, *Linguistik der Lüge*, Heidelberg 1966, p. 18.

[3] Cf. N. Chomsky, *Cartesian Linguistics*, New York 1966, p. 72; "... speech perception requires internal generation of a representation both of the signal and the associated semantic content"; cf. also Humboldt: "Die Menschen verstehen einander nicht dadurch, daß sie sich Zeichen der Dinge wirklich hingeben, auch nicht dadurch, daß sie sich gegenseitig bestimmen, genau und vollständig denselben Begriff hervorzubringen, sondern dadurch, daß sie gegenseitig ineinander dasselbe Glied der Kette ihrer sinnlichen Vorstellungen und inneren Begriffserzeugun-

not take place, or if what is evoked is too different, the hearer simply does not understand the speaker, or misunderstands him. But even if he understands him precisely, that is if the same lexical meaning (eventually disambiguated by the context) with the same criterial semantic features is evoked in him, there are differences which belong roughly to two types.

First, the concretization of an applied signification may very between the speaker and the hearer. For example, if somebody who likes abstract art says

"The other day, I saw a beautiful picture"

to somebody whose taste is strictly realistic, the message conveyed by the word *beautiful* as intended by the speaker will differ from what the hearer will understand. But this type is on the periphery of language and linguistics proper, and possibly beyond their boundary: the linguistically relevant designatum with its criterial properties, and generally all the criterial semantic features of beautiful are identical both for the speaker and for the hearer. If the two see an abstract picture and one of them says

"What a beautiful thing!"

while the other cannot understand how the first can say a thing like that, their misunderstanding is purely extralinguistic. As far as language and linguistics is concerned, the sentence has the same meaning for both of them.[4]

The second type of phenomena concerns the fact that different words (and even more their denotata) evoke different "feelings" (in the broadest possible sense of the word) in the speakers of a language. If this effect is rather uniform, strong, and negative, i.e. if the feeling aroused is fear and/or aversion etc., such words are sometimes avoided and euphemistic expressions are used in their stead; this is the so-called linguistic taboo. It is because of this taboo that we say that somebody is *gone* when he is *dead*, etc.[5] Similar cases are rather simple and easy to understand. Their rather uniform effect causes that they overlap with connotative values. But in other cases, the evocative power of a word varies from one speaker to another much more.

This power of different words to evoke "feelings" is used in many texts. We shall discuss an example which is very simple, because the evocational

---

gen berühren, dieselbe Taste ihres geistigen Instruments anschlagen, worauf alsdann in jedem entsprechende, nicht aber dieselben Begriffe hervorspringen" (quoted on the preceding page of *Cartesian Linguistics*).

[4] The fact that this is one of the mechanisms of linguistic (in this case semantic) change is of only m inor importance in connection with the lexicographer's work.

[5] Linguistic taboo may exercise an influence strong enough to make the usage of the euphemisms stabilized in the interpersonal system of a language. The respective non-euphemistic or taboo-words get sometimes lost.

intention and technique is rather primitive. We read in the Manhattan Telephone Directory the following sequence of firms:

Atomic Cleaners & Dyers
Atomic Dress Co.
Atomic Energy Commission
Atomic Handbag Co.
Atomic Music Co.

Obviously, only the third institution has a connection with real atomic problems. It seems that all the other firms use the attribute *atomic* only because they suppose that it will evoke in some prospective customers a positive feeling, that it will suggest that the firm is super-modern, super-effective, and what not. I would not think that there is some real semantic effect to observe here, not even semantic depletion; it would seem that the meaning of *atomic* is totally unchanged, but that the word is used here not with its usual communicative purpose but only because of its evocative power.

A good part of commercial advertising and political propaganda is operated on this principle; but some highly artistic texts, such as, for example, lyrical poetry, also use these effects, though in a less conspicuous way. Some of the affective o v e r t o n e s of different artistic texts can be traced back to this evocative phenomenon.[6]

These evocative phenomena are highly individual, because they depend on the individual sensitivity, imagination, cultural background, education, personal attitude to the respective denotatum, and similar individual factors. Since, however, they can be grouped so that there is some observably if only partially uniform effect, these phenomena overlap to some extent with connotation (cf. § 1.3.2).[7]

Both types of these rather individual phenomena just characterized are connected with lexical meaning or even interfere with it, but do not directly belong to it, or at least not to its core.[8] But it seems that even some criterial semantic features of a word may vary from one speaker, i.e. from one idiolect to another. Not all of them, of course: interpersonal understanding would be

---

[6] Cf. S. Ullmann, *The Principles of Semantics*, 2nd ed., Glasgow–Oxford 1957, p. 98f., on the emotive or sentimental overtones; ibid. a good bibliography of the subject, particularly K. O. Erdmann, *Die Bedeutung des Wortes*, 4th ed., Leipzig 1925 (Gefühlswert, Stimmungsgehalt: feeling-tone; Erdmanns' conception, however, is strongly different from that suggested in the present book; the range of the phenomena discussed is also different).

[7] C. E. Osgood — G. J. Suci — P. H. Tannenbaum, *The Measurement of Meaning*, Urbana 1957, is probably the most important and comprehensive book dealing with the evocative power of words; reports of experiments made with individual single speakers and groups of them. (Cf. also my review in Archiv Orientální 29, 1961, 325ff. on the authors' erroneous assumption that it is lexical meaning what they "measure".)

[8] The opinions of different scholars on this subject vary (cf. Ullmann, loc. cit. footnote 6).

impossible or severely hampered; but just a few of them. For example, it seems that in the idiolects of those speakers of English who do not distinguish *definitely* and *definitively*, the respective designate have lost some criteriality still present in the designata of those speakers who discern the two words without having to look them up in a prescriptive dictionary, say in Fowler's *Modern English Usage*. On the other hand, if one Czech coauthor of the present book protested against Czech *chlapec* "boy" and *hoch* "boy" being quoted above as absolute synonyms and maintained that the two words have slightly different meaning, it seems that in his idiolect the respective designata have some some additional criterial semantic features, absent in those idiolects on which the treatment of the two words in Czech dictionaries is based.

Different criteriality frequently co-varies with the speaker's education. A group of listeners (including the author of the present book) heard in a commercial announcement of the television in Urbana, Ill. (July 1969), a business firm's advertisement heralding "the six-month anniversary" of their regular fornight sales. The better Latin-educated part of the audience found the expression funny, others did not object.

In consequence of all this, we can posit a hierarchy of the criterial semantic features within a designatum: the majority of them is present in all the idiolects (i.e. in the whole language), some are present only in a group of idiolects (i.e. in a dialect or so), and some are present only in a single idiolect or in a few isolated idiolects; and all of them are surrounded by various and individually varying non-criterial components, such as the evocative effects.

But on the other hand, it would be wrong to suppose that idiolects are absolutely different; in such a case, the speakers would not understand one another. The idiolects of different speakers of the same language are largely identical, but there are differences as well.

If we observe the idiolects of speakers of the same language who have lived together since their childhood in a closed geographical area, we usually perceive (1) a basic identity of the idiolects with the idiolects of other speakers of the same language from other areas (otherwise it would not be one language), (2) some isolated features which are to be found in single idiolects only and which render them individual (otherwise they would not be separate idiolects), and (3) some features which alone or in specific groups are neither individual nor observable in the whole language, but which are typical just for that area, and are the cause that it is, within the language in question, distinguished from other similar areas. The form of language spoken in such an area is then called a dialect.[9]

---

[9] It is not necessary nor usual to specify "*geographical dialects*", but it is possible; the specification has value when some authors speak about "*social dialects*", i.e. slangs, argots, cultivated languages, restricted languages, etc., so that there is a contradistinction.

In some areas, the boundaries between languages are rather sharp (at least linguistically, even if there is a geographical zone where the two languages are interspersed) and it is self-evident to which of the neighbouring languages a concrete dialect belongs. In other areas, however, the local dialect belongs. In other areas, however, the local dialects are rather similar but some of them are considered variants of one of the neighbouring languages, and some as variants of the other. This situation, which exists, e.g., on the linguistic frontier between (Low) German and Dutch, can arise only if the languages involved are related and very similar. The delimitation of one of the languages against the other has, thus roots in the whole tradition, both political and cultural, and such factors must also be taken into consideration also synchronically and in the future perspective.

Languages differ as to degree of dialectal variation. Some of them, like Russian, show only a small degree of dialectal variation and the existing dialects (only insignificantly differring one from the other) are spread over vast areas. Other languages, like German, have many dialects. Sometimes even the dialects themselves show regional, local and rather insignificant variations in very small areas such a local variety of a dialect is usually called a patois.

Languages differ also as to the sharpness of the boundaries of the single dialects or the single patois. Usually there is a broader or narrower territory between two dialects or patois in which the two dialectal areas overlap, with different phenomena of interference of one form on the other

The very existence of dialects is obviously connected above all with the stability of the speaker's life within a clearly circumscribed region and with the relative rarity of contacts with the speakers of other dialects. No wonder, therefore, that in the big, rich cities which attract people from different and distant regions, there is a greater occasion for speakers of a dialect to accept some features of another dialect.[10] The inhabitants of such towns are also usually more clearly distributed in different social groups. In addition, mainly in modern times, the influence of school education one of the results of which is also, as we shall see later, the levelling out of linguistic differences, is more strongly felt in cities than in rural districts. For all these and similar reasons, more or less pure dialects tend to be, in our epoch (as in some others) a rural phenomenon as opposed to urban speech.[11]

[10] The opportunity to acquire the linguistic features of another dialect are also greater in nomadic tribes than among the rural population (cf. the situation in Arabic, as suggested by Petráček).

[11] It is only a matter of terminology if we decide to call the variety of a language spoken in a big city (as distinct from rural speech) a dialect, too. Every variety of language can be called a *dialect*: this is the prevailing American terminology.

THE STANDARD NATIONAL LANGUAGE

4.2 In the history of different languages, one can observe the frequent pheno-menon that for various reasons, mainly of a cultural, political, and economic nature, one of the dialects of a language gains preponderance over the other dialects, or a good part of them. Such a situation has usually one of the follow-ing two results. The first possibility is that the other dialects stop being used and die out. The classical example for this is Greece where in the last centuries B.C., practically all the dialects (with negligible exceptions like the Tsakonian of our day) have died out and only a modified form of the Attic dialect has been used. Sometimes, this language diverges again and new, secondary dialects develop. Probably more frequent is the second possibility: the single dialects or at least a good many of them, do not disappear; they continue to be used, if sometimes only in a reduced scale, but the preponderant dialect develops into the standard national language.[12] This standard national language usually has some variants. The most basic of them are:

(1) The literary language and the cultivated spoken language. This is the language of literature and of official use, written and spoken. We put the two varieties into one category because they are extremely similar. Normally, however they are not absolutely identical. The usual situation is that the cultivated language, as used, e.g. in official public speeches, in edu-cation etc., avoids some more complicated grammatical structures or forms which are perfectly possible in the literary language, and sometimes also avoids all elements, lexical and grammatical, which could be considered obsolete or "bookish", though they are tolerated or even preferred in the writ-ten language.

(2) Colloquial language is the form of the standard national language which is spoken in private and in semi-official situations (business etc.) by people of average and higher education. Both the literary and the spoken culti-vated language and the colloquial language are also used, in their proper spheres, in the areas where there are dialects. The typical situation in countries with compulsory school education is that some knowledge of the standard national language is constantly spread by the schools; this development is fostered by the apparatus of the state administration, by commerce and other interdialectal contacts, and especially by the modern means of mass communi-cation, namely books, newspapers, radio, cinema and television. As a result, a good part or even the majority of speakers of dialects also know the standard

---

[12] There are possible terminological differences. Some linguists term this a *dialect*, too, and reserve the term *language* only for the sum of all the varieties.

national language,[13] at least in some form and to some extent, and are ready to use it in a suitable out-of-the-daily-life situation. Sometimes isolated dialectal features do penetrate into the standard language; they are called dialectisms. Usually only few of them can be observed in the literary language if it is well stabilized and has some tradition,[14] slightly more in the spoken cultivated, and substantially more in the colloquial language. The parallel term colloquialism designates those elements of the colloquial language which are typical for it and which do not occur in the litterary language, at least not as normal means of cummunication, without a stylistic effect.

Sometimes there are observable differences within the standard national language as used in different regions, but they cannot be regarded as dialectisms, because they belong to the standard national language, and they are not foreign elements in it; such elements are frequently called regionalisms. Petráček reports Arabic *mudīrīyatun* "province" in Egypt, *muḥāfaẓatun* "province" in Syria, and *mutaṣarrifīyatun* "province" in Iraq.

(3) Folk speech is the form of standard national language spoken by people of minimum or no education who do not, however, speak a (rural) dialect. Sometimes there are differences between this folk speech as spoken in the original area of the dialect from which the national language developed and as spoken in those areas, mostly in big cities, in which it has ousted the original local dialects. In some linguistic areas, the difference between the colloquial language and the folk speech is minimal or there is no difference at all. The term colloquialism (cf. above) is sometimes used in reference to typical elements of the folk speech. Other scholars use for them the term vulgarism, particularly when the denotatum itself is of an obscene or similar character.

These terms try to give only that basic conceptual framework for an analysis of the situation obtaining in a specific language.[15] The actual situations differ vastly one from the other, in different languages not only in the degrees of difference between the levels of a language, but also in the strength of local dialects and the number of dialectisms (which frequently differ from speaker to speaker and from author to author, is the standard national language is not well stabilized) in the standard national language. There are also other possible situations. Sometimes it is necessary to accept more levels of language than described here, sometimes the local dialects develop a written form of

[13] If we decide to use another terminology in which the standard national language would be one of the dialects (cf. footnote 11), this sentence would have to be re-worded, but its meaning would remain unimpaired.

[14] But it is not a true dialectism if an author tries to give local flavour to history by using dialectical words when describing the province; or even when he uses them in direct speeches of local persons in novels, etc.

[15] The preceding classification is highly dependent on Gleason, *Introduction* 405.

their own, and sometimes there is not one single form of the standard national language but more varities of it, owing to geographical, cultural or other reasons.[16]

STYLES AND RESTRICTED LANGUAGES etc.; DIGLOSSIA

4.3 These variations are in language of very different types. Practically omnipresent is the variation of style. When communicating in the standard national language, and also when speaking any dialect, a speaker has the possibility to choose among different levels of style, from the stiffest to the most careless ones. But as the use of dialects is functionally restricted, dialectal texts (spoken or written) in our times usually show a smaller degree of stylistic variation. The standard national language is functionally much more diversified, and the urban population is much more stratified that the rural one. All this diversity has a correspondence in linguistic diversity. We can discern different social dialects according to the different social groups for whose speech they are typical. We can discern different functional languages according to their function: for example scientific language, poetic language etc. We can discern different restricted languages: hunters' language, miners' language, soldiers language, etc. The term "language" in the last group of terms is used only because it is traditional; in reality, it is a misnomer because all these "functional languages" and "restricted languages" are only variants of a particular language.[17]

The term "restricted" language has a double justification. These "languages" are restricted to small parts of the whole society. And then, only restricted parts of the whole lexicon belong to them; for example, only things which are related to hunting have special terms in the restricted language of hunters.

---

[16] L. Bloomfield, *Language* (revised ed., London 1935), p. 52, discerns the following stratification of language: (1) literary standard (used in the most formal discourse and in writing, e.g. Eng. *I have none*): (2) colloquial standard (the speech of what Bloomfield calls "the privileged class", e.g. Eng. *I havn't any, I havn't got any*); (3) provincial standard (the same English examples, but with a different intonation); (4) sub-standard (e.g. Eng. *I ain't got none*); (5) local dialect (e.g. Eng. *I hae nane*).

[17] Extreme cases of such restricted languages are the different codes by which ordinary language is artificially changed or reduced, usually in private, intimate conversations, or in presence of foreigners etc. Minn Latt reports the *Săkaleim code*, nationally known in Burma and used in familiar discourses. Its basic principle is to interchange vowels of two tonic syllables, while keeping the initial consonants intact; e.g. *ălis θout* gives *ăloupθis* "to steal; to snatch something secretly" (verbatim "new job"). The whistled languages reported by Pike from Mexico (only the suprasegmental tones are whistled in clandestine communications) are probably the representative of the strongest reduction of ordinary language.

It seems to belong to a speaker's command of languages that he is able to switch from the general lexicon to that of a restricted language (within the range of his knowledge) just as he is able, in the range of his ability again, to use different styles, etc.[18]

Restricted languages of the debased classes of society are frequently called jargons; for example, criminals' jargon etc. The term slang is frequently used in reference to the other restricted languages, particularly when they are spoken; for instance, the slang of the hunters, the slang of the students, etc. But the term "slang" is used also in reference to the general colloquial language, particularly if it is really full of colloquialisms; in this sense, one can speak, for example, about "the slang of the London society in the thirties". No need to say that the two acceptations have a broad area of overlapping. It is rather typical for the slang (particularly in the second sense of the term) that it is subject to quick changes caused by the occasional and ephemeral character of a good number of its lexical elements.

The lexicographer should know all the specificities of the variants mentioned above as well as possible; otherwise it might happen that he could regard as a lexical unit of the general, standard national language a lexical unit specifically and typically used only in one of the restricted varieties. The results of such a basic mistake can range from a purely mistaken misrepresentation of the data in a monolingual descriptive dictionary to a bad influence upon the user of a bilingual dictionary. This person would then speak or write a strange personal variant of the target language, he would use a strange mixture of obsolete and poetic words with some quasi-funny expressions from slang, and perhaps with some vulgar words added. Although it is by no means an easy matter to indicate the lexical specifities of all these variants, it is one of the fundamental tasks of the lexicographer.

Particularly difficult is a situation which is frequently called diglossia. By this term we designate with Ferguson a situation found in some languages where the more formal forms of speech differ vastly from the less formal ones, sometimes to the degree of a low mutual intelligibility. The boundary usually goes between the literary and the spoken cultivated language, on one side, and the colloquial language on the other. (In this case, the colloquial language usually varies considerably from one dialectal area to another; sometimes, the colloquial language has another dialectal origin than the written and culti-

---

[18] Cf. D. DeCamp, *Toward a Generative Analysis of a Post-Creole Speech-Continuum* (in: Conference on Pidginization and Creolization of Language, 1968, forthcoming) on the speaker's ability to choose from a continuum of possible varieties, various forms of language. In this connection, cf. E. Hamp, *Acculturation as a Late Rule* (in: Papers from the 4th Regional Meeting, Chicago Linguistic Society, Chicago 1968, p. 103ff.) who finds that some accultured forms (in the sphere of phonetics) can be handled by additional rules, superimposed on those that govern language in general.

vated spoken one; and sometimes, the standard national language does not have a colloquial form and only dialects are spoken at this level). But there are also cases where the written language is so archaic that even the cultivated spoken language is found to be considerably different.

Usually, this situation can be observed in those languages in which the literary language enjoys an influential and long tradition, so that it tends to be highly archaic, or where the local dialects are very different, or both. Classical examples of diglossia can be observed in modern Greek and in Arabic, but it is a rather general phenomenon in many languages of Asia which enjoy an old tradition and possess and old reputed literature. Minn Latt reports, for example, that a division between classical and Modern Burmese exists today. Classical Burmese literature has a continuity of tradition going back many centuries, but texts in Modern Burmese began to appear only in the 18th century. At present, the two "languages" may be used separately or mixed (Modern in dialogues and Classical in other parts of a literary work). Writers actually tend more to old fashions and archaisms when writing in Classical Burmese, whereas in Modern Burmese their styles become more in accord with the living language of the people. Classical Burmese is never spoken even on the most formal and auspicious of occasions.

THE DEVELOPMENT OF A STANDARD NATIONAL LANGUAGE

4.4 Another difficult situation is found in those cases where there is no standard national language, or even no written form of a dialect with an important literature, but where there are only spoken forms of several dialects. There are different developments possible in such a situation. If the area is very large and has several cultural and political centers, some of the dialects can develop into different languages. This is, broadly speaking, the situation of the Romance languages which were at one time dialects of (Vulgar) Latin, but developed into different languages in the early Middle Ages.[19] If the area is not too large, and especially if there is a single center of culture, or politics, or some other preponderance, the dialect spoken in this center (and eventually later used in its literature) can develop into the standard national language. In Europe, but also in many other areas, this seems to be the normal, most frequent development in the last millenary. This development is without any doubt connected with the emergence of centralized European states. But the example of Italy where the dialect of Tuscany (above all as the basis of the literary work of Dante and the authors of the XIVth century) gained absolute

---

[19] The real development was more complicated than this, but probably no concrete phenomenon is as simple and as homogeneous as the generalized conceptual discussion of theory.

preponderance without a political or economic preponderance in this area and even without a single unified state being established in the country (the unification of Italy came centuries later) shows that the correlation between linguistic and non-linguistic developments is not one-to-one. In any case, developments of this type have taken place in many languages of our time and it is to be expected that they will take place or even that they will be put into operation by decision also in the future.

In the majority of cases it happens that during the development of a dialect into a national language some features of other dialects find their way into the standard national language. If they are of considerable numerical importance, we call the resultant language a koiné. Thus, it was basically the Attic dialect of Greek which ousted the other dialects (cf. above) but as there are numerous elements of the Ionic dialect in the language finally adopted through-out the greatest part of Greek territory, we usually say that it was the Greek koiné. This term is sometimes also applied when the national language deve-lops not from one overwhelmingly preponderant dialect, but from different dialects merged into one form of speech. This development is, in our day, sometimes put into operation by decision; if this is the case, then the resultant form of speech is usually called a union-language.

One case of the development of a union language is well described by Gleason:[20] "the Shona group of dialects occupies a large part of Rhodesia and adjacent Portuguese Africa. There are six reasonably and clearly marked groups of dialects, each showing appreciable local variation. Five of these were reduced to writing by missionaries, and in four of them the whole New Testament was translated. An appreciable amount of publications was done in each. However, all the Shona dialects together are spoken by only little over a million people. This is hardly enough to support and adequate output of printed materials in five different languages. Accordingly, in 1929 a com-mittee began work on a survey of the language problems in the area. As a result of their work, a new written language known as Union Shona was designed. It has since largely replaced the older written forms and is now quite generally used throughout five or six dialect groups. The committee decided that it was impractical, for reasons as much social and geographical as linguistic, to bring the Kalanga dialects into the scheme. A unified grammar was set up, based largely on the Karanga and Zezuru dialects. The vocabulary was drawn largely from four of the dialects, and it was agreed to discourage the intro-duction of new words from others. A new and improved system of spelling

---

[20] *Introduction* 429f. The material correctness of some details in the following discussion is doubted by Zima; we use the whole passage, nevertheless, for its methodological clarity to which the eventual trifling modifications are irrelevant. — Cf. V. Tauli, *Introduction to a Theory of Language Planning*, Uppsala 1968, p. 165 ff. (section "New national and literary languages": theoretical discussion of the pertinent problems).

was introduced... Since that time Union Shona has become well established. There has, of course, been opposition, both in general and to specific features, but it has not been serious. Numerous publications have appeared, including the entire Bible. The scheme is proving its value in many ways. Not only has the course of development been greatly speeded, but a natural group of dialects has been selected for inclusion. In time the artificiality of the design will become less obtrusive and a highly satisfactory written language may be expected to develop. Continuing his discussion, Gleason also describes a less sucessful attempt at a similar solution: "Such union languages are not always equally successful. Union Ibo for a large and linguistically very diverse area in southern Nigeria had a very different outcome, and has been largely abandoned. The failure seemed to be due to poor selection of the features to be included, and to inadequate attention to the social and political differences in the area. That is to say, there was inadequate field investigation both in linguistics and anthropology on which to base the proposal".

To develop the written standard national form of a language which does not yet possess it yet and which shows little or no dialectal variation is a task which is less complicated, because there is not the necessity of choosing among the different possibilities, but it is also very difficult. Not infrequently, specific difficulties are caused by the state of the respective society which does not yet need the functions performed by the written language.[21]

Languages which do not have standard national forms are frequently called vernaculars. Languages the standard national forms of which are in the process of being developed or the standard national forms of which have been developed only recently so that there is yet much uncertainty, vacillation, and change, can be called unstabilized or not yet stabilized languages.[22]

LINGUISTIC CHANGE

4.5 The preceding discussion of the development of the standard national form brings us to the necessity of mentioning also the variation of language in the temporal dimension.

The fact that each language changes constantly is so well known that we shall not discuss it in detail. We shall mention only those things which are directly important for the lexicographer.

[21] Cf. Garvin's experience with Ponape, footnote 36 and the passage to which it refers.

[22] If this term is used, it is necessary to realize that it is, at least in the present book, just the (modern, contemporary) standard national form which is meant. The term implies nothing else; the language in question may have a fully stabilized classical form, or an archaic literary language still used which is fully stabilized, etc., but that does not matter. Understood in this way, the term obviously has no pejorative connotation.

If the language in question has a longer history, it will be possible to discern different periods in it. Very frequently, one of such periods is called Old, or Classical or Ancient, another Modern, or Contemporary, and so on. Each language has its own periodization according to the facts of its history. That the lexicographer must know this periodization and decide, when planning the dictionary, which periods he intends to cover is so obvious that to state it is a platitude. But the lexicographer must know the development of "his" language in great detail, at least as far as those periods which he intends to cover are concerned. One of the important circumstances is that boundaries between the single periods are not sharp. For instance, the advent of a Modern, or Contemporary period is usually heralded, still within the realm of the preceding, older epoch, by some significant changes in the lexicon of a writer or of a group of writers. And on the contrary, there may be writers or whole literary genres whose lexicon seems to belong more or less to the preceding period.

Since the linguist is concerned with the lexicon of a given language, it is above all the changes of the lexical units which interest him most. Each and every property of any lexical unit may change. If the planned dictionary is a historical one, many of these changes should be registered and indicated by the lexicographer, if they can be perceived with a sufficient certainty. One should, for instance, register the eventual changes in the paradigm, changes in the combinatory power of the lexical unit, etc. The authors of historical dictionaries should also indicate, if necessary, that a lexical unit ceased being used or at least is not attested, after a certain period; an explicit statement to this purpose is always better than mere silence. This principle should be observed both if a lexical unit ceased being used at all ("is lost") and if only one or some of its senses are not used any longer.

If the dictionary prepared is a historical one, the lexicographer must give great attention to the semantic change (§ 1.4.4) and must try to present, in each entry, the history of semantic changes of each lexical unit included in the dictionary.

But even in an absolutely synchronic dictionary (and we shall see in § 5.2.2 that this term itself is highly relative, the lexicographer is concerned with historical considerations, and specifically with semantic change. First, we have seen (§ 1.4.4) that knowledge of historical development is not indispensable but helps one to understand the multiple meaning of a lexical unit and similar questions. Second, the lexicographer is constantly concerned with the phenomena caused by actual applications of the lexical units, with vacillation of usage etc. (cf. above § 1.4). These phenomena can be observed "at the same time" and their study is, therefore, a synchronic one. (Unless one is prepared to accept the position that each and every smallest change, such as the appearance of an occasional expression, implies a change of the system of language and that, therefore, their observation belongs to the historical study of language; cf. § 5.2.2 again). The dynamism of these different applications and vacillations implies, however, the germ of development, a historical or diachronic study in itself, because this dynamism is probably the main mechanism or at least one of the main mechanisms of semantic change: the stabilization of an originally abnormal application causes a change in the meaning and the sum of such changes is perceivable in the whole system of language. In other words, the boundaries between the synchronic and the diachronic historical study are, in this sphere of the lexicographer's work, more fluid than an orthodox believer in sharp differentiation of the two approaches would be prepared to believe.

Three terms connected with the historical study of lexicon are of an outstanding importance for the lexicographer, viz. the archaism, the obsolete word and the neologism.

Archaic and obsolete lexical units are used in the language described in the dictionary only exceptionally, they were formerly used more frequently. Two types of situation should be discerned. In the first type of situations the denotatum itself lost frequency in the extralinguistic world and therefore, the respective lexical unit is no longer a part of the active lexicon. Harnesses and halberds are rare objects in our days; therefore, the words *harness* and *halberd* can be considered archaisms, at least in the general language. But if need be, these words can be used without any connotation. Lexical units of this type can be called archaisms (in a restricted, specific sense of the term); were I not afraid of terminological innovations, I would, however, prefer to call them time-bound words.[23]

The other type of situation can be illustrated by the following example. There are young, unmarried women among the speakers of English in our days just as there have been since times immemorial; but not English speaker of our days will use the word *maid* in reference to one of them (unless he intends to produce some effect of style and connotation), though some decades ago such an application would have been quite normal. Such a word can be called obsolete.[24]

Let us mention here that archaisms and (less frequently) obsolete words are sometimes "revivified" and begin to be used frequently again, usually but not necessarily in a new sense: cf. Eng. *turnpike road* "toll highway" (archaic until the construction of divided highways without level crossings in America).

---

[23] Cf. The "*culture-bound words*", § 7.1. These "*time-bound words*" are a subspecies of the "culture-bound" ones: after all, we have a difference of culture before us.

[24] A good, sharp distinction of the two types in R. A. Budagov, *Vvedenie v nauku o jazyke*, Moskva 1965, p. 99. — Both types are very frequently called *archaisms*, or, alternatively, *obsolete words*. The time-bound words are sometimes called *historical words*. I am unable to decide which hyperonym of the two categories to choose.

On the other hand, neologism is a term which can refer to any new lexical unit,[25] the novelty of which is still felt. We have seen above (§. 1.4) that there is a broad range of possibilities between a hapax, a mere occasionality, and the full stabilization of a lexical unit in the system of language. Any expression which can be classified on this scale, with the exception of the extreme value (full stabilization) can be called a neologism.[26]

Considered from the point of view of another dimension, it follows from our above discussions that there are neologisms

(1) among combinations of words (§ 3.2.3),

(2) among compounds (§ 2.3),

(3) among derived words (§ 2.2),

(4) and neologisms constituted by new applications of words (§ 1.4.2.3).

We could add, for the sake of completeness, that there are also neologisms constituted by

(5) absolutely new words which are coined not by one of the processes just mentioned, but by more or less pure invention. E.g., when the word *robot* "automatic apparatus or machine" was invented (by K. Čapek, 1920), it certainly was a neologism until it acquired the status of a fully stabilized lexical unit.

All these neologisms can be, and very frequently are, constructed out of elements (morphemes and/or words) which exist in the respective language.[27] There is, however, a vast area of interference with foreign languages. Neologisms of one language can be formed under the influence of another language or by the use of its elements. The whole area is so relatively well known that it is hardly worth-while to present yet another discussion of it. It may suffice to say that we can discern:

(a) The direct transfer of a foreign element, usually a word. The form of such a borrowed word (or loan-word) can attain different degrees of adaptation to the phonemic and morphological structure of the language into which it has been accepted, but it can also remain unadapted. The status of a loan-word in the lexicon of the "new" language can also differ vastly, from a pure and ephemeral occasionality to full stabilization. In the majority of cases, a fully stabilized loan-word is also fully adapted in its form, but this is

[25] Incidentally, the term is sometimes used in a still broader way, so as to cover also innovations in syntax; but we are concerned only with the lexicon.

[26] Different scholars use the term with different degrees of restriction.

[27] Category (5) is exceptional and transitional, because these words are not really formed but rather freely created and because if there is any element by which the creators have been inspired, it may be both native (as *robot*: inspired by Czech *robota* "hard work") or foreign (as Eng. *gas*: inspired probably by Greek *kháos* "chaos"). But this category is so rare and exceptional that it is not worth-while to discuss it apart from the usual categories.

12*

only a frequent not a necessary coincidence. Such a loan-word, which is not felt as a foreign element any more, can be called a domesticated loan-word (or even an etymological loan-word if it was borrowed long ago and it is so strongly adapted that its origin is revealed only by etymology). On the contrary, a nonadapted or only slightly adapted loan-word which is still clearly marked as a foreign element and is felt as such can be called a foreign word.

New lexical units can be formed from such a borrowed element, either by derivation, or by composition, or by combination of words (and by the transitional types of these processes). Not unfrequently, compounds or multiword lexical units (but only very seldom derivations) which consist of elements the different origin of which is obvious are called hybrids. A compound word like Czech *uhlohydrát* "carbohydrate" can be called hybrid, because its first part is of native, its second part of foreign origin. Sometimes, the notion of the hybrid is so extensive that it is not based on the difference *native*::*foreign*, but on the difference of any two languages; e.g., the Eng. adjective *monolingual* (as in *monolingual dictionary*) can be called hybrid, because its first part is of Greek, its second part of Latin origin.[28]

(c) A new derivation, a new compound, or a new combination of words (or any transitional type) can be created out of native morphemes and/or words, but by a more or less precise imitation of the equivalent lexical unit in another language. This phenomenon is called loan-translation.[29] The degree of imitation of the foreign language may differ vastly. On one end of the scale, we have absolutely precise loan-translations: e.g., Russ. *utkonos* "platypus" is a compound the parts of which are *utka* "duck" and *nos* "nose" and Ossetic *babyzvyndz* "platypus" (*babyz* "duck" + *ſyndz* "nose") is an exact loan translation of it. But there are also more free loan translations (e.g. Russ. *zabastovka* "strike" derived from *basta* "stop, that'll do, that's enough": Ossetic *kwysturäd* "strike" derived from and compound of *kwyst* "work" + *uromyn* "to stop, to hamper"). Sometimes it is difficult or impossible to decide whether we have to deal with a case of a very free loan-translation or whether the neologism was created independently.

(d) Still another type of neologism can be seen in the phenomenon that the meaning of a native word is changed by the imitation of its equivalent in the foreign language. E.g. Oss. *älxync* "knot" is equivalent to Russ. *uzel* "knot". Since this latter has developed a special sense "(railway) junction", the Ossetic word developed the same sense, too. This phenomenon can be called imitative

---

[28] For examples of hybrid multiword lexical units, see Z. Novotná, *Contributions to the Study of Loan-Words and Hybrid Words in Modern Chinese* (in: Archiv Orientální 35, 1967, 613ff.; with the bibliography of the subject).

[29] In French (and sometimes also in English), a lexical unit coined by loan translation is called a calque.

semantic change.[30] Again, the degree of precision of the imitation varies considerably.

Unless he is preparing an etymological dictionary, or a dictionary with a strong historical and etymological interest, the lexicographer ist not too much interested in the problem of the origin of the lexical units. For him, the dimension *stabilized* : : *non-stabilized* is much more important that the dimension *of native origin* : : *of foreign origin*. These foreign or foreign-inspired neologisms are, however, a special source of trouble, above all if its is necessary to fill up considerable onomasiological gaps in the language one is dealing with and/or if there is a strong puristic movement in the respective community.

If the speakers of a language, living in a cultural setting in which modern civilization (including science, technology commerce, administration etc.) is unknown or not accepted come at once into contact with it, or even if they decide or are forced to accept it, the language in question will lack many expressions necessary for the new needs.[31] Very probably, such a language will lack the scientific terminology, the technical terminology, etc. Since it is onomasiology which studies such coherent groups of expressions, we can call such considerable areas of lack the onomasiological gaps.

The necessity of filling up the onomasiological gaps[31a] usually leads to the creation of a vast number of neologisms of different types which vary both in the dimension of form (above, 1—5) and in the dimension of provenience (above, a—d). Sometimes the task of filling up the onomasiological gaps, or some of them, is solved by some official decision: an official body either prepares the necessary neologisms or has them prepared by linguists or a joint committee of linguists and specialists of the respective field, and introduces them into use by its own authority. For example, when the Czechoslovak Republic was founded in 1918 and Czech was introduced as the official language of the army after some centuries of exclusive use of German in this sphere, it was necessary to create in the above way the whole military terminology, till then lacking in Czech. A proceeding like this cannot automatically guarantee that the "invented" terms will be the best possible ones, in each single case; but it has the great advantage that the terminological neologisms chosen usually become quickly stabilized. In a similar way, different institutions (Academies, Language Boards, etc.) in different countries take care of these

[30] This phenomenon is sometimes called semantic borrowing (Ullmann; from German *Bedeutungsentlehnung*, Wellender); Wellender's conception is, however, narrower than the one advocated here. Some scholars consider this imitative semantic change a subcategory of loan translation; both of them taken together are sometimes called *loan-shifts* (Haugen).

[31] It would be easy to re-word the statement so that it would cover not only the modern situations. For obvious reasons, however, these modern situations seem to be much more difficult and the extent of the onomasiological gaps considerably greater.

[31a] Cf. V. Tauli, *Introduction to a Theory of Language Planning*, Uppsala 1968, o. 120f. (section "Vocabulary planning tactics").

problems; very frequently, the institution which takes care of terminology is identical with or closely related to the institution concerned norms in the sphere of orthography. But it would be unwarranted to except that the foundation of such an institution must automatically lead to a quick and successful creation and stabilization of terminology. The Ministry of Defence can introduce the new terminology into the whole army by an order; but the authority of the different Language Boards, Terminological Committees, etc., can command different degrees of respect. It is inevitable that a neologism, even a neologism which is coined according to the productive tendencies of the respective language (we call such a neologism **organic**) must strike the users, at the beginning, as unusual. And we have seen above (categories 1—5 and a—d) how many theoretical ways of new coinage of neologisms there are: the practical possibilities in a concrete case are even more numerous, because the neologism needed can be coined, within the same category, from different constituent parts. Therefore, different neologisms of synonymous meaning can be and are coined by different speakers and authors according to their preference, knowledge, and ability. The normal situation, in consequence of these reasons, is that when the onomasiological gaps are being filled, different **competing or synonymic neologisms** are coined in order to designate the same segment of the extralinguistic world, and are thus synonymous.

The phenomenon is so frequent and so well-known that one example may suffice: Petráček reports from Arabic the following synonymic expressions all of which designate the storage battery: *ǧāmiᶜatun, maǧmūᶜtun, ǧamma-ᶜun, muǧammiᶜun, mudachchiratun, mirkamun.*

Another source of synonymic neologisms is the borrowing of two words of identical meaning from two different languages. E.g., Zima reports from Hausa *gwamnatìi* (from Eng. *government*) and *gouhernamà* (from French *gouvernement*) "government"; cf. also Pshtu *sāyins* (from English) : : *siyāns* (from French) "science".[32]

Different synonymic neologisms can come into existence also by different adaptations of the same borrowed word. All this causes that these competing and unnecessary synonyms are sometimes onerously abundant. As an extreme but not atypical example, I quote from the foreword to an English-Irish Dictionary:[33]

"The prefix *hydro-* was variously Gaelicized as follows (all examples are from text-books or examination papers): *hydro-, hidro- hiodro-, hudro-, íor-, íodhro-, -udar, údro-, udra-, uidr-.* Apart from these, use was made of native prefixes, e.g., *dobhar-, bual-, uisce-, fliucht-, leacht-.* "*Telescope*" was variously rendered: *cianarcán, cianamharcan, ciannarcán, ciandarcán, ciandearcán,*

---

[32] O. L. Chavarria-Aguilar — H. Penzl, PL 244.

[33] T. de Bhaldraithe, *English-Irish Dictionary*, Baile Átha Cliath 1959, p. V., footnote 3.

cianradharcan, ciandracan, ƒadradharcan, ƒadamhrcán, ƒaidearcán, radharc-
ghloine, súilghloine, súil-ƒhiodán, gloine ƒadradhairc, gloine ƒhéachaint, telescóp,
tealoscóp, teileascóp.''

Obviously, such a number of synonyms serves no real purpose and the
majority of them is doomed to be forgotten. (For example, the dictionary
just quoted chooses only one of the synonymic neologisms, viz. *teileascóp*,
which is presented among the entries.) But until the use is stabilized, a considerable vacillation, or fluctuation can be observed; this is one of the reasons
why such languages are called unstabilized. This term does not imply
anything derogatory. Nor does it imply that the language in question is
necessarily one without tradition. For example, Burmese has a long history
and tradition, but its modern form is unstabilized in this sense of the word.

When planning a dictionary of a not yet stabilized language, the lexicographer must make up his mind which policy he will follow. If his dictionary
is to be primarily used in a registrative and descriptive manner in order to
understand the existing texts, he will have to list all, or at least the most
frequently used synonymic neologisms. On the other hand, if the lexicographer
intends to exert a greater normative influence by attempting to help to
stabilize the (immediately future) usage, he will have to choose among the
synonymic neologisms. The single choices in particular concrete cases should
be governed by an identical, or at least coherent general policy; but there will
always be exceptions. For example, even if a general policy is formulated
according to which loan-translations are preferred to borrowing, there will
always be cases in which loan-words will be adapted and domesticated. Unless
he has good reasons to expect that his dictionary will enjoy high normative
authority on its own strength, the lexicographer will be well advised to enter
upon the normative activity only in cooperation with the proper normative
institutions (if there are any), such as the ministry of education, the different
language boards etc. But in any case, the problems connected with the terminological neologisms are very thorny, and it is a very frequent phenomenon that
use stabilizes other expressions than those approved of by the normative
bodies.

Different languages and above all different language communities have
different attitudes toward particular types of neologisms. The most neuralgic
point is usually the loan-words. In each known language there are loan-words.
But if there are many neologisms of foreign origin, the linguistic community
(or at least the normative authorities) sometimes react against them and try
to coin other neologisms in their stead. Since the usual situation is that many
of them must be coined at a rather rapid pace, the usual solution is that loan-
words are ousted by loan-translations: instead of Germ. *Telephon* (loan-word,
composed of parts which mean "far, distant" and "voice") the approximative
loan-translation *Fernsprecher* ("far, distant" + "instrument for speaking") is

introduced. A strong wave of such a tendency to expel the foreign elements is usually called purism.[34]

Purism is a frequent phenomenon and there are numerous types of it. It was probably petty purism when instead of the international expression *theatre* (Germ. *Theater* etc.; derived from *Greek theân* "to look"), the Czech loan-translation *divadlo* (derived from *dívati se* "to look") has been introduced. Such petty purism is especially irritating if its potential victims are loan-words which are known in many languages. For example, many scientific and technical terms are formed from Greek and Latin bases and have a very similar form in different languages, e.g., *telephone*, *television*, etc. Such terms are frequently called internationalisms; they should not be the target of puristic tendencies.

On the other hand, it was probably quite a legitimate purism if in the situation mentioned above, a Czech military terminology was coined, instead of the eventually possible introduction into official terminology of foreign words necessarily existing in the soldiers' daily jargon.

Up to now, we have discussed only the most general species of purism, which is concerned with foreign elements; we could call this species interlingual purism. The other species, the intralingual purism, is concerned not with foreign elements, but with elements which, though not foreign, are considered alien to the norm of "good" language. This type of purism is usually of the "petty" type; it develops generally in languages with observable diglossia and tries to conserve the more archaic form.

A borderline type of what we call "intralingual purism" and "interlingual purism" could be termed "anti-calque purism" which tries to abolish those expressions which are coined too closely on the model of (or, particularly, by the "translation" of) the equivalent expressions of another language. For example, the equivalent of German *handeln* "to act" is Czech *jednati* "to act". The Czech expression *jedná se o* (verbatim "it acts about" = "the matter, question is") is undoubtedly a word-for-word translation of the German expression *es handelt sich um* (verbatim "it acts about" = "the matter, question is") and can be considered an unnecessary calque, the more so that there is the original Czech expression *jde o* (verbatim "it goes about" = "the matter, the question is"). This type of purism in not always illegitimate, particularly if there is a flood of such calques and if they are not functionally necessary; but this anti-calque purism very frequently degenerates into the petty type which can, then, be cantankerous if it is combined with strong nationalism, and ridiculous if it lacks a really deep knowledge of the purist's own language, of its history and derivational possibilities.

---

[34] Purism, i.e. attempts to oust loan-words by other expressions, usually by loan-translations, is a frequent phenomenon. The other tendency, i.e. the planned eviction of loan-translations for the benefit of loan-words, is far less frequent but not unknown.

In all respects involving normative activity, the lexicographer will try, if possible, to operate in a consensus with the other normative authorities, and he will not overestimate the probability of his success in this field: in reality, it is only use in language which decides which lexical units will be stabilized.

LEXICOGRAPHIC PRACTICE; THE NORM

4.6 It is to be expected that in the future, lexicographers will have to help in making decisions concerning the establishment of different national languages. There is no guaranteed prescription for such a decision. Obviously, preference will be given, in our day, to one of the two solutions which bring only one standard national language into existence (i.e. either the selection of a dialect or the creation of a union-language, as few unified communities of today will like the prospect of an unnecessary emergence of different standard languages when it is possible to develop one standard national language from different dialects of the same language.[35] The functions of a standard national language are well recognized by Garvin;[36] the unifying function (several dialect areas are united into a single standard-language community), the separatist function (a speech community is set off as separate from its neighbours) the prestige function and the frame-of-reference function (the prestige resulting from the possession of a standard language, and ... the function ... to serve as a frame of reference for correctness and for the perception and evaluation of poetic speech).

Quite apart from any eventual feelings which different linguistic problems may excite in different areas of the world, the communicational need of a modern society, or of a society that is developing into a modern one, suffices to make the standard national language a means of communication much more desirable than the particular dialects. Therefore, the development of a standard national form from the different dialects of a language will be considered, in the majority of cases, a highly desirable task of such a language community. If such a development is more or less planned, it is not always clear whether preference should be given to one of the dialects, or whether a merger in a union-language should be planned (A good result can never be absolutely

[35] There is no necessity to emphasize that we are speaking about different dialects of one language, and the development of one standard national form of the same language; the situation of different languages spoken in one community (as, e.g., in one state) is quite different.

[36] Garvin, *The standard language problem — problems and methods*; in: Hymes, Language in Culture and Society, p. 521 (based to a degree on Mathesius and Havránek); here also a good bibliography of "case studies", i.e. of reports on and analyses of different standard national languages. — Cf. also O. Jespersen, *Mankind, Nation and Individual from a Linguistic Point of View*, Oslo 1925, especially Chapters III and IV.

guaranteed in advance), unless the prestige of one of the dialects is quite overwhelming and in consequence of this position the respective dialect is somewhat predestined to this development.[37] Most important for the lexicographer
is that he should never try to make such a decision or put such a plan into
execution alone.[38] The task is so complicated that he must not try to solve it
without the cooperation of other linguists who will study the situation in the
field, who will evaluate the differences of the individual dialects and the
relative degree of their proximity, who will analyze the different possibilities
of combinations best suited to arrive at a homogeneous whole etc. But the
cooperation for other experts from other fields is also absolutely necessary: the
cultural and religious situation, the political forces, the trends of economic
development, the geography of the territory and many other important factors
must be taken into consideration. Otherwise it may happen, for instance, that
one will try to form a union-language from dialects spoken by people who are
basically hostile; or that one will try to develop a dialect into the national
language whereas it will be the territory of another dialect which will gain an
overwhelming economic and political importance in a few years; or that one
will make some other frustrating error. Another circumstance to be carefully
considered is the general level of the society for whose communicative purpose
the standard national form is to be developed: Garvin[39] has described a
very interesting case that shows clearly how the development of the standard
national form in itself is of only minor importance and use if the community
simply does not have those ecommunicative needs fulfilment of which is the proper
province of the standard national form.[40]

Another very delicate task is to compile a dictionary of a language with a
strong diglossia. Again, the lexicographer will have to formulate a unified
policy before beginning his work on the manuscript of the dictionary. But in
order to formulate such a policy, it will be necessary for him to consider not
only the immediate problems of the dictionary or points of interest in the lexicon,
but also to form a well-considered appraisal of the future development of the
situation, taking into consideration the whole trend of cultural development.

In both situations discussed in the preceding paragraphs, the lexicographer
will do well to understand his locus standi properly. The lexicographer's, and

[37] We do not discuss here the fact that the usual functions of the standard national language,
or at least some of them, are performed, in different areas, by a language originally foreign to
the area and country in question. An impassionate analysis of such a situation is, in such a case,
as difficult as it is necessary.

[38] These different tasks can be performed, physically, by one person who operates in more
than one capacity. They cannot, however, be solved by lexicography qua lexicography alone,
though the dictionaries are one of the main tools of standardization. At any rate, it is always
better to have more people working on tasks of this delicacy and complexity.

[39] Cf. footnote 36.

[40] Cf. also footnote 36.

generally the linguist's work can be enormously helpful in such tasks. It is, however, in the majority of cases only a help, not a creation. There are exceptions, but this statement is correct as a general rule. Lexicographers can coin new expressions, they can normalize their form and meaning, they can systematize and clarify the old ones, they can help in an endless number of such exceedingly useful and necessary tasks. The real life of a language, however, is in its use; and the definitive, full-fledged stabilization of the standard national language is brought about by its being really and extensively used in literature and in oral communications of all types.

The typical situation is that the lexicographer's work involves a language which already has a standard national form. This situation is so typical that in the majority of other cases, the lexicographer works either on the model of the typical situation or with the desire to bring it into existence. In a general way, it is usually only ethnolinguistic dictionaries and those dictionaries which intend to describe the respective language for purely scientific purposes which stand apart.

It is possible and useful to give a description and analysis of any form of language. There are admirable treatments of single idiolects, of local patois, of single dialects, argots, etc. For the lexicographer (in the usual sense of the word), however, the most important task is to handle the standard national language, either in a monolingual or in a bilingual dictionary.[41] It is no undue pedantry if he does this and if he, more than that, concentrates his task and his work around the literary and the cultivated spoken language, and around the colloquial language. This is mainly the case if the dictionary is to be a short one. The bigger the dictionary, the more elements of folk speech or of dialects can be taken into consideration. Why should this be so?

If the dictionary is not intended to be of a specifically documentary, registering character, it should be as homogenous as possible. The literary and the cultivated spoken language, and the colloquial language as well, are the most important variants of a language (in the broader sense of this word), because it is in them that the majority of the more important communications take place.[42]

This opinion does not militate against lexicographic treatment of folk speech or of dialects; on the contrary: these tasks are of immense value, irrespective of whether the results of such studies are published separately, in the form of dictionaries of the single dialects or of some groups of them, or of the folk speech, or whether they are published together with the lexicographic treatment of the standard national language. But it is necessary to understand one other thing: a dictionary which contains heterogeneous material, such as, say,

[41] More on this in the discussion of the different types of dictionaries in the following chapter.

[42] This point of view (which is strongly Prague-inspired) will be considered hingly if not irritatingly controversial by adherents of other approaches, such as the descriptivists.

the standard national language (mostly its first two levels) plus the dialects cannot be normative in the same degree as a homogeneous dictionary, even if it labels the difference in the material by marks, glosses or any other means. This is a very important consideration, primarily when the lexicographer is preparing a dictionary of a language that is beginning to develop its standard national language, because in such a case it is just the effort to establish the norm which is the focus of the lexicographer's attention.

The norm is a concept largely overlapping and partly identical with the concept of the system of language, but seen from another point of view and conceptualized for another purpose.[43]

The norm can be conceived as that part of the total possibilities offered by the system which is considered "good", i.e., functionally most adequate.[44]

This is the first difference between the norm and the system. The second difference can be stated as follows. As we have seen in the whole preceding discussion, a language cannot be conceived as a homogeneous, unique system: since there is variation in language (dialects, restricted languages, styles, etc.), there must be (partial) subsystems of these varieties within the whole system. It is possible to posit a norm for each of these subsystems, or to posit a parallel variation within the norm (with, say, subnorms or something like that), or to seek a similar solution; but it is usual to use the concept of the norm preponderantly into connection with the standard national form of language.

We know that there is a difference between the *lexicon*, i.e. the total stock of lexical units of a language, on the one hand, and the *dictionary*, i.e. the linguist's description or presentation of it, on the other; the same difference obtains between the grammatical *system of a language* on the one hand, and *grammar*, i.e. the linguist's description or codification of it, on the other. In the same way, we can posit a parallel difference between *norm*[1], i.e. an objectively existing part of the system of a language on the one hand, and *norm*[2],

---

[43] For number of lexicographers, above all Ščerba, the two concepts are more or less identical.

[44] The functional approach to the norm is partly inspired by Havránek, in: J. Vachek, Prague School Reader in Linguistics, Bloomington 1964, p. 413ff. — Cf. also *Jespersen, Mankind, Nation and Individual from a Linguistic Point of View*, Oslo 1925, Chapter V (Standards of Correctness) and VI (Correct and Good Language); B. Trnka, Časopis pro moder. filologii 13, 1927, 193ff. (here also some remarks on the broader issues of purism and on what we might call, intralingual purism": elimination of dialectisms etc.); E. Coseriu, *Sistema, norma y habla*, Montevideo 1952 (reprinted in *Teoria del lenguaje y linguistica general*, Madrid 1962). All these works are concerned with modern languages. It is important, however, to understand that the notion of the norm is applicable to (some) old languages as well. We even get from the classical authors at least partial insights into the activities which fostered the development of such standard languages as Classical Latin. Cf. G. Neumann, *Sprachnormung im klassischen Latein* (in: Sprachnorm, Sprachpflege, Sprachkritik [Jahrbuch des Instituts für deutsche Sprache 1966—67], p. 88ff.). — We do not discuss here the question how, by what mechanism, a speaker who uses more variant forms of a language switches from one variant to another, and how his knowledge is organized.

i.e. the linguist's description of it, on the other; the term *codification of the norm* is sometimes used in this latter sense.[45] The difference between *norm*[1] and *norm*[2], however, is not as sharp as that which obtains between lexicon and dictionary, because the factor of the linguist's influence (exercized in our day primarily by the prescriptive and prohibitive drill in school) seems to be much stronger in this sphere; and this is the reason why we shall not try to contradistinguish sharply the two notions in the following discussions.

It is very important how the linguist codifies the norm.

There is always a strong element of tradition in the norm and nobody can object against it, because without respecting the tradition, language would lose its communicative power too quickly, in the change of generations. But the value ot traditions should not be overestimated by those lexicographers who study the norm and give it expression in their works. The norm must change with changes in the system, otherwise texts respecting the obsolete norm will become too archaic and the whole linguistic situation will eventually develop into diglossia. Another fact of which every student of the norm should be aware is that there are more levels and many functions of language and that the norm should be "functionally adequate" not relatively to one level and one function, but alternatively according to the needs of any and all of them. The colloquial language has needs and purposes of its own, in contradistinction to say, the literary language; therefore, it would be preposterous and vain to try (as it has sometimes been done) to evict from the norm of the colloquial language everything which is not part of the norm of the written language. The interlinguistic communicative power of terminology, for example, especially in its scientific-communicative function, is a highly desirable and valuable phenomenon; therefore, international terms should not be ousted from the norm on puristic and (or nationalistic) principles. These are only a few examples which try to illustrate the functional approach to the linguistic norm.

Some descriptivist approaches, in order to avoid evaluation, are very radical in declining to accept, e.g., the term "level" in language; consequently, the concept of the norm itself is not too much to their liking. But it would seem that even the most radical adherent of such an approach will not be able to reject the functional approach. And after all, it can be and it has been observed that even the most radically egalitarian descriptivist will be very careful not to ridicule or "displace" himself by not respecting the norm of "good" English in his own statements.

But it must be remarked that the ability to decide whether an expression is "correct" or not is not restricted to speakers of languages which enjoy a long philological tradition of their own. Even in the case of a language without

---

[45] Some lexicographers (for example, Havránek, Filipec et al.) conceive the contradistionction of *norm*[1] :: *norm*[2] (i.e. *norm* :: *codification of the norm*) in a sharper way than we point the present book.

such a tradition unsophisticated speakers of it can not only decide what is "correct" and what is not, but they even seem to be able, at least very frequently, to form an opinion of their own as to which expression in their language is "good" and which is not.[46]

Another thing to be taken into consideration by the lexicographer is the constant development of language. The lexicographer must conceive the whole ramified picture of language as being in uninterrupted change. Lexical units change their meaning, their use is discontinued, new ones are either coined or borrowed and there are constant shifts in the different levels of language, to mention only a few phenomena. There are two circumstances the lexicographer should consider.

First, the lexicographer will have to know the development of "his" language. Even if he works on a dictionary which is intended to contain only the "modern", "contemporary" language, the lexicographer will have to know (if not decide) what is meant by these terms. Obviously, he cannot accept as "contemporary" only what was said or written, say, during the time necessary for the compilation of his dictionary (and, nota bene, there would be an element of time even in such a severely limited material!), because that could hardly be a sufficient basis for his work. Therefore, the notion of "contemporary" language will cover literary and oral production of a period of years or decades preceding the lexicographer's work. The length of such a period varies from one language to another, and so does the degree of difference obtaining between the older periods and the "modern", "contemporary" one.

The second thing the lexicographer should be very careful about is, as we have repeatedly mentioned above, the tradition of the language.

On the one hand, the lexicographer must take tradition as such into consideration, as well as the fact that his work and the publication of his dictionary will take several years, so that there will be an element of historicity in his dictionary in any case; he should also be cautious in respect to the latest changes of any kind, if he thinks that they have not yet taken root, lest he publish information on a fact that was only ephemeral and soon forgotten. But on the other hand, the lexicographer will have his own opinions on the correct solutions of problems yet unsolved and a legitimate desire to incorporate them in his dictionary. He will always have to present, in his dictionary, some indications of developments yet unknown to his precedessors. And it may be that he will try to introduce some reforms, or at least to foster them. Even if this were not the case, the lexicographer knows that a really good dictionary

---

[46] I owe this information to Prof. J. Greenberg; his experience concerns Yoruba speakers. According to Zima, one of the dialects of Yoruba (Oyo) had in certain historical periods the function of the supra-dialectal standard.

should be capable of being used many years after its publication and is, therefore, disinclined to compile it in a way which will render it very soon archaic, incapable of being used in the schools, etc.

To understand what is the best in the tradition, to understand the general trend of future development, and to combine this knowledge in a dictionary which is well founded on facts whose roots are in history but whose future development has been foreseen and fostered, that is the real art of the accomplished lexicographer.

APPENDIX

4.7 The preceding general discussion has the purpose only of providing the necessary notional frame-work and terminological apparatus. It must, however, be understood that the real situation varies from one language to another. So that the above discussion cannot be fully adequate for the situation in any particular language. As an illustration of what has been stated, there follow some very short (and therefore reduced) statements about the variation observable in a few different languages.

Zima reports on the rather simple situation in Hausa: The local dialect of Kano has started to be considered — to a certain degree — the norm of the (spoken) language. This norm based on the dialect of Kano did not have a maximum of cultural or administrative prestige, but it enjoyed commercial prestige. It must be taken into consideration that the whole prestige of Hausa has been derived basically from economical factors (the Hausa have always been mainly merchants). Later, however, the economic preponderance of the region of Kano (where there had been big marhets, the starting point of Transsaharan trade, etc.) became weaker and the administrative prestige of another region, viz. of Sokoto, increased. (After the Holy War, Sokoto became the center of the Hausaland dominated by the Fulaws.) But latter, the influence of Sokoto also decreased. The center of administration (both in the general sense of the word and in reference to the modern administration organized by the English) was transferred to the region.
Kaduna, situated just at the frontier of the Hausa area.

The results of all these extralinguistic changes are multifarious, the primary one being that the Kano "norm" is not stabilized and is under a strong Sokoto influence; recently, there is also a certain influence of the Southern "border" dialects, at least in the less formal styles. It is interesting that the Kano dialect has more influence as the norm in the spoken language (the spoken standard was obviously constituted at a time when the prestige of Kano was strong (whereas the written norm — if there is any) seems to show a tendency to accept rather more Sokoto (and other) elements. The recent tendency to introduce Hausa into Niger by means of mass literacy campaigns and by the publication of basic Hausa literature seems, however, to stress also the importance ot those Hausa dialects that are spoken on the territory of this state.

Languages with a longer history naturally show more variation. Motalová reports on *Armenian*:

(1) The first (classical) epoch: 5th—11th cent. The Armenian language of this epoch is called *Grabar* (i.e. the written language). One can assume that this written language was nearly identical with the spoken language of that time, at least at the beginning of the epoch. It was probably constituted on the basis of the language spoken in the central regions, primarily on the Ararat Plateau. The differences between the dialects were minimal, at that time. Towards the end of this epoch, the spoken and the written languages began to be more differentiated.

(2) The middle epoch: cca 12th—16th cent. After the political center was transferred to Cilicia (on the Southern shore of Anatolia), so-called Middle or Cilician Armenian developed. The basis of its constitution was the spoken variants of the Cilician dialects. Old Grabar and Cilician Armenian were used in different functions:

(a) Cilician Armenian: The language of the state and of the administration; the language of scientific (especially medical) literature, partly of historiography; the language of belles-lettres, above all of poetry.

(b) Grabar: the ecclesiastical language and the language of religious, philosophical, logical, and partly also of historical works.

During this epoch, the individual dialects become more differentiated. There was a strong emigration resulting in numerous Armenian diaspora in different parts of the world. After the decline of the Armenian state, Cilician Armenian stops being the language of administration and, deprived of its functions, declined.

Towards the end of this epoch, political independence was lost. The Armenian area was divided into two parts: the Eastern (Persian) and the Western (Turkish) part. Belles-lettres declined rapidly. Two basic groups of dialects were constituted, in analogy to the partition of the whole area.

(3) The recent epoch: 17th—20th cent. One of the most important features of the epoch is the constitution of a new standard national language, the so-called Ašxarhabar (i.e. "worldly" language).

At the beginning of this epoch, there exist side by side:

(a) Grabar, Classical Armenian

(b) So-called Civil Armenian (lingua civilis). In this language, different elements of Grabar and of the various dialects are mixed. It is a generally understandable language. The functions of Grabar and of Civil Armenian were divided in the same pattern as in the preceding epoch between Grabar and Cilician Armenian. Civil Armenian is predominantly used in letters, in the administration, in the courts, in the scientific literature, and later in the newspapers.

(c) The dialects — their ramification is generally the same as today. Owing to different cultural and political factors, the dialect of Yerewan (called also the Ararat dialect) and the dialect of Constantinople develop most quickly. One the basis of these two dialects, the new standard national language is constituted in two variants, the so-called Eastern and the so-called Western variants.

In the 19th century, efforts were being made to revivify Grabar. The positive result of these efforts was that the language was studied in great detail. But attempts at an adaption of this classical language to the new needs (above all by coinage of neologisms, introduction of loan-words and by structural changes in grammar) have proved to be artificial and have remained without results.

In the 19th century, cultural life developed rather rapidly, both in the Armenian area proper and in the diaspora. The result of the ever increasing number of literary works, of newspapers and journals published, and of schools founded was that Grabar continued to lose ground and the new standard literary language was used. At the outcome, the new language, in its two variants, started to be used in all functions of the standard national language. For onomasiological needs, loan-words were not so much used as in the preceding epoch. Nelogisms became more common, as well as elements introduced from the Grabar and from the dialects. The development of the dialects towards a greater differentiation stopped.

(4) The newest epoch, since the foundation of the Armenian Soviet Republic, which has become the political and cultural center of the Armenians. Armenian has again become the language of the state administration. It is the Eastern variant of the standard national language which prevails; it has developed rapidly and become quickly stabilized. The Eastern variant is also accepted by the reemigrees, who originally spoke the Western variant. Under the influence of the standard national language, the dialects decline rather quickly. Scientific and technical terminology is coined. Though there is no unifying center of the Western variant of the standard national language and though the perspective of its further development is, consequently, unclear, the Western variant is spoken and written by the majority of Armenians who live in the diaspora; it is used in books and journals published in different places throughout the whole world. The Western variant has a certain influence on the Eastern one, above all in the sphere of the lexicon. Some elements are positively accepted into the Eastern variant from the Western one, but the influence of

the latter is primarily negative; since the Western variant is rather hostile to loan-words the tendency of the Eastern variant to borrow is indirectly restrained. It is unclear whether a unification of the two variants could be expected. Most probably, the use of the Western variant will tend to be more and more restricted.

Zvelebil discerns the following variants of *Tamil*:

(1) *The standard literary language* is based on ancient and long standing literary and grammatical tradition; the phonological system is roughly that described in the first grammar of Tamil, the Tolkāppiyam (3.—1. B.C.) and the medieval grammar Nannūl (12.—14. A.D.), the morphological system is roughly based on the literary language of medieval texts, esp. the commentaries, and elaborated in the first "modern" Tamil prose of the 18.—19. century. This style is used, with the necessary lexical innovations, in modern creative and technical writing, in high brow platform speech, in education, and sometimes on the stage and in radio.

(2) *The folk speech*, as spoken by the uneducated masses, has a number of *regional dialects* (roughly North, West, East, South and Ceylon) having again a number of local dialects and patois.

(3) *The common colloquial language*, more or less in statu nascendi, is based on the speech of educated middle classes of non-Brahmin descent from the Eastern and Northern regions of Tamilnad. This is used in the ordinary conversation of educated individuals in most platform speech, also sometimes in education, often in movies and on the stage, sometimes in broadcasting.

(4) There are a number of community (caste) dialects; their chief binary division runs between *Brahmin* and *non-Brahmin* speech, and within the Brahmin community between Saiva (Iyer) and Vaishnava (Iyengar) Brahmins.

As far as the development of Tamil is concerned, Zvelebil discerns the following epochs:

A.　　*Pre-Tamil* stage: pre-literary *reconstructed* stage of Tamil-Malayalam sub-group of the South Dravidian sub-family. Cca before the beginning of our era. A few decades of very short hybrid Tamil-Prakitic inscription in Brāhmī.

B. 1. *Old Tamil*, cca 3.—1. B.C.—6—7. (8) A. D.
　　11. Early Old Tamil, 3. B.C.—5. A.D.
　　12. Middle Old Tamil, 5. A.D.—6. A.D.
　　13. Late Old Tamil, 6. A.D.—7.(8.) A.D.

Known chiefly from literary sources: poetry, a few scraps of prose; a few decades of short inscription in Brāhmī.
　　2. *Middle Tamil*, cca 6.—7. A. D.—18. A.D.

It begins with the language of Pallava Inscriptions, in literature with bhakti Saiva and Vaishnava hymns. The language of ancient prose commentaries.

Malayalam separated from Tamil as an independent language by the end of the Early Middle Tamil period.

It ends approximately with the poetry of late 17., early 18. century.

3. *Modern Tamil*, since cca the middle or end fo 18th. Cent. Begins with the prose of documents, diaries, ballads, and later prose of the first "modern" writers of the 19th century.

Minn Latt discusses the different variants of present-day *Burmese*:

Among the regional dialects of Burmese the leading position of the Central dialect is established by the overwhelming numerical superiority of its speakers above the total number of those who speak the other dialects (such as Yăkháin, Dhăwé, etc.), and also by its favourable position in the geographical, economic, political and cultural contexts. It is thus on the basis of the Central dialect that the standard national language is built; one may even say that it is in effect the standard national language utilized and accepted thoroughout the entire Burmese territories. Evidence indicates, for instance in Dhăwé, that the urban populace of the minor dialect areas are drawn closer to the Central dialect speech, while the rural speakers, in turn, imitate the habits of speakers in their cultural centres the towns.

It is not impossible to discern sub-regional variations among the Central dialect speakers who are distributed throughout a huge territory, but, in general, there is a large degree of unity and concord in their speech; where certain discrepancies occur it is understandably often the usages of the city of Rangoon that win the widest acceptance. Therefore it is possible to say that the Central dialect is preponderently uniform with the Rangoon standard serving as the main unifying center.

Within this national standard, however, it is possible to distinguish, at least to a workable degree, three groups of styles.

Since it is not our purpose to deal with all the details we may state broadly that intimate styles are used in conversations among family members, school mates, close friends, fellows in a closely-knit brotherhood etc. High styles are used in sophisticated and artificial monologues and dialogues and are largely removed from the usual types of conversation, both formal and informal. Normal styles are usually employed in conversations, for instance with business or professional colleagues, strangers, or when addressing superiors etc. This group serves as a buffer between the two groups already mentioned, but then it is the most vital and the most important. It is the norm, the standard of spoken Burmese, most widely accepted and understood. It is the base on which the intimate styles, with all their jargons, slangs, abbreviations etc. are built. It is the base on which the high styles with all their laboured structures, high-flown vocabulary, archaisms, artistic tastes etc. are constructed.

13*

On the basis of this division we can establish two sets of linguistic usage, colloquial and literary. The colloquial covers the normal and the intimate styles, whereas the literary covers the normal and the high styles. It must be stressed that the colloquial speech of one social group, a social dialect, can be different from that of another, and also that the literary style of one person can also differ from that of another.

With such a variety of styles the search for an exemplary *norm* is naturally rather complicated. In colloquial speech the preferred norm, for instance in schools, is usually the formal linguistic practice of the educated strata: this should not be confused with the intimate, unofficial conversations of the same people, which are as good or bad as any other. Again, the educated strata as such is rather broad and their speech habits diverse; hence there can be periods in which one of its sections gains more influence than another. These changes and variable trends are even better revealed in the literary language (here we have left room for the differentiation of the literary language and the cultivated spoken language) where the style that wins the widest concensus in one period may lose its position at a later time.

It will be highly rewarding for the lexicographer to take these phenomena into account. Basically, his material has to pivot on the normal styles of the language and extend, as far as his purpose demands, to the areas of the intimate and the high styles, indicating these diversions wherever they are necessary. It is imperative that he indicates which form is drawn from the intimate, subnormal speech of a restricted community, for instance that of the dockers, and which form is used in the literary, high-flown language of certain poets.

Apart from the differentiations above, the lexicographer will do well to keep in mind that, beside the literary language mentioned above, which *can* be spoken on normal and auspicious occasions, there are also literary styles that are never spoken. This distinction is a result of the historical development of Burmese language and literature throughout the centuries: in contradistinction to the variants of Modern Burmese, we may call these unspoken styles Classical Burmese.

Since the two "languages", Classical and Modern, are currently used side by side the lexical units are overwhelmingly identical. What is archaic in one is also archaic in the other. But there are many words, grammatical as well as lexical (for instance *ăkhu* in Modern Burmese, und *jăkhu* in Classical Burmese both of which mean "now") that should be indicated in the dictionaries.

CHAPTER V

THE TYPES OF DICTIONARIES

5.0 One of the best definitions I know of the term dictionary was given by C. C. Berg:[1] "A dictionary is a systematically arranged list of socialized[2] linguistic forms compiled from the speech-habits of a given speech-community and commented on by the author in such a way that the qualified reader understands the meaning ... of each separate form, and is informed of the relevant facts concerning the function of that form in its community." This definition is concerned with the central types of dictionaries, i.s. with those dealing primarily with lexical meaning.

The functions of the linguistic forms (i.e., in our case, words and other lexical units) and their meaning are, as we know from the preceding discussion, so multifarious and ramified that we cannot wonder that there are many different types of dictionaries. Indeed, Y. Malkiel[3] is absolutely right when saying that the word "dictionary" can "apply quite loosely to any reference work arranged by words or names."[4] In this chapter, we shall discuss the most important types of dictionaries.

---

[1] *Report* p. 4.

[2] The term "socialized" is explained by C. C. Berg in the subsequent sentence in the following way: "Linguistic forms are social facts in so far as they result from individual utterances being socialized, i.e. imitated time after time, under similar circumstances, by members of the community where they originated". In the overwhelming majority of cases, the data indicated in a dictionary are "socialized forms" in this sense of the word; what remains beyond the boundaries of the definition would be the indications of different occasional forms, e.g. of hapax legomena in big dictionaries. It is not necessary to loose much time pondering over such exceptions (which confirm the rule); and after all, it can be maintained that each and every hapax can potentially develop into a "socialized form", i.e. into a form which is stabilized in the system of language (as suggested by C. C. Berg in his further discussion, loc. cit.) and also that a hapax is usually understood only on the background of the stabilized, "socialized" forms.

[3] PL 23.   [4] The boundaries against other genera are not sharp-cut. For example, biographical works containing encyclopedic information on outstanding persons organized into individual entries labelled by the names of the personality discussed are called biographical dictionaries (cf. footnote 12). On the other hand, nobody will call a telephone directory a dictionary, though one could maintain that it has some features of a such a work (entries labelled by names, arranged in their alphabetical sequence, some information abouch each entried person [i.e.w. address and number], etc). Shortreference works of the who-is-who type are somewhere in the middle.

ENCYCLOPEDIC DICTIONARIES

5.1 In the first place, we must differentiate encyclopedic dictionaries from linguistic ones. The latter are primarily concerned with language, i.e. with the lexical units of language and all their linguistic properties; we shall discuss them at length in the rest of this chapter. In contradistiction to this, the encyclopedic dictionaries (the biggest and most general of which are frequently called simply encyclopedias) are primarily concerned with the denotata of the lexical units (words): They give information about the extra-linguistic world, physical or non-physical, and they are only arranged in the order of the words (lexical units) by which the segments of this extralinguistic world are referred to when spoken about.[5] It is this arrangement "by words" which gives encyclopedias a similarity to monolingual dictionaries.

As a generally known example of an encyclopedia can be indicated the *Encyclopedia Britannica*.[6] Probably the most venerable publication of this sort is Diderot's old *Encyclopédie ou Dictionnaire raisonné des sciences, des arts et des métiers*;[7] but it would be easy to quote many similar undertakings written in different languages of the world.

The word "encyclopedia" suggests a huge work of many volumes concerned with all the fields of human knowledge. It is important, however, to under-stand that very specialized dictionaries can also be of encyclopedic character provided that they are primarily interested in the denotata. It is irrelevant whether they are huge[8] or whether they are concise;[9] it is also irrelevant by what principle their entries are chosen (terms of a science, important geo-graphical place-names, names of famous writers, etc. etc.): the decisive thing is the interest they display in the extralinguistic world and the sort of infor-mation they give. If we read the entry *bridge* in a linguistic dictionary like the OED,[10] we get (besides a statement of the archaic and etymologically related forms), above all the definitions of the word's different senses (like a structure forming or carrying a road over a river, a ravine, etc., or affording passage between two points at a height above the ground), with quotations of different passages from texts where the word occurs. In *Encyclopedia*

---

[5] It follows from this that encyclopedic dictionaries usually contain only words of designative character (plus proper names).

[6] *Encyclopaedia Britannica*, A new survey of universal knowledge. London–Chicago–Toronto, different editions, mine of 1960.

[7] Paris 1751–1780.

[8] E. g. Pauly's *Real-encyclopädie der klassischen Altertumswissenschaft* (Stuttgart 1894 sqq.) consists by now of more than sixty volumes.

[9] E. g. W. Belardi — N. Minissi, *Dizionario difonologia*, Roma 1962, has some 136 pages in 16⁰.

[10] OED vol. I, 1097 sq.

Britannica,[11] the same word *bridge* is the index of a long entry which consists of the following chapters: I. History. II. Notable bridges by type. III. Constructions by type, A. fixed bridges, B. opening bridges. IV. Materials of construction. V. Bridge design. VI. Manufacture and supports. VII. Erection. The entry is full of pictures, tables, formulae; in short, he who has read it knows what is worth knowing about the various objects of the material world which can be referred to as bridges.

There is no need to stress that encyclopedic entries are not always as long as the one quoted above. But it is not their length which is decisive, it is their focus of interest in the extralinguistic world, in the objects themselves. It must also be remembered that the division of dictionaries into encyclopedic and linguistic ones is not necessarily an either-or matter. In the discussion of the monolingual and bilingual dictionaries (Chap. VI, VII), we shall have occasion to show that there are elements of encyclopedic character in almost all dictionaries. Some of these encyclopedic elements are unavoidable, some are introduced because the compiler of the dictionary wishes to give his work a certain character. Another field of overlapping is the terminological dictionaries of different specialized sciences, where a definition of a term's designatum (i.e. of the respective concept) will not differ vastly from a short description of the respective denotatum. Similar is the case of the dictionaries of names. There are many dictionaries of names of a purely encyclopedic character, with the names serving as indexes: to entries describing the respective places or the life and work of the men in question.[12] But even in the purely linguistic dictionaries of names,[13] there are some elements of encyclopedic character which are hard to avoid, such as, for example, the statement of the more important persons in history who had the name *Henry*, in a dictionary of English Christian names.

Encyclopedic dictionaries as a species, however, are not a subject of the present book's main interest.

LINGUISTIC DICTIONARIES

5.2 If we turn our attention to the linguistic dictionaries,[14] we can divide them into different categories by different criteria.

---

[11] *Encyclopaedia Britannica* (footnote 6), vol IV, p. 123—137 (with ten plates of pictures).

[12] An encyclopedic dictionary of place names is frequently called a *gazetteer*. An encyclopedic dictionary of personal names is frequently called a *biographical dictionary*.

[13] A linguistic dictionary of names is frequently called an *onomasticon*.

[14] The adjective *linguistic* should be taken as pertaining rather to the substantive *language*, not so much to the substantive *linguistics*.

5.2.1 One of the most important divisions of linguistic dictionaries is that between the diachronic and the synchronic ones. Diachronic dictionaries are primarily concerned with the history, with the development of words (lexical units), both in respect to form and in respect to meaning. Among the diachronic dictionaries, we can again perceive two different types, viz. historical and etymological dictionaries. Historical dictionaries focus their attention on the changes occurring both in the form and in the meaning of a word (lexical unit) within the period of time for which there is historical (usually textual) evidence at hand. Etymological dictionaries focus their interest on the origin of the words (lexical units); and as it happens that a good part of the words of any language known to-day[15] came into existence before the beginning of the textual tradition,[16] the etymological dictionaries can be said to deal largely with the pre-history of the words.[17] But the origins of the more recent words are also a legitimate subject of the etymological dictionary.

The two elements, the historical and the etymological, are almost always intermingled, but in the majority of cases a preference for or the prevalence of one point of view can be observed. For example, the entry "father" goes as follows in Skeat's *English Etymological Dictionary*:[18] *father*, a male parent. Middle Eng. *fader*, Chaucer, C.T. 8098. (The spelling *fader* is almost universal in Middle English; *father* occurs in the Bible of 1551, and is due to dialectal influence, which changed *-der* to *-ther*). Anglo-Saxon *faeder* ... Dutch *vader*; Danish and Swed. *fader*; Icelandic *fadir*; Gothonic *fadar*; German *Vater*. Latin *pater*; Greek *patér*; Persian *pidar*; Sanskrit *pitr̥-*; Irish *athair*. Indo-European type* *patēr*. —

The entry *pays* "country" goes as follows in Dauzat's French etymological dictionary:[19] *pays/pais*, Xe siècle, aussi "patrie" en ancien français), du bas latin *pagensis* (VIe siècle, Grég. de Tours), habitant d'un pagus (subdivision de la cité), par ext. le pagus lui-même; a repris le sens "originaire d'un même pays", ...

The etymological and comparative point of view prevails in Skeat, the historical point of view in Dauzat.

---

[15] With the obvious exception of artificialities like Esperanto.

[16] This statement has some validity only as far as the "general words" of the "general language" are concerned; should we take into consideration, for example, the endless cohorts of the special terms of different sciences, the statement could not hold water, because there are hundreds of thousands of the latter, all of them coined within the historical time of the respective cultural languages.

[17] "Conjectural research in the prehistory of lexicon" — Y. Malkiel, PL 16.

[18] Walter W. Skeat, *An Etymological Dictionary of the English Language*, Oxford, first edition 1879, reimpression 1958, p. 209. — The text of the entry is reduced and abbreviations avoided.

[19] A. Dauzat, *Dictionnaire étymologique de la language française*, 10th edition, Paris 1954, p. 541 (cf. the preceding footnote.)

As an example of an entry in which the historical point of view is stressed even more than in the example quoted from Dauzat cf. *Kleid* "clothes" in Paul's German Dictionary:[20]

Kleid "clothes", attested only since the 12th century, but related to Anglo-Saxon (Engl. *cloth*); possible related to German *Klette*. The basic meaning was "stuff, material", as show by Eng. Then it developed in to the designation of a piece of garments made of the stuff, at first quite generally, as it is used till now in Plural (cf. *Kleiderschrank*) and in the composed word *Beinkleid*...

The entry quoted from Skeat shows that the "prehistory of the word" requires very frequently a comparative study of related words from different languages. As a consequence of this, big etymological dictionaries logically tend to develop into comparative dictionaries which usually arrive at the original form of a proto-language by comparison of the descendant languages.[21]

The etymological (and comparative) dictionaries are usually more concerned with the form of the words than with their meaning (though semantic correspondence is a vital necessity in the comparison of words). This is certainly a pity, but it generally cannot be helped, because for the study of meaning, rich evidence, i.e. extensive collections of material and mainly contexts are necessary. But at the beginning of the history of a language, contextual quotations are scarce and they are absolutely lacking in the reconstructed period. Therefore, the etymological (and comparative) dictionaries can give only schematic indications in respect to the meaning. In a historical dictionary, the semantic developments are at least as important as those of the form of the word. The historical dictionaries also frequently indicate what new words were derived from the original one during its history. Seeing how useful both points of view are, it is no wonder that some dictionaries try to be both etymological and historical, combining the two aspects.[22]

As far as the etymological dictionaries are concerned, we shall further mention yet the circumstance that there are not only general etymological dictionaries (i.e. dictionaries containing words from the general language), but also special ones, according to the different 'subdivisions' of language.

---

[20] H. Paul, *Deutsches Wörterbuch*, 8th edition, edited by A. Schirmer, Halle (Saale), 1961, p. 330 sq.; reduced and translated from German.

[21] As examples, we can indicate A. Walde — J. Pokorny, *Vergleichendes Wörterbuch der indogermanischen Sprachen*, Berlin und Leipzig 1930ff.; J. Pokorny, *Indogermanisches etymologisches Wörterbuch*, Bern s. a.

[22] As examples, we can indicate A. Ernout — A. Meillet, *Dictionnaire étymologique de la langue latine, Histoire des mots*, 2. éd., Paris 1939 (there are also other editions); V. I. Abaev, *Istoriko-etimologičeskij slovar' osetinskogo jazyka* I, Moskva 1958. The majority of big historical dictionaries (like those quoted in the following footnote) also indicate the etymology of the entry word, though usually only succinctly.

In this way, we have etymological dictionaries of, say, local dialects, restricted languages, different groups of words (e.g. terms designating the flowers), of borrowed words etc.

As far as historical dictionaries are concerned, one important circumstance should be mentioned. The compilers of the very big historical dictionaries[23] frequently cannot indicate the single senses of the words, and above all not the single quotations, in their real historical sequence,[24] because such a presentation would be rather chaotic; they must present their material, not unfrequently, in logical groups, or by semantic connections, or by some other principle, and proceed historically only within these "chapters". This is one of the reasons why there is an important area of overlapping between the historical dictionaries on the one side, and the big monolingual dictionaries on the other. We shall discuss this in connection with the latter (§ 6.5.5.1).

The construction of historical or even of etymological dictionaries is a highly specialized branch of lexicography; as far as etymological dictionaries are concerned, the work is so specialized that very frequently their compilation is not conceived as a lexicographic activity in the narrower, more technical sense of the word.[25]

5.2.2 Whereas the task of diachronic dictionaries is to deal with the development of the lexicon, the purpose of synchronic dictionaries is to deal with the lexical stock of a language at one stage of its development. The difference between the two species is probably fairly clear, when considered generally. Two points must however, be discussed in greater detail.

First, the concept synchronic is not synonymous with "contemporary". Any epoch in the development of language can, at least ideally,[26] be treated synchronically. Grassman's Dictionary of the Rig Vedic Sanskrit[27] is a synchronic dictionary though the language it deals with is certainly not a contemporary one but stopped being used several millenaries ago.

The second point is more difficult. It is impossible to interpret for practical linguistic and lexicographic purposes, the term synchronic as if we were concerned with the state of a language at one point of time. We must imagine

---

[23] E.g., J. Grimm — W. Grimm, *Deutsches Wörterbuch*, I. Leipzig 1854 ff. Oxford English Dictionary, I, XIII (Supplement), 1933 ff.

[24] Cf. Malkiel, PL 16.

[25] On indications of etymologies in general linguistic dictionaries see below.

[26] Practically, there are sometimes obstacles; for instance, texts of an old language or at least some of the single lexical units can be understood with merely the help of historical or even etymological interpretations only. But these are extreme situations caused externally, by the lack of tradition of the language in question, not by the language itself. (Cf. p. on the etymological method.)

[27] H. Grassman, *Wörterbuch zum Rig Veda*, Leipzig 1873.

it so, but we cannot make it so. It would be impossible to make a full, detailed investigation of a single idiolect in one day; it would be impossible to undertake a full, detailed investigation of a local patois in a village in a week; an investigation of a regional dialect in a month etc.: the broader our interest, the more time we need for our task. Apart from this merely technical factor, we must also take into consideration that the texts produced (orally or in writing) during a short period of time, usually, in the case of languages rich at least on the average, are not variegated enough, so that not all words of the language really occur in them. With the exception of the situation where the lexicographer elicits data from his informant, it is necessary to have different texts usually coming from a longer period of time, to be reasonably sure that the lexicon of the language is representatively manifested in them. This observation is equally valid both for the living and for the dead languages (or older stages of development of the living languages). As, however, language is known to change uninterruptedly, though usually in very small steps, this means that the corpus of texts used in this way as the basis of the lexicographer's work is not absolutely synchronic in the strictest sense of the term.

It follows this that the concept of a dictionary being "synchronic" is highly relative. This relativity does not, however, diminish the usefulness and correctness of the concept; this assumption (or rather experience) is necessary not only specifically in lexicography, but generally in linguistics.

But it is not only the element of time necessary first for all the words to have occasion to occur in texts and then for the data to be collected from these texts, which makes the concept of synchrony rather relative. Above (chapter IV) we have had occasion to discuss the variation of language. This phenomenon also must be taken into consideration in this connection. Even if we succeeded in recording all spoken and written texts produced during, say, one and the same day, there is every reason to believe that such a cross-section would contain, for example, highly obsolete expressions (e.g. in legal and religious texts both spoken in courts and churches, and published) and occasional, ephemeral neologisms (e.g. in jocose conversations) forgotten the following day. Considered from this point of view, a really homogenous dictionary could be only a special dictionary dealing with the word-stock of a short, tedious literary work quickly written by the same author on the same subject in the same style in a monotonous, dull tone, preferably in a dead language. This factor is different from the factor of change discussed above, bacause the obsolete elements, let us say, really occur at the same time as, for instance, the recently coined ones. But there is undoubtedly a certain inner tension and consequently a dynamism implied in this situation, because the archaic elements simply are not on the same level as the 'modern' ones, if for no other reason than that they are not as productive as the latter. It is this unavoidable dynamism which brings it about that there is always area of overlapping between a synchronic and a historical dictionary.[28]

5.2.3 As the second division of the linguistic dictionaries, we shall discern general dictionaries on the one side, and restricted (or special) dictionaries on the other.[29] The contradistinction "general" — "restricted" must not be interpreted in terms of the density of the entries; it would be totally wrong to think that general dictionaries try to contain "all the words" whereas restricted ones do not: the density of the entries and their number is a criterion that will be discussed in the section dealing with the size of the dictionaries. In reality, it is the eligibility of a word (lexical unit) for being indicated in a "yrestricted" ("special") dictionary which is restricted, because the compiler of the dictionary decides *a priori* that he will make his choice from only a certain part of the total lexicon of the language.

The restriction can be based on any perceivable (or only supposed or postulated) variation of language, on any classification of its texts, or on any principle or combination of principles determined by the author of the dictionary. This liberty of the author causes that there is practically an endless number of different restrictions, of which we shall be able to mention only some of the more important types.

---

[28] Very strict views are sometimes voiced on this subject. So e.g. Malkiel (PL 16): "The ideal synchronic dictionary would be one least contaminated by acknowledged or, worse, unacknowledged archaisms". If an archaism really occured at a given time, I do not see why it should not be listed in a synchronic dictionary dealing with that epoch. But this theoretical point of view is and must be modified in a concrete case: much depends on whether the dictionary is planned for active use, etc. — But the real fundamentum divisionis, at least in the living languages, seems to be the non-productivity of the obsolete words. Every good dictionary is used a long time after its publication. During this time, the obsolete words will either retain the same status they had during the period described in the dictionary, or they will grow more archaic; the revivification of an obsolete word is a rare (though neither unknown nor too rare) phenomenon. On the other hand, any of the "living" elements, i.e. the non-archaic ones, can become productive (or more productive) in the derivation of new words or coinage of new expressions, during the time the dictionary is used after its publication. Every user of any dictionary is accustomed not to find everything in it and to interpret what is not indicated by what is indicated; he will do the same with the onomasiological innovations posterior to the publication of the dictionary. It can be maintained, therefore, that the indication of an archaism or of an obsolete word in a synchronic dictionary is the indication of a simple fact, where as the indication of a "living element" is not only the indication of the fact itself, but also of a real or potential derivational, combinatorial, or generally innovational pattern.

[29] It would probably be preferable to use only the term "restricted" in this connection and reserve the term "special" for those dictionaries which are compiled for a special purpose but a considerable bulk of traditional use is an impediment to such a precise terminological clarification.

As far as dictionaries restricted on the basis of the variation of language go, we can speak first about dictionaries which describe regional dialects.[30] The existence of these dialects is established by the facts of language, at least to a high degree, and the natural thing is to describe them, in the dictionaries, according to their groups or their real boundaries by dialect areas groups. But as we have seen in chapter IV there are groups within groups and single local patois within greater regional dialects. And so Y. Malkiel[31] is absolutely right when he states that "the dialect area selected as a unit (i.e. for lexico-graphic treatment) may vary from a hamlet to a continent,[32] the controlling factors being the diversification of speech, the configuration of the terrain, the pattern of political allegiances, and the availability of field-workers and informants". These dialect dictionaries are based either on oral material and (eventually) different questionnaires, or on written sources (if there are texts written in the dialect), or on both. If there are numerous written texts and if they have a sufficiently long tradition, the respective dialect dictionary will naturally tend to acquire a historical character. Some entries will have to have an encyclopedic character, because there will be denotata with which the speakers of the standard national language will not be familiar and which are difficult to explain. As these dialect dictionaries deal very much with the geographical distribution of linguistic phenomena, Malkiel[33] is probably right when regarding maps and charts as very useful and even a small-scale linguistic atlas as a desideratum.

The dialect dictionaries can be worked out in two different ways: either, the dictionary offers complete information on the lexicon of the respective dialect or local form of language without reference to any other dialects or forms; or the dictionary lists and explains only what is different from another dialect or, usually, from what is considered the standard national form. It is not necessary to stress that the first method (total description) is more valuable, because its result is a richer picture of the local variety described, whereas the other method has, *praeter alia*, the inherent possible difficulty that the variety of language against which the dialect described is contrasted is itself not sufficiently known and unequivocally described. But practical reasons (above all the eventual great number of repetitions or identical statements and descriptions) cause that the contrastive method will certainly be used also in the future.

---

[30] The variation of language in the domension of time, i.e. the linguistic change, is not conceived as belonging here, because this variation is the basis of the difference between historical dictionaries and synchronic ones. (Though one could, theoretically, regard synchronic dictionaries as restricted in comparison with historical ones.)

[31] Pl. 10. — Cf. Ščerba, *Izvestija* 91.

[32] E.g., Sir W. A. Craigie — J. A. Hulbert, *A dictionary of American English*, London 1960.

[33] PL 22.

The other dimensions of the variation of language are not a less fertile ground for restricted dictionaries: each and every professional restricted language, slang, jargon, argot has a distinctive lexicon of its own which can be described in a restricted dictionary. As, however, these "social dialects" are, in the majority of cases, varieties of the standard national language, the respective restricted dictionaries which describe them are written in the contrastive method even more frequently than those of the geographical dialects.

Within this group of dictionaries, it is above all those which deal with the professional languages the contrastive lexicon of which is predominantly of a designative character.[34] This is true in the case of restricted dictionaries of the trades, crafts, sports etc. But in the case of restricted dictionaries of the professional languages of the arts and above all of the sciences, the lexicon dealt with will be not only of a designative, but even of a terminological character. This fact and other circumstances (above all, the correct supposition that whoever is interested in scientific terms will usually be interested in the realities denoted as well) guarantee that these terminological dictionaries will have an encyclopedic character or at least will contain many encyclopedic elements. Such terminological dictionaries are almost always written by use of the contrastive method, and usually of a very strict variety of it: only the technical terms themselves are accepted as entries and in the case of polysemous words, only the technical-terminological senses are indicated, the other, non-terminological senses being passed over in silence. This method (which is quite justifiable) results very frequently in such a uniformity of indications and scarcity of other than technical information that these restricted dictionaries can be typed as, or are even actually called, glossaries.[35] But on the other hand, the number of terms indicated as entries in these glossaries or restricted dictionaries of scientific terms should not be small. Ščerba[36] is quite right when maintaining this since dictionaries of this type are needed for the reading of

---

[34] An interesting group of dictionaries restricted to the designative words whose denotata belong to the physical extralinguistic world are pictorial dictionaries. They are usually organized on an onomasiological principle. For example, there will be the picture of the human body, or of a ship, or of scenery, of of different plants, animals, utensils, and the expressions by which the single things depicted or their parts can be referred to are indicated by arrows. An alphabetic index of expressions contained in the dictionary can be used to locate the place where an expression applies to the picture of its denotatum when the user procedes "from the word to the thing". These pictorial dictionaries are useful mainly in the cases of denotata which are not generally known and perhaps in learning words of a foreign language by groups; but inasfar as they do not define the designatum, by its criterial features (if they could be said to define it, then only ostensively) they cannot be regarded as being on the same level as the "verbal" dictionaries. In this respect, pictorial material used in some dictionaries in addition to the verbal definition is different from the purely pictorial dictionaries.

[35] Cf. below.

[36] *Izvestija* 106; Ščerba's argumentation, however, deals more with the pedagogical side of the issue.

scientific texts where even an "important" term has a higher probability of occurrence than usual and can gain a sudden importance.[37]

Any classification of the texts of a language can be used as the basis of a restricted dictionary. Such dictionaries can range from short contrastive glossaries which list some words used by an author or by a group of authors but unknown in the variety of language considered standard, to full, lexical descriptions of the total stock of words occurring in one work, or a group of works, or in the complete works of an author; or of a group of authors writing in the same style or on the same subjects etc.;[38] or of a whole literary genre. The encyclopedic interest is sometimes very strong in these dictionaries. The main purpose of a dictionary can be conceived as the explanation of the contents of the text itself (with the entry words used as indexes to the crucial passages and or with broad encyclopedic treatment of the philosophical or other concepts expressed by the works; we usually call such a dictionary exegetic dictionary.[39] Thus, the dictionary of a literary text can consist of elements that belong basically to three categories: (1) linguistic (the meaning of the words), (2) encyclopedic (realia; denotata referred to in the text), (3) exegetic (contents of the text, its nuances and overtones, and the single ideas expressed in it, etc.)[40]

A special group within this group of restricted dictionaries are indices (citations[41] of places where a word occurs in a text, usually with no other or only very scarce information) and concordances (quotations[42] of all passages in which a word occurs).

The principles on which the author of a dictionary may decide to restrict it can vary endlessly. In the final analysis, any property of the lexical units

[37] Y. Malkiel (PL 14) maintains that "the need for ... glossaries of technical terms may soon altogether recede as a result of the invention of electronic translating machines". This may be correct as a perspective, but I would not expect it to happen within the next few years; and the possible storage of complete terminological sets in the data processing machines will hardly eliminate the practical glossaries for the public, even in the future.

[38] These "groups of authors" (or "groups of works" for that) can be established on different principles again. For instance, an important principle of restriction is the selection of those authors (and works) who are read in school.

[39] As in all other cases, the character of the dictionary can be mixed, it can be linguistic with some exegetic elements, etc.

[40] In the classification of philological methods and procedures, exegesis is frequently if not unexceptionally conceived as involving also the explanation of the denotata referred to in the text. The boundary of the exegesis as we draw it here is narrower, because we wish to refer to the encyclopedic treatment of the denotata in the same way, irrespective of the type of the dictionary.

[41] The term *citation* means the statement by which a passage can be localized in a text; this usually happens by numbers of books, chapters, sections, verses or by any other similar expedient. For example: Hom. Il. 13, 51.

[42] The term *quotation* means a verbatim statement of the passage in question, usually with the necessary citation.

and any property of their designata or denotata or any other function could be used, in any combination, as the principle, as the rationale of the restriction. We shall exemplify only some types.

Etymology is the rationale of such dictionaries as, for example, those of loan-words (they are frequently called dictionaries of foreign words) and those of telescoped words, acronyms, and abbreviations (they are frequently called dictionaries of abbreviations), and similar ones.

The circumstance that a word occurs not only in free combinations but also in set groups is the rationale for such dictionaries as those of idioms, set expressions, proverbs, quotations etc. The single word here is usually used as the index for the set combination. The main purpose of these dictionaries is generally the explanation of the overall meaning of the set combination. Furthermore, the identification of the original source of set group can also be an important goal.

The rationale of restriction can also be some semantic properties. The semantic property most frequently exploited is near-synonymy. The dictionaries which select words (lexical units) and which organize them on this principle are usually called ideological dictionaries or dictionaries of synonyms.[43] They indicate chains of synonyms, near-synonyms, and/or groups of semantically related terms. The antonyms are sometimes indicated in the synonymic dictionaries (with due glosses), but there exist even special dictionaries of antonyms. The scientific value of these dictionaries consists in the fact that they help greatly in the discovery of associative ties within the lexicon, areas of a finer semantic differentiation, and similar properties of the lexical stock of language; on the practical level, they help the author to find just the "right" word he seeks but which escapes his memory.[44] Really good dictionaries of this type should not only list the near-synonyms and semantically related items in chains, one after the other, but they should also add glosses in which the semantic difference is explained[45] and if need be show that these differences belong to different dimensions.

The systematic dictionaries indicate the semantically related words in groups according to the onomasiological fields and within them according to the notional structures (proceeding mainly from hyperonyms to the respective hyponyms). Some of them try to do this in the field of the general vocabulary,[46]

---

[43] With the exception of Great Britain it is by now obsolete to call these dictionaries *thesauri*. But cf., for example, J. Hulbert, Dictionaries British and American, London 1955, p. 92: according to this scholar, *thesaurus* is 'a dictionary of slang on the synonymic principle'.

[44] Ščerba, *Izvestija* 110, correctly stresses also their usefulness in learning a foreign language.

[45] Cf. on this Aleksandrov LS 6, 1963, 33.

[46] The most detailed system of this kind is R. Hallig — W. von Wartburg, *Begriffssystem als Grundlage für die Lexikographie* (Abhandlungen der deutschen Akademie der Wissenschaften), Berlin 1952. Note that there is a considerable area of overlapping between systematic dictionaries

but the majority of them treats in this was the terminological sets of the particular scientific and similar branches.[47]

Some of the bigger dictionaries of both these types list a great part of the total lexicon. They should be classified, nevertheless, as restricted dictionaries (at least in my opinion), because they never present the lexicon as fully as their general counterparts of comparable size, and because they treat and present lexical meeaning in a highly reduced way.

It would serve no purpose to discuss more than the most important types. As already staded, the selective restrictions of dictionaries can be based on very different principles and on different combinations of principles. As an example, we can quote the full title and subtile of the following dictionary: G. Vaccaro, *Dizionario delle parole nuovissime e difficili: neologismi, solecismi, barbarismi, regionalismi, dialettalismi, locuzioni* con 8.000 esempi tratti dai romanzi di autori italiani editi per la prima volta nell' anno 1965.[48] The underlying idea of this dictionary is obviously to help the reader with any expression he presumably may not understand. The reasons for this difficulty are various: it may be that an expression has not yet become stabilized (a neologism), that it is a loan-word or even a loan-word bound on a foreign culture (an exotism), that the expression is not correctly used (i.e. not used in the way as used by the majority of model authors (a barbarism, or a solecism), that the expression belongs to a geographical dialect (a regionalism, dialectalism), that the word is part of a set expression with underivable overall meaning (locuzioni); what are passed over in silence are the archaisms, no doubt on the strength of the assumption that they can be found in the already existing dictionaries.

5.2.4 The counterpart of the restricted dictionary is the general dictionary. As mentioned above, the term "general" does not pertain to the size of the dictionaries. The rationale on which this category is founded is the circumstance that these dictionaries are concerned mainly with the general language (as opposed to the different restricted ones), i.e. with the standard

and ideological ones. For instance, Roget's *Thesaurus of English Words and Phrases* (in any of it many editions) is a typical example of combination of the two approaches: the individual group of synonyms are grouped themselves on the principle of a systematic classification of notions

[47] Cf. E. Wüster, Proceedings of the 8th Congress of Linguists, Oslo 1958, p. 102, according to whose bibliography the majority of normative dictionaries of technical terminological sets is organized on the systematic principle.

[48] Roma 1966 — The author plans to publish a new edition of this dictionary every year as a "supplemento annuale a tutti i vocabolari della lingua italiana". If he succeeds in this and if his material is really representative, the series will one day make excellent reading and will be a first-class source for the development of the Italian lexicon; its value could be radically enhanced of one could discover, in future volumes, whether the expressions previously listed as neologisms were dropped or whether they continue being used.

national language as generally used. It is not necessary to stress that the whole
notion defies a precise definition, but it cannot be avoided in the lexicographer's
practice. Within the category of general dictionaries, it is necessary and useful
to discern two different types again, viz. standard-descriptive dictionaries and overall-descriptive or informative dictionaries.[49] As
the terms imply, both these types belong to the broader category of descriptive dictionaries.

Standard-descriptive dictionaries can be characterized as descriptive dictionaries of the standard national language as it is used at the point of time when
the dictionary is being compiled, and to a degree also as it is expected to be
used for some time after the publication of the dictionary. What should be
stressed is the words "as it is expected to be used": this is what gives the standard-descriptive dictionary a certain normative character, because the lexicographer compiles a dictionary of this type assuming that the user will not
only expect in it information concerning words (lexical units) he does not
precisely understand when he reads (or hears) texts, but that the user will
also check in the dictionary some data about words he uses when he himself
produces new texts.

Overall-descriptive dictionaries differ from standard-descriptive ones in
two respects: (1) they describe much more than the standard national language
as it is used at the point of time of the compilation; they are not concerned
with future usage. They are used primarily by users who wish to find information about a word they do not understand when reading (or hearing) a text.

Since both standard-descriptive and overall-descriptive dictionaries are
usually compiled only when there is a literature written in the respective
language (though it would be possible to compile them also without any
written sources), we shall illustrate the two types by using a literary language.

The standard-descriptive dictionary describes the language used
by contemporary authors and speakers. In its purest form, it describes only
regular usage (not the individual author's peculiarities and occasional uses);

---

[49] This basic distinction and its implications were conceived by Ščerba, *Izvestija* 89 sq.;
we do not specify, in the following discussion, all the single points in which our conception differs
from that of Ščerba. Ščerba uses another terminology. For example, what we call a *standard-
descriptive dictionary* is termed by Ščerba and *academic dictionary* (cf. the terminological homonymy with what is usually called an academic dictionary.). P. Garvin (in his review
of Ščerba's paper in *Izvestija*, published in Word 3, 1947, 130) calls this type of dictionary
"*normative*". This is not bad and harmonizes rather will with Ščerba's thought; on the other
hand, it seems to me that "normative" is too strongly linked with "prescriptive", at least in
English. Ščerba's *slovarspravočnik* (which is very close to our *overall-descriptive dictionary*) was
translated by Garvin (loc. cit.) "*reference dictionary*"; in a similar way; Sebeok (Lingua 11,
1962, 365) speaks about Ščerba's *referential type*. Again, the translation would be to Ščerba's
liking, but the homonymy with the general acceptation of *reference-* (as used, for example, in a
book of reference, a reference work) is obvious.

it does not describe dialectical or regional words occasionally used by single authors in order to add some local flavour to the text; it is not interested in archaisms (unless they frequently recur in different set expressions — but in that case they are not really obsolete because they can be expected to be used in future, too); in short, it is not too much interested in those parts of the total lexicon which are connected with any phenomenon that belongs to the field of the variation of language. A standard-descriptive dictionary of this type describes what is generally regular, normal, what is the norm.[50] As there are usually no really sudden and rapid breaks in the development of a language, and above all not in the development of the literary form of the standard national language, the inference is that what is generally and regularly used now will continue to be used also in the immediate future, of course with some changes, some of which cannot be foreseen at all, but some of which are heralded, for example by the circumstance that some occasional usages may grow more frequent, etc. In this way, it can be maintained that the standard-descriptive dictionary tries to anticipate the future; the anticipation, however, is always highly imperfect, because nobody is able to anticipate development with certainty in every single case. Nevertheless, the standard-descriptive dictionary is productive, to a degree, and it exercises an influence on usage. When it has been published, its users do not only use it to get information on a word they read in a text, but they use it also when they draft a new text themselves and are not sure about the usage of an item. And this is the second reason why there is an element of normativity in these dictionaries: by finding out what has been the norm at the time of their publication they set the standard for the future user.[51] Different lexicographers understand this "setting of the standard" in a different way; the general trend of our age, however, seems, in the direction of a liberal understanding of it.

One further remark should be made in this connection. As mentioned above, the principal domain of a standard-descriptive dictionary is the standard national language; descriptive dictionaries of the other varieties of language always tend toward the purely informative or overall-descriptive type. One, and probably the most important of these reasons for this is the fact that the most important communications are couched in this form of language, and such communications at that which require clarity and precision. A gangster will hardly check in a dictionary to see whether he uses a lexical item of the

---

[50] The best example of such a dictionary is undoubtedly *Dictionnaire de l'Académie (française)*, in any of its edition (1st ed. 1694.)

[51] This is the primary difference between the descriptive dictionaries of living languages and of dead languages. In the case of the dead languages, the necessity to find out what is normal and what is occasional is not so great, because there is not an attempt at anticipating future development and at excercizing and influence. For this reason and also because the principal task in the field of dead languages is to understand the texts, and not to produce new ones, dictionaries of dead languages necessarily tend to be of the overall-descriptive type.

14*

thieves' jargon in the same way as his colleagues of the profession; a man who speaks the local patois of a village will hardly feel any uncertainty about the usage of the respective expressions which are so very much bound to concrete situations. But, for instance, a lawyer who drafts a legal document (in the standard national language, of course), will take every precaution lest the text be misunderstood and will, therefore, in a case of uncertainty check in a dictionary to see whether his way of using a word coincides with the regular one. This explains why the standard national language is the focus of the lexicographer's attention and this is also one of the reasons why standard-descriptive dictionary exercises a normative influence on usage after its publication.

In conclusion, this productive power, this power to influence future usage is a basic characteristic of the standard-descriptive dictionary.[52]

But while the productive power of a dictionary which describes only the regular, active usage at present is great, the user will not, on the other hand, find in it, information about everything that occurs in the texts at present. To comply with this need is the task of the overall-descriptive dictionary. The selective principles of such an informative dictionary will be much broader than those of a standard-descriptive one. Such a dictionary will tend to register also the occasional applications by individual authors, the archaism, the dialecticms; it will probably tend to indicate more technical terms, and use more encyclopedic elements in its definitions; and it will tend to be more historical that the standard-descriptive dictionary, because one reads also older bokks written in a generally "obsolete" way. In short, an overall-descriptive dictionary of the general language tries to help the user to understand all the texts and communications likely to be read and heard by him, with the exception of the most technical ones (for instance, chemical abstracts, etc.).[53] Obviously, such a reference dictionary cannot be as homogeneous as the standard-descriptive one; sometimes, it also happens that the single spheres of language to which a lexical item belongs are not sufficiently discerned, so that the dictionary does not comply with its descriptive task as perfectly as we would like. But even if it errs by projecting the whole mass of different and differentiated lexical items more or less on one level,[54] it complies with its informative task and helps the user.

---

[52] It will be clear that practically any dictionary has a normative power (cf. Hausenblas), because a man who does not have a choice of different dictionaries at hand can try to check his uncertainties in any dictionary, monolingual or bilingual; every lexicographer must reckon with this circumstance. But the standard-descriptive dictionary not only reckons with it, but the endeavour to comply with it is one of its central purposes.

[53] As an example of such an overall-descriptive dictionary can be indicated *Webster's Third*, which has also rather strong encyclopedic inclinations.

[54] This is what is meant by Malkiel (PL 9) "The average dictionary not only tends to overlook differences in chronological levels, but, as a rule, represents a medley of diverse social and regional dialects".

Quite frequently, the standard-descriptive dictionary and the overall-descriptive dictionary are combined in one single publication. The usual procedure is that the standard-descriptive part of the resulting dictionary is treated as a box within another box. The dictionary which is published is then basically of the overall-descriptive type, but all obsolete, regional etc. items are labelled as such by a sign or a label. In this way what is not labelled can be considered "normal" in the sense of a standard-descriptive dictionary.[55] This type of dictionary is exceedingly useful, not only for practical (commercial) reasons, but also because the boundaries between what belongs to a strictly standard-descriptive dictionary and what does not are not always clear, and because they are subject to changes: a mistake in a label is less disagreable than a mistake in the selection. In our opinion, the so-called a c a d e m i c dictionary can be considered a conspicuous species of this combined type of dictionaries: it is a big dictionary basically of the overall-descriptive type, usually with a strong historical and even stronger philological predilections; the technical terms are not present, in the majority of cases, in such a great number, and the encyclopedic element, though present in many definitions, is not over-stressed. The standard-descriptive nucleus of such an academic dictionary is elaborated with a varying degree of clarity.[56]

5.2.5 Another dimension on which different types of dictionaries can be discerned pertains to the numbers of languages represented.

In m o n o l i n g u a l d i c t i o n a r i e s only one language is represented. The most important variety of this type is those dictionaries which we discussed in the preceding section; indeed, the usual situation is that a standard-descriptive, an overall-descriptive or an academic dictionary is monolingual.

Two languages are represented in b i l i n g u a l d i c t i o n a r i e s. The usual aim of a bilingual dictionary is to help in translating from one language into another, or in producing texts in language other the user's native one, or both. The usual situation is that the more descriptive tasks are reserved to the monolingual dictionaries, particularly if a living language is to be described.

In those cases, however, when the compilation of a monolingual dictionary is not to be expected soon, a bilingual dictionary assumes some of the descriptive tasks.[57] As bilingual dictionaries will be discussed in detail in chapter VII it is not necessary to add more remarks on them now.

---

[55] The same procedure is sometimes used in the dictionaries of dead languages. An epoch and or a dialect are considered basic ("classical", etc.); the respective items have no labels. The other items ("archaic", "postclassical", "late", "dialectal", etc.) are labelled as such.

[56] Some examples of academic dictionaries: *Norsk Riksmålsordbok* (1930), *Ordbok over det danske Sprog* (1919—1954).

[57] This is most frequently the case of the dead languages: a dictionary like Liddell-Scott-Jones, Greek-English Lexicon, Oxford 1940 not only indicates the English translations, but describes also the Greek lexicon.

Only unfrequently are more than two languages represented in one dictionary:[58] as we shall see in the discussion of bilingual dictionaries, the fact that there is no great isomorphism between single languages makes it a hard task to find the lexical equivalents of two languages. To indicate the lexical equivalents of more than two languages simultaneously is usually possible only if we alsolutely neglect polysemy and take into consideration only the dominant senses of the single words. The situation is easier if the languages in question are closely related, but even in this case the difficulties are formidable.

If we do not take into consideration such specific works as comparative dictionaries which have etymological aims we can say that the only domain in which multilingual, more-than-bilingual dictionaries have a justification is the field of technical terminology. The meaning of technical terms is usually much more precisely defined than that of a general word, so that semantic equivalence can be established more accurately. It is also possible to neglect polysemy, to neglect, in the indication of a term's meaning, all other senses than the terminological ones, so that it is easier to find the precise equivalents in the other languages. This is why there are some successful multilingual dictionaries of different technical terminologies. But even in this field, the difficulties are great and the "false friends" (see above) more numerous than one would casually assume.[59]

5.2.6 The purpose for which a dictionary is intended is a powerful determining factor. Some types of dictionaries are conspicuous for the severe restriction of their purpose. Probably the most important among these are the pedagogical dictionaries. They usually restrict either the number of entries and the indications of the words' single senses, or the phraseological indications so as to cover only what somebody learning a language may be expected to say, write, and read; dictionaries of this type frequently contain more explanations, translations, glosses etc. than their more general counterparts.[60]

Other pedagogical dictionaries are of a prescriptive (or prohibitive) character. Very frequent are orthographical and orthoepical dictionaries:

---

[58] Some examples of trilingual and quadrilingual dictionaries and of the reasons for their compilation can be found in Malkiel, PL 13.

[59] Zima reports different interesting situations where a multilingual dictionary could be useful. For example, the speakers of Hausa live both in Anglophone and Francophone states. Therefore, a Hausa-English-French dictionary would be useful. The situation is of particular interest, because the usefulness of such a dictionary has not only practical reasons. Such a dictionary could also have some unifying influence on speakers of Hausa in different areas. The problems of anisomorphism, however, would probably force the eventual compiler to conceive such a dictionary as a rather small one.

[60] For example A. S. Hornby — E. V. Gatenby — H. Wakefield, *The advanced learner's dictionary of current English*, 2nd ed., London 1963 — Cf. the detailed discussion of the pedagogical dictionaries of this type in LS 2, 1957, 110.

they concentrate for the most part on giving indications as to how to spell and how to pronounce the lexical units.[61] When the norm of a standard national language is being constituted, reconstituted or simply changed, and above all when there is a puristic movement in the society or even a situation characterized by diglossia, many prohibitive and generally prescriptive dictionaries are published: the two aspects, the prescriptive and the prohibitive one, are usually combined. The purpose of these dictionaries is to enforce the regular usage of the lexical items. Considered from one point of view, these prescriptive dictionaries show a logical connection with standard-descriptive ones: the tone of the latter may verge to prescription, or there may be isolated prescriptive and prohibitive elements within the standard-descriptive dictionary. There is no reason to wonder or to object if the matter is treated with reason and delicacy; very frequently, however, the task of prescription is discharged with a remarkable pettiness which is to be avoided.

Scientific and other similar purposes may produce lists of words which are frequently called dictionaries but whose real status as dictionaries is open to question. The two most outstanding members of this class are probably the reverse dictionaries (indices a tergo) which are alphabetically arranged, but from the end of the word to its beginning[62] and the dictionaries indicating the frequencies of occurrence of the single words in different languages.[63]

These are only some examples of those cases when the purpose of the dictionary gives it a very conspicuous character. But it is important to realize that every dictionary, even the most general one, pursues a certain aim or set of aims. For example, the presentation of the material depends very much upon whether the dictionary is planned to serve primarily one's scholarly colleagues, or the students, or the man in the street.[64]

---

[61] For instance, Duden, *Rechtschreibung der deutschen Sprache* (many different editions); S. I. Ožegov — A. B. Šapiro, *Orfografičeskij slovar' russkogo jazyka*, Moskva 1956; N. Bagaev, *Osetinskij orfografičeskij slovar'*, Dzaudzykau 1947.

[62] A Greek dictionary of this type (P. Kretschner — E. Locker, *Rückläufiges Wörterbuch der griechischen Sprache*, Göttingen 1944) begins with the following sequence of entries: *a, a, ba, hyperba, korba, ..., da, ... panstratia, aka, kouka, epipola, analfa, ma, hama, homa, katana, mna, ou, pa, papa, papapa, ra, bra, kra*, etc. — Cf. Malkiel, PL 17; Swanson, PL 76; J. Štindlová, Cahiers 2, 1960, 79ff.; T. Sebeok, Lingua 11, 1962, 371ff. — The rhyming dictionaries (in older time frequently called *Gradus ad Parnassum*) are the predecessors of the reverse dictionaries: they indicate words which form rhymes. Dictionaries of this type flourished mainly when the composition of verses was though a very elegant pastime. — It is not without interest to note that old Arab dictionaries were generally based on the reverse order, or on some modification of it (Petráček).

[63] See Swanson, PL 65.

[64] Cornyn (PL 274), who makes this distinction, is certainly right in observing that the groups are not mutually exclusive. But the tone of the presentation, the language in which it is couched will depend very much upon the supposed users: cf. Harrell, PL 53. Cf. Also Martin, PL 153 and Householder, PL 279.

The purpose of a dictionary varies in yet other respects. As mentioned above, the character of a monolingual dictionary depends observably upon whether its purpose is descriptive and normative or whether it is descriptive and purely explanatory. The difference between a bilingual dictionary the purpose of which is to help to translate foreign texts into the user's native language and a bilingual dictionary which is to help to produce texts in a foreign language will be discussed in § 7.3.

The dictionary may pursue most different purposes in any respect. If it deals with a language with diglossia, it may try to present the two forms in a detached way, or to merge them, or oust the "vulgar" form, or to banish the "mummified" one, or to restrict both of them to functionally different styles, or an endless other number of possibilities. If it deals with a language whose standard national form is still unstabilized, it may try to describe it as it is, or it may try to make it richer by introducing newly coined words and expressions to fill up the onomasiological gaps, or it may try to unify neologisms coming from different sources, etc. If a dictionary deals with a language which does not as yet have standard national form, it may just present a dialect of it, or more of them (if there are any), by comparison or by contrast, and possibly but not necessarily, with an emphasis on the encyclopedic explanation of the folkloristic culture-bound items, or it may try to establish a standard national form, etc. Or the purpose of a dictionary may be just a general one, to be a descriptive dictionary of the standard national language.

In short, the possible aims of dictionaries show a variation as great as that of the language and of the society's needs and their subjective interpretation.[65] It is clearly impossible to pursue all these purposes in one dictionary.[66] The decision concerning the purpose or the combination of purposes of a planned dictionary is one of the most important ones. A good part of both the scientific and the commercial success of the dictionary will be a result of how reasonably this decision was made and how adroitly it was carried out.

5.2.7 The last dimension which we shall discuss is the size of the dictionaries. It is one of those dimensions where no precise statements, but only "impressionistic appraisals" (as Malkiel[67] calls them) are possible: size is not mere bulk and so the number of the entries of a dictionary, numerically precise as it may be, is only a rough indication of its informative power. Very much depends upon how the entry itself is worked out.

Much more important than the statement of the absolute number of the entries would be the indication of how great a part of the total lexicon (stock of lexical units) is presented in the dictionary; even if formulated in this more

---

[65] Cf. Malkiel PL 8.
[66] Martin PL 153.
[67] Malkiel PL 8.

correct way, the size of the dictionary cannot be indicated precisely, because the precise value of the lexicon remains unknown.[68]

We must not forget, either, that there is a certain relativity in different languages themselves: a language with only an unconsiderable variation and no literature spoken in a culturally simple milieu, can be treated rather exhaustively in a dictionary whose size is not necessarily too bulky, whereas a medium dictionary of a language spoken in a diversified society may be several times as big.

It would probably be better to speak about the degree of completeness, or exhaustiveness, or density of a dictionary. But while these new terms would bring new troubles of their own, "size" is a traditional term which can be safely used if it is correctly understood.

5.2.8 Though single dictionaries show as great a variation in this respect as in other dimensions, we can perceive several traditional types.

A big dictionary which tries to be exhaustive is called a thesaurus. When we take into consideration what we know about the constant innovations caused in language by new applications of lexical units, we are not surprised that it is only the dead languages (including, of course, languages like Middle English) which is represented by a finite set of texts[69] and which, therefore, can be studied, analyzed, and presented in its totality. This finiteness of the set of texts makes the thesaurus at least theoretically possible, but there is yet another, and probably more important, aspect of the situation: no new sentences are produced in a dead language.[70] Consequently, the generative power of the dictionary will not be one of the lexicographer's first concerns (though if the descriptive work is done throughly, the descriptive statements plus the examples can be used as patterns to be imitated). The other consideration is as important: in a finite and thus limited set of texts, each and every application,

---

[68] Malkiel PL 8.

[69] Even in this context, the term "finite" has only a relative value: there are always new finds of manuscripts, inscriptions, etc., i.e. of new texts.

[70] The real situation is more complex than this statement: for example, Latin is still written and to some extent also spoken; but of course nobody is a native speaker of Latin today. Motalová reports a similar situation in Armenian: sometimes it happens that two highly educated speakers, one of the Eastern and one of the Western variant of Armenian, prefer to converse in Grabar, i.e. in Classical Armenian, though this form can be regarded as a dead language. We probably do not have to discuss all these questions at length as everybody will intuitively agree that this shadowy after-death life of classical languages like Latin is not comparable with the way languages like English or French or Hausa or Marathi are used. Greater difficulties sometimes arise with a strong diglossia, because the adversaries of the older variant of the respective language (such as, for example, Greek Katharewusa) will maintain that it is a dead language only artificially used, whereas the adversaries of the modern form (such as, for instance, Greek Dhimotiki) will maintain that the classical form still enjoys uninterrupted life in its own sphere.

every nuance, every hapax is more important than in an open set (i.e. a living language) where each new book an every new conversation may bring new, different applications. Therefore, a theasaurus[71] tries not only to indicate all the lexical units which occur in the texts, bult also tends to indicate all their occurrences, or all the important ones, ideally with at least abridged quotations of the relevant contexts (i.e. the "good" ones, cf. § 6.3.1.1).[72]

As far as the living languages are concerned, it must be remarked that this degree of exhaustiveness, of density, can be reached only in finite texts, like for example, the texts produced by single authors: a special dictionary of, say, Shakespeare can be based on the principle of the thesaurus. A dictionary of a living language with always new texts coming into existence and with an endless number of spoken utterances which cannot be completely and exhaustively recorded cannot be built on the principle of a thesaurus.[73]

Even the biggest dictionary of a living language cannot indicate everything, such as every occasional application of every lexical unit: it necessarily must try to abstract the regularities, the norm. It is, however, possible to regard a corpus of authors writing in a language as a (finite) set of texts, and treat it accordingly. This is the way most of the big, academic dictionaries proceed: they abstract the regularity of use and present it mainly on the basis of and illustrated by numerous quotations from the authors; and they register also the more occasional applications, occuring in the text of an important authors.[74] If they are of an historical character, it happens that the old texts are treated in a way which approaches that of a thesaurus.[75]

The fact that in a big, academic dictionary not all occurences of a lexical unit are quoted and not all its occasional applications are presented is not the only difference between this type of a dictionary and a thesaurus. The other difference consists in the fact that even the biggest academic dictionaries do not list all the lexical units of the language in question. It is above all the endless ranks of scientific terms (chemical terminology alone is said to consist

---

[71] E.g., *Thesaurus linguae Latinae*, Lipsiae 1900ff. (not yet completed).

[72] More or less extensive quotations of all passages in which every word of a text occurs are given in the so-called concordances. The usual situation is that such concordances cannot and do not elaborate the semantic analysis of the words. A book of reference which indicates all passages of a text (or of a group of texts) in which a word occurs by the mere enumeration of the citations (without quotations; see on the difference, generally without any other forther information, is usually called an index verborum.

[73] This important distinction and the whole discussion of the thesauri is based on Ščerba, Izvestija 101, 104, 105. — Cf. footnote 43 on another terminological value of *"thesaurus"*. Garvin (Word 3, 1947, 128; review of Ščerba, Izvestija (calls this type of dictionary the *general concordance* (Cf. the preceding footnote).

[74] The motive for this is usually reinforced by the circumstance that these big academic dictionaries use to belong to the type of the overall-descriptive dictionaries.

[75] For example, *The Oxford English Dictionary*, Oxford 1933ff.

of more than 400.000 terms) which are not listed. This is a reasonable and correct policy: because these dictionaries are of a general character, they can leave unmentioned what belongs to the restricted, special languages only.[76] But we shall have occasion to see (cf. 6.4) that the respective decisions belong sometimes among the most difficult and subjective ones.

The medium dictionary is usually of a rather more standard-descriptive character, because it saves space above all at the expense of the obsolete and dialectal lexical units and of more occasional, less regular applications, so that it may be expected to list the lexical units of the standard national language in its contemporary form (without the restricted languages). Thus, it frequently happens that the medium dictionary has a higher generative power than a large on (unless the latter has a special standard-descriptive nucleus — see above. This character is frequently also stressed by the circumstance that the medium dictionary has fewer quotations from literature but more "typical combinations of words" than the large one.[77]

A small dictionary usually has no quotations or examples (with the exception of the more important set expressions), so that its generative power is rather low. The vocabulary of the small dictionary is reduced in comparison with that of the medium one; the reduction usually eliminates not only the obsolete and similar lexical units (absent also from the medium dictionary), but also the less frequent and unimportant lexical units which belong to the standard national language, and the less frequent senses of the polysemous lexical units.[78]

It would be useful but it is not possible to convert the above characteristic into concrete numbers of entries: single dictionaries vary because what some of them present as subentries are independent entries in others, and different languages also require different forms of presentation. If we were to make a

---

[76] Cf. on some present and possibly also future developments in this field below.

[77] Cf. Filipec LSB 198 who classifies the dictionaries by this criterion; for him, a big dictionary is the one with the quotations from *belles-lettres*, a medium one indicates the typical combinations of words, and a small one is even more condensed. Cornyn PL 274 classifies the dictionaries in a similar way (but he puts together things we keep apart in the present discussion): dictionaries with encyclopedic indications and dictionaries with indications of usage (morphological and syntactic features), and glossaries, lists of forms with only some minimal information.

[78] The whole discussion of the size of the dictionaries is concerned only with dictionaries which at the same time are general. Special dictionaries are not so variegated in this respect, at least in the majority of cases, because they are based on restricted material. But what we said about size can be applied mutatis mutandis also in the case of the special dictionaries; e.g., as far as the special dictionaries of linguistic terminology go, one can regard J. Knobloch, *Sprachwissenschaftliches Wörterbuch*, Heidelberg 1961 ff., as a big one, O. S. Akhmanova, *Slovar' lingvističeskich terminov*, Moskva 1966, as a medium, and J. Marouzeau, *Lexique de la terminologie linguistique*, Paris 1951, as a small one. — It is also worthwhile to observe that the bilingual dictionaries are, so to speak, one degree lower in the whole gamut, because the really big dictionaries of living languages are usually monolingual: Havránek LSB 49.

very rough estimate (with which everybody is free to disagree), we would be inclined to say that medium dictionaries usually do not have less that 40.000 and small dictionaries not less than 10.000 (but preferably more) entries.

Smaller than this are usually only special dictionaries (e.g. of the works of single, not too prolific authors) and similar special word lists. Among such "subminimal" dictionaries we can discern, for example, a vocabulary (which is a bilingual word-list with translation, e.g. as an appendix to the edition of a foreign author (or a glossary) which is a word list with explanations of words supposedly difficult for the reader to understand, though they belong to the reader's language.[79] Apart from such specialities, a yet smaller general dictionary of the standard national languages seems to be useful (if is a language of a diversified society and rich literature) only if it is planned and worked out as a special pedagogical tool for the absolute beginner who learns the language.[80] In other sociolinguistic situations, such a very small dictionary may serve similar purposes, such as , for example, to teach people read and write in a alphabetisation campaign (as suggested by Zima), etc.

This is only a skeleton of a classification[81] of dictionaries. The single dictionaries show different combinations of the properties mentioned above. Some

---

[79] Malkiel PL 8 sq.

[80] Ščerba, *Izvestija* 106, 107.

[81] Another important classification is that of Malkiel PL 5 sqq. According to Malkiel, dictionaries can be classified (1) by their range (2) by their perspective, and (3) by their presentation. The first category is subdivided into (a) the density of entries, (b) the number of languages covered, and (c) the degree of concentration on strictly lexical data, at the expense of realia, proper names, etc. In the second category (classification by perspective), Malkiel discerns three basic perspectives, viz. (a) the fundamental dimension (diachronism versus synchronism) (b) the basic arrangement of entries (conventional, i.e. usually alphabetic, semantic, and arbitrary), and (c) the level of tone (objective, preceptive or prohibitive, and jocular). In the third category, the attention is focused on the definition, on the verbal documentation, on the graphic illustration, and on the presence of special features (for example, the localizations, the phonetic transcription, etc.). — T. A. Sebeok, *Materials for a typology of dictionaries* (Lingua 11, 1962, 363ff.), finds that the following 17 properties are decisive when we try to decide to which type a dictionary belongs. A dictionary can be (1) generated (a native scholar produces a list of words he feels should constitute a glossary), or it can be (2) abstracted (from texts); there are different (3) limits of the corpus (of excerpted texts); (4) the internal diversity of the corpus may be envisaged or not; (5) single forms of multiple forms can be indicated. The dictionary can be (6) based on form, or it can be (7) based on meaning; it can be (8) organized by form; or it can be (9) organized by meaning. (10) Cross references can be given according to form; or they can be given (11) according to meaning. (12) Documentation can be (a) dialectal, or (b) geographical, or (c) textual. (13) Exemplification, (14) glosses, (15) frequency data, (16) etymological commentary, (17) encyclopedic commentary: all this information mentioned in (13)—(17) can be given with various wealth of detail, or not at all. — Ščerba started a classification of dictionaries in his paper in *Izvestija*, but to my knowledge he never completed this work. His dimensions were (a) academic dictionary (i.e. a dictionary similar to the type we call "standard-descriptive") :: reference dictionary (cf. footnote 49); (b) encyclopedic :: general dictionary; (c) thesaurus :: normal dictionary (mono-

of the combinations are rather typical, as, for example, the tendency of an overall-descriptive dictionary to develop towards a historical one. European overall-descriptive dictionaries, large and medium, are much more purely linguistic that their American counterparts (cf. the pictorial and generally encyclopedic material in Webster or any American dictionary of this sort). Some of the different combinations are given by the "logic of the things" (e.g. the historical tendency of overall-descriptive dictionaries), but some are brought together purely by the authors' decision (e.g. decision to indicate the etymology as an appendix to each entry of a synchronic dictionary.[82]

In planning the preparation of a dictionary, it is of vital importance to decide as early as possible what character the dictionary should have, in all these dimensions.

In the present book, we focus our interest on what we consider the most important dictionaries, viz. the monolingual general dictionaries of the standard national language, and the bilingual ones.

lingual or bilingual); (d) normal dictionary (monolingual or bilingual) : : ideological (i.e. synonymic) dictionary; (e) monolingual : : translational (i.e. what we call bilingual dictionary); (f) non-historical : : historical dictionary.

[82] Cf. Barnhart PL 161 for a highly constructive discussion of the possible decisions in the planning of an English overall-descriptive dictionary with a strong encyclopedic *teint*.

CHAPTER VI

THE MONOLINGUAL DICTIONARY

BASIC DECISIONS

6.1 When planning a monolingual dictionary, we must make two basic decisions at the very beginning.

First, it is necessary to analyze the language in question and find out what varieties of it there are and how they are interconnected. Among other things, it is necessary to know (at least impressionistically, at the beginning of the work, but the more thoroughly the better) the difference between the literary and the spoken form of the standard national language; are there frequent obsolete words in the literary form of the standard national language? Are there many (different) dialectisms to be found interspersed in texts couched generally in the standard national language? Is it self-evident to a speaker of the language in question what form these dialectisms would have in the standard national language, and does he generally understand them? How far back goes the literature which is still read by the generally educated people, and that which is read in schools of general education;[1] what is the difference between the oldest texts that belong here and the texts written in the contemporary literary standard national language on one side, and the contemporary spoken standard national language on the other?[2] When these and many similar questions (all of them concerning variation in language, see Chap. IV) are answered, at least intuitively, or, if even this is impossible, when the lexicographer realizes where problems of this sort will probably be located, it is necessary to decide which varieties of the language the prepared dictionary will have to cover, and which criteria will be used to distinguish them. If the (preliminary) answers were only of the "impressionistic" and "intuitive" character, much care must be given to the observation whether the subsequent study of the concrete material corroborates or modifies them; if they are modified, it is vitally important to make the necessary change of policy when the work is not yet too progressed.

---

[1] What is meant are literary works that are conceived as belonging to the same language; not, e.g., Sanskrit texts read in schools in India. For instance in French, this covers texts as far back as, e.g., Molière, but certainly not *chansons de gestes*.

[2] Cf. Cornyn PL 274 on the different historical and other background of languages like Pashtu, Greek and Turkish, and on the consequent necessity of different solutions.

Second, it is necessary to decide to what type the prepared dictionary should belong. What questions are to be asked and aswered follows from the preceding chapter about types of dictionaries.

The character of nearly all the lexicographer's subsequent work and his subsequent decisions on single points and problems follow (or should follow) as a consequence of these two vital decisions. For example: If his dictionary is to be an overall-descriptive one, the lexicographer will be less troubled by the presence of dialectisms and archaisms among his entries than if he prepares a standard-descriptive dictionary which has to have great generative power, etc. There is no general reply to a question like whether a dictionary should contain obsolete words or not; the choice among the different possible answers depends upon the two basic decisions mentioned above. A clear decision in both respects cannot guarantee freedom from error in every single case where such questions arise, but it will spare the lexicographer much vacillation from one case to another and much nervousness when he sees similar things solved in a different way in other dictionaries that pursue other aims: and above all, it will give the dictionary the necessary conceptual and methodological unity.

The lexicographer who is concerned with languages which are not fully stabilized, either because their standard national language is of very recent origin (or even only *in statu nascendi*), or because they are going through a period of rapid development (usually under the impact of the new patterns of life brought about by the civilization of our time), will be confronted, at least in the majority of cases, with several quite neuralgic problems such as the following. Which form of language is to be considered as setting the standard, if there is not a clear prevalence of a dialect, of a group of texts, or of one of the layers in diglossia? Questions like this cannot be answered by the isolated effort of the lexicographer, nor will he be able to offer his part of the solution before he has gone through his material; he must, however, be aware of such problems before he starts his work in order to be able to observe the data from the very beginning.[3]

ARTICULATION OF WORK

6.2 In the following paragraphs, we discuss the work to be done by the lexicographer. This discussion will be articulated as follows:

(1) the collection of material;

(2) the selection of entries;

(3) the construction of entries; and

(4) the arrangement of the entries.

[3] More on this in § 4.3.

This articulation is given, to some degree, by the succession of the single phases of the work itself; we must first have the material to be able to do any further work, and we must first select the entries for inclusion in the dictionary before we can construct them. In real life, however, there is a good amount of overlapping between the phases. Because, for example, only few lexicographers (especially those who work in the field of the living languages) stop the whole excerption absolutely when they have selected the entries and have started work on their construction, they will have to anticipate the necessity of adding some new indications to entries preliminarily regarded as finished. The lexicographer should not be unduly embarrassed by this circumstance, because it should be apparent from the whole preceding discussion that (a) all the facts of language do not appear in the data simultaneously, and that (b) language changes constantly, so that there will always be new data. On the other hand, the amount of overlapping between the phases should not surpass a certain limit, because if it is necessary to re-work frequently und repeatedly what has been done and if always new changes of previous decisions are found necessary a considerable loss of time and money is almost inevitable. It is impossible to state precisely what is a necessary, reasonable amount of overlapping and what is not. Impressionistically, one can state the following "rules": if the posterior excerption or information only infrequently adds to the entries which have been constructed by them, and if these additions consist generally of specifications, mainly in contextual nuances and figurative meaning, there is no reason to worry; if, however, posterior excerption of information frequently compels the lexicographer to change the whole construction of some entries, or shows him that there are some direct senses of some lexical units in the sphere of general language (the sphere of technical terminology is not so important and dangerous, in this respect) which he did not know, then probably the material on which the lexicographer based his construction of the entries was not ripe enough, was not sufficient. The same applies to the selection of the entries: new, previously unknown, lexical units will appear constantly; if the majority of them are not selectionable for inclusion into the dictionary by the principles which governed the original selection and if there are only occasional additions, the lexicographer can be content; on the other hand, the selection of entries was probably made from an insufficient material if constantly new additions appear to be necessary, unless the additions are undoubtedly recently coined, successful and therefore quickly stabilized neologisms.

COLLECTION OF MATERIAL

6.3 If the lexicographer is working on a bigger project, he will be well advised to work out some samples of entries when he thinks that his material is sufficient. The collection of the material is, however, continued and the lexicographer observes the effects the new material will have on the samples of entries. If the results of his observation are negative (in the sense of the preceding remarks), the collection of material must remain the main task and new samples should be made later. These samples may differ in size (for example one can work out only some isolated entries, or, preferably, some sequences of entries) and they can be used in different ways: in smaller projects, they are rotated among and discussed by the members of the team, but in bigger projects it is worth-while to have them published and discussed by more scholars.

6.3.1 The basic form of the collection of material is the excerption of texts. When he excerpts, the lexicographer takes out of a text lexical units (words) which are of interest and puts them on single slips of paper;[4] the excerption is of value above all if — or rather only if the lexical unit (word) in question is quoted with its lexicographic context and preferably if other indications are added, such as the citation of the source of the excerpt etc. Since both monolingual and bilingual dictionaries of the type that is the focus of our interest (general, either standard-descriptive or overall-descriptive) are usually compiled for languages which have at least some written literature, it is primarily the written texts which are excerpted; but if there are no or few texts written in the language in question, the situation is not fundamentally different: one begins generally with those oral texts which can be called "oral literature", i.e. narrations and such things the text of which is more or less fixed. But (as Zima reports from various regions of Africa) the language of this "oral literature" is frequently different (and sometimes very considerably different) from the really spoken one. Therefore, the lexicographer has to collect also the colloquial material in the true sense of the word (not only monologues, but also elicited answers, and preferably also dialogues, talks, discussions, negotiations of affairs in business and office, etc.).

---

[4] This is the classical method; recently, new techniques have been developed which use the possibility of getting many xerox copies or photographs of a text or of a passage cheaply and quickly. Instead of copying (only) the context on a slip of paper, the excerptor underlines it (or at least the prospective entry-word), or marks it in a similar way, in the xerox copy or photograph of the whole passage (usually a page or a part of a page). Cf. de Tollenaere, Cahiers 6, 1965, 109ff.: a detailed discussion of these new techniques, with comparative information concerning their application in different lexicographical projects. — A radically different method of collecting contexts is offered by the automatic data processing machines; see below § 8.5. Cf. also Wahrig, *Wörterbucharbeit*, p. 59.

The decision as to what texts should be excerpted is a consequence of the lexicographer's two basic decisions concerning the scope and the type of the dictionary: if it is to be an overall-descriptive dictionary, the repertory of the excerpted texts must be broader, in the different dimensions of the variation of language, than if we decide to prepare a standard-descriptive dictionary (or a dictionary the main purpose of which is to constitute the norm, or even a prescriptive one). In the latter case, we primarily make the excerption from only those texts which are written in the standard national language of the sort which is considered good standard and which we expect to be used in the immediate future. If possible, all such texts should be excerpted; if this is not possible because of the limitations of time and money, the selection of the texts to be excerpted should be — within the eventual limits set by the preceding two sentences — as broad and should cover as diverse texts as possible. It is, above all, the *belles-lettres* that are to be excerpted, but the more pragmatic texts (legal, administrative, etc.)[5] should also not be neglected.[6] The excerption of newspapers implies the danger that journalistic texts make a rather frequent use of many occasional expressions and ephemeral neologisms, and that the newpapers seldom have the literary standard of many other texts. But the excerption of newspapers has the great advantage that newpapers (and periodical journals like weeklies, monthlies, etc., as well) consist chiefly of very recent, contemporary, even dated texts on most variegated topics.

Though written texts also contain passages written to imitate the spoken language (such as some dialogues in novels and dramas, etc.), it cannot be doubted that this procedure, this putting of the written texts into focus, implies as its consequence a certain understressing of the spoken language, and above all of the more colloquial form of it.

If we are dealing with a language that has a very strong diglossia, i.e. if the written texts differ vastly from the spoken ones, we have two possible courses of action. Either we can decide that we shall compile a dictionary of

---

[5] Scientific texts have their special problems; usually not much is gained by their excerption. In the majority of cases, it is more to the purpose of a general dictionary to excerpt the respective school textbooks.

[6] No need to stress that all this is full of problems. When discussing these questions, Horálek (LSB 197 sq.) is right when he says that in reality, the spoken language differs from what one gets when one excerpts *belles-lettres*, even those written in the most colloquial style. Kahane and Kahane (PL 253) discuss these problems in a similar tone: is fiction a realistic basis for a description of the frequent and typical patterns of the spoken languages? Should we not be afraid of a return to the 17th century principle of the authorities? But Filipec (LSB 198) is quite right when stating bluntly that "the basis of the excerption must be the classical authors" — only the word "classical" hides the danger of being understood as "old", so that our formulation which uses the idea of "setting the standard" (cf. Filipec, loc. cit., end of the page) is perhaps better.

the literary standard national language,[7] or we decide that we shall take into consideration the spoken forms, too; in the latter case, it is necessary to explore the spoken variety as a language of its own, i.e. excerpt the oral texts, etc.[8]

If the spoken form of a language is not vastly different from the written one, the emphasis laid on written texts does not leap to the eye, though indeed a dictionary which does not give as full an account of the colloquial forms as of the literary ones is not fully descriptive in the precise sense of the term. But since colloquialisms are frequently more or less occasional, or ephemeral, a dictionary, with the probable exception of a special restricted dictionary of colloquialisms, would have many of them aside in any case, even if they were excerpted. But it is certainly correct if the more important and — which is the first concern — the stabilized colloquialisms are included in the general dictionary; the technique of their acquisition is described below.

6.3.1.1 The lexicographic context which should or even must be quoted on the slips is that part of the verbal context which allows us to perceive in which signification the word in question is applied, and to perceive at least some of its semantic features and grammatical properties; the lexicographic context should be as short but, primarily, as clear as possible.[9]

Not all verbal contexts have the same value. A context like *he painted the window* shows at least that a window can be the object of painting; but the context fails to give us a hint how to understand the verb (1⁰. "to colour the surface of something", 2⁰: "to produce a picture of something", etc.) so that its value is rather low. If we study, for example, the different Hindi words for different types of rain (Ccf. above, a context like *jis rāt bāriš hotī, usse agle din use chuṭṭī ho jātī,* "he used to get his free day after those nights when

---

[7] In this way, we have, for example, dictionaries of Literary Arabic. This solution is usually preferred in those cases where the standard national language is little other than the literary form, only the local dialects being used in speaking. These dialects can be, and in frequent concrete cases also really are, described in special dictionaries of their own.

[8] If there is such a situation in a language, the spoken form is usually on the verge of becoming the medium of written communications also — The word "texts" refers here to any sentence or group of sentences couched in the spoken language in question.

[9] A similar definition: "un contexte limité et clair qui nous permet de dire que tel «mot» est employé dans tel «sens». This is the definition of "lexie" (which we call "lexicographic context") as stated by de Tollenaere, Cahiers 3, 1961, 104; this statement is inspired by A.-J. Greimas who in his turn is inspired by Hjelmslev. M. Joos, *Semology: A Linguistic Theory of Meaning* (in: Studies in Linguistics 13, Nr 3—4, p. 53ff.) uses the term *collocation* in a similar way: "a word-combination which through light on the meanings of the words involved"; cf. chapter 3 on the overlapping value of the term *collocation* in British (Firthian) linguistics. Some lexicographers (for example, scholars who might be summarily called the Czech lexicographic school in Prague) use the term *minimal context*; I do not use it because it could lead the excerptor to an unwelcome scarcity in his slips.

15*

there was rain"[10] tells us nothing about the type of the rain, *bāriš*. On the other hand, if we study a context like *adṛśya pluhār jaise niḥsvar pankhõ ke sahāre uṛ rahī thī* "the invisible rain flew as if on noiseless wings we learn much about the word *pluhār*, because this could not have been a torrential rain, but rather the contrary.

It is quite impossible to indicate how long a lexicographic context should be. Very frequently, one can understand the real signification of a word only if one takes into consideration not only the immediate context, but also things stated many pages before or afterwards.[11] Let us suppose that we try to establish the meaning of a lexical unit like *palsy-walsy*. If we read, in a novel, a sentence like *"They were quite palsy-walsy, you know!"*, we do not get much; it may happen that there is a distance of many chapters between the description of the conduct itself of the persons involved and its summary characterization as *palsy-walsy* in our sentence; or it may even happen that there is in the book excerpted, no passage giving a clue to the meaning of the word. A sentence like the one quoted is, then, no good lexicographic context, though it shows at least some things of minor importance, e.g., that *palsy-walsy* stands alone, without, say, *together* following it. Therefore, only if there are no better contexts, passages like the one quoted must suffice.[12]

In the study of dead languages it happens quite frequently that there is simply no good, illustrative context preserved from which the lexical meaning of an otherwise unknown word could be ascertained. In such a case, the so-called etymological method is used: the linguist tries to understand the meaning of the respective word from the meaning of the words with which it is related, from the general meaning of the stem from which it is derived, etc. Though the interpretation of, for example, Rig-Veda and Homer shows some successful cases of application of this method, it is better to use it only if there are no contexts or only for the eventual corroboration.

It will be clear that the lexicographer's attitude towards poor, uninformative contexts will be different: if (and only if) the prepared dictionary tries to approach the status of a thesaurus, it is necessary to quote everything. In a historical dictionary, a context which itself tells nothing may be very important simply because it is old, or because it testifies to the occurrence of a certain sense at a certain date, though the sense cannot be established from this

---

[10] The example is taken from P. A. Barannikov, *Osnovnye čerty leksičeskoj sinonimii sovremennogo Xindi*, Leningrad 1963, 15 sq., who quotes it in another connection.

[11] Cf. de Tollenaere, Cahiers de lexicologie 3, 1961, 105 on the different length of lexicographic contexts; p. 112 sq., he rightly says that it is sometimes necessary to read the whole text (say, the whole novel) in order to understand a word.

[12] In a case like the one described here, it is to advantage to note on the respective slip the citation of the remote passage which is relevant for the signification of the word, and eventually also its summary.

context alone, without the help of other passages; a large overall-descriptive dictionary may have to give evidence of the word's occurrence in different spheres. But for the lexicographer's task itself, i.e. for the establishment of the word's meaning, it is those contexts from which the concrete signification can be obtained which are of prime importance.

As already stated, the really significant lexicographic context of a word is not necessarily to be found close to it. On the contrary, it may occasionally be misleading to consider only what immediately precedes or follows. One example will suffice to illustrate the point.[13] The Eng. adjective *semantic* occurs first in the second edition of John Spencer's *A Discourse concerning Prodigies* (published in 1665). The Oxford Eng. Dict. (s.v.) duly indicates this fact and defines the meaning of the adjective as follows: "relating to signs of the weather". The sentence in which the adjective occurs (and which is quoted, in a slightly reduced form, by the OED) is: (a) *"Twere easie to shew how much this Semantick Philosophy, in all parts of it, was studied ... etc."* It is not necessary to stress that we find no clues for the meaning of *semantic* in this sentence. The indication of the meaning in the OED is without any doubt based on what immediately precedes this sentence, viz.: (b) *"Thus Castor and Pollux (those twin-lights, so called, seen sometimes about ships in the silences of the night) were anciently received as the indications of a quiet passage; because any disposition in the air to motion would soon have divorced those gentle fires."* On the strength of this passage, the definition of the meaning of semantic in OED ("relating to signs of the weather") seems to be quite correct. If we, however, go four pages back, we find the following statement: (c) *"Moreover, Philosophy will very probably direct us to the true Original of Divination by Prodigies, and the other Species thereof, Chiromancy, Capnomancy, Oneiromancy, Haruspicina, Augury .... all these curious arts .... contain under them the good liquor of a useful Philosophy."* There follow four pages of elaboration of the single points; sentence (b) is the last of these different examples and sentence (a) is the conclusion of the whole passage. Therefore, (a) "Semantick Philosophy, in all parts of it" (note the explicit reference to the fact that the concept is a complex one) does not refer only to the immediately preceding passage (b) "indications of a quiet passage" (i.e., weather), but to the whole preceding exemplification, and with it to the remote passage (c) which is the really conclusive lexicographic context of the adjective *semantic*: "concerned with the interpretation of various phenomena as symptoms of future events."

The lexicographer must also be very careful about the real purport of the passage out of which a context is excerpted. For instance, if a sentence like French *C'est joli!"*, Eng. *"What a nice thing to say!"* is excerpted, nobody can

---

[13] The whole example and the elaboration of its single points are taken from A. W. Read. *An account of the word "semantics"*, Word 4, 1948, 78 sq.

say whether *joli, nice* are to be understood in the ironical sense or not: only a much broader context can decide this. Very frequently, such contexts show only occasional contextual nuances of the meaning; but even if this is the case, it is good for the lexicographer to know about it, because it could be disagreable or even misleading, for example, to quote just such a passage as if the word in question were used in it in a direct sense. Sometimes, however, such applications are so frequent that the ironical sense can be considered stabilized: cf., for instance, Eng. nice, the ironical sense of which is regarded and treated as stabilized by many English dictionaries.

Therefore, a really good excerption requires one to know the whole excerpted text, to take into consideration all the relevant passages, not only the immediate environment of the word, and to understand thoroughly the purport of the relevant passage and consequently the eventual concrete contextual nuance of the word in its concrete application.

Another thing to consider during excerption and in the use of contexts is the following difference. When studying a word like, for instance, Eng. *horse*, we may meet on the one hand, a sentence like

The horse jumped over the fence with easiness,

and on the other hand a sentence like

The English word horse *has the same meaning as* cheval *in French.*[14]

In the first sentence, the speaker used the word to speak about the thing designated by it; in the second sentence, he speaks about the word itself. Obviously the two types of occurrence are different, but the difference is not so great for the lexicographer's purpose. Indeed, the second sentence is a statement of an opinion and as such is open to possible mistake, error bias, falsification or the like on the part of the man who produced it. But these cases are not so dangerous as they would seem if we use such statements with due caution.[15] On the contrary, very frequently such contexts that contain short, spontaneous, parenthetical explanations of a word are the most useful,

---

[14] The difference was established (for lexicographic purposes) by F. Hiorth, Sprache 4, 1958, 17. Hiorth calls the first type of a word's occurence in a sentence *Gebrauchsvorkommen*, the second type *Metavorkommen*. (Hiorth's paper is in German, and so are his examples which are translated here. The difference is said to be based on the semantic philosophy of Arne Naess, which I do not know. In other papers (Studia linguistica 9, 1955, 63 sq.; 10, 1956, 57), Hiorth develops other ideas from Naess and makes the distinction between the "actual" and the "intended" meaning. The difference seems to be much more important for Hiorth than for the present writers.

[15] The important thing ist not to treat similar statements as if they were more valid that they are. If a legal text explains the meaning of the word *prison*, we can take it as evidence for the restricted language of the law, but not necessarily for the standard national language; a similar statement coming from the 19th cent. is not necessarily valid today, etc.

just as the contexts in which one can study the synonyms (near-synonyms) or antonyms, etc., of the respective word.[16]

6.3.1.2 Good lexicographic contexts which have a high illustrative power are rather rare. Even more rare is a single context which shows the lexicographer really all the semantic features of a word and the whole range of its application, at least in one of its senses if it is polysemous. The usual situation is that more, and frequently many, contexts are necessary: one context will show, for example, that the sort of speech called *oration* is a public one, another that it is a formal one (i.e. that these two criterial features are parts of the disignatum), one context will show that a *register* is kept about marriages, another that it is used about funerals, yet another will show ships or voters as items of a register.

Just how many slips are needed if the lexicographer wishes to be reasonably sure that he has everything that is important in his material, is a problem beyond calculation. The archives of the big academic dictionaries of languages which have rich, ramified literatures and whose speakers form a complexely ramified society usually contain millions of slips. But even the lexicographer who prepares a monolingual dictionary of a language with a not very rich literature spoken by people with simple and not too diverse patterns of life should be prepared that there will be hundreds, or at least scores, of thousands of slips in his drawers.

More important and more useful than the quantitative aspect of the excerption is the lexicographer's ability to exercise a qualitative judgement: if new slips bring no new information, they are not necessary (if it is not a thesaurus we are preparing). The strategy of the excerption is very well described by F. Havlová:[17]

One begins with the total excerption i.e. one excerpts the whole lexical stock occuring in the writings of the most important authors, irrespective of the probability that some of the later slips will give no new semantic information.

This total excerption is carried out either on the thesaurus scale, or, more frequently, on the principle that if a word's signification is sufficiently attested in one author (or in a more detailed modification of the scheme, in one work of

---

[16] J. Hulbert, *Dictionaries British and American*, London 1955, p. 81, states as a part of his lexicographical experience that excerptors should be instructed to look for such contexts. He quotes the following passage (from Catlin, Indians, 1933, I, 219) as an example of a good context illustrating the meaning of the expression *salt meadow*: "We came into contact with an immense *saline, or «salt meadow», as they are termed in this country* [America] ... *some hundreds of acres of the prairie which were covered with an incrustation of salt.*"

[17] LSB 190f. — Cf. also Gleason, Monograph Series on Languages and Linguistics 14, 1961, p. 115ff.: an elaborate account of his conduct of a highly specialized excerption, with calculations of time, of probable density, and with many other technicalities.

an author), slips attesting the same signification are not collected from the same author (or the same work); they are, however, collected if they attest the same signification in another author (or in another work).

What follows is the partial excerption: only those words and significations are excerpted which are not yet attested in the material, or which are attested by a few slips but are generally very rare. Also excerpted are passages which attest for a word a signification identical to that of other slips at hand, but a different formal, combinatorial property of the word, such as the prepositional rection or case-rection. Passages showing different ranges of application should also be collected irrespective of whether the signification itself is new (i.e. not yet present in the slips) or not.

The special excerption is chronologically independent from the two types already described. What is recorded are the typical words of the restricted languages, be it the political, economical, and scientific terms, or slang words, or jargon expressions, or any other similar material according to the type of the dictionary under preparation.

When all these three types of excerption are completed, one goes on with the "gleaning": not yet excerpted texts are read and extraordinary, i.e. not yet attested data are collected.[18]

The conduct of such excerption is a task which requires no small delicacy and knowledge. As excerption is usually done by a staff of specialized and frequently outside workers, it is useful to write special instructions (i.e. a set of rules or policies) for them, in which not only the general intentions, but preferably also as precise rules as possible are given for the single steps. Such instructions should also contain statements on the lexical units to be excerpted (e.g. on the multiword ones), on the format of the slips and on the disposition of the single notes on them. To write such instructions is a very difficult task; it is almost impossible to compose the definitive draft of it before collecting some experience. The usual policy is to write a provisional draft first and then to observe, in the initial stages of the excerption, its lacunae, unclarities, and other deficiencies. The lexicographer will hardly get a really intimate knowledge of all these problems if he does not do an amount of excerption himself (preferably, of course, in the initial or even preparatory stage of it), even if there is a staff of special excerptors. The difinitive draft if the instruction is written only when the lexicographer has accumulated sufficient experience; it should be conceived and written in such a way that it can be supplement by a more detailed rules if a newly arising case brings the necessity of specification of a more general rule, but real alterations of the final, definitive version

[18] Among the "not yet excerpted texts", there will be also texts published after the main excerption has been stopped. The bigger the lexicographic project, the more important it is to go on with excerption of the gleaning type in order to keep the material up to date.

should be avoided. One of the points to be mentioned in the instructions is that if there arises a legitimate doubt whether a context should be excerpted or not, the decision should be positive: it is easy not to take into consideration an unnecessary, superfluous information contained in the slips, but it is practically impossible to re-examine what has not been excerpted.

A rich collection of contexts is frequently called the lexicographic archives. Such archives develop usually in connection with work on large, academic dictionaries and grow into a permanent institution which collects new contexts, prepares new editions of the original dictionary, or collects material and plans new dictionaries derived from the original project. Such archives contain millions of collected contexts; they are, therefore, an important source of information for different linguistic investigations.

Both the conduct of the excerption and the evaluation of the excerpted texts presuppose an intimate knowledge of the texts. It is not sufficient to classify a text, for example, by its author and the time of its origin; it is necessary to know the linguistic variation within the text. For instance, it is a well known fact that a lyrical passage in a Greek tragedy is written in another form of language than that used in the dialogues; or that a word occurring only in the 10th book of Rig-Veda is probably younger than those which occur in the other books. But there is a strong element of stylistic and generally linguistic variation in modern authors as well: different persons in a novel are characterized by the language they speak, etc.[19]

6.3.2 The excerption, though it is usually the main source of the fundamental material for the dictionary, never suffices in itself, irrespective of the number of the collected slips. The factor of the lexicographer's knowledge of the language is of vital importance.[20]

The lexicographer who compiles a monolingual dictionary is very frequently himself a native speaker of the language in question. In that case, it is a matter of course that he uses his knowledge of his own language in his work. It is no undue "introspection" if the lexicographer confronts each piece of information gained by excerption, or from any other source, with his own knowledge.[21] Indeed, a lexicographer who knows his language really well and who has a good critical sense can complete many a lacuna left in the

---

[19] Cf. Migliorini, *Vocabolario* 60, and Rey, Cahiers 7, 1965, 94, on the stylistic variation in individual literary works and its implication for lexicography.

[20] Cf. Janský LSB 131 and 138f.; Havlová LSB 192f.

[21] For the purpose of the present discussion, it is rather unimportant whether we speak about the lexicographer's "knowledge of his language", or about his "native speaker's competence", or about his "speech habits", or his "Sprachgefühl", or whether we use some other similar terms. Great as the differences implied in these and other terminological sets are, they need not be taken into consideration in our present context.

material, eliminate many misunderstandings as they may occur in the excerption, and prevent many other mistakes. In short: in lexicography a good knowledge of the language in question is not only as important as in any other field of linguistics; it seems that if the lexicographer has a so to say philological knowledge of the language (i.e. a well trained ability to understand all the more difficult texts spoken and written, in all their details and stylistic, exegetic and other intricacies, applicational occasionalities, nonces and contextual nuances and overtones), he has a greater chance of compiling a really good dictionary.[22]

But on the other hand, even the lexicographer who is a native speaker of and a firstclass specialist on the language in question must not forget that what he speaks is only one idiolect of the language and that his passive knowledge of it has some limits, too. Therefore, if the dictionary which is planned is not to be a very small and restricted one, it is preferable that he should check his own opinions and his own knowledge against those of other people. In this way, if everything or nearly everything is mutually controlled, the criterion of interpersonality can be attained.[23]

In big lexicographic projects, there will usually be several lexicographers who have joined forces; in smaller projects, the lexicographers will do well to have some consultants. But it is not only this interpersonality which can be attained by such a lexicographic team; it is also very useful to choose the perspective members of the lexicographic team in such a way that they can mutually complement one another. For instance, if the standard national language a dictionary of which is to be compiled is used in different dialect areas, it is useful to choose the members of the team in such a way that the main areas are covered;[24] if an overall-descriptive dictionary of a language with rich, variegated, and difficult literature is to be compiled, it is useful if the single members of the team are experts on the single branches of the literature; etc. But it is not always possible to comply with all these requirements and it would be a bad policy to choose people who are otherwise substandard only in order to comply with them.

The lexicographer is not always a native speaker of the language whose dictionary he intends to compile. First, there are the so-called dead languages,

---

[22] But the reverse is not true: an accomplished philologist is not necessarily a good lexicographer. If a really learned lexicographer who has a first-class knowledge of his language fails to compile a good dictionary, it is usually because of embarras de richesse: by giving too much information and too abstruse indications.

[23] Cf. Weinreich, PL 43; cf. also Weinreich PL 33 who distinguishes "individual introspection" and "collective introspection". — The advantage that a lexicographic team usually can compile a bigger dictionary more quickly than a single scholar with the consequent reduction of the danger that the facts of language will change before the dictionary is compiled is so obvious that it is hardly necessary to stress it.

[24] Cf. Kahane and Kahane PL 255.

i.e. languages which have in our day no native speakers at all. The lexicographer can dare to compile a dictionary of such a dead language only if he is an accomplished expert on the existing texts of it: as has been mentioned above, the texts are of such paramount importance, in this situation, that any dictionary of dead language necessarily tends to the thesaurus type more strongly than a dictionary of a living language. But even for the compilation of a dictionary of a dead language, the lexicographer must be able not only to understand the texts and the concrete applications of the single words (lexical units) in them, but he must also be able to indicate their meanings as he assumes them to have been in the system of the language: it is only his own knowledge and his own ability to abstract the potential generality from the concrete cases which can help him to do this work.

6.3.2.1 But very frequently, it is a living language whose dictionary the lexicographer is preparing, though he is not a native speaker of it. This happens above all if the language in question has no considerable lexicographic and generally literary tradition.[25] In this case, the usual procedure is for the lexicographer to cooperate with some native speakers of the language in question who are called **informants**.

It is better to have one informant than to have none; but because of the greater interpersonal objectivity gained by mutual comparison and control, it is highly preferable if the lexicographer can cooperate with several. As far as the choice of informants goes, it can be said that well-educated informants are usually (but not always or automatically) better than less educated ones:[26] the general experience of the profession seems, to my knowledge, to agree with this. If institutional education does not play a role in the pattern of life of the respective society, the obvious thing is to choose as intelligent and able people as possible.[27] The capital thing is for the informant to know his native language as well as possible; general education helps to foster this knowledge considerably. An eventual linguistic sophistication of the informant is not a

[25] Let us not forget that in this chapter we are discussing primarily monolingual dictionaries; it is rather rare that a monolingual dictionary (standard-descriptive or overall-descriptive) of a language like English is compiled by a native speaker of another language, at least I do not recollect such a case.

[26] Kahane and Kahane PL 255. All problems connected with work with informants are well discussed in E. A. Nida, *Morphology* (Ann Arbor 1946, 2nd ed. 1949), Chapter 7, (p. 175ff.), Field Procedures, especially § 7.23, The Informant (I owe the reference to Zima); A. Healey, *Handling Unsophisticated Linguistic Informants* (Linguistic Cercle of Canberra Publications, Series A, Nr 2), Canberra 1964; W. J. Samarin, *Field Linguistics*, New York 1967.

[27] But if the lexicographer prepares a dictionary of a language spoken by a society with patterns of life strongly different from the European ones, he must be aware of the possibility that the "institutional education" afforded by European institutions may have different effects on the language of the speakers who possess it.

circumstance which would make his choice to the function impossible, provided
this sophistication has a solid, if limited, basis; but any cooperation is impossible with a prospective informant who imagines that he has "ideas" about
his language which are not substantiated by the facts or even who simulates
knowledge he does not have. The informant's basic task is to reveal as much of
his native speaker's competence by his performance (i.e. to reveal as much of
his idolect's system by concrete utterances) as possible; we shall see later that
an experienced informant can be allowed to summarize his knowledge or to
comment upon it. If it is possible to choose more informants, it will depend
upon the character of the planned dictionary how we shall choose them: we
could repeat here the remarks we have made above concerning the
choice of the lexicographic team. Informants should be as representative as
possible speakers just of those varieties of language that are to be covered
by the planned dictionary. The broader, for instance, the intended average
of the different dialects in an overall-descriptive dictionary, or even in a
comparative dialectal dictionary, the broader the choice of speakers of the
different dialects, and vice versa. If it is possible, both sexes and different age
and social groups should be represented.

The functions of informants in lexicography are so numerous and important
that even the lexicographer who compiles the dictionary of his own native
language is sometimes said to be "his own informant."[28] The main reason
why the informants are so extremely useful is that information can be elicited
from them. When written texts are excerpted, one may have to excerpt
thousands of pages until some necessary data occur, and one can never be sure
that something which does not occur in the slips really does not exist: the
argument that something does not occur in the excerpted texts is an *argumentum e silentio*; it may be pure chance that a lexical unit or a rection or a sense
etc., does not occur in the literature.[29] But because the informants can be
asked direct questions concerning the problem just in hand, their cooperation
can save an enormous amount of time and work, and their eventual negative
replies of the type "I do not know that", "I would not say it so", "I have
never heard it", are more conclusive, at least as far as their own idiolects are
concerned, than the eventual silence of the excerption.

[28] There is some bias in the conception of the situation: if such a lexicographer is conceived
of as performing two functions, that of the scholar and that of the informant, it is not necessary
to mention the term "introspection", so very much hated by the behaviourists. But we can use
the conception because of its clarity without committing ourselves on the broader issue. That
we have to do with behaviourist bias can be shown by the following quotation from Skinner
(*Verbal Behavior*, New York 1957, p. 12): "The speaker and listener within the same skin engage
in activities which are traditionally described as »thinking«." We repeat that we use the term
"one's own informant" without accepting the bias implied.

[29] The validity of this statement is, however, reduced if both the bulk of the literature existing
in the respective language and the bulk of the literature excerpted are very great. On the possi-

Almost any lexicographic problem can be studied with the help of informants. For example, the informants can be asked to indicate how the different objects of the extralinguistic world which can be shown to them are designated; they can be asked to describe different situations of life so that expressions can be gathered; they can supply objects to verbs, substantives to their attributive adjectives, form different sentences to show the use of grammatical words, etc.[30]

In carefully controlled situations, informants can be asked to supply information by translating expressions into their own language;[31] it goes without saying that this requires a relatively high degree of knowledge and ability on their part. In any case, all such translations should be substantiated by some examples of sentences which show that the respective expression really has the meaning implied by the translation.

Informants are also one of the main sources of really colloquial material for the dictionary.[32] To get this material from them, it is necessary to discuss with them the respective lexical fields as wholes (greetings, emotive words, eventually the terms of abuse and disgust, etc.). It is also useful to ask them always to indicate the eventual colloquial synonym of any expression discussed with them, if there is any, or even to read with them some dialogues in the written texts and ask them, to restate them in more colloquial form.

It is not possible to give a full list of the possible uses of cooperation with the informants, because of the number of possibilities, of differences between the languages, and of diversity of intentions of different lexicographers. Basically, informants' indications have the same standing as excerpted contexts, and should be treated in the same way: the informant is the source of (spoken or written) texts (short and informal as they may be) which show concrete applications of the lexical units. The lexicographer observes and studies these applications in the same way as if were excerpted from the written sources, in order to abstract from both of them what he considers the systematic properties of the lexical units in the system of language.

At the beginning of their cooperation, the lexicographer is much less interested in the informant's opinions concerning his own language. This attitude

bility and advisability of "asking the informants questions", see also Nida, IJAL 24, 1958, 288.

[30] A theoretical discussion of the techniques used in work with informants is in Mathiot 18 sqq. She discerns elicitation within the deictic field ("How do you call this?") from the elicitation within the symbolic field (verbal categories: "How do you call the various types of ...?"; nonverbal categories: "Describe a game, dance, etc."). These are, as the author correctly stresses, techniques of elicitation especially for those lexical units which have the designative function; they will have to be applied primarily when we compile a dictionary of a language whose written texts are negligible in quantity.

[31] Cf. Mathiot 21.

[32] Even highly conservative lexicographers admit this; cf. Janský LSB 138 sq. on the practice of Jungmann (first half of the 19th cent.).

should not, however, be carried to the extreme. If we suppose that the lexico-grapher studies, for example, some near-synonyms, he will not try to elicit from the informant a direct statement of his opinion concerning their diffe-rence, but he will ask him to produce some sentences or short lexicographic contexts in which the words are used in such a way that the relevant semantic features can be discovered. If the informant is a really good and intelligent one, he will inevitably understand the lexicographer's tricks and know the purpose of his questions, especially if their cooperation goes on for some time or even for some years. He will, then, tend to give statements of the type "The difference between ... and ... is ...", or "... is used if ...", etc. If the lexicographer knows from experience that the informant's indications are usually correct and that they are always based on the informant's honest endeavour to state what he knows — and only what he knows well at that — there is no reason why statements of this type should not be taken into con-sideration; but they should be substantiated by some examples.[33] It is gene-rally easier and more reliable to get answers of this type when lexical units with designative function are concerned than when lexical units with prevalent grammatical functions are studied.[34] The informants' statements of this type should be taken into consideration with due caution; above all, they should be checked with the indications of other sources and of other informants; but it would be a pity to refuse to take them into consideration at all, because this would deprive the work with the informants of their very specific power-fulness: a descriptively abstractive statement of the informant of the type: "... is used if ..." has the value of many excerption slips with contexts out of which the indication would otherwise have to be abstracted. Supposing that a highly experienced and well trained informant has a certain intellectual ability, it is even possible to consult him on more complex things like the whole construction of the entry (i.e. on the way how the lexical meaning of the words is presented in it), or on the definition's, in order to ascertain how far, if at all, they agree with his own native speaker's insight.

Similar living sources of information are the staffs of experts from diffe-rent special branches of knowledge who are frequently asked to cooperate when a big dictionary is compiled; it is primarily the different terms of the single sciences which usually need elucidation by such experts. This situation has its own specificity again: these experts are not usually asked to produce sentences or lexicographic contexts in which the respective term would occur, but rather to give a definition of its meaning. If these experts are well chosen

---

[33] Informant's statements of this type have the same status as the "Metavorkommen" (Hiorth) of words in written texts (cf. footnote 14). When the informant has the requisite experience, it is not necessary to ask him to produce whole sentences; it suffices if he indicates very short lexicographic contexts.

[34] Cf. Mathiot 12 who is even more energetic on the point.

and known their respective sciences well, it is frequently less necessary to check their statements with other indications than in the case of the statements of informants — native speakers. There is, however, another danger of which the lexicographer will have be to be aware, viz. that the definitions (or explanations) given by these experts will be of a too encyclopedic character, and that the term in question may also have a similar but different sense as a general word (e.g., Eng. *water* as a general word and as a chemical term).

The lexicographer may also decide to have a broader staff of native speakers with whom he does not cooperate constantly but who can be contacted and asked in cases of uncertainly.[35]

6.3.3 An important source of information can be found in other dictionaries of the language in question, if there are any. Sometimes, one dictionary is the basis for the compilation of another; this is the case especially when a shorter version of a big dictionary is to be prepared[36] and if a monolingual dictionary is used as the basis for a bilingual dictionary the purpose of which is to describe the source language (cf. § 7.3); these are, however, only the extreme, if not unfrequent cases. The usual situation is, however, that the lexicographer has to confront his own material (and also his own statements, definitions, treatment of polysemy etc.) with the other existing important dictionaries of the language in the field of which he works.[37] His attitude should be that of the usual scientific criticism: nothing is to be accepted from another source without a constant checking up of every detail.[38] But on the other hand, if the older dictionary thus used is a really good one, known to have been prepared in

---

[35] Cf. Weinreich PL 33: according to him, this questioning can be handled as a poll.

[36] The reverse situation, the expansion of a shorter dictionary into a bigger one is rarer. In this case, the expanded dictionary usually differs more from the original, shorter one, and the work on it is usually more independent than when the shorter dictionary is an abridgement of the original bigger one.

[37] When one is deciding which dictionaries are to be compared and when (i.e. at what stage of the work), it is necessary to take into consideration that there are different types of dictionaries (e.g., an older overall-descriptive dictionary must contain many indications which a prepared standard-descriptive one must not give) and that language varies and rapidly changes: a few years will suffice to make some indications obsolete, etc.

[38] It is necessary to check really everything. Apart from the differences caused by linguistic change and other phenomena of language, each known dictionary contains its allotment of errors, be they simple misprints. An extreme case of an error is the so-called *ghost-words* (or *bogeys*): words (lexical units) indicated bona fide as entry words and treated in the usual way though they do not really exist and are based only on a mistake in the literary tradition, its mistaken interpretation, or any other similar circumstance. Migliorini, *Vocabolario*, 78, quotes among the examples of ghost-words also Italian *settilineo* "having seven lines", present in different Italian dictionaries, which is only an original misprint for *rettilineo* "having a direct line". Malkiel (PL 9) discerns another category, viz. the *latent words*: words which could exist because they are formed according to the usual rules, but which never have existed. Neither category should find access into a really good, critical dictionary, but it is not always quite simple to detect the mistake

a solid way by a lexicographer or a lexicographic body enjoying authority, its indications should be given serious consideration, above all when one's own excerption and other sources are admittedly more limited than those of the work compared and when the variation of language and other similar factors cannot explain the eventual difference.[39]

SELECTION OF ENTRIES

6.4 The next step in the lexicographer's work is the selection of entries, i.e. the choice of the lexical units which are to be embraced in the future dictionary, as against those which are not. The individual factors which influence the lexicographer's decision can be grouped into the following two broad categories:

(1) the form of the lexical units,

(2) the density of the lexical units included in the dictionary.

6.4.1 As far as form goes, the majority of the entries in the dictionary will be concerned with the lexical units as they were discussed in the preceding chapters. The most usual lexical units of the Indo-European and many other languages are the words as they are constituted both by the facts of the respective languages and by their eventual linguistic (above all orthographical) traditions:[40] The lexicographer is fully entitled to accept the tradition, with eventual minor modifications, as it is manifested in those texts which are the basis of the dictionary.[41]

in the predecessor's indications. Yet the mere decision as to whether some lexical units indicated by the predecessor are sufficiently obsolete by the time of the compilation of a new dictionary or whether they should be retained is sometimes very difficult. Cf. also p.

[39] The importance of the existing (big) dictionaries is stressed by Sledd PL 144; Hulbert, *Dictionaries* 47f.

[40] Cf. Swanson, PL 64. Mathiot 2 sq.: "The grammatical unit best suited to the purpose of a practical dictionary is the word, and not the morpheme, since the user cannot be expected to know how to identify ... morphemes, wheras words are traditionally set off in the orthography by spaces." Garvin, Anais 3. — The suggestions to make the morphemes the basis of dictionaries (as e.g. Malone PL 113) would make the situation more difficult for the linguistically unsophisticated reader without much helping the linguist. For example: ought German *Handschuh* "glove" to be listed under the morphemes *Hand* "hand" and *Schuh* "shoe", or as a morpheme of its own?) Significantly enough, the few dictionaries based on the morpheme (as e.g. H. Hoyer, *Analytical dictionary of the Tonkawa language*, Berkeley—Los Angeles 1949; quoted in Garvin, loc. cit.) are intended mainly for linguists and deal with languages of undeveloped societies only.

[41] The longer the tradition, the greater its importance. Recently established orthographical conventions (and lexical units) are changed more easily; this is particularly true if the respective standard national form as a whole does not have a long tradition. Similarly, the impact of "tradition" is only small if written texts of the respective language are not numerous.

Apart from some borderline cases which are present in every language, I do not think that the decision to regard what is considered a word in each of the respective languages as the basis of the entries in the dictionary could cause any major difficulties.[42] The necessary thing is, however, not to neglect those words which have other than designative functions; sometimes they are neglected or the lexicographer feels some disinclination to treat them in the same way as the "full" words, mainly if they have some formal properties which seem to give them a "lower" status than that of the other words: this is occasionally the fate of elements such as for example proclitics and enclitics, in contrast to the words with full accents.[43]

Multiword lexical units (cf. above § 3.3.1) are lexical units of the same standing and function as single words; therefore, it is necessary and a matter of course that they should be selected, treated, and indicated as wholes.[44]

The fact that we regard the words (*qua* lexical units) and multiword lexical units as the basis of the lexicographer's selection of entries does not, however, mean that we should leave units smaller than the word out of consideration.

In those languages where the boundary of the word is not sufficiently clear, the lexicographer will meet morphemes about which he cannot easily and unequivocally decide whether they are words of their own or not; in the majority of cases, he will be well advised to allow them their own entries as if they were independent words, eventually with some further special indications and specifications. But sometimes the lexicographer also indicates as an entry a mere morpheme even if there is no uncertainty about the word boundary and when it is clear that it is only a morpheme. This is the case, for example, of highly productive prefixes or compositional elements. For instance, a prefix like *anti-* or *pseudo-*[45] is so highly productive in many European languages, that it is impossible to indicate all the instances where it occurs; even if they were listed, new creations, and many of them only occasional, could be expected to arise at any moment. Therefore, it is fully legitimate to indicate the single morpheme, i.e. in this case the isolated prefix, describe its meaning, and add some of the more important and stabilized words in which it occurs.[46]

---

[42] The lexicographic tradition of some languages is different from what is described and suggested here. In some cases the difference is caused by the structure of the language itself; for example, the boundaries in Chinese lexical units are not always well-defined and always discernable as clearly as those of lexical units in a language like German. The problems connected with this are rendered even more difficult by the character of the Chinese script. The regular derivational patterns of Arabic and the character of the Arabic script cause that the Arabic dictionaries are based rather on the (abstract) consonantal root than on the word which are derived from it.

[43] Cf. Swanson PL 64.

[44] Cf. Swanson PL 65; Országh LS 5, 1962, 149.

[45] It is irrelevant whether we consider this example, or any other similar one that could be quoted as a prefix or as the first part of compound words or as anything else.

[46] Cf. Janský LSB 141; Chapman, *Lexicography* 27.

In the same way, for instance Oss. *sant-* is indicated as a reinforcing prefixed particle or Hausa (as reported by Zima) *maỳ*, pl. *màasu* as a possessive prefix (cf. for example, Hausa *jirgii* "ship", *maỳ-jirgii* "the owner of a ship", *màasu-jirgii* "the owners of a ship"), etc. Such a listing of prefixes is made easy by the fact that they fit well into the usual alphabetical order of the entries. There is, however, no reason why the very productive suffixes should not be treated in precisely the same way and why they should not be inserted in alphabetical order by the sequence of their letters.[47]

In all cases of such "summary indications" of morphemes and subword units it is, however, necessary to study all the words in which the respective morpheme occurs in order to see whether the semantic effect described by the summary indication in really identical in all cases. For instance, if Eng. *pseudo-* has a "summary indication", it is correct to have a special entry for *pseudonym*,[48] even if the semantic difference were not considerable.[49]

In the chapter "Formal variation of words", we saw that some processes of the derivation of words are so productive and uniform that they verge on the grammatical or that they really constitute a grammatical category of words. If there is a category of words constituted by a uniform derivation (say, by the same suffix), and if the membership of this class is quite open) i.e. if always new members of the class arise and are easily understood, it is not necessary to indicate in a dictionary, unless it is a big one, all the known members of the class, if the semantic effect of the derivation is as uniform as its form. Examples have been quoted above (§ 2.2) so that it is not necessary to repeat them here. It is, however, important to stress again that if the lexicographer reduces the selection of a uniformly derived category of words, he is obliged to check every member of the category which would otherwise be eligible for selection, in order to see whether some of the members do not have semantic "specialities" of their own, not shared by the other members of the class. Any word that shows a semantic speciality should be indicated in the dictionary, unless it is eliminated for other reasons (rareness, obsoleteness, etc.).[50]

It is useful if the lexicographer elaborates all such selective principles and restrictions before he begins work on the construction of single entries so that he can develop a unified policy. It is also useful to fix, in connection with this, the general policy concerning other similar problems like the selection of compounds, of telescoped words, atc.[51]

---

[47] Hoenigswald PL 107 with a general requirement that (all) the morphemes with a grammatical meaning should be listed.

[48] Hornby s. v.

[49] The eventual difference or identity of the etymology is of only minor importance here.

[50] Cf. Isačenko LSB 47; Swanson PL 67; Gleason PL 102; Hoenigswald PL 106.

[51] Editorial paper in LS 1, 1957, 4.

All decisions made in all these and similar respects should be fully stated in the foreword to the dictionary. The first concern is to help the reader to use the dictionary as quickly and as efficiently as possible. But the second concern is to inform the lexicographer's future successor, who may prepare a new edition or a new dictionary.[52]

6.4.2 The problems connected with the density of entries are, unfortunately, far more complicated than those connected with their form; and Malkiel[53] is completely right when speaking about the absence of generally accepted norms for the selection of entries.

Some possible choices and decisions are determined by previous fundamental decisions concerning the type of dictionary which is to be prepared.[54] A dictionary planned to help the reader to understand older texts will necessarily have to contain more occasional expressions, obsolete words, and regionalisms than a standard-descriptive one.[55] But even if the dictionary is planned to cover, say, texts with frequent regional expressions, it may happen, on the other hand, that it must be only small. In such a case, different compromises are possible, for example that regional words which cannot be understood on the basis of the knowledge of the standard national language be indicated, but that those regional words which are morely (regular, predictable, intelligible) phonetic variants of their respective standard national counterparts be omitted;[56] such a dictionary would lose much of it descriptive but not of its informative power. In short, an infinite number of attitudes and variants of decisions is possible, in all these and similar problems.

Two problems seem to be of outstanding importance. In the first place, the question of colloquialisms. Havránek[57] is certainly right when he maintains that the colloquial variant of a language must not be forgotten in a large or a medium dictionary and when he deplores the fact that many of the older dictionaries are based too exclusively on written texts. It is certainly a pity if the archives of some large, academic dictionaries are limited to only printed

[52] Cf. Gedney PL 321.

[53] PL 7. — The selection of entries is discussed by W. Mańczak, *Zeszyty naukowe Uniwersytetu Jagiellońskiego* 60 (Prace jezykozn. 5), 1963, p. 447ff. (non vidi).

[54] Cf. the editorial paper LS 1, 1957, 4 — The mutual interdependence of the decisions has been repeatedly stressed above, in different connections.

[55] But Malkiel (PL 8) is right when he maintains that the use of older dictionaries during the compilation of a new one allows many an archaism finds its way also into a dictionary which is intended to cover the contemporary language only. These, however, are illustrations rather of the fragility of the profession, not of its principles; cf. footnote 38.

[56] Cf. Tietze PL 269.

[57] LSB 207.

16*

material.[58] The description of the colloquialisms does certainly belong to the description of the lexicon of a language. But on the other hand, one must not forget that some of these colloquialisms are extremely ephemeral: if other words are excluded from the selection because they are not stabilized, it would be a disproportion not to eliminate a colloquialism on the same principle. But stabilized, usual, frequently used colloquialisms are certainly eligible for selection.[59]

The other problem that will cause the lexicographer much trouble is that of the technical terminology of the sciences.[60] It goes without saying that the importance of a term and its eligibility for selection must be decided upon not from the point of view of the respective science, bur from that of the general language.[61] It is, however, not easy to decide whether the term is used generally or only in the specialized texts.

The foreword to the *Dictionnaire de l'Académie (française)* (8ᵉ édition), Paris 1932, (which is certainly one of the most venerable works of our profession), begins with the question of why the preparation of new editions of the Dictionary requires an increasing amount of time. (First edition 1694, then four editions during the XVIII century, but only two in the XIXth century the last of them 1877; and then an 8th, in 1932.) It is stated that work on the Dictionary has never suffered an interruption, but that "l'Académie a du faire face à une tâche que ses prédécesseurs avaient sans doute connue, mais que des circonstances particulières rendaient singulièrement plus ample et plus délicate." This difficult task was the selection of the technical terms; we read about these problems the following words (p.I.): «Aux dernières années du XIXᵉ siècle, quand l'Académie s'occupa de préparer une nouvelle édition de son Dictionnaire, elle se trouva en présence d'une brusque pénétration des vocabulaires des Sciences et des Arts dans le parler de tous, qui de puis ne devait plus cesser de s'enfler démesurément d'année en année. Non seulement les sciences déjà constituées se renouvelèrent, mais d'autres prirent naissance, comportant en bien des cas des applications à l'industrie. D'autre part de notables transformations s'opéraient dans l'ordre économique, social et politique. De là un grand nombre de mots nouveaux aussitôt vulgarisés par la conversation, par la presse et par l'école. Quel

---

[58] Havlová LSB 192 sq.; her remark is said to be based on the Czech academic dictionary archives.

[59] Colloquialisms are sometimes so exclusively colloquial that their written form is not fixed. Cf. Martin's (PL 55) complaint that the "bad pennies of everyday conversation" like *uh, Hi there!* are shunned by dictionaries, despite their frequency, and Gedney's (PL 229) remark that they should be included in a colloquial dictionary but that generally one is uncertain even how to spell them.

[60] Note that the whole present chapter is concerned with the general-purpose type of monolingual dictionary, not with restricted dictionaries of technical terms.

[61] Cf. Sorokolebov LS 1, 1957, 124.

adolescent de nos jours ne connait pas par leur nom les différentes pièces d'une automobile? De quel artisan, de quel paysan de France restent ignorés des termes tels que *microbe, sanatorium, otite, diphtérie, hydravion, commutateur, carburateur, court-circuit?* Mais dans cet afflux de vocables nouveaux, il en est beaucoup dont l'existence ne peut être qu'éphémère. Les uns disparaîtront avec les objets, eux-mêmes éphémères, qu'ils représentent; d'autres, qui se sentent de l'improvisation, seront remplacés par des dénominations plus exactes; d'autres enfin ne dépasseront pas le domaine où ils sont nés et, n'étant compris et employés que par des initiés, n'ont point chance de pénétrer dans l'usage commun. C'est ce départ qu'a essayé de faire l'Académie dans la préparation de cette nouvelle édition. Travail minutieux, qui ne pouvait être exécuté a la hâte, et qui exigeait un double effort d'adaptation au mouvement modernes et de prudence avisée.»

There is every reason to believe that during the last thirty or forty years which followed the 8th edition of the French Academic Dictionary the number of scientific terms used in the general language has kept on increasing, and that this trend of development will continue. Therefore, the compiler of a medium or large monolingual dictionary of a living language will be well advised to follow the example set by the French Academy and select the technical term for indication in the dictionary without any undue penury, above all those which occur also in texts used for general (and perhaps also secondary) education;[62] and he will have to expect that his work on the task will not be less difficult than that of the French Academy. Indeed, he will have to anticipate that his work will be open to doubt: there are no criteria generally agreed upon in this field. Consequently, the lexicographer should not be unduly dispirited if he feels that he is on very uncertain ground and he should not lose time unnecessarily by changes of policy.

A good policy is to prepare preliminary inventories of technical terms from the single sciences etc., to rotate them among different specialists (not only specialist concerned with the single sciences but also pedagogues, etc.), and above all to compare them mutually so that the degree of exhaustiveness or rather density does not vary too much from one science to another.

A minor but irritating problem is whether a monolingual dictionary should contain proper names. (cf. § 1.8.2). It goes without saying that they must be indicated if they have developed and appellative meaning, such as, e.g., Russ. *Khlestakov* (1) name of a person in Gogol's "The Government Inspector", (2) "liar, confidence man",[63] or if there is a derivation with an appellative

[62] Cf. Borovkov LS 1, 1957, 153. There is, however, no possibility of registering all the technical terms (not even in a very big dictionary) because they are too numerous and their number increases practically every day.

[63] Ščerba, *Izvestija* 99; cf. also p. 98 on the whole problem of names. Cf. also Householder PL 281.

value, e.g., Russ. *Evropa* (1) "a continent (with a high culture)" *evropejskij* "cultured, cultivated".[64]

Apart from such cases, it is probably of some importance to indicate the personal names primarily if we compile a dictionary either of a dead language or of a language without a long literary tradition, and then only with a short indication of the categorial membership. The indication of place names seems to be more important and the user expects to be informed where the place is situated.[65]

All that has been said up to now has been concerned with some partial subsets of the total lexicon of a language. Apart from all these questions, there is the basic problem of what to select and what to leave out in dictionaries of different sizes. Up to now there seem to be no theoretical points elaborated to cope successfully with this problem; therefore, we shall have to limit ourselves to some remarks only.

It would be a mistake to think that a big academic dictionary lists "everything" and that the shorter variants are quantitative reductions from this basis. In reality, only a dictionary of a dead language can be complete as far as the repertory of the lexical units recorded in the preserved texts goes. Even the biggest dictionaries of living languages cannot register all the occasional words (or even all their occasional applications).[66] The following circumstance is, however, to be taken into consideration" the dictionary of a language with scarce literary texts, or of a language in which the standard national form is only beginning to be developed usually tends to be more exhaustive (though the number of its entries is smaller) than that of a language with a long, rich literary tradition.

The frequency of occurence of the single words is certainly a powerful factor in the selective decision[67] when the lexicographer is compiling a smaller

---

[64] Ščerba, loc. cit. In this second type of case, the inclusion of the proper name itself is not so necessary as in the first type. Cf. also Haas PL 46 with good French-English examples; Chapman, Lexicography 27 sqq.

[65] There is no need to stress that the lexicographer's attitude will be quite different from the one advocated here if he is compiling, form example, a dictionary with a strong exegetic component; encyclopedic indications will be, in that case, an important part of the exegesis.

[66] Cf. the highly instructive statement of R. W. Chapman, *Lexicography* (London 1948), p. 11 sq.: The question what we shall admit, what exclude, perhaps gives the lexicographer his most splitting headache. A dictionary of an ancient language can afford to embrace everything that can be called a word ... But if the lexicographer of English should include all he finds in G. M. Hopkins and the Daily Mirror, that would be a phantasmagoric *olla podrida*. He must, however reluctantly, omit *drear-nighted* and skies of *couple-colour*. At the other end of the scale he must draw the line, however willingly, at neologisms ... But between these extremes the choice may by very hard." (Mr. Chapman's impressions are based on his experience gained in work on the supplement volume to the OED.) — Cf. also Doroszewski 62: a dictionary cannot register all really occurring words.

[67] Cf. Malkiel PL 10. — Cf. Wahrig, *Wörterbucharbeit*, p. 9 (a similar, if not stronger, point of view as that advocated by the present author: statistics is at the moment no reliable tool for

dictionary, though it can usually be appraised only impressionistically since there are generally no precise counts at hand, with the exception of some of the better known languages. Frequency is, however, not the only decisive argument. When we compile a short dictionary for the understanding of texts, we may have to include a rare word occurring in an author whose works we are trying to cover, though we omit some more frequent words occurring in some spheres of language which we do not try to cover.[68] If we compile a short standard-descriptive dictionary, we may include some terms of the standard literary language which are not as common as the ommitted colloquialisms.

It would seem that in the absence of a more theoretical elaboration of these problems,[69] respect to the purpose of the dictionary should be the guiding principle in these decisions. In the same way, the lexicographer will be well advised to test the results of his decisions in a preliminary way. It will be useful to prepare a preliminary inventory of the future entries, i.e. at least a partial list of the prospectively selected entries, and to read with it some texts which are supposed to be covered by the future dictionary; or to try to produce with it some texts similar to those frequently occurring in the standard national language. Such a test will not only show the extent of the eventual lacunae, but also where they are located; the test can be applied at different stages of the work and with different intentional restrictions of purpose.

Another useful test is the comparison of an (eventually partial) preliminary inventory of prospective entries with a dictionary of another language which is similar to the one under preparation.[70] This type of test is particularly useful when we prepare a monolingual dictionary of a language without a long literary and lexicographic tradition and if our main aim is not the folkloristic specificities of the respective society. In such a situation, the comparison with a similar dictionary of a language with a longer literary tradition may have the additional advantage that it shows the real lexical lacunae of the language itself, not of our excerption or knowledge: those designata (practically all of them connected with modern civilization) for which there are not yet any expressions coined: in short, the onomasiological gaps.[71]

It is also useful to ask a sample of educated speakers of the respective langague to read and to comment upon such a preliminary inventory of prospective entries.

---

the selection of entry-words as there are practically no reliable counts at our disposal, above all not exhaustive counts of different word-combinations).

[68] After all, even a hapax ist "not an illicit entry, but a legitimate border-line case": Malkiel PL 9.

[69] Cf. Akhmanova IJAL 31, 1965, 157 (the basic lexical inventory, the types of words, the kinds of derivations, etc. which must be included in different kinds of dictionaries).

[70] Sometimes one dictionary serves as the basis for the preparation of the preliminary list of entries of another dictionary; cf. the extremely instructive discussion of Harrell (PL 57): an English-German dictionary used as the basis for an Arabic one.

[71] Cf. on designative neologisms.

In any case, the selection of the entries for the dictionary is a highly delicate task. Though no precise or even rigorous statements are yet possible, the lexicographer should try to state in the foreword to the dictionary what he has tried to accomplish and by what principles. Statements of this character will inform the user about what he may seek in the dictionary and what not (and thus spare him much inconvenience), and they will prepare the ground for the lexicographer's sucessor.[72]

THE CONSTRUCTION OF ENTRIES

6.5 Single lexical units are treated in single entries. All the entries of the dictionary should be constructed in as uniform a way as possible. Each entry should be treated as a compartment of its own, containing all the information about the respective lexical unit considered necessary for the purpose of the dictionary. There are basically two notable exceptions to this rule. First, it is not necessary to state, in the entry all the properties which the lexical unit has a member of a class (morphological, syntactic, or any other): the entry should concentrate upon just the opposite, upon the individual properties of the lexical unit in question, so that a general indication that it is a member of the respective class will suffice to inform about the shared properties.[73] As the second exception, one can consider the fact that cross-references from one item to another are sometimes necessary and that some entries are conflated into nests; cf. § 6.6.2.

6.5.1 In a monolingual dictionary, only one language is used in the entry. This circumstance should not, however, hide the fact that this single language has two different purposes: on the one hand, it is the object of the lexicographers work (irrespective of whether the purpose of the dictionary is description, interpretation, or explanation, etc.) but on the other hand, it is the instrument by which this work (description, explanation etc.) is done.[74] This double

---

[72] Cf. Gedney PL 231.

[73] Membership in a class can be indicated in a negative way. Most German dictionaries, for instance, operate on this principle in respect to verbs. The absolute majority of German verbs belongs to the big category of "schwache Verba", i.e. what we call in English "regular verbs". Consequently, if there is, in a German dictionary, no indication that the verb is "stark", i.e. irregular, it is understood that it is a regular one. The majority of English dictionaries handle the regular and the irregular verbs in the same way as the German ones. — Martin (PL 159) offers a similar case in Chinese: appropriate classifiers for nouns are indicated only when a specific (not a general) classifier is preferred, optional, or obligatory.

[74] In some terminologies, the language (any language) which is used as the instrument by which another (or the same) language is described, analyzed, or handled, is called a *metalanguage*; other terminologies use the contradistinction *language under description* (*l. u. d.*) :: *language of description* (*l. o. d.*).

purpose and double use must be constantly taken into consideration; some of the more important points will be mentioned below.

It would be wrong to identify this difference between the object-language and the instrument-language with the difference between the facts (or data) and their handling, the difference between the concrete and the abstract. In reality, the whole activity of the lexicographer is highly abstractive and its results are abstractions of different degrees and of different character. For instance, quotations of (literary) passages, as they frequently appear in bigger dictionaries, are highly concrete, to be true: these sentences really were pronounced or written in a concrete situation and with a definite purpose; but yet to select them and to quote them as evidence of the occurrence of a lexical unit with a certain signification which belongs to a certain sense is an abstractive work. There is no necessity to stress that, for example, the indications of the senses are of an incomparably more abstractive character: they are summarized and generalized from many concrete occurrences and they will be projected into the future use particularly in a standard-descriptive dictionary. The indications of connotative values, the classification of the lexical unit as belonging a restricted language, all this is founded on an abstractive work of the lexicographer. It is, therefore, not without justification if the whole entry is conceived as the lexical abstraction of a lexical unit. The lexical abstraction is, in this conception, the lexicographic approximation and representation of the status of a lexical unit in the lexical stock of a language.

The other argument for this conception of the entry as a lexical abstraction is that the entry contains a cumulative information which does not always completely and exhaustively coincide with any single speaker's idiolect. This is self-evident in the case of a historical dictionary or of a reference dictionary: no single speaker's idiolect comprises all the lexical units with meanings as known in, say, the XVIIIth century and as known to-day, or all the lexical units which belong to the diverse dialects. But the character of the most scrupulously synchronic and standard-descriptive dictionary (like the *Dictionnaire de l'Académie Française*) is not less abstractive in this respect, because general experience shows that no single speaker knows or even actively uses all the lexical units which can be considered as belonging to the general language and in all their senses as they are indicated in the single entries at that.

6.5.2 The entry consists of two parts: in the first part (which is frequently called the lemma), the lexical unit itself is indicated; the second part contains all the other information.

The most important part of the lemma is the entry word (or head word), which is the indication of each respective lexical unit in its canonical form.[75] The other indications of the lemma inform the user about the (usually morphological but — above all in the case of uninflected words — also the syntactic or combinatorial)[76] class of which the entry word (i.e. the respective lexical unit) is a member. This can be indicated either by the cardinal forms of each respective paradigm, or by the number of the paradigm (according to their numeration either as generally accepted, or as numbered in the grammatical sketch appended to the dictionary), or by an abbreviation or sign (e.g. *n.* — *noun* in an Eng. dictionary)[77], or by any other similar means. With the possible exception of yet underscribed or only unsufficiently described languages, these indications should not cause much trouble, because the lexicographer will usually accept the classes and categories as established by tradition.[78] Two things are, however, important in this connexion. First, it is necessary to state fully and explicitly, in the foreword to the dictionary, what classes and categories are indicated, and by what means. Second, the bigger the dictionary, the more imperative the necessity to indicate all eventual aberrations of the respective lexical unit from the usual paradigm, i.e. to indicate all its "irregular forms". It is irrelevant whether these irregular forms have some semantic peculiarities or not. The purpose of the lemma is to identify the lexical unit, to locate it in the (formal, frequently specifically morphological) system, and to describe its form;[79] therefore, the "irregular forms" should be indicated, even if they have no observable effect on the meaning.[80] The non-existence of a form etc. (e.g. "no plural") should also be indicated.

[75] On the choice of the canonical form, see above § 2.1.1. Cf. also Garvin, *Anais* 4 sqq: discussion of procedures applied in the choice of canonical forms for the dictionary of an undescribed language (Kutenai). — On the necessity of indicating some forms of one paradigm as different entries, see above; Gedney PL 229; Garvin, Anais 3.

[76] Sometimes, morphological and syntactic criteria are combined. For example, the indication "verb transitive", in an Eng. dictionary, combines the morphological and the syntactic (or at least combinatorial) criteria (and information). — E.g., the case government can be taken care of in the lemma: cf. Hoenigswald PL 109 sq.

[77] A grammatical sketch will be necessary primarily if the language in question does not yet enjoy a long tradition of linguistic work and is not yet absolutely stabilized, because such a dictionary will be used very frequently as a normative manual; the user will, then, find all the necessary information in one book (Majtinskaja LS 1, 1957, 170). Cf. also Householder PL 279.

[78] This does not mean that the lexicographer is absolutely bound to tradition up to the last detail. On the one hand probably nobody will change, e.g., the traditional conception of the five declensions of nouns in a Latin dictionary. But on the other hand, the tradition should not preclude the seeking of new ways how to convey more, or more detailed, information in a more compact form, how to make some indications more precise, etc.

[79] "Form" is here not the singular of "forms of a paradigm", but rather the "expression" of the glossematic terminology.

[80] Cf. Gleason PL 91, 92, 94; specifically Kopeckij LSB 34; Helcl LSB 38 (with Czech examples).

Other similar information can be given in the lemma, provided it concerns primarily the form of the lexical unit. The most frequent indications of this type are about pronunciation. Indeed, "pronunciation", i.e. the spoken form to which the written one (the one basically indicated in the dictionary) is correlated, should always be given when the orthography does not give an unambiguous information about it. In some languages (e.g. Finnish), there will be only occasional cases which present trouble of this kind but other orthographies (as e.g. English spelling) are not so closely correlated to the phonemics of the languages, so that the indication of pronunciation is always useful.[81]

The indication of pronunciation should not be a narrow phonetic one (i.e. one which tries to express every phonetic subtlety irrespective of whether it is phonemically relevant or not), but a possibly phonemic one: it should indicate basically the phonemes or, where the need is really imperative (i.e. where the user may be expected to go seriously wrong unless he is given a more phonetic guidance), the most important allophones.[82] In any dictionary that indicates pronunciation, there will be as a matter of course a list of the phonemic and phonetic values of the letters and signs used in these indications. In a discreet and unobtrusive way (lest the unsophisticated reader be horrified and disgusted), the list should be conceived basically as a presentation of the phonemes and their eventual chief allophonic types which can then be described with some (but not absolute) phonetic precision.[83]

In normal cases, it is sufficient to indicate the pronunciation of the entry-word in its canonical form, but further indications are necessary if there is some unpredictable variation within the paradigm. For example, Germ. *Knie* "knee" has the plural form *Knie* "knees"; not only the "regular" (i.e. predictable) pronunciation of the canonical form [kni:], but also the unpredictable pronunciation of the plural [kni:e] should be obligatorily indicated.

A concise information concerning the etymology of the entry-word can belong to the lemma — unless it is given separately, as an appendix to the whole entry. This etymological information is a matter of course in the historical dictionary, but many dictionaries of the overall-descriptive, informative type also give it. In some cultural areas, such as, for example, the United States, a short etymological information is expected even in the smallest

[81] The examples here are taken from languages which use Roman script. The situation is, however, not basically different when other scripts are taken into consideration: Sanskrit written in the Nagari script enjoys a one-to-one correlation between orthography and pronunciation; but such a good situation is not the rule, rather the exception. On the other hand, Chinese script (as reported by Novotná) gives very few cues to pronunciation; only the phonetics of phonoideograms offer a certain though unreliable guidance as to how the character in question is to be pronounced.

[82] Cf. Malone PL 115f., 117; Kahane-Kahane PL 256, 257; Sledd PL 149.

[83] Cf. Malone PL 115.

dictionaries. But it is without any doubt not obligatory to give such etymological information in the purely standard-descriptive dictionaries.[84]

6.5.3 What follows the lemma is the main part of the entry its basic purpose
is to indicate the meaning of the lexical unit in all its aspects.

In the first chapter of this book, we had occasion to perceive how complex
all the problems connected with the lexical meaning are and how difficult it
is to ascertain; no wonder that the task of presenting it in a simple way is no
light one.[85]

The basic instruments for the description of lexical meaning are:
    1[0] the lexicographic definition;
    2[0] the location in the system of synonyms etc.;
    3[0] the exemplification;
    4[0] the glosses.

6.5.3.1 The lexicographic definition overlaps to some extent with the
logical definition, but there are some striking differences.[86] Probably the most
important of them consists in the fact that whereas the logical definition must
unequivocally identify the defined object (the *definiendum*) in such a way
that it is both put in a definite contrast against everything else that is definable
and positively and unequivocally characterized as a member of the closest

---

[84] Hulbert, *Dictionaries*, p. 57ff. argues that the general dictionary should give etymological
information. "Etymology is important ... because vestiges of the original meanings of words
often remain in present senses (e.g. one conscious of the etymology of *virile*" [from Lat. *vir* "man"
"will use it of a woman only humorously or pejoratively, and because ... [etymology is] ...
significant in the cultural history."

[85] Cf. the correct remark of Weinreich (PL 26): "There is no known discovery procedure for
correct semantic descriptions." — Rich experience is collected in the paper of Ph. B. Gove,
Subject Orientation within the Definition (in: Monograph Series on Languages and Linguistics 14,
1961, p. 95ff.). The paper contains much more than its title promises; the main topics are: the
wording of the definition, parenthetical adjuncts within the definition, typical objects and subjects of verbs, verbal illustrations, quotations. The paper contains many good examples, collected
during the author's practice as editor of *Webster's Third*.

[86] Indeed, these differences are so important that I use the term "lexicographic definition"
only because it is by now traditional. In Russia, the (logical) definition is called definicija, but the
lexicographic definition, tolkovanie, i.e. something like "interpretation, explanation", which is
very good. — Cf. T. Knudsen — A. Sommerfelt, *Principles of Unilingual Dictionary Definitions* (in: Proceedings of the 8th Congress of Linguists, Oslo 1958, p. 98ff.); A. Rey, *A propos de
la définition lexicographique* (in: Cahiers 6, 1965, 67ff.); B. Pottier, *La définition sémantique dans
les dictionnaires*) in: Travaux de linguistique et de littérature III 1, Strasbourg 1965); J Rey-
Debove, *La définition lexicographique: recherches sur l'équation sémique*) in: Cahiers 8, 1966,
71ff.); Wahrig, *Wörterbucharbeit*, p. 24ff. (the lexicographical definition consists of the main
semantic features of the lexical meaning of the respective word).

class,[87] the lexicographic definition enumerates only the most important semantic features of the defined lexical unit,[88] which suffice to differentiate it from other units.

The difference between the logical definition and the lexicographic corresponds closely to the difference between the scientific concept and the designatum (cf. above, § 1.3.1). Designata of different lexical units frequently overlap: consequently, lexicographic definitions of Eng. *agreable* and *pleasant* which would not show that there is a vast area of overlapping between the two words and would stress only their differences would be entirely wrong.[89] The designata sometimes lack not only the precision but also the systematic coordination of the scientific classification: therefore, Eng. *whale* can be lexicographically defined[90] as "kinds of large sea-animal some of which are hunted for their oil".[91] When the lexical units are applied in concrete sentences, one can frequently observe very different specifications of their lexical meaning: the lexicographic definition must be sufficiently general to imply all the single possibilities without stating them;[92] e.g., a definition like Eng. *beautiful*: "giving pleasure or delight to the mind or senses"[92a] is not sufficient from the point of view of logic (a pipe may give pleasure or delight to the senses without being beautiful[93]) but it laudably does not try to state all the necessary attributes of beauty.

But on the other hand, it would be wrong to deny that there is a similarity and affinity between the lexicographic definition and the logical one. Perhaps the strongest similarity between the two is caused by the fact that it is sometimes possible and useful to indicate, in a lexicographic definition, the closest hyperonym or another close near-synonym, and the semantic feature (or features) which makes the difference (with the resulting impression that we

[87] This statement is based on the so-called classical definition (*per genus proximum et differentiam specificam*), which can be considered the logical definition par excellence. Analytical, contextual, genetic, etc., definitions are not considered here; all of them differ from the lexicographical definitions more or less in the same way as the classical one.

[88] Cf. Janský LSB 135.

[89] The overlapping of designata and definitions is correctly stressed by Országh LS 5, 1962, 143.

[90] A. S. Hornby c. s., *The Advanced Learner's Dictionary of Current English* (2 ed., London 1963), s. v.

[91] What kinds of animals? ("*animal*" could be taken as *genus*, but a logical definition requires the *genus proximum*). If only some of them are hunted for their oil, what is the difference between the non-hunted ones and the other sea-animals? (Insufficient *differentia specifica* from the point of view of logic).

[92] Cf. Trávníček LSB 60; Trávníček also makes here the excellent point that the concrete implementation of the designatum sometimes varies with the speaker's education, preference, etc.

[92a] Cf. p. 122.

[93] It must be stated, however, that shorter dictionaries (like the one from which we quote this definition) inevitably must suppose some knowledge on the part of the user.

have before us the *genus proximum* and the *differentia specifica* of the logical definition. For instance, let us discuss the following example, adapted from a smaller Eng. dictionary:[94]

    to intone: "to recite in a singing tone".

The term to *recite* is obviously a hyperonym which functions here as the *genus proximum*, and *in a singing voice* is the additional semantic feature which functions here as the *differentia specifica*.

When constructing these definitions, the lexicographer will have to avoid several dangers.

The definition should be sufficiently specific, but not overspecific. Weinreich[95] indicates the following good examples. If we find in an English dictionary, the loan-word from Russian *verst* with the definition "a Russian measure of length", then it is insufficiently specific because the difference from other Russian measures of length is not indicated. A lexicographic definition of the word *triangle* "a figure that has three sides and three angles, the sum of which is 180°", is, on the other hand, overspecific, because the indication of the number of sides would suffice. In the majority of cases, the overspecific definitions verge on the encyclopedic.[96]

A good example of a definition that is not sufficiently specific is discussed by T. Knudsen and A. Sommerfelt:[97] the OED defines Eng. *pedestrian* as "one who goes or travels on foot", but a better definition would be "person who goes or travels on foot".

The indication of semantic features is based on what appears to be relevant to the general speaker of the language in question, not on properties that can be perceived only by a scientific study.[98] Therefore Eng. *water* (as a general word) is much better defined as "liquid as in rivers, lakes, seas and oceans" (Hornby), than, say, as "the liquid that when pure consists of an oxide of hydrogen H_2O".

The greatest difficulty in this respect will be caused again by technical terms.[99] Biržakova[100] is completely right when she demands that the lexicographic

---

[94] Hornby s. v.   [95] PL 32.

[96] Cf. Získal SS 4, 1938, 27; Weinreich PL 32 (with the direct equation *excessively specific-encyclopedic*; cf. Urdang, Languages 39, 1963, 587 sq.) — The disinclination to indicate too many semantic features is one of the reasons why near-synonyms are used: instead of "absolute" lexicographic definition (i.e. with fairly complete enumeration of all the important semantic features), the lexicographer indicates the near-synonym as representing the majority of the semantic features, plus the additional feature (s). (Cf. Weinreich PL 30).

[97] Proceedings of the 8th congress of Linguists, Oslo 1958, p. 94.

[98] This is probably the main point of difference between the lexicographic handling of meaning and the Bloomfieldian semantics which was ultimately based on a study of denotata „Circumlocution is not, as Bloomfield thought, a »makeshift device« for stating meanings, but *the* legitimate device par excellence": Weinreich, *Universals* 153.

[99] Cf. Országh LS 5, 1962, 147.   [100] LS 2,1957, 74.

definition of technical words should be scientifically correct, should describe the object correctly, should reflect the generally accepted notion of the object, and difficult be generally intelligible. It will, however, frequently be difficult to satisfy all these requirements: Above all, the scientific correctness and general intelligibility will often clash. No wonder that it is above all in this sphere that lexicographic definitions tend to become encyclopedic, or at least to contain some encyclopedic elements.[101] It may also happen that a lexical unit can be used either as a general word or as a technical term: such a situation will often have to be handled as a case of polysemy, i.e. by the construction of two definitions.

Very similar difficulties must be solved in respect to the lexical units designating plants, animals, etc.[102] They must be explained by a lexicographic definition in general-language terms; but it is only natural that some lexicographers like to identify them with the respective Latin technical terms, above all when the dictionary concerns a language which is not the lexicographer's native one and is spoken in a milieu where the respective denotata are different from those of the milieu of the modern Indo-European languages.[103] Opinions may differ as to the correctness of this procedure:[104] as far as language (as used by the general speaker) is concerned, it is not necessary to add these identifications. It is, however, only natural that the larger the dictionary the greater the inclination to indicate the precise identification by means of the Latin nomenclature. And if denotata that belong to some distant culture are to be really identified, Latin terms is the only practical means. If the lexicographer decides to use the Latin terms, he must not forget that he must then respect the whole classification of the respective science and tackle the fact that there is, in many cases, no one-to-one correlation between the general words and the scientific terms. For instance, it will suffice, from the point of view of general language, to define Eng. *cactus* as "(sorts of) plant with a thick, fleshy stem, usually no leaves, usually covered with clusters of spines or prickles";[105] if, however, the lexicographer decides to add the Latin identification, he will find that there is no single term with which the word *cactus* could be identified, but that he will have to indicate several different genera, such as *Cereus, Mamillaria, Echinocactus*, etc.[106]

[101] Cf. Weinreich PL 32.

[102] What we are speaking about are the general-language expressions (like Eng. *mushroom*, etc.), not the respective terms of zoology, botany etc. (like, e.g., Eng. *edible boletus*).

[103] Cf. Országh LS 5, 1962, 147: in the sphere of botany etc., words (not technical terms) should be defined for the general speaker and identified by the Latin technical term.

[104] Cf. the discussion in PL 280 as summarized by Householder: Ianucci favoured the Latin nomenclature, but it was opposed by Conklin as not sufficent and by Weinreich as neither necessary nor true to the status of natural languages.   [105] Hornby s. v.

[106] Our discussion concerns mainly monolingual dictionaries, above all those of languages which have a literature. It is not necessary to stress that the role of the encyclopedic elements

As regard the problem of the encyclopedic elements within a dictionary, a neat either-or solution will be possible, if extremely difficult, only in a dictionary with purely scientific aims. In the case of a monolingual dictionary that is prepared for a broader public, there will always be some, preferably not too many, such elements.

The definition of Eng. *water* shows us another lexicographic technique, viz the o s t e n s i v e d e f i n i t i o n.[107] Sometimes, it would be difficult or cumbrous to indicate a lexicographic definition of the type discussed up to now. Instead of it, and mainly instead of the differentiating semantic features, the ostensive definition indicates an example or some examples from the extralinguistic world. Cf. the lexicographic definition of Eng. *water* (above) or *white*: "of the colour of fresh snow or common table salt."[108] It goes without saying that it is above all the lexical units which have clearly perceivable denotata in the extralinguistic world that can be dealt with by the ostensive definitions.

The extreme case of an ostensive definition is a p i c t u r e of the denotatum. Such a picture is an absolutely extralinguistic element within a dictionary. It is, however, true that if used with delicacy, the pictorial material can add quite substantially to the informative power of a dictionary.[109] If, therefore, the informing of the user about unusual words is one of the main purpose of the dictionary, it would seem that the pictures have a similar status as the encyclopedic elements: they are foreign to the nature of a monolingual dictionary, but they are not incompatible with it if kept under control. The pictorial material must not be too abundant: only denotata really unknown to the majority of users should be depicted. The pictures should not be over-specific but only general lest the user accept a feature only accidental to the picture as criterial to the designatum;[110] as far as possible, the picture should indicate

---

within a dictionary will increase if the lexicographer finds it necessary or desirable to inform the reader about the respective culture: in a reference dictionary which covers also the older epochs of the language in question or dialectal areas, the encyclopedic tendencies will be, as it is quite reasonable, stronger just in these areas than in those spheres where a greater familiarity of the user with the respective denotata can be supposed.

[107] Cf. Janský LSB 135 sq; Weinreich PL 31.

[108] Hornby s. v. — "*table salt*" is probably added for the benefit of those users of the dictionary who live in regions where "*fresh snow*" is not a commonplace enough white thing: a nice illustration of the principle that the user must be always taken into consideration by the lexicographer.

[109] Cf. Chapman 21, 22.

[110] For instance, let us suppose that a word like Eng. *metope* "square space between triglyphs in Doric frieze" is illustrated by a picture, in a dictionary. A picture cannot indicate "a square space": there must be some surface which is either void or is embellished with a relief (as metopes usually are). If such an over-specific embellishment is stressed too much, in the picture, the user can be led to believe that it is criterial though it is not.

the criterial properties of the denotatum. And in any case, the pictures should be treated as an additional material which they really are.[111]

The circumstance that the language of the definitions is the same as that of the lexical units to be explained must also be taken into consideration by the lexicographer.[112] The lexicographic definition should consist exclusively of words which are explained in the dictionary. For example, if a dictionary defines one of the senses of Eng. *bollard* as "post on a traffic island", the user does not gain much if there is no definition of *traffic island*.

Nor should the lexicographic definition contain words more difficult to understand than the explained word itself;[113] above all there should be no archaic, dialectal, vulgar, rare etc. words in it. And it should be a matter of course that the defined entry-word must not be used in its definition; the same applies to its derivations and combinations, unless they have their own, independent definitions in the dictionary. For instance, J. Hulbert[114] quotes (with full right) as an inadmissible definition:

Negro: "an individual of the Negro race".

This could be admitted only if the dictionary contained an independent definition of the expression *Negro race*.

Particular care should be taken of the fact that the words used in the lexicographic definition will themselves be polysemous. A good part of them will be disambiguated just by the context of the definition itself, and this can be helped by the addition of a disambiguating adjective or adverb to a crucial term which would otherwise remain ambiguous.[115] This method will be sufficiently effective and relatively easy in the majority of cases, because the necessary qualifications will be automatically suggested by the criterial

---

[111] Apart from any other consideration let us not forget that only some of those lexical units can be illustrated by pictures which designate physical denotata of clear shape and of static character. The verbal explanation of the meaning is fundamental in any monolingual dictionary, and should be given in all entries, if only for the sake of consistency. If a monolingual dictionary indicates, in the entry *pig* "domestic and wild animal as shown here" (a picture is added; Hornby, p. 731), nobody will doubt that it is very practical: but it is a *metábasis eis állo génos*, a sudden change of the genre at least.

[112] The majority of the following statements are valid also if the lexical units are defined in another natural language. — On an "absolute metalanguage" (independent of the object language or of any natural language) and on the consequences of its absence, cf. Weinreich PL 37. Cf. also Országh LS 5, 1962, 144 on the properties of the language of the definitions.

[113] An interesting attempt at a vigorous handling of this is M. P. West — J. G. Endicott, *The New Method English Dictionary*, 4th Edition, London 1961, "explaining the meaning of over 24.000 items" exclusively by means of "1490 words". These 1490 words used in the definitions are listed in the dictionary, but they are not defined themselves, nor is their polysemy indicated.

[114] *Dictionaries British and American*, London 1955, p. 68f.

[115] Cf. Országh, LS 5, 1962, 144.

semantic features of the defined lexical unit itself. Should the definition remain unclear or ambigous, or should it become unnecessarily long, the lexicographer can use the following procedure: As the definitions of the single senses of a polysemous word are usually numbered, it is possible to disambiguate the signification of a polysemous word used in a definition of another lexical unit by the indication of the number of the respective sense in which it is applied. For instance, Eng. *crib*[116] can be conceived as having two senses: (1) "something copied dishonestly from the work of another", (2) "word-for-word translation of a foreign text used by students of the language". It is, then, possible to write, in the definition of the verb *to crib* "to use a crib (def. 2); ..."[117]

The definition usually has the form of an endocentric phrase.[118] Since lexical units of a language are defined in the same language, it follows that the definition will frequently take into consideration the grammatical status of the defined lexical unit: a substantive will be defined by a substantival construction (e.g. Eng. *pension* "regular payment etc."), a transitive verb basically by another transitive verb or a syntactically equivalent construction (e.g. Eng. *to pension* "to grant or pay a pension to"), etc., according to the respective system of the language in question.[119] But this circumstance must not be conceived as an absolute requirement to be observed in every case: Weinreich[120] is quite right when maintaining that "a claim of interchangeability between the term and its definition ... is preposterous for natural language".

All the definitions in a dictionary cannot be uniform and homogeneous, because the lexical meaning is concerned (cf. above, § 1.3.1.1). The definitions as discussed here are suitable primarily for dealing with the lexical meaning of the designative words. Though the matter is largely unexplored, it seems that it is less easy to construct definitions of the lexical meaning of, say, grammatical operators, which would be identical with the definitions of the lexical meaning of designative words. In any case, the lexicographer has both the right and the duty to describe the function(s) performed by such nondesignative lexical units in a sentence; and it is quite legitimate to indicate such succinct statements of the word's functions in the same way as the definitions of the designative units are indicated. For instance, Eng. *oho* "exclamation of surprise or triumph"; Oss. *där* "coordinative conjunction".

---

[116] Homonymous with Eng. *crib* "baby's bed etc.". Different dictionaries conceive the (homonymy and) polysemy differently, but differences are immaterial to the point taken here.

[117] Hornby C. S. p. 230.

[118] Cf. Weinreich PL 39; cf. Hiorth, Lingua 8, 1959, 304 sq. on the different relational phrases between the definiendum and the definiens.

[119] Cf. Országh LS 5, 1962, 143; Weinreich PL 39.

[120] PL 39.

The definitions should be abstracted (at least as far as possible) from the contexts the lexicographer has at hand. If there are some other monolingual dictionaries of the same language,[121] their definitions should be consulted, but only when the lexicographer's own attemps have been sketched.[122] The drafted definitions should also be submitted to the well-experienced informants in order to be tested as to their eventual over-specificity or lack of specificity, general correctness, and acceptability.[123] That the lexicographer must use, when constructing the definition, his own knowledge of the language in question should be a matter of course.

6.5.3.2 The second means of the lexicographer for explaining the lexical meaning in the entries of a monolingual dictionary is the synonyms (and near-synonyms). There seem to be basically two different ways of using them.[124]

[121] It is not quite legitimate to compare one's own definitions with the definitions of equivalent words in other languages: the semantic anisomorphism of different languages is to great to allow such a comparison. The only purpose for which a monolingual dictionary of another language can be legitimately used, in this respect, is its perusal or study in order to get acquainted with the defining techniques and usual formulations, not with the content of the definitions themselves. Such a legitimate study of the defining techniques of different monolingual dictionaries must be recommended, above all if the different techniques are analytically compared.

[122] Hiorth, Studia linguistica 11, 1957, 21 (with a report on the identical practice of the Danish Academic Dictionary).

[123] Cf. Weinreich PL 42 sq.

[124] Hiorth, Studia linguistica 11, 1957, 2 sqq. also differentiates two different categories; but they are established in another way in his conception. According to him, if a dictionary indicates, for instance, Eng. *to contravene* = *to disagree with*, then it can mean two different things, viz. either (1) *to contravene* is synonymous with *to disagree with*, or (2) *to contravene* is adequately described by *to disagree with*; therefore, there is an important difference between the two relational phrases assumed by the indication of a synonym. Irrespective of the material correctness of his example, Hiorth is right: in the first case, the explaining synonym can be conceived as belonging rather to the object language, whereas in the second case, it should be taken as belonging rather to the language of the description, to the metalanguage. Very frequently, however, it is not possible to discern to which category the explaining synonym belongs; or rather, it is one of the interesting features of lexicography that such an explaining synonym can be taken as belonging to both categories at the same time. Cf. also Hiorth's summary of his opinion (Proceedings 8th Congress of linguists, Oslo 1958, p. 105f. (and the reply of T. Knudsen (ibid., p. 115). Hiorth discussed the matter more thoroughly in a later paper *"Origin and Control of Meaning Hypotheses"* (in: Lingua 8, 1959, 294ff.). He found that there are thirteen different relational phrases connecting the definiendum and the definiens (at least from the point of view of logic; factually, in practice, they generally remain implicit and unexpressed). These relational phrases are: (1) "... means the same as ...", (2) "... denotes the same as ...", (3) "... designates the same as ...", (4) "... expresses the same as ...", (5) "... is used in the same way as ...", (6) "... is synonymous with ...", (7) "... has the same sense as ...", (8) "... has the same signification as ...", (9) "... is interpreted identically with ...", (10) "... may be defined as ...", (11) "... is understood in the same way as ...", (12) "... may also be formulated as ...", (13) "... is often abridged to ...".

17*

First, the synonym or near-synonym can be indicated as an addition to the definition. This is the usual practice of some big dictionaries.[125] In this way, one can indicate, for example, Eng. *to position* "to put in a or the proper position; *to place, to situate*".

The important feature of this method is that the respective lexicographic definition necessarily is or should be constructed in such a way that it is sufficient alone (eventually with the help of the examples and glosses), without the addition of the synonym. It follows, then, that the lexicographer can also indicate, in these additions, the partial synonyms, in particular those whose difference consists in the different polysemy. E.g. Eng. *girl* "(1a) a female child, (b) a young unmarried woman; *maiden*, (2a) a female servant; *maid*"etc.[126]

The definite advantage of such an indication of synonyms and partial synonyms is that the lexical unit dealt with in the entry is located in the subsystem (or at least group) of the semantically most related words. Apart from the purely scientific value of this, such indications will render the whole entry much more useful, because the resulting contradistinctions and comparisons of the (partial) synonyms will clarify the whole semantic description; as a by-product, these indications of (partial) synonyms may occasionally help the user to find an expression more suitable for his purpose than the one he originally had in mind and checked up in the dictionary. This latter circumstance is very important if the lexicographer prepares a monolingual dictionary of a language whose standard national form is only recently or not yet fully established. In these languages, it is not unfrequently very hard to find a precisely statable difference between some synonyms, yet the lexicographer will have, in many cases, the elusive impression that there is a difference; or opinions will vary from one informant to another without any clear shape or preponderance of the differences.[127] In such a situation, the indi-

---

[125] E.g. *Webster's Third*. The following examples of this paragraph are taken from this dictionary and are reduced.

[126] Sometimes, antonyms can be used for the same purpose with advantage; e.g. Eng. *light* as in *light rain* can be opposed to *heavy* (*rain*) but *light* as in *light complexion* can be opposed to *dark complexion*: Swanson PL 68. One of the rare dictionaries which try to indicate systematically the antonyms and to use them in the indication of the senses, is S. Ristić — Ž. Simić — V. Popović, *English-Serbocroatian Dictionary*, Belgrade 1963. For instance, the entry *girl* has the following form (vol. I, p. 477; here strongly reduced): *girl* (1) *devojka* (anton. *muškarac* [i.e. "boy"]); (2) *devojka* (anton. *žena* [i.e. "woman"]), *neodrasla žena* [i.e. "woman not grown-up"] ...; (3) *devojka* (anton. *žena* [i.e. "woman"]), *žena ispod srednih godina* [i.e. "woman under her middle age"]; (4) *devojka, služavka, kućna pomoćnica* [i.e. "girl, servant, kitchen-help"]. We see that the antonyms have some use, but that they cannot differentiate sense (3) from sense (2) and that they cannot differentiate sense (4) at all. — Cf. also footnote 161.

[127] Cf. Ščerba, *Izvestija* 97 sq.: in such cases, according to Ščerba, it is sometimes hard to perceive a norm, simply because it is very broad. It is, however, because of not only the "breadth" of the norm, but also because of the real variance from one speaker to the other and the lack of precision of the designatum, usually caused by an insufficient criterial specification.

cation of the eventually only partial or near-synonyms is useful: the attention of the users of the dictionary will be drawn to their very existence. One might take the optimistic point of view that the increased use of the single synonyms may eventually lead to a stronger differentiation of their lexical meanings. If this happens (which is not always, only sometimes, the case) it is a gain for the respective language, because the semantic differentiation) with the desirable increase of precision) is usually badly needed in these languages, at least in some spheres of the lexicon.

Synonyms are, however, frequently indicated not as an addition to the definition, but alone without the definition. Opinions vary in regard to this method;[128] in any case, one can state as a general observation that, usually, the smaller the dictionary the more frequent the mere indication of synonyms. If handled with due care, this method can yield good results. After all, there is a broader area of overlapping between the lexicographic definition and the indication of the synonyms than one would think. If we compare

(1) *mare* "female horse"

(2) *to bump off* "to murder" (slang)

(3) *nifty* "smart, stylish"

we see that (1) is an example of a very concise lexicographic definition, in which the term *horse* (representing what would be the *genus proximum* in a logical definition) can be taken as a compendious expression of all the semantic features which constitute it and which would have to be repeated in a more analytic definition of *mare*, and in which the term *female* (representing what would be the *differentia specifica* in a logical definition) can be taken as the statement of the semantic feature which causes the semantic difference. If this is so, then in the example (2) above the term *to murder* can be taken in the same way as the compendious expression of all the semantic features that the two expressions have in common and the indication of the connotative value (in this case the circumstance that it belongs to a slang) can be taken as the statement of the additional semantic feature that makes the difference. In this way, the overlapping between (1) (definition) and (2) (the closest near-synonym plus the difference) is obvious. Example (3) can, then, be taken as a case of the total identity of the semantic features of the synonym and of the entry-word so that it is neither necessary nor possible to state a difference.[129]

[128] Cf. Weinreich PL 40 for a very negative point of view; on the contrary, Filipec LSB 89. Cf. also Hiorth, Studia linguistica 11, 1957, 23 who discerns two basic types: (1) the indication of an absolute synonym (e.g., Eng. *nifty* "smart, stylish") and (2) the indication of a near-synonym with a statement of the difference; to him, both possibilities (and also the other theoretically possible ones) are valid.

[129] One of the greatest dangers to which this type seduces is the circularity of two entries. We speak about circularity if in entry (a) A is explained by the synonym B, and in entry (b) B is

In reality, all this is much more complicated, not only because the explanatory near-synonyms are frequently polysemous themselves and must or should be disambiguated, but above all because more than one near-synonym must be indicated not only to disambiguate one from another but in order to convey all the criterial features.

The simplest type of the use of synonyms is that exemplified above by example (2): all obsolete, dialectal, colloquial, vulgar etc. lexical units can be explained in this way, provided there is a connotatively neutral synonym. If the synonymy is only partial, it is not necessary to disambiguate the synonym if it has only one absolutely dominant sense; e.g. if we indicate Eng. *to bump off* "to murder (slang)", there is no necessity to disambiguate the polysemy of *to murder*, because the non-dominant, transferred sense of *to murder* (i.e. "to spoil by lack of skill or knowledge") will probably occur to nobody. Polysemous partial synonyms which have no dominant sense or which have more of them should be disambiguated by the indication of more than one partial synonyms, by a specifying attribute, or by the number of the relevant sense as stated in the respective entry (e.g. Eng. *maiden* "girl, young unmarried woman (liter.)", or they should be avoided if not required by the general plan of the dictionary.

The other type of application of synonyms was exemplified above as (3): *nifty* "smart, stylish". In some cases, the type discussed in the preceding paragraph and the one under discussion here overlap, but they are nevertheless distinguishable. The present type of application of synonyms is generally avoided by the bigger dictionaries, but probably no small one will be able to afford never to use it. In the majority of cases, one single synonym will not suffice and it is necessary to indicate more of them. Their eventual polysemy is usually disambiguated by their being quoted as a group (or by any other of the usual means). A very frequent situation is that the single synonyms explain some semantic features of the entry word; in this way, the Czech word *boj* ("fight"), etc. can be explained by the synonyms *bitva* ("battle"), *srážka* ("skirmish"), *utkání* ("contest"[130]), and others. This method can be applied with similar clarity above all when the explaining synonyms are or approach the status of hyponyms of the entry-word. On the other hand if we consider an example like Eng. *nifty* "smart, stylish", we cannot say that the synonyms are hyponyms of the entry word. On the contrary, it seems that either one or the other could be used in any sentence instead of the entry-word without a considerable semantic effect; but there seems nevertheless to be an elusive

explained by the synonym A; e.g., *nifty* "smare", *smart* "nifty". At least in one of the entries, one of the synonyms must be explained morefully.

[130] The example and also partly the conception are taken from Filipec LSB 89; the English translations of the Czech words (in parentheses) are only approximative, and have themselves a slightly different polysemy and different synonymic relations.

difference. These two examples tend to exemplify two categories: in the first of them (Czech *boj*) the sum of the synonyms) setting aside the disambiguated senses explains the entry-word, in the second (Eng. *nifty*), any of the synonyms is (nearly) capable of effecting the explanation. Efforts are sometimes made to discern the two types; e.g., the synonyms of the first category are separated by the comma, synonyms of the second by semicolon. These efforts are certainly laudable and useful. But in very numerous cases, it is not possible to make the difference so explicit.

Synonyms are particularly useful when different contextual nuances are to be explained. The lexical meaning of Czech *břeskný* can be described, with the necessary generality (and some unavoidable inaccuracy), by Eng. "shrill, ringing". The contextual nuances are of course different if the adjective is applied to qualify, say, a laugh, and if applied to qualify a type of music. Under the principle of generality of meaning it would be wrong to give these differences the status of different senses; therefore, it is useful to indicate and explain or at least suggest the difference by different near-synonyms; e.g., in the combination of words *břeskný smích* ("laugh") by the near-synonym *pronikavý* ("piercing"), in the combination of words *břeskný pochod* ("march") by some near-synonym like "vigorous".[131] This method of the application of synonyms is used above all in connexion with the next means of lexicographic explanation, viz. with the examples.

6.5.3.3 The purpose of the examples is to show how the entry-word functions in combination with other lexical units. The absolute majority of dictionaries indicate examples. The bigger the dictionary the more examples it generally contains. Only very small dictionaries can afford not to indicate them; but absolute absence of examples is usually accompanied by a severe lowering of the standard of the dictionary (unless its purpose is a strictly restricted one, such as for instance that of a glossary of technical terminology or of a purely orthographical or similar dictionary). Practically only the technical terms (in the strictest acceptation: the precisely, scientifically defined ones) can be presented without examples, even in a large dictionary; but even in this case it is preferable if some examples are nevertheless indicated, primarily if the term has multiple meaning (i.e. if it has terminological value in different branches of science) and in order to show the eventual terminological multiword lexical units formed with it, if they are treated as subentries (cf. § 6.6.3).

Almost everything can be illustrated by the examples: for example, the different contextual nuances,[132] the range of authors in whose works the entry-

---

[131] The example and also partly the conception are taken from Zima LSB 96 sq.

[132] In this case, the quoted examples frequently need a further explanation (usually by means of a gloss or by a synonym); e.g. Eng. *mushroom* "fast growing fungus etc."; example: *the mushroom*

word occurs, the first occurrence of the word, the range of application, the attributive combinations, the typical objects of verbs, the adverbial combinations, the applicational differences of synonyms or near-synonyms, etc.[133]

Exemplification is always useful. Very frequently, many of the examples illustrate what is stated in the other parts of the entry, above all in the lexicographic definition. Even in this case, it is no mere re-statement or repetition, because the examples, being more concrete than the definition, which should be rather general, always add some new information. So for instance, if we read, after the definition of Eng. *beautiful* "giving pleasure or delight to the mind or senses", also the examples *beautiful face, flower, voice; beautiful weather, music,* we certainly gain much information, though these examples indicate nothing that is not covered by the definition and not everything that is covered by it. The series of these examples is certainly not complete by far. But completeness is out of the reach of the lexicographer, in the majority of such cases: how could he be expected to collect and elicit a complete list of items which can be characterized as beautiful? Therefore, he indicates only some examples which he considers typical and leaves it to the abstractive power of the user of the dictionary to form other combinations by analogy:[134] restrictive statements like "used only ..." are sometimes necessary but always dangerous. A bigger dictionary will indicate more examples than those given above; but exhaustiveness can be reached only in the sphere of older texts (which form a closed corpus). This aspect of exemplification is concerned above all with the generative power of the dictionary. If the lexicographer works in the sphere of a dead language (or in the sphere of older texts of a living language), he will not have to anticipate, as in the preceding situation, the creativity, of language, i.e. the possibility that new combinations will continue to arise but on the contrary, he will have to realize the fact that the corpus of his texts is closed and that he has no native speakers, informants at hand from whose linguistic competence to elicit some additional information to complete what he finds in this contexts. This circumstance adds value to each context and, in its turn, induces the lexicographer to approach more or less the thesaurus-type and quote, if possible, all examples attested in the corpus of texts, both for the sake of completeness and because of their factual character.[135]

It is frequently necessary to add to such examples a short explanation of the nuance of meaning in which they are used in the given context.

(rapid) *growth of London suburbs* (Hornby), where *rapid* is the explanation of the concrete signification in this example.

[133] Cf. Janský LSB 136, Martin PL 156, Borovkov LS 1, 1957, 142 sq., Feldman LS 2, 1957, 83 and 89.

[134] Cf. also below, § on the overlapping with the glosses.

[135] This is, incidentally, another reason why the dictionaries of dead languages tend to the thesaurus type. Cf. Ščerba 103 sq.

The examples included in the entry should not be treated by the lexicographer as some additional material but as an integral part of the entry. The examples should not supersee the lexicography in definition,[136] but should illustrate and complement it; it follows as a matter of course that if there are more definitions within one entry, i.e. if the entry-word is polysemous, the examples should be distributed according to the single senses.

Examples can be taken from the (usually written) texts of the language, or they can be constructed by the lexicographer with the eventual help of informants. The first type of example has the great advantage that it has a highly factual character: evidence can be produced that the word in question really was used in a certain passage by a certain author. Therefore, these what can be called "quoted examples" are preferred by any philological dictionary and above all by the big ones. In the case of an overall-descriptive dictionary, and especially that of a dead language or of an older stage of a living language, the quoted examples are the only ones which are even possible; there is ex definitione no native speaker of such a language and therefore no possibility of producing new texts and consequently also no possibility of constructing really authentic examples.[137]

The form of the quoted examples can differ in different dictionaries; the main variations can be observed in the length of the quotation and in the precision of the citation.

As far as the length of the quotation (i.e. of the quoted passage) goes, probably the best thing to do is to quote the whole lexicographic context (cf. § 6.3.1.1), i.e. a reduced part of a passage in a text from which those parts which are irrelevant are omitted.[138] The degree of reduction can vary; the bigger the dictionary the longer the quotations, but even the shortest exemplification (e.g. only the verb with its object) is very useful. The places of reduction (i.e. some omitted words) may be indicated by dots, but it is not absolutely necessary to do it. On the other hand, if it is the policy of the dictionary to quote sentences which are grammatically complete (even if they are quoted in a reduced form), it is sometimes necessary to supply, for example, the subject;

---

[136] Even if a quotation has the form of a definition, the lexicographer should try to abstract his own form of it. This should above all be the case with the so-called contextual (or implicative) definition: see the discussion in Weinreich PL 40 sq.

[137] Cf. Országh LS 5, 1962, 152 for whom only the quoted examples are admissible.

[138] There are, however, isolated voices maintaining that whole, unreduced passages must be quoted. For example, according to M. Cohen (Proceedings of the 9th Congress, p. 503), it is necessary to quote, as the illustration of French *apposer*: "*Le garde-champêtre a apposé une affiche sur le panneau devant la mairie (il l'a appliqué en la collant)*." This is certainly richer than a mere *apposer une affiche* (quoted by Cohen as an example of a nefarious reduction of the context); few dictionaries, however, will be big enough to allow this, because, after all, even if we decide to quote only whole sentences, we shall soon find that many of them contain parts absolutely irrelevant to the understanding of the entry-word, so that to print them is a real waste.

this should be indicated by brackets.[139] A simple example of such a supplement is the quotation

"(*They*) *started lectures and secured a large following*".

The quotation is used as an example in the entry following in OED s.v. The supplement (*They*) is necessary only because the quotations in OED are reduced but not grammatically truncated.

Much more important is the other type of supplement. In the entry *follower* (sense 2, c), the OED has the following quotation from R. S. Surtees (1858):

"*She granted* (*the servants*) ... *every indulgence* ... *in having their followers.*"

In this (reduced) quotation, the indirect object (*the servants*) is supplied from the broader context. The supplement is necessary not only from the grammatical point of view (a mere grammatical word, e.g. *them*, could be supplied of this were the case), but also because the lexicographer maintains that a *follower* is "a man who courts a maidservant" (not a girl of another profession), so that without this supplement, just a criterial feature of the designatum would remain without illustration. It is no pity if a smaller dictionary decides to truncate the sentences in the quotations and does not, consequently, indicate the purely grammatical supplements, either. But it is a grave loss if the supplements of the other type, i.e. those which supply a criterial feature, or at least which are instrumental to a good understanding, are omitted.

The precision of the citation (i.e. of the indication of the source of the quotation) can also vary. The best thing for a big dictionary, above all if it is of the reference type, is to indicate the precise locus, i.e. the author, the work, the page, verse, or line (as conventionally indicated in the respective literature).[140] But few dictionaries will be able to afford the space; in such a case, the mere indication of the author is very valuable, because it gives at least basic orientation about the time when and the type of text where the word occurs.[141] This is especially necessary in those dictionaries which combine the normative purpose with the broader purpose of the reference type.

There is one danger connected with quoted examples, viz. that the lexicographer will indicate too many and that there will be "empty" ones among them. A context like

"*Unlike her more learned colleagues, she was very beautiful*"

---

[139] Cf. Janský LSB 137 sq.; Malkiel PL 20 sq.; Householder PL 281.

[140] This opinion is supported (with the restriction made by the present author) by Havlová LSB 196; Malkiel PL 21.

[141] It is necessary to point out again that a single author's works can belong to different types (cf. § 6.3.1.2, last paragraph). The statement above is valid only as a generalization in the bird's-eye-view; if the differences within the work of one author are very considerable, the indication should be more specific.

is no good lexicographic context at all because we learn next to nothing about any of the words; examples of this type, however, are not unfrequently quoted.[142] Unless one is compiling a thesaurus, or has a chronological or other reason for the quote, a similar context is better to be omitted.

The real difficulty of quotation, however, is that sometimes it is impossible to find a good informative context at all.[143]

The great advantage of constructed examples is just that the lexicographer can either construct them himself (by his competence as a native speaker) or elicit them from his informants precisely according to the purpose, to illustrate the difficult points. Therefore, these examples can be constructed in such a way that they invite analogical applications by the user of the dictionary, if adroitly prepared, and consequently, they often have a great generative power.[144] Constructed examples are usually very short, for example only the verb — its object, the adjective with the substantive or vice versa. etc. For instance, s.v. *incipient*: *incipient decay*; s.v. *to rest*, *waves that never rest*; s.v. *signal*: *signal victory, defeat, reward*, etc.; s.v. *to round*: *round a sentence, estate, career*. When the informants are well trained, they can be allowed to produce only such minimal combinations of words as illustrations, but for a considerable time they should be required to produce whole sentences (from which the minimal combinations are then reduced by the lexicographer) as a partial precaution against too great a imagination or good will.[145]

As we have seen above (cf. § 3.2.3), we can discern free combinations of words and set ones; what has been said in the preceding paragraphs was concerned with the free combinations. As far as set expressions are concerned, it is quite natural for a dictionary to explain the meaning of idiomatic expressions especially if it cannot be deduced from the meaning of their constituent parts by an unsophisticated speaker of the language and if they are stabilized and frequently used.[146] Apart from the problem of their selection, however, there is the question of where to list these expressions. In smaller dictionaries, it is usual to list them at the end of the whole entry; not unfrequently, this "phraseological" part of the entry is separated from the preceding part by a special sign, or these expressions are set in another type than the examples of the free combinations. This method has the advantage that the reader can find an idiomatic expression quickly and that the lexico-

[142] Cf. Janský LSB 136 sq. (with good Czech examples, both positive and negative).
[143] Cf LSB 59 sq.
[144] Martin PL 156. Cf. also Weinreich IJAL 20, 1964, 407.
[145] There is no need to stress that the lexicographer can choose these examples from the material prepared by the informants for the study of the lexical meaning (cf. above, § 6.3.2.1).
[146] Cf. Barnhart PL 177 (with an interesting comparison of the attitude of different dictionaries to the same idiomatic expressions etc.); Országh LS 5, 1962, 150; in a more restrictive sense Malíková LSB 123 (rather free combinations only).

grapher is not troubled with having to decide to which of the senses of a poly-semous word the respective set expression belongs. On the other hand, the bigger dictionaries generally list idiomatic expressions at the end of the examples of free combinations of words which illustrate the definitions of the single senses; the large dictionary's treatment of the lexicographic meaning is more detailed and refined, and consequently the location of the idiomatic expressions within the polysemy of the word more obvious and understandable (though frequently only in a partly historical, partly logical way).[147]

6.5.3.3.1 Besides the idiomatic set expressions, there are also the multi-word lexical units and similar combinations of words (most frequently of a terminological character) which approach their status. We have seen above (§ 3.3.1) that it is not always easy to decide what is a multiword lexical unit and what is not. For the practical purpose here at hand, the problem can be stated as follows. In any languages I know or am informed about, the lexico-graphers will meet cases like Eng. *heavy water, black market*. A very frequent solution is that the lexicographer avoids an either or decision. On the one hand, he does not list them as special entries of their own; on the other hand, while inserting them among the examples of the free combinations, he treats them as so-called subentries: he has them set in a special type (usually a more conspicuous one than that used for the other examples but less so than that used for the entry-words, if necessary, he adds the grammatical lemma (usually only if it differs from the lemma of the entry-word itself), and then he describes their lexical meaning by the usual means.[148]

We have seen above, that the entry can and should he regarded as what we call the lexical abstraction; it follows, then, that a subentry must also be regarded as a lexical abstraction, but of a lower order. It would seem that such insertion of subentries into the main bulk of the entry is not practical and will confuse the user of the dictionary. But on the contrary; if the choice is done with care and if the subentry-word and the lemma are typographically well expressed (i.e. in a well-balanced way), the method of subentries is good both for the lexicographer and for the user. It should also be said that quite apart from the material correctness of the single concrete cases, this graded approach appears to be correct because it seems to be in keeping with the graded stabilization of a multiword lexical unit.

---

[147] Only the latter solution is advocated by Janský LSB 139.

[148] There is no reason why idiomatic set expressions should not be treated as subentries, and sometimes they are. It is, however, the multiword lexical units (or expressions approaching their status) which require this treatment more, because they tend to need an exemplification of their own and sometimes they have even their own polysemy. — Borovkov LS 1, 1957, 141 seems to put the multiword lexical units on the same level as the other examples.

If some set expressions, and above all some multiword lexical units are dealt with in subentries, the question arises into which entries these subentries should be inserted: shall we insert the subentry *black market* into the entry *black*, or *market*, or both? There is no single and unequivocal reply to this question, but the following points can be adumbrated.

(1) Elements like the prepositions, the article, usually also the forms of the verb *to be* (and its equivalents in different languages) are generally not suitable or the purpose: nobody will probably insert the eventual subentry *castles in the air* into the entry *in* or *the*.

(2) In the case of a set group like Eng. *cat burglar*, there is every reason to expect that the user will have no trouble with the word *burglar* (because *cat burglar* is a burglar of a certain kind), but that he will not understand the meaning of *cat* in this group; the insertion of the subentry into the entry *cat* is thus very strongly suggested.

In a similar way, one could argue that in the set group *Englishman's house his castle*, it will be the word *castle* about which the user will need the information in the first line, since there is nothing baffling in an Englishman's possession of a house, but it is an everyday experience that a normal house is not a castle, so that it is the signification of the word *castle* which is the first (but not the only) purpose of the subentry. The insertion of such a subentry into the entry *castle* suggests itself, then, very strongly.

(3) In the case of a set combination like Eng. *castles in the air*, *castles in Spain*, both the main constituent elements (*castles*, and *air*, or *Spain*) will not be immediately clear to the user of the dictionary. If it is not possible, for reasons of space, to insert the subentry into both entries, it is probably slightly better to insert it into the entry *castle*, because *in the air*, or *in Spain* are only attributive to it, so that one could assume that the word *castle* will claim the user's first attention, by force of its central position.

(4) There will, however, be many set combinations which will offer little or no arguments for the preference or one of their elements; e.g., Eng. *black market*, *cash register*, etc. The best solution is to insert the subentry into both the entries. If the size of the dictionary does not allow this, the choice of the entry into which the subentry is inserted should be as mechanical as possible;[149] the mechanical choice of the first designative element as the entry into which the subentry is to be inserted is probably the most advisable decision. One of

---

[149] More sophisticated principles (e.g. "*headword of the attributive syntagma*", "*verb in the verbal phrase*") will inevitably lead to yet further borderline cases and will confuse and irritate the user, at least in a general-purpose dictionary. A more scholarly dictionary may afford more sophistication in this as in other respects.

the reasons why this is so is that those multiword lexical units which are inserted as entries of their own will be alphabetically ordered in the same way.[150]

6.5.3.4 The last means the lexicographer uses in the entry is the gloss.[151] It is a very heterogeneous category; we can call a gloss any descriptive or explanatory note within the entry. There is a certain amount of overlapping between the glosses and the other categories; the most important probably being that of the examples and the glosses. For instance,[152] Eng. *fugitive* has another sense (1) when used in reference to persons ("running away") and (2) when used in reference to different things ("of temporary interest or value"). Both senses can be sufficiently clarified by suitable examples, as (1) *fugitive slave*, (2) *fugitive verses*, etc. Since, however, it is not only slaves who may turn fugitives, the lexicographer may prefer a more general clarification and may gloss sense (1) by a note to the purpose that it pertains to persons. The note "persons" (or any other formulation of it) is then a gloss which indicates the range of application of the entry-word. The overlapping between such a gloss and an example is given by the fact that the word *person* can be used itself in the respective context, so that it can be taken as an example (for which its hyponyms could be substituted). This overlapping between gloss and example is more frequent than one would think. Indeed, it is within my experience impossible to make, in a monolingual dictionary, the neat distinction between the "object language" and "metalanguage" or "language of description" which some theoreticians are inclined to postulate. The lexicographer should be aware of this overlapping and should anticipate the user's inclination to understand seemingly unambiguous formulations in most unexpected ways. One further observation is necessary — that while it is at least as delicate to indicate a restriction of the application by means of such a gloss as by some examples, these glosses are much more, both descriptively and generatively, powerful. Indeed, it is possible to view an important gloss of this type as a lexical abstraction of a lower order again.

Another important function of the glosses is to give grammatical indications in the broadest sense of the word. Those indications by the means of which the paradigm of the entry-word is identified are given in the lemma; within the text of the entry, it is necessary to indicate especially those grammatical properties which disambiguate the single senses of polysemous

---

[150] Cf. Janský LSB 139; Országh LS 5, 1962, 151; Phal, Cahiers de lexicologie 4, 1964, 58 sq.

[151] The term *gloss* is rather frequently used to designate the target-language equivalents in a bilingual dictionary. In the present book, we use it only in reference to what could be described as short comments, explanatory remarks, semantic characteristics or qualifications, etc.

[152] The example is based on Hornby, s. v.

words.[153/154] If, e.g., Lat. *petere* has two senses, viz. (1) "to rush to", (2) "to ask for", it should also be indicated that in sense (1), the verb is followed by the simple reference to the place in the accusative case, whereas in sense (2), the object required will be in the accusative, but there must be the person from whom the object is required in ablative with the preposition *ab*. In this sphere, the glosses show a broad range of contact with the examples (e.g., the example *petere Romam* "to rush to Rome" would suffice for sense (1), in a shorter dictionary), and there is also a considerable amount of overlapping: e.g., if sense (2) of the verb *petere* is accompanied by the formula *aliquid ab aliquo* "Something from somebody", the note seems to have partly the status of a gloss, partly that of a (formulaic) example.[155] Besides this overlapping within the limit of one language, there is also a broad area of variation from one language to another, since what is expressed by a grammatical construction can be expressed by lexical means in another language, and since opinions on what is to be considered grammatical and what lexical vary strongly from one linguist to another. Adroit handling of all these phenomena either by examples or by glosses or by both is, however, one of the prerequisites of the lexicographer's success, above all if his dictionary is to be generatively powerful.

All indications which concern the whole field of connotation and the field of restricted languages, styles, etc., are usually made by means of the labels which can be regarded as a species of glosses, a more formal type of them. In this way, the lexicographer indicates by a label that the entry-word (or one of its senses, or one of the set expressions in which it occurs) is emotive, vulgar, colloquial, etc. In the same way he indicates that the word belongs to a local dialect, to an older stage of the language, to a restricted language, to a set of terminology of a special branch of knowledge, etc. These labels usually have the form of short abbreviations (e.g. *liter.*, *coll.*, *vulg.*, *arch.*, *dial.*, *botan.*, *zool.*, etc.) used in the whole dictionary in a uniform way. Their number and their handling depend primarily upon both the really observable variation of the language in question and the degree of descriptive finesse and generative power with which the lexicographer intends to invest his dictionary.[156]

---

[153] This is the minimal requirement; no need to stress that a big descriptive dictionary should also indicate those individual grammatical properties of the entry-word which are not coordinated with an observable variation of meaning.   [154] Cf. Householder 279, Weinreich PL 39, Weinreich, *Universals* 143, Kotětova LS 1, 1957, 105 and 118.

[155] The formulaic, abstract character of such statements should not be overdone, with respect to the general user. For example, Weinreich PL 40 and 37 maintains that the relational nature of a word like Eng. *end* should be displayed by using algebraic variables (x, y ...) in the term, and again in the definition: (y is the) *end* (of x) "there is no x after y". I do not think formulations like this will render good services to the general user, especially not when the concrete value of the symbols used is limited to only one or a few entries.

[156] Let us mention in this connection that in many dictionaries, we can also find the "rare" or some other similar expression. Purely statistical considerations of the frequency of occurrence

Prescriptive and prohibitive glosses, which have a similar status as the grammatical ones, will be mentioned below (§ 6.7) in connection with the other normative activities of the lexicographer.

We should at last mention the encyclopedic glosses which are interspersed in the text of the entries in some dictionaries. From the point of view of pure theory, encyclopedic glosses should have no place in a purely linguistic description; indeed, no linguistic dictionary should give too many of them. But on the other hand, a useful dictionary of a dead language or of a contemporary one spoken in an exotic culture will have to give encyclopedic notes on the denotate unknown to us; and there are dictionaries (e.g., Larousse, Webster) which delicately combine both the linguistic and the encyclopedic aspect. In any case, there is a considerable range of overlapping between very detailed or possibly over-specific lexicographic definitions and encyclopedic glosses.

6.5.4 What has been discussed is the usual situation, the usual methods the lexicographer uses to describe the lexical meaning of the entry-word. The entries constructed in this way are usually self-contained: all the necessary information is contained in them. There are, however, reduced entries which describe the entry-word by stating the difference (usually some additional semantic feature) from another entry-word.

This is notably the case with series of derived words which are produced by the same word-formational means and are regular both as far as their form and as far as their meaning go; cf. above (§ 2.2). It is primarily dictionaries of languages with a rich and regular morphology in general and word-formation in particular which can spare much space in this way. In small dictionaries, the regularly derived words can be left out if the dictionary contains an appendix on derivation and word-formation.[157] A better procedure, however, is to list them as entry-words and indicate how they are derived from another word which has a full entry of its own in the dictionary.

If there is, for example, in Czech an endless series of feminine nouns in *-ka* derived from masculines which do not have this suffix (*vesničan* "male inhabitant of a village" :: *vesničanka* "female inhabitant of a village", *občan* "male citizen" :: *občanka* "female citizen", *učitel* "male teacher" :: *učitelka*

are seldom the basis of the use of this gloss; within my experience, this label is frequently used when the lexicographer wishes to convey the idea that the phenomenon thus labelled verges on the occasional, or that it is somehow outside the norm, though occurring in a "good" author with authority, but when the lexicographer does not wish, on the other hand, to be too explicit. Though such phenomena really used to be "rare", it is not their rarity which invites the label. This crypto-prohibitive use of the label ought to be discontinued.

[157] Swanson PL 66 is right when maintaining this. His example, however, could have been better chosen: Eng. *goodness* (which he uses as the example) is formed in the same way as *likeness*, *prettiness*, etc., but should be selected as an entry-word (except by some smallest dictionary), because of its own polysemy and phraseology (*to have the goodness to, Goodness knows*, etc.).

"female teacher", *profesor* "male professor" : : *profesorka* "female professor", etc.), it is sufficient to indicate, in the entry *ostrovanka*, the lex. meaning as "fem. to *ostrovan* (inhabitant if an island)".[158]

In cases similar to the one used as the example here, it would seem that one does not spare much space by this procedure. If we have, however, to deal with long series of basic words and derived word with rich polysemy (as, e.g., the aspectual verbs in Russian), the space spared is considerable. It cannot, however, be stressed enough that both the formal regularity and the semantic identity of such pairs of words must be checked and re-checked with the utmost care. Sometimes the situation is so complicated and the acceptance of this procedure would entail such a quantity of cross-references that some lexicographers prefer to treat the basic and the derived words separately, even if a good amount of repetition is involved. In big dictionaries, the separate treatment of all entry-words should be preferred in any case.

Both from the notional and from the practical point of view it is interesting to observe that there is an area of overlapping between this cross-reference of the words and the description of the meaning of connotative words by their connotationally neutral synonyms (§ 6.5.3.2).

6.5.5 As nearly all the lexical units (and above all the most usual and frequent ones) are polysemous, the presentation of polysemy in the dictionary is one of the lexicographer's important and delicate tasks.

The first and basic decision must concern the depth of detail with which the polysemy is to be presented; practically, this decision implies a selection of the senses for inclusion in the dictionary. This selection of the senses must be fully coordinated with the selection of entries for inclusion: In a big dictionary, there will be many entries and there will also be a detailed presentation of polysemy; in an overall-descriptive dictionary, dialectal, obsolete, etc., lexical units will be listed, and so will also be dialectal, obsolete, etc., special senses of polysemous words; in a purely standard-descriptive dictionary, lexical units not occurring in the standard national language will not be included, nor will be special senses not known in the standard national be mentioned in the presentation of polysemous words; if the dictionary lists many technical terms among its entries, it will also indicate many special terminological senses of the polysemous words. In short, the selection of entries and the selection of the single senses of the polysemous entries must be in as good a proportion as possible and governed by roughly the same principles.

Another important observation is that the lexicographer should not see polysemy where there is none. A not infrequent error is that differences caused

---

[158] Jánský LSB 136, Országh LS 5, 1962, 145. Cf. also S. di Blasi, Linguistics 18, 1965, 89 for a very thorough discussion of the derivational relations between the definiendum and the definiens, in a lexicographic definition.

by different applications of a lexical unit are taken for its different senses. For instance, if we read contexts in which *a mother's love for her children* is mentioned with other contexts in which a *man's love of adventure* is described, we shall probably see that they have not much in common: the situations, the actions, the symptoms of the feelings, everything tends to be rather different. It would, however, hardly be correct to see in these different applications a difference of senses: we must be aware of the generality of meaning which causes that the range of a lexical unit's application can be rather broad and its designatum not too specific.[159] It is certainly never easy and sometimes impossible to discern such different applications of a word with a general meaning from a differentiation of its senses;[160] generally, large dictionaries can afford a more extensive ramification of the single senses in their presentation more easily than small ones.[161]

Another danger which should be avoided can be illustrated by the following example. Let us suppose that the lexicographer discerns among the senses of Eng. *to dissipate* (1) "waste foolishly (e.g. time or money)" and (2) "engage in foolish or harmful pleasures".[162] If he has a sufficiently rich collection of material, the lexicographer will certainly find some contexts in which it will not be clear whether the verb is used in the one or in the other sense; in a medium dictionary which indicates some examples, it would be wrong to indicate such "transitional" contexts. It is much better to quote only examples with what has been called above "good lexicographic contexts"[163/164]; the

---

[159] Cf. Havránek LSB 141 sq.; Poldauf, Poznání 207; Weinreich, *Trends* 75. On the other hand, Ščerba, *Izvestija*, 101 maintains that the dictionary should indicate every single nuance of the lexical unit's meaning; this is, however, possible and justifiable only in the case of a big dictionary whose main purpose is to help the user to understand some difficult texts.

[160] Note, for example, that in the entry *love* (subst.), Hornby sets the feeling between two persons of opposite sex apart, as having a sense different from that accepted for the love for children, of adventure, etc.; on the other hand, in the entry *to love* (verb), it seems that there in only one sense accepted for all these applications. Another concrete example: one of the senses of. Eng. *queue* is according to Webster "a line esp. of persons or vehicles"; Hornby divides this into two senses (1) "a line of people waiting for their turn", (2) "line of vehicles waiting to proceed". It can be doubted whether the division indicated in Hornby is really well founded.

[161] Filipec SS 18, 1957, 145 finds a criterion for the constitution of the single separate senses in its autonyms. E.g., if Czech *líný* (something like "lazy", etc.) has the antonyms *pilný* "diligent", *rychlý* "quick", *svěží, čilý* "fresh, brisk", it may be assumed that it has at least those single senses which are themselves antonymous to these antonyms. I like the criterion because it is based on an observably existing linguistic opposition, but the yet insufficient study of the antonyms does not allow its general application at the moment. Cf. footnote 126.

[162] The example is based on Hornby s. v. In a smaller dictionary, this probably could be treated as one sense as well.

[163] Získal SS 4, 1938, 218.

[164] The situation would not be much different if only one sense of the verb instead of two were accepted; the examples indicated by the lexicographer would also tend to show two focuses of application, one around the aspect of "waste", the other around the aspect of "idle pleasure".

abstractive-generalizing ability of the user will supply the transitional possibilities between these "polar" examples and around them: let us not forget that the monolingual dictionary is written for a user who has a good knowledge of the language in question, who is in the majority of cases a native speaker.[165]

In the same way as it avoids mere contextual nuances, the dictionary should avoid mere occasionalities, unless it is a thesaurus or verges on that type.[166]

6.5.5.1 The s e q u e n c e in which the single senses of a polysemous word are to be indicated is another problem which must be tackled by the lexicographer. Shall he accept the sequence
Eng. *queue* (1) "line of persons waiting for their turn",
(2) "pigtail",
or vice versa?[167]

"Various arrangements are possible, the determining factors being for whom the dictionary is intended and for what use or uses" — this statement of I a n u c c i[168] is undoubtedly correct: a dictionary having rather a historical character will try to imitate in the sequence of its indication the succession of the historical developments, a dictionary with strong encyclopedic predilections will stress the technical senses, etc.

In reality, there is no single principle by the exclusive application of which all polysemous entries of a dictionary could be arranged as to the sequence of the single senses. The historical and the statistical principles cannot be uniformly and evenly applied, if for no other reason than for lack of data.[169] But even if these data were always known, these principles could not be applied

---

[165] But on the other hand, in the treatment of meaning, the lexicographer should not try to generalize simply by a logical abstraction to the detriment of the facts of language. French *pied* "foot" seems to have also the following two senses: (1) "un certain organ du corps", (2) "pied d'une lampe, d'une chaise". A. R o s e t t i (from whom we accept the example and its treatment: *Linguistica*, The Hague 1965, p. 35; with an important quotation from M e i l l e t) comes to the conclusion that "pour le sujet parlant, *pied* désigne ce sur quoi porte un objet donné". Conclusions of this type seem to be too exclusively logical; for a lexicographic treatment, the sense *pied* (1) "leg, part of the body" offers itself as the dominant one from which the other is derived.

[166] Z í s k a l SS 4, 1938, 25; Š č e r b a, *Izvestija* 101; M a l k i e l PL 20.

[167] Webster: (1) pigtail, (2) a line of persons; Hornby: (1) a line of persons, (2) pigtail. In a historical dictionary, the situation is clear: OED knows *queue* "pigtail" in 1748, but *queue* "line" only in 1837; in our days, "line will probably be the dominant sense".

[168] PL 204; cf. also G e d n e y PL 233.

[169] "Documentation is seldom sufficient to enable the lexicographer to make more than an educated guess as to priority": U r d a n g, Language 39, 1963, 587; the history of many languages is unknown: N i d a, IJAL 24, 1958, 280, and many others. Even in a historical dictionary, the historical order must be combined with the empirical order as advocated by C a s a r e s: Hiorth, Lingua 4, 1954, 423 and 418. Migliorini, *Vocabolario* 46: The best thing is the coincidence of

in all cases. For example, no lexicographer (with the exception of purely historical dictionaries) will doubt that that the sequence of senses of French *débattre* should begin with the dominant sense "to debate, to discuss", not with the historically oldest sense "to struggle" (which is present today only in se débattre; it is not without interest to see that this observation was made by Littré himself, in the Preface to his Dictionary). There is no single logical or epistemological system which would be both powerful and detailed enough to be used unequivocally and alone as the basis for the ordering of the senses and which would command a general authority and recognition.[170]

The grammatical properties of the lexical unit are not sufficient as a unique principle for determining the sequence of senses: We have seen above that though the single senses are frequently differentiated by some variation in the grammatical form, this is not always the case. Consequently, though it is important to take such formal or grammatical criteria into consideration,[171] they are not always present when they would be needed.[172] There are indeed whole categories of lexical units which can be dealt with by the purely grammatical principle of ordering the sequence of the senses. Such categories are, for example, in many languages, the prepositions and conjunctions;[173] but even in the treatment of these lexical units, purely semantic considerations cannot be disregarded.[174]

If the polysemous word has a dominant sense, this should be the first sense indicated; if it does not have any dominant sense, the sense which has the broadest application and no marked connotation should be indicated first.[175]

---

the logical criterion with the historical one; J. Dubois, Recherches lexicographiques: esquisse d'un dictionnaire structurale (in: Études de linguistique appliquée 1, 1962), p. 43 (Attempt to construct the entry nearly exclusively by formal criteria, mainly on the basis of the different possible combinations of the entry-word).

[170] This is even more true if we have in mind dictionaries of vastly different languages: "logical criteria drawn primarily from one language-culture complex cannot be easily or validly applied to another" (Nida, IJAL 24, 1958, 281). — This does not mean, however, that the lexicographer should not study monolingual dictionaries of other languages, to the contrary. Cf. footnote 121.

[171] An important discussion of different methods: Kahane-Kahane PL 260 sqq.

[172] Cf. Janský LSB 131 on the failure of some older efforts to order the sequence of senses in the entry on the basis of the different grammatical rections only.

[173] Kopeckij LSB 142.

[174] Cf. Bosák LSB 143: the sequence of the senses of a preposition should begin with the most lexical ones and end with the most grammatical ones, i.e. with pure rections.

[175] From time to time, the lexicographer will meet a word no sense of which will appear as a really good choice to begin the sequence with. In such a situation, the sequence of the senses should be at least as neat as possible, the single senses forming the closest groups possible. For instance, Eng. *trolley* (1) "two-or four-wheeled handcart", (2) "small, lowtrack running on wheels", (3) "small table on castors", (4) "small contact wheel between a tram-car or bus and an overhead cable" (reduced from Hornby). Senses (1)—(3) form a group of "vehicles" in the broadest sense, sense (4) is a more modern technicality; consequently, this seems to be a better sequence

All other senses which are more specialized, more specific, or technical, or which belong to the restricted language or styles, or which are obsolete, regional or vulgar should then follow in the order which seems to be optimal to the lexicographer: it is such an order in which those senses which follow each other usually differ from each other by fewer semantic features or by less important ones than those which are situated further apart in the sequence. If a lexical unit has more than one dominant (or at least broad, most general) sense, these dominant senses should *not* be placed all at the beginning of the sequence, with all the other senses following; it seems that it is more effective and to the advantage if each of the dominant senses is followed by the more specialized, specific, technical, etc., ones which seem to be semantically related to it.[176]

Let us discuss a concrete example.[177] In the *OED*, the sequence of senses of the Eng. word *queue* (cf. above) is given as follows:

(1) *Heraldry*. The tail of a beast. 1592

(2) Pigtail. 1748

(3) A line of persons. 1837

(4) A support of the butt of a lance. 1855

(5) (a) The tail-piece of a violin or other instrument.
        (No year indicated.)
    (b) The tail of a note. 1876.

In *Webster's Third*, we have the following sequence:

(1) Pigtail.

(2) Line of persons.

(3) A metal piece attached to the side of the breast-plate of a suit of armour and used as a rest for the butt of a lance.

(4) The tailpiece of a violin or another stringed instrument.

(5) The tail of a musical note.

than if we put the mechanical gadget between the vehicles (*Webster's Third* and others). In similar situations, some unobtrusive historicism (if possible) is not out of place; in our case, OED has roughly the same sequence of senses as the one preferred here on purely semantic grounds. But on the other hand, the lexicographer may feel that sense (4) is by now the most widely used one (what with trolley-buses, etc.); in that case, he will put this sense at the beginning and will lead all the "vehicular" ones follow (thus *Funk-Wagnall*).

[176] Probably the best discussion of this is Janský LSB 133 sqq.; cr. also important points made by Hiorth, Lingua 4, 1955, 418 sq and 423 (with quotations from Casares); Householder PL 281, Feldman LS 1, 1957, 25; very important also Filipec SS 18, 1967, 129 ff. and Országh LS 5, 1962.

[177] In the following discussion, some of the lexicographic definitions of the different dictionaries are severely reduced.

In *Funk & Wagnalls New Standard Dictionary of the English Language* (New York — London 1928; the changes in the newer edition are immaterial), we have the following sequence:

(1) Pigtail.

(2) A file of persons waiting in the order of their arrival.

(3) The tail-piece of a violin or a similar instrument.

(4) The stem of a note. *Music.*

(5) The tail of an animal, especially of a lion. *Heraldry.*

(6) A lance — rest.

We see that the OED, being a historical dictionary simply proceeds by the date of the first occurrence of the single senses.[178] Webster and Funk-Wagnall agree in putting the two non-technical senses at the beginning. It would seem that the dominant sense is by now (1) "a line of persons or vehicles"; there should follow the non-technical but in our days slightly obsolete sense (2) "pigtail"; the sequence of the following more or less specialized technical senses (which can be omitted in a smaller dictionary) is not very important; my preference would be: (3) "the tailpiece of a violin" (*mus.*), (4) "the stem of a note" (*mus.*), (5) "the tail of a beast" (*her.*), (6) "the support of the butt of a lance on a suit of armour" (*obs.*).

We can observe that the final sequence of senses proposed here does not differ too strongly from the one accepted in the historical dictionary, at least not in respect to the relation of the technical, special senses to the non-technical ones: with the exception of the heraldic, all the technical senses follow the non-technical ones, in both treatments. This is not incidental: technical senses frequently develop from general ones.[179]

It should also be remarked that the sequence of the senses does not necessarily imply that one of them could be derived whether historically, logically or semantically from the other, in their succession.

---

[178] Incidentally, this is not always the historical method par excellence: chance may cause that a very old sense is attested only in more recent texts.

[179] In this connection, I feel tempted to remark that within my experience, there is more coincidence between the independent results of the historical approach and those of the purely descriptive one than the more bellicose advocates either of historism or of "synchronism" would care to admit. But on the other hand, the two approaches may lead to radically different points of view. The Ossetic Dictionary *Osetinskorusskij slovar'*, Ordžonikidze 1962 (which is not a historical one) discerns the following five homonymous words I *fyd* "meat", II *fyd* "millstone", III *fyd* "father", " IV *fyd* "evil, bad", V *fyd* "very". But from the historical point of view, there is no homonymous V *fyd* "very": historically it is a case of polysemy of IV *fyd* "bad". V. I. Abaev's *Historical Ossetic Dictionary* lists, under *fyd* "bad", also this sense, with the example *fyd rasughd čyzg* "very pretty girl", transferred from some originally only contextual nuances which could be illustrated, in this case, by a translation like "badly (> devilishly) pretty girl".

If we consider the example discussed here, we see that (6) is not derivable from (5), (5) is not derivable from (4), and (4) is not derivable from (3); and this observation is valid if we change their sequence. In reality, (3), (4), (5), and (6) all go back to (2). In a graphic chart, their relation is not (2) → (3) → (4) → (5) → (6) but rather someting like

$$
(2) \qquad
\begin{aligned}
&\to (3)\\
&\to (4)\\
&\to (5)\\
&\to (6).
\end{aligned}
$$

As far as sense (1) is concerned, it is clear that at some stage of the development, the chart was

$$
(2) \qquad
\begin{aligned}
&\to (1)\\
&\to (3)\\
&\to (4)\\
&\to (5)\\
&\to (6)
\end{aligned}
$$

but it seems that in our day, the chart should have the form

$$
(1){-}(2) \qquad
\begin{aligned}
&\to (3)\\
&\to (4)\\
&\to (5)\\
&\to (6)^{180}
\end{aligned}
$$

[180] The dash between (1) and (2) shows their connection. 148 sq. (who seems, however, to prefer the location of all what we call dominant senses or of all the broadest, most general senses at the beginning of the sequence. Y. Lebrun, *Revue belge de philologie et d'histoire* 41, 1963, 815ff. — G. Wahrig, *Wörterbucharbeit*, p. 31, 36ff. advocates the opinion that the entry should be arranged according to the formal combinatorial possibilities of the entry-word. The same lexicographer applied this principle in his big German monolingual dictionary (G. Wahrig, *Das große deutsche Wörterbuch*, Gütersloh 1966); for example, the entry-word *Weg* "road, journey", is treated in 6 sections, viz.: (1) "*allgemein*" [i.e. "generally"], (2) *mit Substantiven* (e.g. *Mittel und Wege finden*), (3) *mit Verben* (e.g. *den Weg abkürzen*), (4) *mit Adjektiven* (e.g. *ausgetretene Wege gehen*), (5) *mit Partikeln* (e.g. *Glück auf den Weg!*), (6) *mit Fragewörtern* (e.g. *wohin des Weges?*). Non-designative words are treated in the same way; e.g., the entry of *wie* "how" is articulated as follows: (1) *Interrogativadverb*, (a) *in direkten und indirekten Fragen*, (1) *alleinstehend* ... etc. Richly ramified entries have a short conspectus of these sections indicated between the lemma and the main bulk of the entry. This arrangement has the main advantage for the lexicographer himself, because it spares him the necessity to think long, and possible without a neat result, about the purely semantic relations; if the user gets accustomed to the principle, he can also find things easily. This principle of arrangement, however, is no panacea, first because it is not so absolutely unequivocal (e.g. *Mittel und Wege finden*: why is it treated as a combination with the substantive *Mittel* and not as a combination with the verb *finden?* — the more so that in *den richtigen Weg finden*, and in "*Ich habe einen Weg doch gefunden*", the entry-word has the same sense, and is combined with the same verb, but would have to be listed on quite different

The sequential presentation in the dictionary is necessarily linear, so that these different dimensions cannot be indicated; that does not, however, matter too much since it is really not necessary to express all these intricacies in the presentation.[181]

Let us discuss now the more complicated case of a word with two dominant senses. We know from chapter I that this is the case of Eng. *crane* (1) "a certain bird", (2) "a certain machine". In a more developed sequence of the word's single senses, it is not possible to indicate the two dominant ones first and then go on with the other senses. The specialized "ornithological" senses must be indicated in connection with (1), the specialized "mechanical" senses in connection with (2); disconnected senses should then follow. In Webster's Third, the sequence of the senses is roughly as follows:[182]

(1) any bird of the family Gruidae

(2) great blue heron (*Midland*)

(3) the common heron

(4) a machine for raising heavy weights

(5) a bent pipe for drawing liquid out of a ship

(6) a davit for handling lifeboats etc.

(7) an iron arm for supporting kettles over fire

(8) = water crane

(9) a machine for weighing goods

(10) = mail crane

(11) a boom used for holding a film or television camera

(12) = crane gray, a purplish gray etc.

We see that senses (2) and (3) "belong to" (1), whereas senses (5)—(11) "belong to" (4). The synchronic connections of (12) remain unclear to the unsophisticated; the end of the sequence is the proper place.

The presentational linearity of the simple sequence of numbered senses can be made richer and more instructive by the use of more than one series of symbols, with an established order of hierarchy between them.[183] The usual hierarchy of such symbols is: Roman figures, Arabic figures, letters; semicolon, comma. A general convention is created only as far as the two last symbols are

places of the entry), and second, because it tends to tear apart expressions (combinations) which are formally different but semantically related or identical (cf. the preceding example).

[181] Cf. Janský LSB 133 — Nida IJAL 24, 1958, 281 stresses much more the difficulties caused by the linearity of the presentation and by the different relations of the single senses than we do in the present discussion.

[182] For the purpose of the present discussion, we indicate here only the numbered sequence of single senses as they appear in *Webster's Third*, not the further articulation of the Websterian entry.

[183] Havránek LSB 142.

concerned: it is generally accepted that the comma indicates the least considerable semantic difference and that the semicolon indicates the next, slightly more considerable degree. Roman figures nearly always indicate broader categories and greater semantic differences that the Arabic ones; sometimes, however, they are used to distinguish homonyms and thus should not, be used in the presentation of polysemy. The use of letters (both capital and small ones) and their location on the hierarchical scale vary from one dictionary to another. And there are on the other hand even academic dictionaries which use no numbers and letters at al land present the singlesenses simply in unnumbered but separate divisions marshalled in a successive linear sequence.

To illustrate a highly ramified entry with several hierarchical levels of symbols, we resume here the treatment of the Czech word *hlava* (roughly "head") by J. Filipec.[184]

hlava "head" I A a part of the body ... B 1 (in the broader sense) the location (basis) of thinking, understanding and feeling; mind 2 (in the narrower sense) reason, deliberation, judiciousness 3 will; obstinacy 4 the center of memory, memory C 1 the seat of life, life 2 *obsol*. murder, killing; (the penalty for murder), death penalty

II 1 a single person, individual, person
   2 who is at the head of a thing, who controls, is the main person somewhere: the superior, representative, chief, boss, chieftain, leader etc.

III things which are similar to or suggestive of the head, espec. 1 by the form (the head of a screw) 2 by the function or the importance (*obsol*.) 3 a by the situation above: summit, top b *obsol*. the superior part of manuscripts or printed papers, top of a page, heading, caption 4 by the situation in front of something, the frontal part, fore part, face

IV a part, division of a book or paper: chapter, section, paragraph

V *arch*. a measure of length.

---

[184] SS 18, 1957, 143. What is given here is a rough English presentation of the polysemy of the Czech word. It is not meant as an entry in a Czech monolingual dictionary and could not be used as such; nor are the descriptive formulations to be understood as lexicographic definitions. The only purpose of the example is to illustrate the sequence and hierarchical grouping of the senses, and to suggest the reasons the lexicographer had for his decision. Cf. K. Horálek, *Filosofie jazyka*, Praha 1967, p. 88f. (critical discussion of the scheme proposed by Filipec). — Cf. a similar discussion in Wahrig, *Wörterbucharbeit*, p. 49ff. and 66ff. (a thorough, detailed discussion of the arrangement of the entry *Wurzel* "root" in the *Deutsches Wörterbuch* of J. and W. Grimm; another sequence of the senses is proposed p. 75ff.).

When he prepares this articulation of the entry, the lexicographer must be aware of the fact that he is not preparing a logical classification of notions nor a scientific systematization of classes; he must stick exclusively to what he finds in the linguistic facts and present the lexical meaning as a continuum the articulations of which may be strange, or insufficient, or overlapping or disconnected.

The lexicographer will also find that the presentation of the same lexical unit may vary from one dictionary, or scholar, to another. He should not be unduly dispirited by this. There are sequences which leap to the eye: probably nobody would indicate, in our day, the sequence of senses of Eng. *crane*, say, in the following way: (1) "a bent pipe for drawing liquid out of a ship", (2) "the common heron", (3) "water crane", (4) "any bird of the family of Gruidae", etc. But there are other things on which the opinion may very (apart from real material error): this is a result of the continuous and sometimes rather elusive character of the lexical meaning and by the considerable breadth of possibilities of each unit's application which causes that different parts of the broad range present themselves with different strength and clarity to different speakers. This variation also demonstrated by the reciprocal fact that different dictionaries with different presentations of the same thing can render equally good services, provided they are materially, factually correct.

ARRANGEMENT OF ENTRIES

6.6 The single worked out entries must be arranged in a sequence, as wholes. For those types of dictionaries which are here the focus of attention, the only practical possibility in the majority of language is arrangement by alphabetical sequence of the entry-words. Any other arrangement, such as, e.g., arrangement by semantic connections, or by the derivation of the words, have great advantages for different purposes and for different dictionaries (e.g. for a dictionary of synonyms, or an etymological dictionary); but for general purposes, alphabetical order is optimal, because it is the least ambiguous and the simplest method now in existence.[185]

[185] Cf. F. de Tollenaere, *Alfabetische of ideologische lexicografie*, Leiden 1960; cf. also Wahrig, *Wörterbucharbeit*, p. 11 ff. (preference of the alphabetical sequence, thorough discussion of different other possibilities). An opposite view is advocated, for example, by Kahane-Kahane PL 257 f. — If the respective language uses two scripts in the same historical epoch (for example Hausa in our days, as suggested by Zima: Roman and Arabic), the lexicographer must make a similar decision as in the case of diglossia: he must choose which of the two scripts he will use. A compromise is also possible if, for example, one script is chosen as basic for the whole dictionary but the entry-words, arranged in the alphabetical order of the basic script, are indicated also in the script. The use of two scripts implies sometimes a break in the tradition; cf., for instance,

6.6.1 This statement applies not only to Roman script; alphabetical order will be followed also in Cyrillic, Arabic, etc. writing. Indeed, in the case of each script, methods have been developed for the unequivocal sequential arrangement of the single signs; even scripts with such complicated single characters and signs as cuneiform or Chinese have methods of their own "alphabetization" (by the location, number, and form of the strokes in each sign). The dictionary will be arranged according the alphabet or sequence of signs accepted by consensus in the respective language.

It is seldom that the lexicographer finds that he must develop an alphabet for the language in question, because it lacks this tradition. This can today only in language only recently reduced to writing. In the majority of such cases, such a language will be written in the Roman script, possibly with some diacriticized or other symbols. The alphabet will, then, be basically the usual Roman one, with diacriticized letters put next after their undiacriticized counterparts (e.g. *č* following *c*). If there are elements of another script, or absolutely unusual symbols, they can be put either at the end of the alphabet, or inserted in it at a graphically or phonemically suitable place.[186]

The real difficulty is with the diagraphs, i.e. with combinations of two letters which taken together express a single phoneme. E.g., the letter *s* symbolizes a certain phoneme in Eng. *son*, the letter *h* a certain phoneme in Eng. *hill*, but the digraph *sh* yet another phoneme in Eng. *shy*.[187] The alphabets of the single languages differ in the treatment of the digraphs. E.g., the digraph *ch* in Germ. *hoch* "high", in Czech *hoch* "boy" and in (some variants of) Eng. *loch*, is pronounced roughly in the same way. But whereas it is treated as two separate letters in Eng. and Germ., i.e. as *c* followed by *h*, it is treated as a single symbol in all Czech dictionaries: in the Czech alphabet, there is not the sequence of letters ... *g, h, i, j,* but ... *g, h, ch, i, j* ...; a word like *chudý* "poor" will not be found, in a Czech dictionary, among the words which begin with *c*-, but there is a special section of words which begin with *ch*-, etc. Digraphs can be treated in this way in different other scripts, too. E.g., the Ossetic (basically Cyrillic) alphabet has separate letters which we transcribe *dž,* and *z*; but the diagraphs *džz, dz* are considered single signs and have their own place in the alphabet, viz.......*d, dž, dz, e, ë, ž, z, i* ...[188] Armenian *ow* (pronounced

---

the situation in Mongolian where the older, primarily religious texts are written in the native script, and the more modern and rather wordly texts are written in Cyrillic. If such a break is a severe one, if the use of the two script is mutually exclusive, or even if there a strong element of linguistic change implied, the situation is better treated by two different dictionaries, or by one with a historical character.

[186] Cf. Garvin, Anais 7. [187] The discussion is greatly simplified; only the essential points needed by the lexicographer are taken into consideration — There are also more complicated combinations like the trigraphs (e.g. Germ. *sch*), but they will hardly occur in new alphabets.

[188] Diacriticized *dž, ž* are seen to precede the nondiacriticized *dz, z*. This, however, must not be katen as a testimony against the principle stated above (diacriticized signs should follow), because

[u]; reported by M o t a l o v á) is treated as two separate letters in older dictionaries, but as a single sign with its own place in the alphabet in the more recent ones. It is difficult to say whether it is better, in the new alphabet, to treat, the digraphs rather as sequence of two letters or as single signs: the first solution is the customary one, traditionalized by the languages of Western Europe, and seems to be more practical in a purely pragmatic way, whereas the other solution brings the alphabet into a closer correspondence to the repertory of phonemes of the language in question.

6.6.2 Irrespective of the alphabet used, entries in the dictionary should be arranged by the alphabetic sequence of the entry words. Basic differences from this principle are observable in languages with other lexicographic traditions; but some differences are observable in any language.

Most important in this respect are the so-called n e s t s (though they do not necessarily, only very frequently, cause disturbances in the alphabetic order). A nest is a group of entries which is conflated into one; the conflation is effected almost always by the typographical presentation as a run-on (i.e. the single entry words do not begin at a new line) and very frequently by the abbreviation of the entry-words. As far as the presentation of meaning goes, the most conflated nests present the second and following entries only by reference to the first member of the nest; but the more frequent situation is that the single members of the nest are presented separately as any other entries, with their own eventual polysemy and sometimes even with their own examples, etc.[189] The main purpose of this procedure is to save space, but an illustrative presentation of the derivation and composition are sometimes also taken into consideration. In a very broad generalization, it can be observed that on the whole, nests containing derivations tend to be more conflated than those which deal with different composed words.

For example, the Eng. adj. *posthumous* and the adv. *posthumously* differ only in respect to their grammatical categories, otherwise they have precisely the same meaning. Since there is an endless and rather open series of English pairs like this in which the adverb can be treated (not without some historical justification) as derived in a simple way from the adjective, and since in the overwhelming majority of such cases, the meaning of the member of the pair which is conceived as the derived one is absolutely predictable, it is possible to present the two entries in a conflated form, for example as follows:

it is only a consequence of the transcription. The seemingly strange sequence of the letters is caused by the sequence of the Cyrillic alphabet.

[189] But is is clear that even in the isolated presentation of the meaning of the single members of the nest, the text can be so couched as to stress the common elements of the whole nest.

posthumous adj. (1) "born after the death of the father", (2) "coming or happening after the death"; -*ly* adv.[190]

The *conditio sine qua non* of a nest of this type is that apart from the categorial difference, all the members of the nest really have the same lexical meaning, at least at the level of description generally chosen by the dictionary.[191]

What we have described here is the most rigid type of nests. The meaning of the nested entries is so predictable that it is possible to state it simply by reference to the meaning of the first entry, with the indication of the categorial difference.[192]

If such pairs or groups of words are very frequent in the language in question (so that the user of the dictionary may be expected to get accustomed to some nests of a certain type) and if the dictionary is a very small one with short entries which are easy to survey, it is even possible to disregard, for the sake of such a nest, the alphabetical order. One can, for example, form a nest

just adj. (1) "fair ...", (2) "well deserved ...", (3) "reasonable ..."; -*ly* adv. -*ness* n.
justice n. (1) "just conduct ...", etc.[193]

We see that the alphabetical order is disturbed, because the sequence should be ... *just, justice, justly* ... This may be done only under the conditions stated above; otherwise, or if there is any reason to doubt whether the user will quickly and unambiguously find what he seeks, the nest should not be formed and the alphabetical order should be preserved.

A nest conflated from entries whose entry-words cannot be conceived as derivations from the first word can never be as rigid as the one described above;[194] the main difference, is that each of them must have its won statements of meaning.

---

[190] The form and the text of the nest may vary and the number of its members as well. For instance, the second (etc.) member of the nest may have a lexicographic definition of its own; but such that its central part is a reference to the first member of the nest.

[191] Let us suppose that a lexicographer decides to make nests of adverbs + adjectives in the way described. If, then, an adverb differs, as far as its lexical meaning "minus the category" goes from the meaning of the adjective only in one respect, say, in one sense, it cannot be indicated in a nest, but must have a full-fledged entry of its own. If, however, this one sense is, for example, an absolutely obsolete one, so that the dictionary would not indicate it in the full-fledged entry either, then it is possible to make a nest of the two entries and disregard the obsolete sense, as it would be disregarded anyhow. This principle should, however, be applied with the utmost care and circumspection, and not too liberally.

[192] This does not mean that the lexicographer must indicate it in this compound way. There may be reasons why he states more; but nests should always be as short as possible.

[193] Reduced from Hornby s. v.

[194] In the majority of cases, we have to deal with different compositions which have the same first member, or with different words formed by the same prefixed element, etc. In different languages, there are many intermediate types which can be handled according to either pattern.

For instance, if there is a German element *Anti-, anti-*[195] "against", one can form the following nest:

Anti-, anti- "against"
    -alkoholiker "adversary of drinking"
    -biotikum "antibiotic"
    -christ "Antichrist"
    -christlich "opposed to Christianity"
    etc.

Nests of this type are more dangerous than those of the first type, because the single entries will tend to develop a polysemy of their own, so that the single members of the nest will show more variation. Generally speaking, a nest of this type should be formed only if its members show a high degree of uniformity and are not too polysemous so that the single statements will be short.

There are some particular requirements and dangers connected with the formation of the nests. First, the abbreviation should always respect the morphemic boundaries within the nested units; nests whose entries are abbreviated with disregard of the morphemic boundaries are absolutely illegitimate and no dictionary, not even the smallest one, should accept them. And it should be out of the question for a nest to be based on some purely graphic coincidence only, without a real morphemic identity. For instance, we can consider the following Ossetic words: *zulk″* "worm", *zulk″xwyz* "worm-like" (morphemic boundary *zulk″xwyz*), and *zulk″wymon* ("oblique-angled") morphemic boundary *zulk″wymon*: *zul* "oblique", (*k″wymon* "angle"). The best sequence of these entry-words is, in my opinion, the alphabetical one[196],

zulk″ "worm"
zulk″wymon "oblique-angled"
zulk″xwyz "worm-like"[197]

If the dictionary is based on the principle of the nests, it is possible to have the following sequence:

zulk″ "worm"
  -xwyz "worm-like"
zulk″wymon "oblique-angled".

---

[195] In German, all substantives are written with initial capital letters, irrespective of their location in the sentence.

[196] This is the arrangement of the "*Osetinsko-russkij slovar*", Ordžonikidze 1962, s.v.

[197] In the Ossetic alphabet, the letter we transcribe as *w* precedes the letter we transcribe as *x*.

But it would be illegitimate to treat all these words in one nest, i.e. in the following way:

zulk″ "worm"
  -wymon "oblique-angled"
  -xwyz "worm-like".[198]

In some languages, above all in the highly flective ones, the single morphemes do not have such clear boundaries as in the preceding examples. Unless they are absolutely coalesced, the abbreviation in the nest can be made on the basis of the approximative morphemic boundary as it may be supposed to be accepted by the general speaker of the language. For instance, it is not easy to decide with absolute certainty whether the first morphemic boundary in the Czech verb *nimrat se* "to dabble" is before the *a*, behind it, or whether the *a* belongs to both the morphemes. As the general user of a Czech dictionary can be safely supposed to accept *-t* or *-ti* usually preceded by some vowel (about which he does not care much, because practically all of them are permitted in the position) as the ending of the infinitive (i.e. as the morpheme), it is possible to have a nest,

nimra "dabbler"
-t se "to dabble".[199]

In languages with numerous and regular derivations and particularly in those with numerous composed works, it is possible to construct very rich and extensive nests. In that case, there are two particular difficulties. First, such nests can disagree rather considerably with the alphabetical order.

In German, words beginning with *Anti-, anti-* can be put together into a nest 284. Such a nest will begin with, say *Antialkoholiker* "anti-drink campaigner" or *Antibiotikum* "antibiotic" and will end, after a score of words, with *Antitoxin* "antitoxin" or *antiwissenschaftlich* "unscientific", "opposed to the principles of science"; words like *antik* "antique" will then follow.

Composed words beginning with *Hand* "hand" can be treated in a nest which may begin with a word like *Handarbeit* "manual work, handmade" and may end with words like *Handwerker* "craftsman" or *Handwurzel* "wrist"; words like *Händedruck* "handshake";[200] *Handel* "business" will follow the nest.

The second difficulty is caused by words the morphemic status of which is unclear, whether only to the general user or to the savant himself. Is the proper

[198] Though the present example is constructed only for the sake of the argument, there are dictionaries of different languages which actually proceed in this way.

[199] It is irrelevant, for this type of nest, whether the verb is derived from the noun, or vice versa; the alphabetical sequence is decisive.

[200] In the majority of German dictionaries, *ä* is alphabetized as if it were simple *a*.

place of Germ. *antichambrieren* "to lobby",[201] *Antipode* "antipode" in the nest of *Anti-, anti-,* and that of *Handschuh* "glove" in the nest of *Hand-, hand-,* or not?

Different dictionaries obviate these difficulties in different ways. Some do not care about them; this implies that a certain degree of analytic ability is expected on the part of the user of the dictionary. Some dictionaries go on with the nest up to the point where another word which does not belong to it must be entered, according to the alphabetical order, and then continue the nest. In this way, the German nest, *Anti-, anti-* would begin with *Antialkoholiker* and would go on to, say, *Antiimperialismus* "antiimperialism"; the entry *antik* "antique" would then follow, and the rest of the nest would then continue with, say *Antikriegsdemonstration* "demonstration against war", *Antimilitarismus* "antimilitarism" etc. This solution, however, implies that one of the advantages of the nest is lost, viz. that it presents the repertory of pertinent words as a whole. Or the nest is presented as a whole with the dubious cases, but the "unclear"; i.e. morphemically not transparent words, are entered once more in their alphabetically proper places among the other entries, frequently rather far away from the nest itself, and have a cross-reference to the nest; this method implies the loss of another advantage of the nest, viz. that it saves space; and additionally, it compels the user to seek what he wishes to find in two places subsequently.

There is yet another type of nest (or what can be considered nests). In some languages, the central, radical part of the word (irrespective of whether it is root, or stem, or base, in the grammatical tradition of the respective language) is very clearly distinguished from the prefixes. In some of these languages, there has developed a lexicographic tradition in which the prefixed forms are presented as members of a nest the first member of which is the unprefixed form.

For instance, the canonical form of Sanskrit verbs is the root. The entry in a Sanskrit dictionary usually begins with the indication of the root and the necessary lemma; the bulk of the entry is devoted to the presentation of the meaning of the verb without any prefix; in the subsequent nest, the single verbal prefixes with which the root can be combined are enumerated, and the meaning of each of these prefixed verbs is presented. E.g.,

kar- (1) "to make", (2) ... etc. (follow the single senses of unprefixed *kar-*);
adhi- (+ *kar-*) (1) "to put someone at the head". (2) ... etc.;
anu- (+ *kar-*) (1) "to imitate", (2) ...;
abhi- (+ *kar-*) "to make something for someone", (2) ... etc.;
ā (+ *kar-*) (1) "to bring, to fetch", (2) ...; etc.[202]

---

[201] The equivalence of the German and of the English verb is not precise.

[202] Based on O. Böhtlingk, *Sanskrit-Wörterbuch in kürzerer Fassung*, I (St. Petersburg 1879), s.v.

Few lexicographers will be inclined to introduce such nests into their practice, unless they are sanctioned by a venerable tradition. It seems, however, that there are languages in which such "nests by the stem" are a good practical solution for different problems caused by the structure of the words, the usual problem being too great an abundance of prefixes. Pertinent cases are reported by Haas[203] (Malayo-Polynesian languages) and Garvin[204] (Kutenai). If the lexicographer decides to use these "nests by the stem", he will have to warn the reader in the introduction and give a list of the prefixed elements. Cross-references to the nest from the points where the reader would seek the word in its alphabetical order should also be given, at least in the more difficult cases.

On the whole, the practical disadvantages of nests seem to be greater than their practical advantages. Really big dictionaries use them either only exceptionally or not at all; and there is no reason why they should. But on the other hand, they are necessary when space limitations are more severe. And there are also dictionaries which deliberately use the nests for pedagogic or descriptive purposes.[205]

6.6.3 Another source of difficulty is the multiword lexical unit. Theoretically this should not be so. It should be quite irrelevant what morphological structure a lexical unit has; each should have its own entry which should be inserted at the proper place in the alphabetical order. In reality, however, the situation is much more complicated and ambiguous. First, we know that it is not always easy to decide that a group of words is really stabilized; consequently, there will be a hesitation as to whether the group should be treated as a subentry (see § 6.5.3.3.1), or as an entry of its own. The second consideration is of a more practical order. It is easy to insert a subentry into any entry, irrespective of whether it is the first or any of the following words of the multiword lexical unit, but it is difficult to insert entries by the second etc. word into the proper place in the alphabetical order. For instance, the lexicographer decides that the term *sea anemone* will be included in his dictionary. It is easy to insert this subentry both into the entry *sea* and into the entry *anemone*; the alphabetical sequence of the entries and their structure remain intact. If he lexicographer, however, treats this set group on the higher level, it will be easy to

---

[203] PL 49.

[204] *Anais* 6.

[205] Cf. Ruzička LSB 49; Janský LSB 140 sq.; Kankava, *V. I. Dal'kak leksikograf* 19; Čikobava LS 1, 1957, 64 sqq.; Cohen, Proceedings of the 9th Congress of Linguists (The Hague 1964), p. 502 sq., pleads very strongly for the nests; but a dictionary in which one would find French *pleuvoir* "to rain" and *pluie* "rain" grouped together (as suggested by Cohen) would require either too great a sophistication on the part of the reader or a special alphabetical index in the appendix. — Chapman, *Lexicography* 19 develops similar ideas on what he calls, *portmanteaux* or *omnibus articles*; he is, however, more interested in the possibilities of a coherent explanation of denotata which belong together.

insert the entry *sea anemone* where it belongs when the first word is considered first; but to insert it into the proper place for the user who may seek it under the second word will require either a cross-reference (*anemone*: see *sea anemone*) or a special type of lemma (e.g. *anemone*: *sea anemone* "popular name of a creature living in the sea etc.").

This type of lemma is particularly useful when the first word of a set expression is rather formal or semantically depleted. For example, the Eng. expression *at large* should be indicated under *large*. If the lexicographer decides to treat it as a subentry of the entry *large* he will have no difficulty. If, however, he decides to treat it as an entry of its own, he will have to use a similar lemma, e.g. *large*: *at large* "at liberty, free, etc."

This discussion could be taken as an argumentation for the opinion that it is easier to deal with the set expressions and the multiword lexical units in subentries than in entries of their own. There are certainly advantages in the use of subentries. They are not only of practical character (for instance, easy alphabetical insertion under the second [or third, etc.] word, gradual differences between the free combinations of words and the set ones, etc.). Another advantage is that in one bigger entry in which also the subentries show the ramification of the meaning of the respective entry-word in the set expressions and multiword lexical units, generality of meaning and its character of a continuum can be depicted more clearly than in single, short, isolated entries. But on the other hand, if a set expression or multiword lexical unit seems really to have the status of a stabilized lexical unit, there is no reason why it should not be treated and indicated in the same way as the other lexical units; it will be primarily the terminological multiword lexical units which will invite treatment by special entries of their rather than by subentries.[206]

NORMATIVE ASPECTS

6.7 The last section of this chapter will be devoted to the normative aspect of the lexicographer's work (cf. above, § 4.6). The lexicographer should be aware that all his indications may have some normative influence, because the user may sometimes tend to follow them. In some respects, however, the lexicographer must be absolutely conscious that he is performing a normative activity on purpose. This is palpable in the field of orthography and pronunciation and to some extent also in the field of rections, etc. But labels classifying an expression as "obsolete" or "colloquial" or even "vulgar" will also tend to

---

[206] Cf. Országh LS 5, 1962, 151; A. Welter, Jazykovědné aktuality 2, 1965, Nr 2/3, p. 43f.

[207] The lexicographer's normative activity in the field of spelling is well described in Hulbert, *Dictionaries* 50ff.

have, if they agree with the real norm, i.e. with the real usage of a good number of educated speakers, some restrictive influence. In the sphere of lexical meaning itself, though, the influence of indications in the dictionary is more subtle, but it is present and it operates in the same way: hesitating users of the dictionary will sometimes follow its statements.

The preceding remarks are made in the order of ease with which the lexicographer can influence the users of his dictionary: it is relatively easy to exercise an influence on orthography (above all if the dictionary's indications agree with those of other similar basic books of reference), but it is extremely difficult to exercise an extensive influence in the domain of the lexical meaning itself. Indeed, it is usually only in the special scientific terminology that a definition of a term's meaning can be expected with some confidence to be followed — and not even here is it always the case.[208] The Scylla and Charybdis of the lexicographer seems to be, on the one hand, the danger that he will stick too truculently to some obsolete codifications of the norm; in that case, his rulings will be either neglected, or he will foster the development of eventual diglossia. The other danger is that he will draw the line too broadly and accept also stray aberrations as part of the norm. In this case, his picture of the real state of the standard national language will not be correct.

The best method of dealing with what seems to be outside the boundaries of the norm is to be silent about it. Direct recommendations or prohibitions should be offered only exceptionally:[209] sometimes they are considered necessary because of some sociolinguistic or absolutely extralinguistic reasons; e.g. Eng. *nigger* "(impolite word for) Negro; member of any dark-skinned race" which is labelled by Hornby by the sign "to be avoided."[210] Instead of the direct prohibition, however, glosses and labels of the type mentioned above are frequently used. For instance, a descriptive gloss like "impolite" could be expected to discourage the user of the dictionary from using the word, if not as strongly as the prohibitive one.

The purpose of a dictionary of the type we are discussing here is to describe the standard national language and its norm. A few negligible contexts which show an aberration (any aberration) from the norm can be treated as cases of occasionality, i.e. by silence (unless the prepared dictionary approaches the type of the thesaurus. But it is one of the most delicate tasks to recognize the moment when an aberration (which could be treated by silence) has changed its status by frequent application and should be listed (cf. above). For example, the meanings of the pairs of the English adjectives *alter-*

[208] A stronger attitude is advocated by Hausenblas LSB 38 (with excellent Czech examples).

[209] This opinion is held against Ščerba, Izvestija 105f.

[210] The descriptive gloss "impolite word" (or something to the same purpose) is a necessary part for the statement of the lexical meaning; it is the prohibitive gloss "to be avoided" which interests us in this connection.

native : : *alternate, definite* : : *definitive, intense* : : *intensive* overlap vastly
and the members of the pairs can be observed to occur in identical contexts.
A prescriptive dictionary such as that of H. W. Fowler[211] may regret it and
may try to persuade the user to discontinue such (mis) use. But a standard-
descriptive (or even an overall-descriptive) dictionary which would not present
the members of the pairs as (partial) synonyms would probably not fulfil its
descriptive task and would stress too much the normative, or rather prescriptive, side. And not infrequently, there are, for example, two variants of
the same phenomenon, or two possible ways to apply it, and no definite arguments for preferring one to the exclusion of the other; in such a case, both
should be indicated in the dictionary[212] if both are stabilized and equally
frequent. For example, both possible pronunciations of Eng. *animate*, viz.
[animit, aenimeit] should be indicated. The same applies to orthography,
forms, rections, etc.

Up to now, the whole discussion has been aimed at the lexicographis work
in the sphere of languages with a stabilized standard national form. Our
linguistic epoch seems to have a rather liberal if not sometimes even an
egalitarian outlook; or at least many linguists display it: description is preferred to prescription. One wonders, however, from time to time whether such
a simple statement of preference covers all the problems and whether there
are not more dimensions to be discerned, such as, for example, the contradistinction of the nagging, narrow-minded prescriptivism, particularly of a
puristic type, as opposed to a broad-minded, functional prescriptivism,
necessary as one of the unifying forces in a well-functioning language of a
variegated, complex society. One could also wonder whether a rather strong
prescriptive component of linguistic (and inclusively lexicographic) activities,
e.g. at the school level, is not a necessary part of the linguistic situation in the
sphere of languages with stabilized standard national forms. In any case, the
lexicographer's situation is much more delicate if he compiles a dictionary of
a language with a not yet stabilized standard national form. *Volens, nolens*,
lexicographer will more frequently have to try his hand at helping to discern
or even create the norm. This will not be too complicated as far as the orthographical unification goes, or as far as the standardization of forms is concerned: they will all be indicated by the lexicographer in the standard form.
The grammatical indications as well will be made according to the chosen or
accepted standard national form[213]. But as far as lexical meaning itself is
concerned, the lexicographer will hardly be able to do more than to describe
it as it is; attempts at making it "more precise", usually by adding into the

[211] H. W. Fowler, *A Dictionary of Modern English Usage*, Oxford 1926; 2nd ed. (by. E. Go-
wers), Oxford 1965.
[212] Ščerba, Izvestija 97.
[213] Cf. Čikobava LS 1, 1957, 67.

definition criterial features which cannot be maintained by observation of contexts to be in the designatum, generally fail and the users of the dictionary do not follow suit. But a delicate, comparative and contrastive, indication of the synonyms and near-synonyms (cf. § 6.5.3.2) may be of some use for the eventual polarization of their meaning.

Languages the standard national form of which is not yet absolutely stabilized usually lack many expressions needed for the more modern and complex patterns of life and for the denotata of modern civilization. The situation has been discussed at greater length above (§ 4.5). For the lexicographer, it is particularly disagreeable if there are many competing synonyms of a terminological or quasi-terminological nature. For instance Drozdík[214] reports ten different Arabic terms for the tape-recorder, which terms he found in different contemporary Arabic sources and which we shall not quote here in extenso. Usually, no language tolerates ten synonyms for a tape recorder; it can be expected that sooner or later, some of them will be eliminated. It is just in this sphere that the lexicographer should make a quite clear-cut decision as to whether his dictionary will have a more descriptive character (in that case, all the variants, or in this case synonyms, will be listed or whether it will try to foster development by indicating only one or a few of them, according to his preference. If he decides to adopt this attitude, the lexicographer should cooperate with a linguistic normative body (if there is any) and/or with specialists in the single scientific and technical branches. In any case, until the language itself reaches a greater stability, the lexicographer who decides to make such choices and normative decisions must anticipate that they will not be to everybody's liking and that the real development of the language itself may decide against his choice.

[214] L. Drozdík, *Studies in Arabic Word-Formation*, Bratislava 1966, p. 126 (unpublished typescript of a thesis).

CHAPTER VII

THE BILINGUAL DICTIONARY

THE PURPOSE OF THE BILINGUAL DICTIONARY

7.0 The basic purpose of a bilingual dictionary is to coordinate with the lexical units of one language those lexical units of another language which are equivalent in their lexical meaning. The first language, to whose lexical units the lexical units of the other language are co-ordinated is called the source-language; the order of the entries in a bilingual dictionary is given by the source language. The other language whose lexical units are coordinated to the first ones, is called the target language.

THE ANISOMORPHISM OF LANGUAGES

7.1 The fundamental difficulty of such a co-ordination of lexical units is caused by the anisomorphism of languages, i.e. by the differences in the organization of designate in the individual languages and by other differences between languages.

What leaps most to the attention of even the average layman are the cases of the so called culture-bound words: if, say, some plants live or some things exist only in the area where the source language is spoken but not all in the area of the target language, there will be no really equivalent lexicas units ready in the target language. It would be a mistake to think that this can happen only if the two cultures are vastly different, above all if one of them is "exotic" or old. On the contrary, this situation can occur in any two pairs of languages: there is nothing similar to the American *drug-store* in Europe and there is no suitable equivalent lexical unit in the European languages, either.

It would be another mistake to think that it is only the difference in the material extralinguistic wold, the absence of the denotatum which is of basic importance; to the contrary, it is the designatum which has the fundamental role. The material extralinguistic world may be more or less identical but the same „things" are conceived as parts of no designtum in one language but not in another. For example, the Ossetic word *agawyghd* has the meaning "hearth + cauldron + chain": there is no unified designatum in English which would cover all the three components, there are only designations of the single segments of the extralinguistic world.

Again, the distance between the two cultures may cause these cases to be more frequent, but they are observable in any language.

But if there is no equivalent lexical unit in the target language, the bilingual dictionary must use other means than the coordination of lexical units mentioned above. The usual thing is that the meaning of the respective lexical unit of the source language is described by an explanation which is not dissimilar to the definition of a monolingual dictionary but is worded in the target language. In this way, we can read in a Latin-English dictionary, e.g., *consul, -is, m.* "the highest executive dignitary of the Roman republic".[1]

Up to now, we have discussed only designative words. As far as non-designative words go, the lexicographer treats them, as in all other cases, according to the model of the designative ones. For instance a grammatical operator like Greek *an*, the function of which is, in the first place, either to mark the apodosis (second clause) of a conditional sentence, or the iterative aspect of the verb, has no lexical equivalent in English, or in any other language I know, for that matter. In such a situation, the bilingual dictionary will not indicate its equivalent but will explain its grammatical function in the words of the target language. Any other non-designative words can be dealt with in the same way.

Very frequently, it is possible to find an equivalent in the target language, but there are difference caused by the different cultural connections. This is the case, for instance, of Greek *theós*: Eng. *god* is the best possible and the only possible equivalent, but there is a vast difference between the polytheistic world of the Greeks' rather ungodly gods and that suggested by and inherent in the English equivalent.

Cultural change within the same society can also modify these cultural connections; the usual slowness of this process adds to the lexicographer's worries: is the extralinguistic factor of good birth and, or considerable wealth still of importance for the lexical meaning of Eng. *gentleman*, or is it irrelevant or less relevant by now, as in the majority of languages in which the word is borrowed?

Words like Greek *areté*, Latin *virtus* have at least an approximative equivalent in Eng. *virtue*; but many other near-synonyms, explanatory glosses, and if possible also examples will be necessary to show their entire lexical meanings.

These "culture-bound words" pose very difficult problems for the lexicographer.[2] He should not despair if he finds that it is not possible to give all

---

[1] More on these cases and their solution below § 7.6.2. — Cf. Feldman LS 2, 1957, 96, with Japanese-Russian examples.

[2] See on them Swanson PL 70ff.; Nida, Word 1, 1945, 194—208 (= *Language in Culture and Society*, ed. Hymes, 1964, p. 90ff.).

the detailed information on them in his dictionary. After all, he cannot insert long encyclopedic articles with detailed discussions of the other culture. But the basic information on linguistically relevant points should be given.

It would, however, be completely wrong to limit the concept of anisomorphism and the discussion of it to the "culture-bound words" only. On the contrary, anisomorphism must be expected in all lexical units and can be found in most of them. Ščerba[3] is right when he stresses that it is an error in principle if one supposes when compiling a bilingual dictionary, that the notional systems of the two languages are identical. Even in those areas where the two cultures overlap and where the material extralinguistic world is identical, the lexical units of the two languages are not different labels appended to identical notions. In the overwhelming majority of cases, the designata are differently organized in the two languages. Then, too, there is variation in the other components of lexical meaning. The result is that only very few equivalent words which have no polysemy in either language really do have precisely the same meaning; in the majority of cases, they are defined scientific terms. Equivalent lexical units with identical multiple meaning in both languages, and with precisely the same lexical meaning are a real rarissimum.

In chapter I we saw how complex the lexical meaning is: when we compare lexical units of two languages, we must remember that there may be some differences in any of the dimensions mentioned above. Eng. *to pour* has a good equivalent in Germ. *gießen*, but the German verb can pertain only to liquids, whereas the Eng. verb covers also the area of application (and has the criterial features) of Germ. *schütten*. Eng. *pig* has a good equivalent in French *cochon*; but whereas the former is connotatively rather neutral, this is decidedly not the case of the latter. In Eng., snakes "cast" their skins whereas in Czech, they "take them of" (Czech *svlékati*, the verb used about people taking their garments off). The English pronouns *this*, *that* have not two but three Latin equivalents, viz. *hic*, *iste*, *ille*; therefore, there is no one-to-one equivalence and the whole area of application is divided differently in the two languages. In short, the anisomorphism can be manifested by any component of the lexical meaning, in any degree and dimension.[4] Nearly all the problems of equivalence (discussed in detail § 7.6) are caused by the anisomorphism of language.

This lexical anisomorphism causes that the task of translating texts from one language into another is not easy; still, it is possible, because the translator is not obliged to produce a word-for-word translation. To take an over-

---

[3] *Izvestija* 113; cf. also Harrell PL 53: "Different languages are self-contained systems exhibiting only limited isomorphism with one another".

[4] Cf. different remarks made an examples produced by Ščerba, *Izvestija* 113 (polysemy, phraseology), Feldman LS 2, 1957, 98 (style levels; Japanese-Russian examples), Weinreich, Universals 134.

simplified example: a person in a novel is characterized by his impolite speech; in a passage, this is expressed by his use of impolite words referring to, say, eating. If the target language happens to have no full equivalents (i.e. no equivalent words designating eating with the connotation of being impolite), the translator cannot but use those words of the target language which have the same designation (eating), and characterizes the speaker by the choice of some other impolite expressions. In this way, there is on absolute one-to-one correspondence between some single words of the original and those of the translation, but the whole meaning of the original passage is conveyed by its translated counterpart.

MULTILINGUAL DICTIONARIES

7.2 The preceding paragraphs suffice to show that the coordination of the equivalent lexical units of two languages is not a simple task. One of the consequences of this complexity is that there usually is some explanatory apparatus in the entry (such as glosses, explanations etc.), not only the lexical units themselves, plus their equivalents in the target language. The other consequence of it is that the difficulties connected with the construction of a dictionary in which equivalent lexical units of more than two languages would be coordinated (i.e. of a trilingual, or quadrilingual, etc., dictionary) grow so rapidly with the number of languages that it simply is not worth while to undertake such work. Indeed, such multilingual dictionaries either deal only with some restricted sets of words without polysemy, such as the scientific terminology,[5] or they simply neglect it an indicate only the dominant senses of the respective words. As both a pioneer and a chef d'œuvre of this category can be quoted P. S. Pallas, *Linguarum totius orbis vocabularia comparativa*, Petropoli 1786 (comparative glossaries of two hundred languages).

The multilingual dictionaries of different technical terminologies have a high, if limited, usefulness within their own field: they usually have a strong encyclopedic component and help much to guarantee the precise use of the terms in different languages. It would, however, be a mistake to think that the coordination of the equivalent terms in them is plain sailing: the scientific

---

[5] In this case, polysemy either does not exist or it can be legitimately put aside, only the technical-terminological senses of the respective word being taken into consideration. A very good bibliography of technical dictionaries (K.-O. Sauer, *Handbuch der technischen Dokumentation und Bibliographie*, 3. ed., München 1966) quotes a technical dictionary which coordinates terms in 17 languages: Engl., French, Ital., Span., Port., Germ., Dutch, Norw., Swed., Finn., Pol., Russ., Modern Greek, Chinese, Japanese, Malay, Esperanto: F. Meyboom, *Quaestionarium Medicum*, Amsterdam 1961.

terminology has an "anisomorphism" of its own,[6] manifested not only when terminological sets of different languages are compared, but sometimes also when terminological acceptations of the single "schools" or "approaches" are analyzed in contradistinction, though the respective texts are couched in the same language. The lexicographer who intends to compile such a multilingual dictionary, of course, must be a first-class scholar in the respective scientific field in order to have the necessary encyclopedic knowledge of the denotata themselves) but he must not exercise less caution and circumspection in the generally lexicographic side of his work.

The non-terminological multilingual dictionaries also serve only some restricted purposes. Usually, it is either some general orientation in a group of languages (such as in traveller-guides and other practical uses) which is aimed at, or, on the other hand, such multilingual dictionaries are used for purely scientific tasks such as cross-cultural comparisons etc.[7] Their quality is a result above all of the skill with which the lexicographer chooses the really dominant senses of the words and avoids the pitfalls of polysemy.

In any case, a general dictionary for the public, uninitiated or professional, requires a treatment of polysemy and is, therefore, bilingual par excellence, not multilingual. The bilingual dictionary will also be the subject of our further remarks.

TYPES OF BILINGUAL DICTIONARIES

7.3 When planning a bilingual dictionary, the compiler must decide to which type it will belong. At the boundaries of the single types are rather fluid, we shall discuss primarily the more important dimensions of the observable variation.

The choise of the source language and of the target language is in itself a powerful factor. It is, for example, quite obvious that the bilingual dictionary of a dead language will necessarily tend to have a rather philological character, with quotations from the authors (texts), etc. But there are not only these obvious cases; in reality, the lexicographer should always try to find out what

---

[6] Cf., for instance, O. Kettridge, *French-English and English-French dictionary of technical terms and phrases used in civil, mechanical, electrical and mining engineering...*, London 1955, p. VII: "...it is fallacious to suppose that there is necessarily a corresponding term in a foreign language".

[7] It should be mentioned that the "dictionaries" prepared for purposes of machine translation are usually also only bilingual. There are, however, some interesting attempts at a multilingual translation (and consequently, at a multilingual semantic coordination of lexical units) via a general algorithm.

consequences are entailed by the choice of the two languages to be dealt with in the dictionary. If the two languages belong to very distant cultures, there will be a greater need to give some encyclopedic explanations. If the grammatical structures of the two languages are very different, it will be more difficult but also more necessary to decide in advance in what forms the respective lexical units are to be coordinated. If at least one of the two languages shows diglossia, it will be necessary to decide which of the diglottic levels is mainly to be stressed, or how the situation will generally be solved.[8] But even if there is no diglossia involved, the two languages must be compared in respect to the single style levels observable in them. We shall see (§ 7.6) that the indicated equivalents should have the same style level in both languages. But seemingly identical levels are not always absolutely equivalent: words which belong preferentially to the written language are more "high-brow" in Czech than they seem to be in English, but they are by far not so much "high brow" as they are in Burmese. The equivalence of the style-levels in the two languages must be decided upon and adhered to in a unified way in the whole dictionary. All such circumstances must be taken into consideration when a dictionary is planned, and the questions arising must be solved, before the real work begins.

A very powerful factor in the constitution of the type of dictionary is the difference between the way the native language can be treated and the requirements necessary to deal effectively with a foreign language. There are innumerable covert facts which the native speaker knows about his language and about his culture. If the dictionary is written primarily or exclusively for him, information about such covert facts can be omitted; but since a foreigner cannot be supposed to know them, he will require much more information. This is particularly important to remember if the lexicographer compiles a dictionary which is to be used by native speakers of another language. If, for example, the native speaker of a language A compiles a bilingual dictionary A—B or B—A to be used primarily by the speakers of B, he will always have to check whether a linguistic and semantically relevant phenomenon in A which he takes for granted, sometimes to the degree of not noticing it at all, will not be a source of difficulty to the speaker of B. This dimension overlaps with the following one see the next paragraph), but only partly; the overlapping is caused by the fact that in the majority of cases the lexicographer prepares the dictionary for his own linguistic community.[9]

Probably the most important dimension of the typology of the bilingual dictionaries consists in the lexicographer's intention to compile the dictionary either as an aid to the comprehension of texts in the source language or of the

[8] Cf. Harrell PL 55.
[9] Cf. Haas PL 47; Harrell PL 51ff.

description of the source language, or as an aid to the generation of texts in the target language.[10]

Let us discuss these three main possible intentions with the help of a simple (or rather strongly simplified) example, in which we take into consideration only the purely semantic part of the entry. The lexical meaning of Oss. *čyzg* comprises two senses (1) *girl*, (2) *daughter*. Let us now consider the following six situations.

(1) In an Oss.-Eng. dictionary (Eng. being the "native" language), the intention of which is only to help the comprehension of the Ossetic texts, the minimum treatment is a statement like

[Oss.] *čyzg*, [Eng.] *girl*; *daughter*[11]

The presentation may be as strongly reduced as this[12], because the user is expected to have a text before him in which the multiple meaning[13] will be disambiguated by the context so that he will see which of the two equivalents is to be used.

(2) If, however, the same dictionary (Oss.-Eng. [nat.]) is intended as a means to describe Ossetic, typical contexts should by given which will show the application of the word in the two senses:

[Oss.] *čyzg* (1) "With sixteen years, she was prettiest *čyzg* of the village"[14], [Eng.] *girl*

(2) "Bappo refused to give his *čyzg* to such a poor suitor as Tigran", [Eng.] *daughter*.

(3) If the Oss.-Eng. dictionary is intended as an aid to the native speakers of Ossetic to generate English texts, the English equivalent will have to have a gloss to tell the Ossete the difference between them and to instruct him how to use them:

čyzg (1) (anybody's female child, a young woman), *girl*

(2) (one's own female child), *daughter*[15]

---

[10] Different remarks on this topic Ščerba, *Izvestija* 112ff.; Feldman LS 2, 1957, 89; Harrell PL 54; Ianucci PL 204.

[11] Or (1) *girl*, (2) *daughter*, etc. In the following examples, we put the names of the languages into brackets: they would not be contained in any form in any entry.

[12] The degree of conciseness is naturally given also by the size of the dictionary; but here, for the sake of clarity, we do not take this into consideration.

[13] Even if the example discussed be understood not as a case of multiple meaning but of the generality of meaning, it would not effect the presentation in the entry; only the comma (*girl*, *daughter*) would probably be preferred to the semicolon.

[14] The contexs are given here not in Ossetic (which would be the case in a real dictionary), but in the Eng. translation; the word *čyzg* itself is left untranslated.

[15] In an actual case, the glosses would probably be given in Ossetic, the dictionary being determined for the Ossetes; we give them here in English to make the discussion more clear.

(4) If an Eng.-Oss. dictionary is compiled with the intention to aid the Ossetic speaker to comprehend English texts, it will be possible to give the two entries the reduced form

[Eng.] *daughter*, [Oss.] *čyzg*
     girl   *čyzg*[16]

Again, the English contexts occurring in the texts read (or heard) may be supposed to disambiguate the Ossetic polysemy.

(5) If the same dictionary intends to give a more descriptive statement on the English words, it should either give some illustrative contexts in which they occur, as e.g.

[Eng.] *daughter* (daughters are similar to their fathers), [Oss.] *čyzg*
     girl (there are boys and girls in the class),   [Oss.] *čyzg*

or it should disambiguate the Ossetic polysemy by a semantic gloss:

[Eng.] *daughter* [Oss.] *čyzg* (one's own female child)
     girl   *čyzg* (anybody's female child, a young woman)[17]

(6) If the Eng.-Oss. dictionary is intended to help the speaker of English to generate Ossetic texts, the sufficient minimal treatment will be

[Eng.] *daughter*,   [Oss.] *čyzg*
     girl   *čyzg*

This is possible because the Ossetic polysemy is, in this case, irrelevant: whenever the English user wishes to speak about a daughter and applies to word *čyzg*, he will be right, irrespective of the fact that the Ossetic word has yet another sense.

This example is as reduced as possible, in all respects, for the sake of illustration and simplicity. The reduction, however, is only factual. This may be sufficiently clear if we compare the entries of some dictionaries.

H. G. Liddell — R. Scott, *A Greek-English Lexicon* (new ed. by H. S. Jones and R. McKenzie), Oxford 1940, is a dictionary which tries to describe Greek as thoroughly as possible. With some immaterial omissions, an entry in it has the following form:

augé... (1) *light of the sun*, and in pl. *rays beams*, péptato d'au ēelíou[18] Ilias 17.371, cf. Odyss. 6.98, 12.176; ēelíou íden augás[19], i.e. was born, Ilias 16.188; hup'augàs

[16] We do not take into consideration the multiple meaning of Eng. *girl*; there would be no considerable difficulties, anyhow.

[17] The glosses would probably be in Ossetic; it is also quite possible to use both the examples and the glosses.

[18] Rough translation of the quotation: "the light of the sun has fallen". We give here a verbatim translation only of those quotations which are not translated verbatim in the dictionary itself.

[19] "He saw the rays of the sun."

ēelíoio[20], i.e. still alive, Odyss. 11.498; Dios augás[21] Ilias 13,837; augàs esideîn see *the light*, i.e. to be alive, Theogn. 426, cf. Europ. Alc. 667; leússein[22] Aesch. Pers. 710; blépein[23] Eur. Andr. 935; hup'augàs leússein or ideîn ti hold up to *the light* and look at, Eurip. Hec. 1154, Plato Phaed. 268a...; duthmaì augôn[24] *sun*-set Pind. I.4.65; xúnorthron augaîs dawning with *the sun* Aesch., Ag. 254 (lyrical passage); klúzein pròs augás rise surging towards *the sun* ibid. 1182; lamprotátē tôn pareouséon augēōn brightest *light* available Hipp., Fract. 3, cf. Arist. Pol. Ath. 658a3...: metaphorically, bíou dúntos augaí[25] "life's setting *sun*" Aesch., Ag. 1123 (lyrical passage); ...

(2) augaì ēelíoio[26] or augaí alone, *the East*, Dion. Perieg. 84,231.

(3) *dawn, day-break* Act. Ap. 20.11...

(4) generally, *any bright light* puròs augē[27] Odys. 6.305, cf. Ilias 2.456; arízēloi dè hoi augaí[28] of lightning 13.244; brontês augaí[29] Soph., Ph. 1199 (lyrical passage); of a beacon, Ilias 18.211, Aisch., Ag. 9; lampádos[30] Cratin. post 150 ...

(5) of the eyes, ommátōn augaí[31] Soph., Aj. 70; augaí alone, *the eyes* Eur. Andr. 1180 (lyrical passage), Rh. 737: metaph. anaklínantas tēn tês psukhês[32] Plato, Rp. 540a.

(6) *Glean, sheen*, of bright objects, au.khalkeie[33] Ilias 13.341; khrusòs augàs édeiksen[34] Pind. N.4.83; ambròsios au. péplou Eurip. Med. 383 (lyrical passage); ... of gems, Philostr. Im 2.8 — Mostly poet., but freq. in Arist., chiefly in the sense of *sunlight*.

The example shows how the lexicographer studies each context, quotes the most important ones (with precise citations), and comments on the contextual nuances.

The Eng.-Czech. dictionary of Osička and Poldauf[35] is a dictionary of a pure type; its only intention is to help the Czech user to comprehend English texts. A typical entry of this dictionary goes:[36]

[20] "under the rays of the sun".
[21] "the rays of Zeus".
[22] "to regard".
[23] "to look at".
[24] "the setting of the rays".
[25] "the rays of the setting life".
[26] "the rays of the sun".
[27] "the light of the fire".
[28] "the conspicuous rays".
[29] "the rays of the lightning".
[30] "of the torch".
[31] "the rays of the eyes".
[32] "having lifted the light of the soul".
[33] "the gleam of copper or bronze".
[34] "gold shew the gleams".
[35] A. Osička — I. Poldauf, *Anglicko-český slovník*, Praha 1956.
[36] P. 384; here only negligibly reduced.

[Eng.] *slight*, [Czech] *tenký*; *štíhlý*; *mírný, nepatrný, nevelký*; *bezvýznamný, nezávažný*; *nevážnost, přezírání, podceňování, neúcta*... It is necessary to give rough, approximative translations of the Czech equivalents in order to illustrate how the entry is constructed: [Eng.] *slight*, [Czech] "thin; slender; moderate, immaterial, smallish; unimportant, insignificant; disregard, disrespect, underestimation, undervaluation; ...". We see that the dictionary really indicates only the equivalents; apart from them the English polysemy is taken into consideration only by the difference between the comma and the semicolon; and even the difference between the adjectival and the substantival use of the entry-word is indicated only by the morphological class of the Czech equivalents: *tenký*, etc., are adjectives, *nevážnost*, etc., substantives.

I. Poldauf, *Česko-anglický slovník*, Praha 1959, is a dictionary whose basic intention is to help the Czech user to generate English texts. We shall quote here, with immaterial reductions, a typical entry;[37] with the exception of the lemma, the Czech parts of it will, however, be approximatively translated into English and will be printed here between quotation marks.

[Czech] *dílo* n. (*děl*):[38] [Eng.] *work*; ("what was achieved nothwithstanding difficulties"), *achievement*; ("somebody's deed"), *doing* (It's his doing), see *čin*; ("the way of the carrying out of the execution"), *making, workmanship, make*; ("profession") *job, employment*, see *práce*; ("musical") *work, opus* ("other artistic") *work* (*of art, of fiction*); ("in curses") *business* (*The devils b.!*) ..., etc.

We see that the multiple meaning of the Czech word is here analyzed rather thoroughly and instructions are given, in the way of parenthesized glosses, as to when, in what sort of contexts, the single English (partial) equivalents are to be used. But for these glosses, the Czech user could easily form English sentences like "Professor X. Y. has been awarded the Nobel prize in recognition of his life-long scientific business."

In the majority of cases, the lexicographer stresses one of these possible intentions, but he tries also to take the other ones into consideration. An "intentionally pure" dictionary like, example, the English-Czech one quoted above (destined only for the comprehension of the English texts), is a rather rare phenomenon. It can be useful only if there are other descriptive dictionaries of the source language, and aids for translating into it. Such a dictionary supposes that the user has quite a good knowledge of the source language. It must also nevre be too small, otherwise it is ridiculous.

Generally speaking, a dictionary which pursues exclusively one of the possible intentions is a rare phenomenon. It is justifiable and fully useful

---

[37] Entry *dílo*, p. 97.

[38] The information that the Czech substantive is of the *n(euter)* gender and that the form of its gen. plur. is *děl* does not belong to this type of the dictionary in its purest form; this information is given as an element of the description of the Czech entry word with respect to the English user of the dictionary who is also taken into consideration, but only secondarily.

only in languages with abundant lexicographic resources (otherwise it is work wasted and opportunity lost) or in situations which do not allow another solution. The usual situation is, however, that the dictionary is planned so as to be helpful in more than one respect. But the lexicographer should, during his whole work, be aware which of his statements and indications pertains to which of these intentions. He must also decide which of these intentions should be stressed most and which will be secondary: usually, only the intentions to aid description and to aid comprehension of the source language can be combined "on the same level", since the two tasks are largely interdependent (but even here "description" precedes "comprehension"). In all other cases of "combined intentions", an order of preference and stress must be decided upon, because the single tasks are frequently contradictory.

Another dimension of variation is, obviously, the size of the bilingual dictionary (cf. above, § 5.2.7). One of the important insights of our age is that really small bilingual dictionaries are useful only for rather limited purposes, as the primitive needs of a tourist or the difficult beginnings of the pupil. But in all other cases a bilingual dictionary should not be too short, otherwise it is irritating.[39] Size is, however, not only the question of the number of entries (which is nearly always smaller than that in a comparable monolingual dictionary), but also of the richness of the information given in each entry.

The last dimension of variation which we shall mention is the purpose of the bilingual dictionary. This dimension overlaps to some extent with that of the intention, but the two do not coincide.

"Purpose" is a very broad category, and the lexicographer should conceive it broadly. What will be his public (learned, educated, general?) and how will it use the dictionary (literary translation, business contacts, general use?); these and similar questions must be posed by the lexicographer.

In a more special sense, the term "purpose" can imply different restrictions (cf. above, § 5.2.6), which we shall not discuss in detail.

We shall not discuss here the bilingual dictionaries which serve, for example, the purely pedagogical purposes (note that they can have different intentions: to help to read texts, or to produce texts in the foreign language), because they are usually severely reduced; nor shall we discuss technical dictionaries which are restricted, when it is the general dictionaries which are the focus of our attention. There are, however, three groups of dictionaries with a remarkably outstanding concentration upon some purpose we wish to mention. They are:

1° philological bilingual dictionaries,

2° the ethnolinguistic bilingual dictionaries,

3° onomasiologically productive or quasi-normative bilingual dictionaries of not yet fully established standard national languages.

[39] Cf. Ščerba, *Izvestija* 106.

These three classes have in common that all these dictionaries also take upon themselves some tasks which but for different circumstances would belong to monolingual dictionaries, in the first line the description either of the source language (usually 1° and 2°, sometimes also 3°) or even of the target language (3°).

Philological bilingual dictionaries are usually compiled when the source language is dead. For instance, the biggest Latin dictionary, the Thesaurus Linguae Latinae, is a monolingual dictionary. But on the other hand, it would not be very useful to compile a monolingual Greek,[40] Sanskrit, Akkadian etc. dictionary. Therefore, these languages are treated in the respective dictionaries as source languages which are explained by the means of the target language. As examples of such bilingual thesauri or paene-thesauri can be quoted the *Chicago Assyrian Dictionary*[41] and the *Lexicon des frühgriechischen Epos.*[42] In the same way, different languages are treated which possess an interesting literature (recent or ancient) and which are explored chiefly by foreign scholars. The intention of describing and comprehension of the source language is here preponderant. But it would be wrong to think that it is the exhaustive or the thesaurus-like character of these dictionaries which constitutes them as a category, from this point of view. Rather it is the circumstance that they are based on texts, texts which are frequently difficult to interpret, so that the interpretative and exegetic side of the dictionary, the listing and interpretation of — if possible — each nuance in every passage within the canon of the texts treated is quite necessary. It is not only the bilingual thesauri which have this property: every shorter dictionary, say every Latin-English, Greek-French etc. dictionary must necessarily tend in this direction, except that the corpus of texts taken into consideration is more limited than that of a bilingual thesaurus. This what we call "philological aspect"[43] is frequently present in different general-purpose bilingual dictionaries of modern source languages compiled for the native speaker of the target language, since he may legitimately be supposed to read the more important literary texts of the source language.[44] The characteristic feature of such a "philological approach" is not only the preference for literary contexts, preferably as quotations within

[40] It is important to note that in the nomenclature of languages, Greek makes an important exception. If we say *English, French, German* without any specification, we mean the modern stages of these languages; otherwise we must state specifically *Old English, Old French, Middle High German*, etc. On the contrary, *Greek* usually means, without specification, *Old Greek*; any other reference must be explicitly specified, e.g. *Byzantine Greek, Modern Greek*, etc.

[41] I. J. Gelb, B. Landsberger, L. A. Oppenheim, *The Assyrian Dictionary of the Oriental Institute of the University of Chicago*, Chicago 1957ff. (many volumes yet to be published).

[42] B. Snell — H. J. Mette, *Lexikon des frühgriechischen Epos*, Göttingen 1955ff.

[43] "philological" should be taken as "concerned with the interpretation and exegesis of texts".

[44] For example, the big Russian-Czech Dictionary (Velký rusko-český slovník) Prague 1952ff.

the dictionary, but also a certain proclivity to semantic and exegetic glosses and explanations which are frequently of an encyclopedic character.

The ethnolinguistic dictionary seems to be the minor brother of the preceding type. It is compiled for languages which have little or no really important literature and are spoken in societies with cultures widely different from most of the centers of lexicographic activity. Again, the descriptive tasks of the monolingual dictionary must be assumed by this bilingual one; and the proclivity to explanations which verge on the encylopedic is also caused by the existence of designata which have no equivalents in the target language.[45]

A not yet stabilized or only recently developed standard national language usually lacks many a designative lexical unit present in such languages as English, French, or Russian. In such a situation, it is frequently useful not to compile at once a monolingual dictionary, but first a bilingual one, in which the respective recently established standard national language is the target language. As the source language should be chosen that language through whose medium the respective local society gets most information on modern scientific, technical, etc., developments. Apart from the circumstance that a not yet stabilized standard national language frequently does not yet have the abstractive powers necessary for a monolingual dictionary, there is the advantage that the entry-words of the source language directly show the "onomasiological gaps" of the target language, the lacking designative lexical units. How to fill these gaps is not a question for the lexicographer but rather for the language planner. The minimum for the lexicographer to do in any case is to describe the meaning of these lexical units of the rich, fully established source language by means of the target language. If he decides to try to fill the gaps, he has basically two possibilities before him: either to introduce loan-words into the target language or to coin innovations of any type in it. The situation is not without interest for the theory of lexicography. When the lexicographer tries to fill the onomasiological gaps by indicating new loan-words or other innovations as equivalents of the entry-word, it can be maintained that in this case, the lexical meaning of the units of the target language is described rather by reference to the source language, at least unless or until the innovations and loans take root in the target language. As already stated the coinage of innovations is not a purely lexicographic activity in the proper sense of the word (cf. § 4.4), though lexicography usually is vastly useful in filling these semantic gaps. It should be mentioned that dictionaries of this type for many different target languages were compiled in the U.S.S.R. in

---

[45] Cf. Nida IJAL 24, 1958, 280. — As example of a dictionary of this type can be quoted the forthcoming Papago dictionary by M. Mathiot, or, as Petráček reports, Ch. Le Coeur's ethnographic dictionary of Teda (Central Sahara).

the late twenties and in the thirties, the source language being, obviously, Russian.[46]

In different other parts of the world, various institutions cope with similar tasks, as examples, Zima reports the *Hausa Language Board*, the *Bureau of Ghana Languages*, the *Sierra Leone Language Bureau*, the *Translation Bureau in Gambia*, etc.

COLLECTION OF MATERIAL

7.4 In the following sections, we shall discuss some points relevant to the lexicographer's work on a bilingual dictionary. These sections should in no case be read or understood in isolation, but only as complementing or modifying what has been stated in the respective discussions of the monolingual dictionary.

As far as the collection of material goes, the bilingual lexicographer is in an enviable situation if there is already a good, comprehensive, descriptive monolingual dictionary,[47] preferably of the standard-descriptive type or an overall-descriptive one with a standard-descriptive nucleus at least of the non-native language of his pair of languages, but even more if there are such dictionaries of both of them. The absense of such a dictionary is always a serious handicap, because the lexicographer himself must then do much descriptive and other work which should in fact be done by the monolingual dictionary. This remark pertains not only to the collection of the material but has more general validity: in the absence of the monolingual dictionary, the lexicographer will have not only to decide for himself what are to be considered stabilized lexical units and what not, but he will also have to deal with the multiple meanings of each lexical unit, etc. All this will make his work considerably more difficult and longer.

As far as the collecting of material goes a good monolingual dictionary can be used as the basis for the planned bilingual one. If there are more several monolingual dictionaries at hand the one should be chosen which is most similar to the planned bilingual dictionary: for example, a strictly modern standard-descriptive monolingual dictionary is chosen if the planned dictionary is intended to cover only the contemporary language; a more overall-descriptive, broader monolingual dictionary is chosen if the planned dictionary is to be

---

[46] Cf. the remarks in Ščerba, *Izvestija* 112ff. and the discussion with examples by Borovkov LS 1, 1957, 138.

[47] Cf. Berg, Report 9. — As we have stated above, the tasks of such a monolingual dictionary are sometimes fulfilled by a bilingual one of a certain type. This remark should be taken into consideration in this whole discussion.

used for the comprehension of older texts, etc. The material (i.e., the entry-words of the future bilingual dictionary, and their multiple meaning found in the monolingual dictionary) is usually reduced, during the selection. But on the other hand, even if there is an excellent monolingual dictionary at the lexicographer's disposal, the material contained in it must not only be compared with that of other eventual monolingual dictionaries, but it must be completed from other sources, too. In the first place, there may be a difference in the area covered by the two dictionaries: e.g. the monolingual is based more on literary texts whereas the bilingual one intends to be useful also for the generation or comprehension of administrative or technical, etc., texts; or the bilingual dictionary is intended to be useful also for reading some dialectal, or older texts not taken into consideration in the monolingual one. All these gaps must be filled by a specialized excerption of the respective texts. If there is some monolingual dictionary which can be used as the basis for the planned bilingual one, then it is usually older than the planned bilingual one, be the difference only a very short one. But two or three years suffice to make necessary a checking of the newest texts to see whether there are the new lexical units or new senses of the old ones; if so, a special excerption must close the gap again. Apart from all this and in any case, the bilingual lexicographer should excerpt the existing good literary translations of texts both from the source language into the target language, and vice versa. In the excerption for the monolingual dictionary these translations are frequently neglected as not being authentic enough; for the bilingual lexicographer, these translations have the special value that they show how the translator handles the culture-bound and other difficult words.[48]

It is not necessary to stress that the whole material should be checked (coincidence of the evidence, of different dictionaries, of the excerption; the lexicographer's own knowledge; and that of the informants) in respect to its correctness and above all in respect to the question whether it is not obsolete.

If there is no monolingual dictionary at hand, the material for the bilingual dictionary must be gained in the same way as it is gained for the monolingual one (§ 6.3). This is necessary for the source language irrespective of whether it is the lexicographer's native language or not, and for the target language if it is foreign to the lexicographer. Material collected for the target language should, however, be indexed and filed under the (provisional) entry-words of the source language.

---

[48] Cf. Veselitskij, *Principy podači predlogov* 13f. (with a quotation from Ščerba).

SELECTION OF ENTRIES

7.5 The selection of the prospective entry-words which will be included in the bilingual dictionary should be governed by the type of the dictionary, above all by its intention and purpose. The same applies to the reduction of the multiple meanings of selected entries. In the case of a dictionary which intends to help the user to understand texts couched in a foreign language, it will be clear that the occurrence of the lexical units in those texts is the first factor which determines the selection fo the entry-words; the more "text-bound" the dictionary is, the more powerful is also this factor. In a similar way, the selection for a bilingual dictionary with descriptive intentions is governed by principles almost identical to those of the corresponding monolingual dictionary.

Some remarks must be made with respect to the bilingual dictionary which is intended to help the user to generate texts in the (foreign) target language. The basis of the list of prospective entry-words is, of course, the lexicon and semantic of the (native) source language. There are, however, several modifications of this general principle.

First, if the planned dictionary is not to be a big one, it is possible to leave out the less known or less used synonyms of the source language if the better known and more used are included; e.g. if a smaller Eng. — x dictionary has the entry *to sail around*, it is possible to leave out the entry *to circumnavigate*.[49]

Second, such a dictionary, especially if it is a smaller one, should be rather reserved in its inclusion of colloquialisms, slang expressions or even vulgarities and similar levels of language; and even the bigger dictionaries of this type should be extremely cautious in this respect, lest the user be put into a ridiculous or painful position. In a smaller dictionary of this type, it is better to omit such "bad pennies of every day conversation"[50] or, in a bigger one, to label them very cautiously in order to warn the user.

Third, if the target language of a dictionary of this type is spoken in a society with a different culture and in a geographical and other extralinguistic milieu vastly different from that of the source language, it will be necessary to take into consideration also the target language when the entry words of the source language are selected.[51] Different social institutions, different plants

---

[49] Cf. Harrell PL 53 (from whom also the example is borrowed). — If however, in a similar pair of synonyms a word like a *to circumnavigate* has developed a special, technical sense of its own in a sphere to be covered by the bilingual dictionary, it should be given, too.

[50] Martin PL 155; Martin thinks more of expressions like Eng. *uh*..., *Hi there!*, *the thing is*, etc., and seems to incline to the opinion that they should, nevertheless, be indicated, because of their frequency.

[51] To some extent, the target language must always be taken into consideration; even an Eng.-French dictionary which intends to help the speaker of English to express himself

and animals may be unimportant or non-existent in the milieu of the source language while being very important or frequent in the milieu of the target language. Because it may be legitimately assumed that the source-language speaker will use the dictionary to generate texts about the milieu of the target language (possibly also while residing in the other surroundings), the respective lexical units of the target language should be indicated. For example, an English-Chinese dictionary will have to contain entries like

| [Eng.] *Red Guards* | [Chin.] *hung wei-ping* |
| *people's commune* | *jen-min kung-she* |

In a similar way, an English-Chinese dictionary may contain words like

[Eng.] *cloisonné*	[Chin.] *ching-t' ai-lan*
tael	*liang*
lichee	*li-chih*

possibly with explanatory glosses such as *liang* (1. unit of weight, ounce; 2. hist., ounce of silver as monetary unit). A frequent difficulty is that there are not always some really suitable equivalent lexical units of the source language at hand to be used as entrywords. If there are not stabilized lexical units of the source language to be used for this purpose, the necessary indication of the target language should be put there where the user can be supposed to seek it. For example, the Chinese expression *kung-szu he-ying* "under the common management of the state and of the capitalist" can be indicated in the entry *management*.[52]

On the contrary, if the lexicographer compiles a very small dictionary of two very closely related[53] languages, he may tend to omit those lexical units which have in both languages an identical or only negligibly and predictably different form and an identical meaning.[54] If pairs like

[Czech] *herec*	[Slovak] *herec* "actor"
herečka	*herečka* "actress"
herecký	*herecký* "actor's; histrionic"

in French must respect some French specialities. But this consideration is much more important if, for instance, the source language is a European one and the other Chinese or Suaheli.

[52] Examples by Novotná.

[53] The term "related" should not be taken, in this connection, in its genetic aspects only. For the purpose of the present discussion, not only such immediately genetically connected languages as Czech and Slovak, and not only such more remotely but still genetically connected languages as English and French are conceived as "related", but also languages which have no perceivable genetic connection but are linked by a strong layer of identical culture, frequent borrowing from each other or from another common source etc. But on the other hand, a close genetic relationship is the most frequent situation.

[54] This necessity should not be confounded with another phenomenon, referred to by Majtinskaja LS 1, 1957, 165: if all members of a class of source-language lexical units cannot be indicated as entries, the selection of those to be accepted is sometimes influenced by the conside-

have the same form and meaning, a lexicographer who must save space very strictly may omit at least some of them. If this is done on purpose and by principle in all such cases the result is the so-called differential dictionary in the two languages. When compiling such a differential dictionary, the lexicographer should be extremely cautious, because even if the multiple meaning of both the lexical units coincides, there may be important differences in phraseology. One of the dangers of the differential dictionary is that since it is necessarily small, the lexicographer will take into consideration only the dominant senses of the two lexical units: these may happen to be identical and so the pair may be omitted, though there may be important differences in the non-dominant senses about which the user will learn nothing.

But even if it is not a differential dictionary which he is compiling, the lexicographer will tend to omit, in a very small dictionary, such internationalism as *telephone, mathematics,* for obvious reasons. Extreme care should be exercised, because there are not a few "false friends" among them; i.e. lexical units with very similar form but different meaning, e.g. Germ. *Phonologie* "phonemics", Eng. *phonology* = Germ. "Lautlehre".[55] These "false friends" can be found not only in technical terminology, but generally:[56] Cf. Russ. *matka* "uterus, womb", Czech *matka* "mother"; Russ. *čerstvyj* "stale", Czech *čerstvý* "fresh". Sharp differences like those observable in these examples are not particularly dangerous, because they will certainly be noticed. Terminological intricacies (Eng. *phonology*: Germ. *Phonologie*) and not too dissimilar senses (Eng. *to realize*, Fr. *réaliser*), are more dangerous because they are not always easy to perceive.

Another situation of peculiar interest is the selection of entry-words for a bilingual dictionary the target language of which is not yet fully stabilized and lacks equivalents of a considerable number of lexical items of the source language. Here again, the selection of the source-language entry-words must be done with a greater than usual respect to the target language; it is usually necessary to compile at first only a shorter dictionary, rather reduced as regards both the selected entry-words and their multiple meaning, lest the dictionary be surcharged with neologisms of all sorts as well as unstabilized attempts at filling up the onomasiological gaps.[57]

ration of whether or not there is a good equivalent in the target language. Though easy to explain by the general fragility of human nature, considerations of this type should not influence the lexicographer too strongly.

[55] Thus in one terminological set. There are different equivalents in different terminologies. Even within one language, such as English or German, these terms are used with different meaning. — Cf. Ščerba, *Izv.* 112. Cf. also Tietze PL 269 on the wrong tendency to omit internationalism on the strength of the assumption that they are already understood.

[56] Nida, Translating 160.

[57] If more such dictionaries are prepared for one area with the same source language and target languages in a comparable situation, it is possible to prepare one provisional list of entry-words for the whole group of dictionaries. Such a common provisional list will, then, be

Generally speaking, it is necessary to take into consideration that it is a language more or less foreign to the user with which we have to deal in a bilingual dictionary. This is important above all when it is the target language in which the foreign-speaking user is supposed to generate texts. But the same circumstance should be taken into account when it is the source language which is foreign to the user: the "irregular forms", the multiword lexical groups and set groups generally, all these complications should be presented in as simple and as unsophisticated a way as is consistent with material correctness.

THE EQUIVALENT

7.6 The bilingual lexicographer's most important duty is to find in the target language such lexical units as are equivalent to the lexical units of the source language, and to coordinate the two sets. We call e q u i v a l e n t such a lexical unit of the target language which has the same lexical meaning as the respective lexical unit of the source language.

We know how complex the lexical meaning is. Absolute equivalence requires, then, that the lexical meaning of the two lexical units be absolutely identical, in all components (designation, connotation, range of application). Because of the anisomorphism of languages (§. 7.1), such absolute equivalents are rather unfrequent (outside the domain of scientific terminologies). The usual situation is that the lexical meaning of the respective lexical unit of the target languages is only partly identical with that of its conterpart in the source language. If it is necessary to be very precise, we speak in such a case of partial identity about *partial equivalents*.[58] Since, however, the absolute and overwhelming majority of equivalents (irrespective of which pair of languages we observe) belongs to the category of the partial ones, it would be cumbersome to repeat the adjective endlessly. Therefore, if we speak about "the equivalents of a lexical unit" or about "the equivalent of a lexical unit in one of its senses", etc., it is the partial equivalents that we mean.

completed and modified during the elaboration of the single dictionaries, but, nevertheless, much work and time is saved. It is, in fact, strange that Soviet lexicography did not perceive and use this opportunity when dictionaries of this type were compiled nearly by the dozen; cf. the interesting polemic on the subject in LS 2, 1957, 199ff.

[58] Feldman LS 1, 1957, 15ff. and 19, makes yet another distinction. For him, the partial equivalent covers only a part of the lexical meaning of its counterpart in the source language, irrespective of the context in which it is to be applied; if the lexical unit of the target language can or must be used only in a limited range of application, Feldman terms it a *bound equivalent*. (The paper quoted different Japanese-Russian examples to illustrate the difference.) Feldman's idea seems to be a fruitful one: we shall, however, not adopt the terminological difference primarily because of the endless number of doubtful cases which would result.

The logical outset of the search for equivalents is a comparative analysis of the structures of the two languages. The lexicographer must ascertain what categories of lexical units (i.e., traditionally, what parts of speech) are present in both the languages, and must decide which pairs of categories will be considered equivalent. This is relatively easy if there are observably similar or identical categories, in the two languages: it will be easy to decide that a French noun will be considered equivalent to an English one, that a Russian verb will be considered equivalent to a German one, etc. The lexical equivalents will, then, be preferably chosen in such a way that they belong to the categories considered equivalent.[59] But this is a mere preference, since if the equivalence of categories is established correctly the pairs of lexical units will, after all, come out automatically; if there is a clash between this principle and a concrete case of real lexical equivalence of lexical units which belong to different classes, the correct equivalence must take precedence over the principle. For example, the Germ. category of nouns will be considered equivalent with the English noun. But the English equivalent of the German noun *Handarbeit* (in its application as a label on wares) will be *hand-made*, which is an adjective, because the noun *hand-work* is used only in reference to the process of the work itself, not in reference to its result.[60]

It is very important to observe the points of trouble at the very beginning and to decide upon a unified treatment of them. To take a simple example. There is a good amount of equivalence between the categories of the Czech and the English lexical units; one point of trouble is, however, the adjective, which can be derived in Czech from practically any noun by a limited number of suffixes, like *-ský -ový*, which is not always the case in English.

Cf. Subst. [Czech] *nebe* [Eng.] *heaven*
  Adj.   *nebeský*   *heavenly, celestial*
but
  Subst. [Czech] *cihla* [Eng.] *brick*
  Adj.   *cihlový*   *brick* (as in *a brick wall*)[61]

---

[59] Cf. Martin OL 157; Householder PL 280 (quoting Weinreich). — The precise meaning of "preferably" is: if there are two or more equivalents in the target language, all of them precisely identical but not all of them members of the "equivalent" category, and if the size of the dictionary does not permit the indication of all of these equivalents, the one will be selected that belongs to the "equivalent" category.

[60] The principle that lexical equivalence is the most important consideration, in a bilingual dictionary has a general validity. Within the morphological categories, the equivalents are usually indicated in corresponding forms; but it goes without saying that if, e.g., Russ. *znamenie vremeni* (sing.) has the equivalent Eng. *the sign of the times* (plur.), this equivalent will perhaps be indicated, if required by the type of the dictionary, with an indication of the grammatical difference.

[61] This statement, couched here in rather traditional terms, could be re-stated in a number of ways, according to the approach and terminology chosen; note that it is not necessary for the

There are several possible ways to handle a situation like this: it is possible to leave the pair *cihlový — brick* as it is (preferably with a note about this type of equivalence in the Foreword or Grammatical Appendix), or one can indicate the class *cihlový — brick* (adj.) or *cihlový* (adj.) *— brick* (adj.) or (attr.), or one can add an example *cihlový — brick* (*brick wall*), etc. — all this according to the decision for whom and with what intention the dictionary is compiled. The crucial thing, however, is that all cases of one and the same type should be treated in the same way, throughout the dictionary, unless there are, in isolated cases, specific reasons to treat them otherwise.[62]

It would be easy to find a great number of examples in different languages.[63] Sometimes it is possible to solve the situation in a restrictive way: for example, if there are two regular grammatical categories one of which can be conceived as derived from the other in the source language, and both of which correspond to only one category in the target language, the single pairs of members of these categories will generally have identical equivalents in the target language; in this case, the second of the two categories can be indicated only by reference to the first category, unless the concrete lexical unit or its equivalent has some semantic properties of its own.[64]

If there is no "categorial equivalence" of the "parts of speech" observable, the lexicographer has to proceed on the basis of the equivalence of the lexical meaning only. In any case, the lexicographer should, at the beginning of the work, prepare as complete as possible instructions on how to treat the single cases of categorial identity or diversity of the single morphological categories of both the languages.[65]

It follows from the first sentence of this chapter that the bilingual dictionary should coordinate the lexical units of the two languages: therefore, the equivalent should be a real lexical unit of the target language which occurs in real sentences. We shall see later that this requirement has its limitations, but has general validity within the limits of the possible.

In order to be sure that he indicates real lexical units of the target language, the lexicographer collects contexts which illustrate the whole multiple meaning

purposes of this discussion, to get entangled in the question of what the second *brick* (in *a brick wall*) really is or what it should be considered.

[62] Cf. Majtinskaja LS 1, 1957, 162f. Let us mention some types of equivalents discussed by this scholar, using her terminology. In Bashkir, there is no formal difference between the noun and the adjective. If the equivalent also does not distinguish them, we can write (Bash.) *baškort*, (Eng.) *Bashkir* (subst. adj.). If the target language discerns them, both should be indicated: (Bash.) *baškort*, (Russ.) 1) *baškir*, 2) *baškirskij*. Let us stress yet another time that the *intention* of the dictionary must be taken into consideration, too.

[63] Cf. Tietze PL 271ff. (Turkish examples.)

[64] Cf. Majtinskaja LS 1, 1957, 164 and 167 (with Finnish examples).

[65] Such an analysis should be made and at least tentative instruction prepared even before one begins to collect the material.

of the respective lexical unit (i.e., all its senses and many of its applications, or all of them) in the source language, in the degree of finesse and detail planned for the future dictionary (the bigger the dictionary, the more numerous the contexts, with subtler semantic differences); he translates these contexts into the target language and observes whether the prospective shortest possible equivalent can be used in all the translations (producing a sentence of the target language that absolutely conforms to its rules) or only in some of them, or in none.[66] If the prospective equivalent can be used in all the contexts and only those contexts, it is an absolute equivalent. If it can be inserted only into a group of the translated contexts, it is only partial, and another equivalent (or more of them) must be sought for the rest of the translated contexts. If it can be inserted into more contexts, its meaning is broader, usually either because the designatum has fewer criterial features, or because there are fewer applicational restrictions. If it cannot be inserted into any context, it is no equivalent at all.[67]

This method of testing (the translation of) all the contexts (in the desired degree of detail) has not only the advantage that it leads to lexical units of the target language; it also helps to cope with the anisomorphism, i.e., in this case, with the differences of the lexical meaning of the two lexical units. It must be remembered that it is not possible to take the (eventually multiple) meaning of a lexical unit as described in a monolingual dictionary of the source language and seek the prospective senses in the description of the (eventually multiple) meaning of the prospective equivalent in a monolingual dictionary of the target language. Such a procedure can give a first orientation, but the real task, if it is to be done with finesse, is more complicated: the comparison of the two lexical units by the contextual method very frequently shows differences between them which consist in phenomena not always stated in monolingual dictionaries. And it must also be remembered that the way the lexicographer handles the equivalence and how he presents it varies largely with the different intentions and other properties of the planned dictionary. Let us discuss some examples.[68]

---

[66] The lexicographer can get the necessary contexts from the monolingual dictionary of the source language, or from his collection of excerpted contexts, or he can use informants (and eventually his own knowledge) for the purpose.

[67] If informants are used for the purpose, the procedure can be short-circuited in a similar way as in the case of the monolingual dictionary. Let us suppose we seek an equivalent of Eng. *to eat* and *to drink*, in some target language. If one works with well-trained informants, it is not necessary to prepare a range of short contexts, say *to drink water, to drink beer, to drink soup* and have them translated, but it suffices to ask which objects can be used, in the target language, in combination with the prospective equivalent of Eng. *to drink*.

[68] The examples were prepared by Mrs. Ch. Schwarz of the Chinese-German Dictionary staff in Berlin. — I use Modern Chinese examples in order to show some of the uncertainties produced by the absence of a standard-descriptive monolingual dictionary. — The English translations of the German expressions are to be taken as only rough indications of the meaning.

Germ. *heiraten, sich verheiraten* "to marry" can be considered equivalents of Chinese *ch'u-chia*. There is, however, one difference: whereas the Germ. lexical units are used irrespective of the sex of the person, the Chinese lexical unit is used in reference to women only. In a Chinese-Germ. dictionary intended strictly for the comprehension of Chinese texts by native speakers of German, the indication of the equivalence

[Chin.] *ch'u-chia*: [Germ.] heiraten, sich verheiraten

would be sufficient: the range of application of the German lexical units is greater than that of the Chinese one and either of them is always applicable, in the translation of the Chinese contexts, so that there is on need to add a gloss; the Chinese restriction need not be stated as it will be inherent in any context met by the user; and it is not necessary to inform the German user about the semantic difference between the two German lexical units. (*heiraten*: Eng. "to take in marriage", *sich verheiraten*: Eng. "to get married").

From what we dicussed above (§ 7.3) it will be clear that a bilingual dictionary of another type[69] will need some further indications. If the lexical meaning of the Chinese lexical unit is to be described more precisely, the entry will have to contain some indication of the restriction, as

ch'u-chia, (von Frauen) *heiraten, sich verheiraten.*

If the dictionary is intended to help to generate German texts, the lexical meanings of the Germ. equivalent will have to be specified, for example in the following way:

ch'u-chia, heiraten ("to take in marriage")
        sich verheiraten ("to get married")[70]

A combination of these intentions would lead to an entry of the type
ch'u-chia (von Frauen), *heiraten* ("to take in marriage")

        sich verheiraten ("to get married").

It is probably not necessary to describe the different possible entries of a German-Chinese dictionary.

The German equivalent of Chinese *hsien-hsieh* can be regarded *beinahe, fast* "almost, nearly". An examination of the Chinese contexts (which we shall quote here in approximative English translations only) shows that all of them are roughly of the type: "he nearly stumbled, fell, starved, died, knocked, down someone, poisoned, someone, crushed someone". We shall not repeat

---

[69] The Dictionary with entries of the type just described has the smallest descriptive and generative power and needs, therefore, the lowest quantity of specificatory information.

[70] Instead of the English glosses written in quotation marks, in a real case we would probably have Chinese or German glosses.

the different forms the entry could have, according to the lexicographer's intentions, beginning with the simplest form;

[Chin.] *hsien-hsieh* [Germ.] *beinahe, fast.*

Let us, however, suppose that the lexicographer intends to describe in his dictionary the source language (Chinese), at least to some extent. He can then, add a restrictive, specifying gloss of the type, say

hsien-hsieh (bei negativen Ereignissen) *beinahe, fast*

"(about negative events) *almost, nearly*".

It will not always be easy to construct such glosses, expecially if the bilingual lexicographer does not have the support of a good monolingual dictionary; therefore, he may prefer to add one or more Chinese contexts as examples. If he chooses them well, he can convey the necessary information concerning the restriction without accepting the commitment that the restriction is absolutely valid. Or, in a bigger dictionary, he can give both the gloss and the contextual examples.

Let us now consider the equivalents; for the beginning let us discuss the English ones (which could serve as equivalents of the Chinese lexical unit, though the example is based on the German material). Both the English lexical units have multiple meaning. If we accept Hornby's description of it, we see that *almost* has two senses: (1) as in: *"He almost fell"*; (*almost* is replaceable by *nearly*); (2) as in: *Almost no one believed her*; (*almost* is not replaceable by *nearly*). On the other hand *nearly* has three senses: (1) as in *It is nearly 1 o'clock*; (replaceable by *almost*); (2) as in *I have £ 20, but that will (ot be nearly enough for my journey* (not replaceable); (3) as in *nearly related* ʌnot replaceable).

If we quote *almost, nearly* together as equivalents of the Chinese lexical unit, they disambiguate each other, because it is obvious to the user of the dictionary that only that sense applies which is common to both of them.

If we consider the German equivalents *beinahe, fast*, we see that they are as close synonyms as one can find, the difference in their meaning being almost imperceptible.[71] The question arises, then, why both of them should be quoted, what purpose does it serve. There are two reasons: First, the indication of synonyms in the target language helps the user to find variant possibilities of expression, if only for purely stylistic variation. Second, imperceptible and hard to state as they are, there usually are some slight differences between such synonyms, so that if more are indicated, the information conveyed is richer. On the other hand, if the dictionary is to be only a small one, synonyms

---

[71] Steinitz-Klappenbach, S. 1229: *fast* "drückt aus, daß die Bezugsgröße in ihrem vollen Umfang eingeschränkt ist; beinahe, nahezu"; S. 490: *beinahe* "fast".

of this type can be omitted; and they should not be indicated too lavishly, even in big dictionaries.

We see that we can discern three types of indications of synonymous equivalents which are not differentiated formally in the absolute majority of dictionaries:

(1) *heiraten, sich verheiraten*: a rule (semantic or grammatical) of the target language makes it predictable which of the two equivalents will be used;

(2) *almost, nearly*: both can be used, but only in the senses of their multiple meanings which overlap, which are disambiguated;

(3) *beinahe, fast*: any of the two can be used, and the two taken together make the information somehow richer.

These are only the polarized types; in the concrete situation there is much overlapping and uncertainly over which category a case belongs to: it is above all types (2) and (3) which are frequently hard to discern.[72] The lexicographer should, however, try to know to which type a single case belongs: if the dictionary must be short, he can reduce type (3) by the omission of one of the synonyms, without a great loss; type (2) can be thus reduced only if the meaning of the remaining equivalent is disambiguated by another means, i.e. if it is clear, e.g. from an example quoted, in which sense it is to be taken; the reduction of type (1) usually causes considerable mistakes or difficulties on the part of the user of the dictionary. Synonyms both of type (2) and (3) are usually joined by the comma. In type (1), either comma or semicolon is used; in bigger dictionaries, the latter is preferable.

7.6.1 The German equivalent of Chinese *jiu* can be regarded as *alt* "old". When the lexicographer collects and analyzes the contexts of the source language (we use again an example of the more difficult situation, where the lexicographer does not have the support of a standard-descriptive monolingual dictionary of the source language), he will perceive that they belong roughly to the following three groups:[73]

(1) old edition of a book, and old malady makes its appearance again, old society, old ideology, old dweiling, old job;

(2) old method, old custom, old dream, old archive;

(3) old industry equippment, old material, old clothes, old house.

If the dictionary does not belong to the type in which the indication of the equivalence Chin. *jiu*, Germ. *alt* "old" is sufficient, viz. if the dictionary is to

---

[72] But some dictionaries indicate the absolute synonyms which can be freely exchanged in another way than the other ones (e.g., by parentheses, eventually with "or", etc.). To do this is a very difficult task; but it is very valuable information.

[73] We give here approximative English translations of the Chinese contexts.

have a greater descriptive power, it will be necessary to disambiguate the German equivalent, i.e. to indicate which of its senses do apply and to state that the sense as in *"Er ist 14 Jahre alt"* "He is 14 years old" does not.[74] Let us now suppose that the usual method of the dictionary would be the indication of synonyms (irrespective whether accompanied by examples or not). One can assume that the entry could have a form like the following one: [Chin.] *jiu*, [Germ.]

(1) *alt, früher, ehemalig*, "old, former, previous";

(2) *alt, schon lange bestehend* "old, already existing for a long time";

(3) *alt, gebraucht, durch langen Gebrauch abgemacht* "old, used, worn out by long use".

When we consider these indications we cannot fail to perceive the difference between an equivalent like *alt* "old" which is undoubtedly lexical unit, ready to be inserted in to a sentence, and *durch langen Gebrauch abgemacht* "worn out by long use" or *schon lange bestehend* "existing for a long time" which are not quite stabilized lexical units and which though they could be inserted at least into some of the contexts are felt as non-minimal, as expansions of what could be said by *alt*; but on the other hand, these latter equivalents have the advantage that they, taken in isolation, give more information about the lexical meaning of the source-language lexical unit.

We call the equivalents of the first type translational or insertible equivalents, those of the second type explanatory or descriptive ones. The basis difference between them is not their status as lexical units (there are some explanatory equivalents which are fully stabilized lexical units, though more frequently they are not). The main distinction is that when choosing a translational, insertible equivalent, the main concern is given (within the boundary of correct possibilities) to its ability to be used in a fluent, good translation of whole sentences, to be inserted into contexts of the target language whereas the explanatory or descriptive equivalent is chosen in order to give more information about the lexical unit of the target language.

Naturally there are many equivalents which combine both the advantages; e.g. *gebraucht* "used" (which occurs in the same example) seems to be a good translational equivalent with a high explanatory power. And it is also certain that sometimes it is difficult to draw a line between the two types.[75]

---

[74] It could be maintained that Germ. *alt* "old" has no conspicuous multiple meaning, nor, consequently, particular senses, but that it shows a certain generality of meaning. This point of view would change nothing as far as the necessary disambiguation goes; one would probably conceive the situation as a case of a different range of application, with the necessity to indicate restriction.

[75] We shall see later that the boundary between the explanatory equivalent and the explanation which is not an equivalent is also not absolutely sharp.

If it is necessary to choose either a translational insertible equivalent or an explanatory one, which of them is to be preferred? Let us discuss a simple example. The entry in an English-French dictionary

girlhood "état de fille"[76]

is in itself correct and it helps one to understand any English sentence in which this word is used.[77] On the other hand, probably nobody would translate English sentences like *"Her girlhood was the only sunny time of her life"*, or *"In her girlhood, she used to read Tennyson"; or "During her girlhood, she has acquired many a bad habit"* into French as "Dans son état de fille...", etc. Therefore, a more translational equivalent like "adolescence" is sought. This is, however, not sufficient, because whereas Eng. *girlhood* is restricted in its application to female human beings, Fr. *adolescence* is not. The respective entry with a more translational equivalent must, therefore, have a specifying gloss on the type.

girlhood, — *"adolescence, période de jeunesse"* (d'une femme);[78]

It will be clear that a dictionary which intends to help the user to generate sentences in a foreign target language does not tolerate the explanatory equivalents. Such a dictionary must try to indicate as translational equivalents as possible; if an explanatory equivalent is to be used, though (for lack of a translational one in order to warn the user.

In the other types of dictionaries, both translational and explanatory equivalents can occur. It possible, they should be discerned by some formal means; this is generally, however, an impossible requirement; only the most obvious cases of explanatory equivalents which are on the borderline of direct explanations (see § 7.6.2) can be labelled as such.

The explanatory equivalent has the advantage of being very general, because it is situated on the notional rather than on the purely linguistic level. If the user understands what is meant by the explanatory equivalent "état de fille" and if he knows that he is not expected to insert it in each and every respective sentence, he will understand very different English sentences and will adapt his translations to the requirements of the different contexts: *Au temps d'adolescence..., Dans sa période de jeunesse..., Quand elle était jeune fille...,* but possibly also: *Quand elle était jeune..., Au temps de sa jeunesse,*

[76] W. James — A. Molé, *Dictionnaire des langues anglaise et française*, 2nd ed. Leipzig 1918, p. 200.

[77] The only exception would be sentences with *girlhood* in the sense of "a group of girls taken collectively"; this sense, however, is obsolete and probably no bilingual dictionary would try to attain this degree of detail.

[78] Reduced from Ch. Pelit, *Dictionnaire anglais-français*, Paris 1934, p. 437. Note that "période de jeunesse" verges again on the explanatory, though in a much less obtrusive form than "état de fille".

etc. The explanatory equivalent makes considerable demands on the user's knowledge of the target language (he is supposed to know the necessary semantically related words and near-synonyms) and on his intellectual powers (he is supposed to be able to discern the limits of the notion indicated by the explanatory equivalent). Therefore, such an explanatory equivalent can be used with success only if the target language is well known by the user, preferably if it is his native one. The explanatory equivalent is very practical when a lexical unit of the source language is to be handled, the designatum of which has no or no precise counterpart in the target language.

The first and foremost advantage of the translational, insertible equivalent is that it is purely linguistic, so that the lexicographer remains within the realm both of his immediate competence and of his task. It is the translational equivalent by means of which the two languages are compared, not the notions expressed; this leads to a minute analysis both of all the components of the lexical meaning of the two respective words and of the applicational restrictions and preferences which are observable in their applications in sentences. Therefore, to establish the translational equivalents is the linguistic task par excellence. On the other hand, we must not forget that translational equivalents usually require much more glosses that the explanatory ones, just because the respective designata have other organization of criterial features. Without these glosses, the information conveyed by the pure translational equivalents is frequently not rich enough to suffice as a description of the source language.

The translational equivalent has also the great advantage that it offers the user ready expressions to be used in sentences. On the other hand, apart from the circumstance that it is sometimes impossible to find a really good translational equivalent at all, this "translational approach" involves a particular danger. Let us return to our Chinese-German (-English) example: Chin. *jiu* Germ. *alt*, "old" and to its multiple meaning.

If one of the senses of the Chinese lexical unit can be represented by Eng.[79] *old, former, previous*, then, if we make a rich enough collection of contexts, there will certainly be sentences which would require translational equivalents like *preceding, foregone, past, obsolete*, etc.; there will be contexts which will require not only *old, existing for a long time*, but perhaps also *ancient, antique, archaic, time-*, etc.; in some context rather than *old, used, worn out by long use*, equivalents like *second-hand, decrepit*, etc., might seem to be the best possible ones. In short, the method of establishing translational equivalents by testing the sentences of the source language entails the danger that the dictionary will grow into a synonymic dictionary of the target language. The lexicographer

---

[79] I used here only the English translations of the eventual German equivalents to make the discussion shorter and simpler. It is immaterial which language is used for this demonstration.

must avoid this danger, because the number of all these equivalents, and the necessity of disambiguating their own multiple meaning and eventually of adding glosses and exemplification to each to them would lead to a dictionary of monstrous dimensions which would indicate many severely restricted applications of the lexical units but which would tend to be on a low level of generality. Indeed, no lexicographer and no dictionary can guarantee that it will offer all suitable equivalents for each possible application;[80] even if he tried, there are always new applications brought about by new extralinguistic situations or by the originality of the speaker. The lexicographer's task is to indicate the most general translational equivalents which have a broader range of application; they should also (with their necessary glosses), if possible, correspond to the multiple meaning of the lexical unit of the source language.

Thus the explanatory equivalent and the translational one are nor so much opposed as one might think" both act as representatives of a group of synonyms and near-synonyms from which, if he knows them, the user may choose the most suitable one. The basic difference between the two is, however, that the translational equivalent is always a possible and sometimes the best possible choice for insertion into a real sentence.[81]

---

[80] Kopeckij, *Poznání* 193. Cf. Feldman LS 1, 1957, 11ff. and 14: in the selection of equivalents, one runs the danger disintegrating the meaning of the source-language lexical unit into too small components by too specific equivalents (Japanese and other examples).

[81] Though the idea of the translational equivalent seems to have been conceived at different places by different scholars without any mutual inspiration (cf., e.g., Martin PL 156: "We should aim at a single translational equivalent ... most broadly applicable"), the lexicographer who first stated the principle and put it into realization was L. V. Ščerba, above all in his *Russko-francuzskij slovar'* — *Dictionnaire russe-français*, 1st edition Moskva 1936. Ščerba's approach was stricter that the one advocated above: he tried to give as few explanatory glosses and explanations as possible, and he was opposed to the indication of synonyms of type (3) (*beinahe, fast*; cf. also Istrina, *Izvestija* 3, 1944; 87, who seems to be even stricter than Ščerba himself, cf. *Izvestija* 115; for a strict avoidance of glosses or explanations, cf. Feldman, LS 2, 1957: Jap. *naku* would need, as translational equivalents, all Eng. words like *to whine, to miaow, to neigh, to moo, to crow*, etc; but even in such a situation when there is no absolute, total equivalent and when it is impossible to indicate all the partial synonyms, Feldman prefers to give only a few, without any explanatory gloss, to any explanation or anything which would be against the translational principle). The precise (if only partial) translational equivalent ought to have the dominant or rather exclusive position. — All these principles were very rigorously applied in the first edition of Ščerba's dictionary; Filipec (LSB 48) is, however, completely right when observing that in the third edition of it (the first half of which was worked out under Ščerba's guidance, before his death), the original approach is rather weakened. It is also important to note that Ščerba had very outspoken ideas on the usefulness of different types of dictionaries and on the sequence in which they should be prepared, ideas which we shall not discuss here in detail; and which few lexicographers would be prepared to share without limitation; in any case, the result of all this was that some of Ščerba's disciples and followers adhered to the translational principle to the exclusion of other possibilities and irrespective of the purpose and intention of the dictionary. Cf. Borovkov LSB 1, 1957, 152ff. on different

While it is the lexicographer's task to find as precise equivalents in the target language as possible, he must anticipate the eventuality that he will not find any. This may happen with any lexical unit; it is, however, in three particular groups that it most frequently occurs, that the lexicographer must use means other than lexical equivalence.

The first group is the lexical units with other than designative functions.[82] We shall discuss only two examples. If we find the following Eng. translations of different contexts in which the Russ. postrepiion *po* occurs:

po pribytii ego	*on his arrival*
po ukhode ego	*after he had gone*
po okončanii	*as soon as he had finished*

probably the only efficient solution of the situation is to state the function(s) succinctly and give some typical examples.[83] Sometimes it happens that a lexical unit performs a grammatical function and has as such no lexical equivalent in the target language, though it may have, in other contexts, a designative meaning with good equivalents. Knudsen[84] quotes as an example the Norwegian sentence *de går og baktaler meg* "they are calumniating me"; *går* has a good equivalent in Eng. *go*, but in sentences of this type its function is to express the constancy, the repeatedness of the calumniation and it does not require an Eng. equivalent. In such cases the respective function should be indicated as a part of the lexical unit's multiple meaning.

Bashkir dictionaries, and on the disadvantages of a too strict application of the translational principle); Havránek LSB 50 (translational equivalent is the best rendering, but it is also slightly narrower); Bosák LSB 127 (a danger of practicism is involved in the translational approach); Jehlička LSB 125 (the indication of synonyms is necessary); Malíková LSB 119 (good discussion of the translational approach and a strong argumentation on its behalf, in its absolute form; excellent Russian and Czech comparative examples). Cf. also the independent (v. above) voice of Martin PL 156 which pleads for the indication of synonyms: they offer a range of choices to the translator and give a semantic spectrum of the source-language lexical unit; sometimes, however, they can be interpreted as the evasion of responsibility on the part of the lexicographer (which is, incidentally, a correct remark), cf. also Borovkov LS 1, 1957, 147, with Uzbek and Kirgiz examples). The translational approach was further developed with the necessary modifications and limitations) by A. I. Smirnickij. The *Russko-anglickij slovar'* — *Russian English dictionary* by A. I. Smirnickij (7th ed. by O. S. Akhmanova, Moskva 1965) is certainly the model of a dictionary intended to help to generate texts in a foreign target language, and which is compiled by a moderate version of the translational approach.

[82] Kopeckij, *Poznání* 193f.

[83] Cf. Babkin LS 3, 1958, 73. The example here is inspired by Veselitskij, *Principy podači predlogov* 16. — It is important to state also the "zero" elements, if the entry-word is not always translated in the contexts of the target language; e.g., Eng. *the* usually remains untranslated in Japanese but sometimes it is translated as if it were *that*: Martin PL 458.

[84] Proceedings of the 8th Congress of Linguists, Oslo 1958, p. 101.

In the same way, it is frequently impossible to find equivalents of interjections; the only solution is, then, to state their functions. The same applies frequently to lexical units derived from such nondesignative words. For example, if the function of Eng. *chick* is "a representation of the click ... used to urge on a horse",[85] then if a lexicographer decides to indicate the verb *to chick* in an Eng.-French dictionary, his only possibility is to state "faire claquer sa langue (pour exciter le cheval)"[86] (or something to the same purpose), unless he finds a real French equivalent.

The second group consists of the "culture-bound words" which were discussed above (§ 7.1). These lexical units do not have a counterpart, i.e. a lexical unit with an identical designatum in the target language.[87] Consequently, there cannot exist a translational, insertible equivalent; the only way to arrive at one is to coin it. The usual way to coin a translational equivalent is either to borrow the word from the source language or to coin a new expression for it. The other possible way is to try to find an explanatory equivalent. But in any case, if the meaning of the culture-bound word of the source language is to be really understood by the foreign user of the dictionary, the entry must contain an explanation of it.[88] Let us consider the following Ossetic examples:[89]

(a) [Oss.] *alam*, [Eng.] *alam* — (borrowing)

(b) [Oss.] *ironvandag*, [Eng.] *Ossetic way* — (new coinage by verbatim translation)[90]

(c) [Oss.] *ziw* [Eng.] *collective help* — (explanatory equivalent).

The explanatory equivalent (c) gives us the richest information. But for a real understanding we need an explanation not only in the case of (a) and (b), but also in this case:

(a) [Oss.] *alam*, [Eng.] *alam* (fruit and candy bound on a twig and carried by mounted participants of a funeral feast)

---

[85] Reduced from OED s.v.

[86] Harrap s.v.

[87] If they do, the target language belongs to the same culture, and these words do not belong to the category of "(foreign) culture-bound words", considered from the point of view of the concrete bilingual dictionary.

[88] The statement is *mutatis mutandis* valid also if the culture-bound word occurs in the target language (which happens primarily for reasons discussed above). An explanatory gloss is, then, necessary.

[89] The examples are based on the *Ossetic Russian dictionary*.

[90] Any other coinage could be used; this passage should not be taken as a suggestion that equivalents should be coined by such verbatim translations: we only say that they sometimes are, and use one case as one example out of a group of possibilities.

(b) [Oss.] *ironvandag*, [Eng.] *Ossetic way* (an ancient Ossetic funeral ritual)

(c) [Oss.] *ziw*, [Eng.] *collective help* (socially expected help, above all during agricultural work, organized within or by a group of people).

It depends upon the lexicographer's decision whether his explanations will be minimal as here, case (b), or whether they will verge on the encyclopedic (case a, c); but they should have a united style within the whole dictionary.[91/92]

The difference which we see between what we call the explanatory (or descriptive) equivalent and the explanation is that the former tends to be similar to a translational, insertible equivalent and can become, if stabilized, a lexical unit of the target language, whereas the latter tends to be very similar to a lexicographic definition (or is even identical with it) and usually cannot aspire to become a lexical unit.[93] It is unnecessary to stress that there is a great number of boundary cases.

7.6.2 The third group of words which will have no translational equivalents are those expressions which were discussed above in connection with the "onomasiological gaps" and the dictionaries which try to fill them. The situation is similar to that discussed in the preceding paragraphs; an explanation of the meaning of the source-language lexical unit is always to be given, irrespective of how the lexicographer tries to fill the onomasiological gap in the target language unless the user is expected to have a good knowledge of the source-language or to make frequent use of another dictionary, especially of a monolingual dictionary of the source-language.

But these three groups are to be regarded only as areas in which words with no equivalents are most frequent. We know, however, from the discussion of the anisomorphism (§ 7.1) that similar cases can be found not only in these areas but in any sphere of language. Still, the usual situation is that an equivalent can be found but not an absolete one, only a partial one.

---

[91] Even the strict Ščerba himself accepted the necessity of explanations in these cases. In Russian, there is a word *oblomovščina* "lazy, idle, apathetic behaviour (typified by the writer Gončarov in Oblomov, a person of one of his novels)". In the first edition of his dictionary (p. 364) Ščerba writes:
[Russ.] *oblomovščina*, [French] *oblomovchtchina, mollesse, indolence*
In the 3rd edition, we read (p. 389):
[Russ.] *oblomovščina*, [French] *oblomovchtchina* (d'Oblomov, personnage d'un roman de Gontcharov qui symbolise la veulerie).

[92] Dictionaries of distant contemporary cultures which contain rather encyclopedic explanations of the principal culture-bound words are sometimes called ethnolinguistic dictionaries; cf. Nida IJAL 24, 1958, 280.

[93] Cf. Feldman LS 2, 1957, 96 (with Japanese examples), who demands that "the explanation of a word without equivalent should be as close to a theoretical translation as possible". This can, however, be legitimately demanded only from what we call the explanatory equivalents.

FORM OF ENTRIES

7.7 Since there are more types of bilingual dictionaries than of monolingual ones, and since they diverge more strongly, the forms of the entries in single bilingual dictionaries are very different, too. The most powerful factor in this variation is the intention of the dictionary; cf. § 7.3. We shall not repeat what is stated there or discuss in detail what obviously follows from it, but shall mention only a few specific points.

The lemma will indicate the entry-word in its canonical form. The absolute majority of dictionaries add grammatical indications to show the entry-word's paradigm, and its specificities. Even dictionaries planned for native speakers of the source language should give these indications in order to help the speaker of the target language if he seeks information in the dictionary. When preparing these grammatical indications, the lexicographer should take into consideration that they are written for foreigners, not for the native speaker. They should, therefore, be more explicit and rather more detailed. The lemma should indicate also the pronunciation of the entry-word in its canonical form; but further indications are necessary if there is some unpredictable variation within the paradigm. The indication of pronunciation can be omitted only if there is a one-to-one correlation between the written form and the spoken one; i.e. if the user will be able to know how to pronounce the written form. Few dictionaries will be in the position to omit these indications in the lemma: even a dictionary with no descriptive intentions must give them to help the user to pronounce texts in the source language, and a dictionary which intends to help the speaker of the source language to generate texts in the target language will also try to be of some use to the speaker of the target language, just as with grammatical indications. An appendix on the pronunciation of the source language is also welcome, and is in most cases a necessity.

The equivalents are quoted in their canonical form. Most dictionaries will supplement the latter by those grammatical indications which are necessary to identify the equivalent's paradigm and to remind the user about the irregular forms; this latter task can be performed by reference to a grammatical appendix. If necessary, an instruction on how to pronounce the equivalent should be added. These indications concerning the equivalent can be omitted only if the dictionary is destined for the speaker of the target language exclusively, without any regard[94] for the speaker of the source language; but even in this

---

[94] This is the general scheme. Within it, different modifications are possible. For example, it is possible to have the following rule: the equivalent belongs to the same morphological category as the entry-word, unless there is an indication to the contrary. Under this rule it is possible to write in an Eng.-Fr. dictionary *avow* v., *avouer*, even if the equivalents should get their grammatical indication within the general scheme. The rules of this type can be decided upon on the basis of

extreme case, these grammatical indications should be given if the (partial) homonymy of the canonical forms of two equivalents (irrespective of where they are located in the dictionary) is disambiguated by the other forms of their paradigm.

The grammatical indications concerning the entry-word should, in any case, be given in the terminology which is usual in the source language, and the indications concerning the equivalent should be given in the terminology usual in the target language; if necessary, one should also use, for this purpose the source language and the target language, respectively, but as the indications are usually given in the form of very compact abbreviations, this necessity does not occur too frequently. The reason for this is that different languages have different grammatical terminology with different phenomena of anisomorphism of its own, so that it is useful to keep the two terminological sets clearly apart.

Just as in the monolingual dictionary, the multiple meaning of the majority of entry-words will cause considerable difficulties in the construction of a bilingual entry.

In this work, the lexicographer tries to cover the whole lexical meaning of the entry-word by partial equivalents of the target language. The multiple meaning of the lexical unit of the source language is, therefore, necessarily the basis of the whole construction of the bilingual entry, of the sequence of the senses. The bigger the dictionary and the more thoroughly it intends to describe the source language,[95] the more will the structure of the bilingual entry have to resemble that of a monolingual dictionary of the source language, even if it implies the repetition of the same equivalent in different senses of the entry-word, but with different examples and phraseology. But even in such a case, there will be divergences between the bilingual dictionary and its monolingual model: nearly all bilingual dictionaries are smaller than monolingual ones, they omit less frequent, obsolete, too technical senses etc., which results in a reduction of the multiple meaning as presented in the dictionary. On the other hand, it is necessary in the majority of cases to indicate more than one equivalent even for one sense of the entry-word in such a bigger dictionary.

Smaller and less descriptive dictionaries will, however, not only reduce the presentation of the entry-words' multiple meanings by omitting some senses, but they will also try to make the entry more compact by "joining" some senses together[96] and by presenting the meaning as a more general one. The limiting factor of such efforts is most usually the semantics of the target lan-

---

the comparison of the respective structures of the two languages. The user's assumed abilities should not, however, be strained too much by such rules and conventions.

[95] The two aspects are frequently correlated, but they are virtually independent.

[96] This is a highly pragmatic statement; cf. on the generality of meaning, the senses, etc., above.

guage: the equivalents have, then, a strong influence on the structure of the
entry.

Let us discuss the following example. For instance, the lexicographer may
try to present the lexical meaning of Oss. *čyzg* as compactly as possible, but
he will not be able to indicate less than two English equivalents, viz. *girl*,
daughter, or *girl*; *daughter*, or (1) *girl*, (2) *daughter*, etc.:

[Oss.] *czyg*, [Eng.] *girl, daughter*.

On the other hand, if French *fille* had not only the sense of Eng. "daughter"
(as in "*Voila' mon fils et ma fille*"), but if it still fully had also the sense of
Eng. "*girl*" which is yet observable (as in "Elle est une très belle fille"),
though it is to a great extent expressed now by *jeune fille*, a short Ossetic-
French dictionary intended to foster the understanding of Oss. texts could be
much more compact and state simply:

[Oss.] *čyzg*, [French] *fille*.

Obviously, the shortest possible entry of an Ossetic-English dictionary conveys
the impression that the Ossetic word has a multiple meaning, but the entry of an
imaginary Ossetic-French dictionary that it does not.

In this sense, the entry in a bilingual dictionary is organized by the equivalent. There is, however, one point of danger which must be avoided. The
user should not be left in ignorance as to which of the senses of French *fille*
apply and which do not, unless the dictionary intends to foster only the comprehension of source-language texts. If Japanese *na* has the Russian equivalent *imja*, it will be to the purpose to indicate that from among the multiple
meaning of the Russian word, the senses "name, reputation" apply.[97] If the
senses are not too divergent and if the dictionary is to be short, it is not necessary to go into all the details. For example, Oss. *avtomat* is the absolute equivalent of Russ. *avtomat*[98] which can be used in reference to different automatic
machines, slot machines, automate generally, submachine guns, etc. In a short
dictionary, it is is useful to add a gloss in forming the user that the equivalence
is valid in different senses.[99]

In practice, the lexicographer will find that strongly differing senses of the
entry-word frequently have different equivalents in the target language, and
on the other hand, that different senses of the entry word which do not require different equivalents can be "combined", "reduced" into onew. The
generality of lexical meaning, however, — both in the source language and in

[97] Cf. Feldman LS 2, 1957, 87 (reduced).

[98] Obviously it is a loan-word.

[99] The example is based on the Ossetic-Russ. Dictionary. Cf. Malíková LSB 129 (eight
senses of Russ. *voda* "water" with equivalent eight senses of Czech *voda* "water").

the target language, causes that in the majority of cases, the bilingual lexicographer will not stand before an either (or decision with one solution absolutely false and the other absolutely correct.[100]

GLOSSES AND LABELS

7.8 The equivalents themselves are the most important part of the entry.
But in the majority of cases, it does not suffice to indicate them alone, first
because most of them have a multiple meaning of their own,[101] and second,
because they are only partial equivalents of the entry-word.

We have seen above (§ 6.5.3.2) that it is not the whole multiple meaning of
Eng. *almost*, nor that of Eng. *nearly*, which is equivalent to that of Chinese
hsien-hsieh, but only one respective sense of each. We have seen also that it is
just by their being quoted together that the meaning of the two equivalents is
disambiguated. The same disambiguation (i.e. the elimination of those senses
of a multiple meaning which do not apply) can be effected by a gloss, e.g.
Eng. *daughter* — Oss. *čyzg* ("one's own child").[102] Such a gloss disambiguates
the multiple meaning of the Ossetic word, because it eliminates the other sense
(*girl*). Such a gloss is not an explanation: whereas the latter approaches the
lexicographic definition, the gloss does not attempt more than to indicate as
succinctly as possible the relevant difference, the criterial features, the sphere
of application, etc. In one case, it is enough to state in the gloss "one's own
child" (as against "anybody's child"), whereas the explanation would need
the statement of other criterial features, at least that the child must be female.

In the same way, glosses are used to specify the partial equivalents: they
specify to which part of the entry-word's multiple meaning the respective
partial equivalent belongs, and thereby also disambiguate its own multiple
meaning.[103]

[100] Cf. Jehlička LSB 126 (the decisive factor is the multiple meaning of the source language;
it should be respected even if equivalents have to be repeated); Ďurovič LSB 128 (a bilingual
dictionary is not a translation of the monolingual one; the basis of the entry's organization is the
equivalents); Malíková LSB 129ff.; Borovkov LS 1, 1957, 138 and 158 (the importance of the
target language).

[101] On the whole problem of disambiguation see especially Ianucci PL 201ff. (with excellent
examples and a rich classification of dictionaries); Ščerba, *Izvestija* 114; Feldman LS 2 1957,
88ff.; Malkiel PL 15.

[102] The parenthesized gloss is put into quotation marks to show that it is a translation of
what would probably be couched in Ossetic in a real dictionary.

[103] It is probably because of this plurality of both their function and their form that these
specifying glosses are refered to by very different terms, ranging from "*meaning discrimination*"
to "*semanticization*". Nor is it clear whether the disambiguation and the specification are as

We have quoted the example of an entry with rich glosses above. It may be clear from that example that these glosses have varying forms and that they are similar to or overlap with other lexicographic means: the gloss "what was achieved notwithstanding the difficulties" is similar to an explanation; the gloss "somebody's deed" to an explanatory equivalent; the gloss "profession" is similar to a disambiguating synonym; etc. It is not very important to give too much attention to the form of these glosses (provided that one does not write uncalled-for encyclopedic explanations in their place; the success of the lexicographer is brought about by his ability to find cut the really criterial feature and) or the limited range of application which make one part of the entry word's multiple meaning equivalent with (a part of the multiple meaning of) the parial equivalent.

Very frequently, it is no easy task to decide upon these glosses, especially when they are based on a restriction of application and when there is no standard-descriptive monolingual dictionary of the respective language at hand.

For example,[104] Chinese *shen -ju* has (in its verbal function) the German equivalents *einsichern, eindringen*, approximatively "to soak (through) to penetrate". Unless one wishes to indicate only these translational equivalents, one has to study the contexts to see whether or not a gloss is necessary. There are two big goups of contexts, in our case: in the first of them (which is smaller) a liquid (usually water, but sometimes also oil) soaks into the ground; in the second group, capital penetrates into countries, markets, branches of industry. There remain, however, many other contexts: somebody penetrates the specificity of a branch of art, something gets into the body, disquietude enters the heart, oxygen gets into the veins, a political problem comes into the frontier territory. The gloss should, not, then formulate the restriction in an absolute way; one of the possible formulations is (in Eng. translation) "*to soak* (through), *to penetrate*" (e.g. capital, liquids).[105]

Sometimes it is useful to add a gloss because of something that is not included in the dictionary but which could nevertheless be relevant.

For example,[106] Czech krátkost "shortness" can be used both in reference to time and to space. In a Czech-Chinese dictionary this would require two Chinese

---

different as the different terms imply. "Disambiguation" can be taken as referring to the elimination of some senses as they are presented in monolingual dictionaries; "specification" can be taken as referring to the singling out of a criterial feature or applicational restriction relevant only in comparison with the equivalent. But these things are far from clear and it is quite probable that the two terms refer to basically the same mechanism. One can also speak generally about *semantic glosses*.

[104] The example was prepared by Ch. Schwartz, cf. footnote 68.

[105] We shall see later that it is not necessary to put the gloss behind the equivalents.

[106] The example is taken from Kratochvíl-Novotná-Šťovíčková-Zgusta, Archiv Orientální 39, 1962, 272.

equivalents, one for each application. Since, however, the Czech word is frequently used in reference to time and only rearly in referece to space, the lexicographer may incline to indicate only the "temporal" equivalent, which is Chin. *tuan -chan*, and omit the "spatial" one. In this case, it is to the advantage to add the gloss:

[Czech] *krátkost* "shortness", [Chin.] *tuan -chan* (temporal)

in order to specify the "temporal" equivalent against. the (absent) "spatial" one.

If only one of a pair of homonyms is indicated in the dictionary, it should in the same way be disambiguated against the absent one.

In this way it happens that entries which do not present any polysemy are nevertheless furnished with glosses. The consequence, especially in very precise dictionaries, is that such a gloss tends to lose its purpose of disambiguation and (or specification and tends more to become an encyclopedic explanation. We read in a Rumanian-Czech dictionary the following entries:[107]

[Rum.] *muezin*, [Cz.] *muezzin* ("Mohammedan")
[Rum.] *muftin*, [Cz.] *mufti* ("Mohammedan priest").[108]

The parenthesized remarks have the appearance of glosses. As there are, however, only Mohammedan muezzins and muftis, we have before us explanations: the rather encyclopedic or at least non-linguistic character of the latter is stressed by the fact that it consists not only of the adjective Mohameddan', but also of the noun priest.

Opinion may differ on the advisability of such remarks. The very strictest method would disagree with them, as they are undoubtedly of an encyclopedic, not linguistic character. But on the other hand, if they are neither too long nor too frequent, they may considerably enhance the user's comprehension of words which may have excellent, absolute equivalents, but which he may ignore both in the source language and in the target language, irrespective of which is his native one.

The Latin terminology which is added in some dictionaries to the botanical and zoological (and only rarely to other) terms can be regarded as belonging here. To some extent, these glosses disambiguate the meaning; so, for example, if an equivalent of Eng. *flax* is sought, it may appear that there are different equivalents according to the different species of flax: the Latin term (*linus*...) can be, then, used as the disambiguating gloss. But it is hard to discern this use from those cases where the addition of the Latin term is of a purely encyclo-

---

[107] J. Staca c. s., Rumunsko-český slovník, Praha 1961, p. 607. The entries are only slightly reduced (primarily by the omission of the grammatical indications of the lemmata). The entry-words and the equivalents are not translated, but the glosses (in quotation marks) are.

[108] *Mohammedan* is adjective in the Czech original.

pedic character. Taken on the whole, the non-terminological, general-purpose
bilingual dictionary should try to find, as equivalent of Eng. *flax*, a word
in the target language which has as general, non-terminological a meaning.
Latin terms are thus of value especially if there is no such general word and a
more special term of the target language must be indicated, or if differences in
the extralinguistic world cause that the general term in the source language
and its equivalent in the target language are used also specifically in reference
to other species of the same genus.[109]

Device very similar to glosses are the classificatory labels by which the
lexicographer indicates that a lexical unit belongs to a certain dialect, or to a
restricted language (technical, terminological) or to a social stratum (argot),
to a stylistic level, etc. The whole sphere of the variation of language and much
of the sphere of connotation is covered by these classificatory labels. There are
two basic differences between these labels and the specifying glosses. The first
difference is formal; whereas the form of the glosses is free and can vary from
one partial equivalent and one entry to another, according to the lexicographer's decision, the number and the form ot the labels must be decided upon
before the main work on the dictionary itself begins.[110] Many labels are well-
known, e.g. *astr(onomy)*, *bot(any)*, *geogr(aphy)*, etc.; *obs(olete)*,[111] *lit(erary)*,
coll(oquial), *vulg(ar)*; *slang*, etc.; *dial(ectal)*, etc. It is impossible to give a list
of all possible labels; at the beginning of his work, the lexicographer must
analyze the two languages on all the axes of their variation and must decide
which labels he will use. This repertory of labels should then be used in the
whole dictionary in the most uniform possible way.

The second difference pertains to the purpose: while the semantic glosses
always disambiguate and (or specify parts of the lexical meaning (otherwise
they turn into encyclopedic explanations), the labels only sometimes disambiguate and (or specify, but very frequently, if not even in the majority of
cases, they simply inform the user about a descriptive fact of language.[112]

---

[109] The point is admittedly controversial. For instance, I. J. Gelb (private communication)
pleads strongly for the Latin terms.

[110] If the lexicographer is not sure that his decisions in this respect are definitive, he should
develop such a system of labels (and of the underlying categories) that a development of his ideas
will cause only some further specification, not real change of the system. In other words, he
should not commit himself to over detailed specificities.

[111] Labels like *obsolete*, *archaic* should be handled with care.

[112] Some dictionaries use also the abbreviation *transf(erred)* (or similar forms). Unless the
dictionary is based on the historical principle and unless it intends to indicate rather systematically
which senses are transferred (and which, by contrast, are not), the qualification of a sense as
transferred is useful if it disambiguates the polysemy, and especially if the different senses
require different equivalents. E.g., the meaning of the Eng. idiomatic expression *to conquer the
field* can be conceived as (1) "to win the battle", (2) "to win the dispute"; since these senses require
different Russian equivalents, it is possible to write, in a Engl.-Russ. dictionary: [Eng.] *to conquer*

For instance, if we write, in an English-Russian dictionary[113]

[Eng.] *perfect* (adj.), [Russ.] (1) *soveršennyj*, *ideal'nyj*
(2) gram. *perfektnyj*,

the label *gram.* specifies that Russ. *perfektnyj* is to be considered equivalent of Eng. *perfect* only if used as a grammatical term.

If we write, in a Russian-English dictionary[114] the entry

[Russ.] *percepcija*, [Eng.] (philos.) *perception*,

the label disambiguates the meaning: the English term can be used also as a general, if "high-brow" word, not as a member of a terminological set, and then without the terminological precision. Therefore, this can be taken as a case of disambiguation against what is not included in the dictionary.

But if we write entries[114] like

[Russ.] *persul'fat*, [Eng.] (chem.) *persulphate*
perkhlorat,   (chem.) *perchlorate*,

we give the user a descriptive indication, but neither disambiguate nor specify the meaning.

The same can be maintained about entries[115] of the type

[Oss.] *xämxittä*, [Russ.] (v̌ulg.) *morda* "mug (ugly face)".

One vulgar word is indicated as the (absolute) equivalent of another vulgar word. Therefore, under the principle of translational equivalence, their mere indication without any label could be considered sufficient. It would suffice to indicate merely the equivalent, if the mere understanding of Ossetic texts were the only aim of the dictionary. But few lexicographers do not give these labels, irrespective of the dictionary's itention: even for the understanding of texts, the explicit descriptive indication of the style-level, etc., is also of high importance.

In any case, a correct selection of these labels and their proper use is one of the most important tasks of the lexicographer, primarily for the description of the source language or for the generation of texts in the target language.

The question arises as to where these glosses (eventually explanations) and labels should be placed and in which language they should be couched.

---

the field, [Russ.] "oderžat' pobedu", (transf.) "vzjat' verx v spore" (cf. Mjuller *anglo-russ. slovar'*, Moskva 1963, p. 378). Although the abbreviation has the form of a label (just by being a uniform abbreviation), it is basically a gloss, because it disambiguates the meaning. The difference is that other glosses specifically state the criterial feature whereas this one is more general; this is its main advantage, since this generality saves the lexicographer much time; on the other hand, it certainly presupposes much more knowledge on the part of the user of the dictionary.

[113] Reduced from V. K. Mjuller, *Anglo-russkij slovar'*, 10th edition, Moskva 1963, p. 731.
[114] Smirnickij-Akhmanova, p. 420.
[115] *Oss.-Russ. Dictionary*; the Eng. words in quotation marks are a rough translation of the Russ. equivalent.

The general rule is that an indication of the type we are discussing pertains to what precedes, i.e. usually either to the equivalent or the entry word; but an indication that precedes the equivalent and is not seperated from it by a comma or a semicolon pertains to the entry-word. The general disposition of the entry should follows this principle.[116]

There are, however, exceptions which do not allow the application of this general rule. This is primarily the case of the explanations. Should the general rule be applied on the entry quoted above we would get

[Rum.] *muezin* (Mohammedan), [Czech] *muezzin* (Mohammedan).

No lexicographer will be prepared to waste space in this way; therefore, these explanations, if they pertain equally to the entry-word and the equivalent, are usually put behind the equivalent.

On the other hand, a gloss like the one in the Czech-English dictionary entry (see above).

dílo, (profession) *job*

can be taken as specifying both the entry-word and the equivalent; but it is more the entry-word which needs disambiguation, and the gloss somehow joins the two by functioning as an instruction as to when to use the equivalent. Therefore, it is usually placed before the equivalent. (Using this arrangement, the lexicographer has the additional advantage that the place behind the equivalent is free for any other indications which pertain to it.) But there are dictionaries which put these glosses behind the equivalent; if it is for good reasons and done with due care, this procedure can also lead to good results.[117]

Labels follow the general rule: they pertain to what precedes. But since it would simply be a loss of space to write, e.g.

[Russ.] *persul'fat* (chem.), [Eng.] *persulphate* (chem.)

[Oss.] *xämxittä* (vulg.), [Russ.] *morda* (vulg.)

---

[116] Cf. Ianucci PL 204.

[117] Very frequently, the same things can be seen differently from two points of view. For instance, let us imagine we are to compile a French-English dictionary with the intention to help Frenchmen to generate English texts. As equivalents of French *président*, the Eng.-words *president*, *chairman* will immediately occur; but we shall soon find, among many other things, that we should indicate also Eng. *Speaker*, for texts dealing with different British and American legislative bodies. In this situation we can take the point of view that it is a property of the Eng. word *speaker* that should be explained; in this case, the entry would have approximatively the following form

[Fr.] *président*, [Eng.] *president*, *chairman*; *Speaker* (dans le parlament britanique).

But on the other hand, we could reason in the following way: when one comes, in the continuum of the possible references of French *président*, to the reference to British and American legislative bodies, the Eng. word *Speaker* is to be used as the equivalent. In the case, the entry could have approximatively the following form:

[Fr.] *président*, [Eng.] *president*, *chairman*; (dans le parlemant britanique etc.) *Speaker*.

and since they sometimes have the same disambiguating function as the glosses, they are frequently handled as the latter; i.e. they precede the equivalent (or more rarely, follow it):

persul'fat, (chem.) *persulphate*

xämxittä, (vulg.) *morda*

If the labels are thus reduced (one instead of two), extreme care should be given to avoid confusion in those cases where a label should pertain only either to the entry-word or to the equivalent. These cases are rare (and should be rare, because they are against the principle of equivalence), but it happens, say, that for an entry-word with a connotation, there is only a non-connotative equivalent, or an equivalent with another connotation. The Russian word *morda* is more vulgar that the milder English *mug* (*ugly face*). In an Oss.-Engl. dictionary, there would be no other equivalent at hand, and the only thing to do (supposing the word is selected for indication) would be to construct an entry like

xämxittä (vulg.), *mug* (ugly face)[118] (slang).

As far as the language of the glosses, explanations, and labels is concerned, either the source language or the target language can be chosen.[119] As we have

---

[118] We write the explanatory equivalent behind the Eng. equivalent, because only the latter needs disambiguation, the Ossetic entry-word having no multiple meaning. In this connection, we may mention that it would suffice to write.

xämxittä (vulg.), *mug* (slang)

because the meaning of *mug* is disambiguated by the label. With word of this type, however, it is better to add a disambiguating unconnotational synonym or explanatory equivalent to make sure that the user will understand correctly.

[119] There are dictionaries which use both languages, i.e. which give each gloss, etc., twice, but this would involve too great a loss of space. The real difficulty is, however, deeper than that: from the translation of the glosses into the other language new problems of their discrepancies and necessary disambiguation would arise, caused by the unisomorphism of the two languages. — Cf. Harrell PL 53 (a compromise on the question of which language to choose is impossible), and above all Ianucci PL 203 ff. (with rich examples of different practices observed in different dictionaries). Ianucci's main idea, viz. to disambiguate the meaning within the entry of a bilingual dictionary by reference to the number of the respective sense of the word in a corresponding monolingual dictionary, is, however, inpracticable. The main reason is not the vast difference in the tratment and presentation of the multiple meaning of identical entry-words which can be perceived in different monolingual dictionaries of the same language; theoretically, a conventional decision to use only one monolingual dictionary could help in this respect. The main obstacle to Ianucci's proposition is that the equivalents of the target language require, by their own semantics, different specifications and arrangements which are not necessary in a monolingual dictionary. — Some dictionaries use *ideographic symbols* instead of some of the labels; e.g. they label a naval term not by an abbreviation like, for instance, nav. but by the picture of a small symbolic anchor. This practice should be discontinued as it produces texts full of heterogenous

seen above in different connections, the lexicographer must, among other
basic things, decide for which user the dictionary is primarily intended:
either for the speaker of the source language or of the target language. The
language of the glosses, etc. should be that of the speaker for whom the dictionary is basically planned. But as the speaker of the other language can be taken
into consideration, if only secondarily, in other respects, so also in this point:
e.g., those explanations which will not be needed by the speaker considered in
the first place, but are necessary to the speaker of the other language, can be
given in the other language. For instance, in a Russian-Eng. dictionary the
intention of which is to help a speaker of Russian to generate English texts,
the glosses etc. will be in Russian; yet a culture-bound Russian word like
oblomovščina which is perfectly understood by any speaker of Russian but has
no English equivalent, can be explained in English:

> [Russ.] *oblomovščina,* [Eng.] *oblomovshchina, sluggishness, inertness, apathy* (as
> of Oblomov, the Goncharoff character with these
> traits).[120]

EXAMPLES

7.9 Let us return to the fictive Chinese-English entry (discussed above).
[Chin.] *shen -ju,* [Eng.] *to soak (through), to penetrate* (e.g. liquids, capital).[121]

The purpose of the specifying gloss is clear: it shows in what sort of contexts
the Chinese lexical unit is used. The word *liquids* can be considered a gloss
without any further discussion: it is used here as an abstraction, as the hyperonym of all the designations of different liquids; the word *liquid* itself will
occur only rarely in a concrete context. But on the other hand, the word
capital is much more concrete, because it does not seem to have hyponyms:
therefore, it could be considered an *example* of context, exemplifying a case of
a typical combination of words in which the English equivalent can occur.[122]
One difference between a gloss and an example is that the gloss is sometimes
more abstract and sometimes does not consist of a lexical unit; the other

---

elements which both confuse the user and attract too much of his attention. (The point is controversial; I. J. Gelb thinks that such symbols will be more used in the future, just as abstract
marks are used in different other sciences in an increasing number.)

[120] Modified from Smirnickij-Akhmanova, op. cit., s. v.; of footnote 91.

[121] There is no need to stress that the gloss could be placed as well (or even better) before the
equivalents: *shen -ju* (e.g. capital, liquids) *to soak (through), to penetrate.*

[122] Cf. above on the possibility fo reducing, of abbreviating the contexts.

difference is that the gloss should be given in the language familiar to the user, the example naturally in the language foreign to him. Since the first of these differences is not obligatory, and since the second difference can be viewed from various points of view, there is a considerable amount of overlapping between glosses and examples. For instance, we read in an entry of an Eng.-French dictionary[123]

> [Eng.] *to realize.* [Fr.] (1) a) *réalisier* (un projet, une espérance); b) *convertir* (des biens), *en espèces, réaliser* (un placement), *liquider* (sa fortune), *mobiliser* (une indemnité); c) *réaliser* (des bénéfices), *gagner* (une fortune)..., etc.

The French words in the parentheses can be considered either glosses (if it is a dictionary intended for Frenchmen) or examples (if the dictionary intends to help Englishmen to produce French sentences). If it is a gloss, it tells the Frenchmen: the English word *to realize* has a meaning equivalent to French *réaliser* (and can be translated by it) when it occurs in contexts in combination with English words which have a meaning similar to French *projet*; if it is an example, it tells the Englishman: in contexts in which French *projet* occurs, French *réaliser* has a meaning equivalent to Eng. *to realize*, and can be used as its translation.

In this way, the example disambiguates and/or specifies the meaning in about the same way as the gloss. The examples can, however, be used for other purposes which can be broadly divided into semantic and grammatical ones.

As regards the first category, we know from the above discussions that in combinations of words, various semantic effects are sometimes observable from different occasional nuances in concrete contexts to lexically stabilized set combinations like the multiword lexical units and the idiomatic expressions, etc. All of them can be quoted as examples. Different dictionaries stress different categories of examples:

A dictionary which is designed to help the user to produce sentences in the (foreign) target language prefers among the examples the typical, free combinations in order to show the user how to use the equivalent "in a normal way" (unless the task is absolved by rich glosses); the stabilized set combinations and especially the multiword lexical units will frequently have their own lexical equivalents in the source language, and will be indicated in their respective entries; this type of dictionary has practically no use for occasional nuances occurring in texts since it is concerned with the future application in texts that will be or may be generated, i.e. with the normal potentiality.

A dictionary designed to help the user to comprehend texts in the source language will have to indicate, within the limits of its size and the corollary

---

[123] Reduced from Harrap, s. v.

degree of detail, the stabilized set combinations of any sor. If such a dictionary pursues some philological purposes, such as comprehension and exegesis of the texts of some difficult classical or even older authors, it may go as far as to quote and explain concrete contexts, i.e. passages from these authors, and will be interested also in occasional contextual nuances.

A dictionary which intends to describe the source language should be interested in both free combinations (to show what is normal and typical) and in set ones (to disentangle the eventual semantic effects).

Much of what has been said about the examples above (§ 6.5.3.3), in connection with monolingual dictionaries, is valid also in this connection, so we shall not repeat it.[124]

The meaning of set combinations should be dealt with by equivalents and by the apparatus of glosses, explanations, etc., as discussed above.

It is probably not necessary to discuss in detail that a designative lexical group like Russ. *železnaja doroga* (word-forward translation: "iron road") will have its Eng. equivalent *railway*, irrespective of whether it is treated in an entry of its own or in a subentry located within the entry of either of the words, or in both.

In the same way, Eng. *to cloud* will have, in an Eng.-French dictionary, equivalents like *couvrir, voiler, obscurcir; troubler; obnuer; ternir*,[125] but an idiomatic expression like *cares have clouded his brow* will have its own translation *les chagrins out assombri son front*.

A set expression can be quoted among the examples also if it shows no observable semantic effect in the source language, but if it is necessary from the point of view of the target language; above all if it need another equivalent, or another rendering in the target language. Above we quoted the Eng.-French entry

[Eng.] *girlhood*, [Fr.] *adolescence, période de jeunesse*
(d'une femme).

The English locution *in her girlhood* ... shows no semantic effect. Yet none of the French equivalents indicated is a full, translational equivalent of it. Therefore, it is useful to show this in the entry:

[Eng.] *girlhood*, [Fr.] *adolescence, période de jeunesse* (d'une femme); *in her girlhood*: quand elle était jeune fille.[125]

---

[124] Note that if these examples of stabilized set combinations grow into subentries, they must have a lemma of their own, with the necessary grammatical indications and eventually with the pronunciation. — Cf. in the examples: Feldman LS 2, 1957, 86 ff.; Ianucci PL 203 ff. (excellent samples from different dictionaries).

[125] Condensed from Harrap, s. v. only immaterial differences irrespective of where some contested frontier territory belongs.

The eventual necessity of indicating another equivalent for such set expressions which are not characterized by any observable semantic phenomena in the source language is frequently neglected, undoubtedly because the lexicographer is not warned by the semantics of the source language and does not really check the validity of the general equivalents (*adolescence*, *période de jeunesse*) for these cases.

A difficulty can arise with proverbs and similar dicta, if they are indicated among the examples, which can be the case only in the bigger dictionaries. A radical application of the principle of equivalence would require one to indicate not the translation of the proverb, but the really equivalent proverb of the target language. The French equivalent of the Eng. proverb *In for a penny, in for a pound is Quand le vin est tiré, il faut le boire*; the German equivalent is *Wer A sagt, muss B sagen*. But few lexicographers will go as far as that; in the majority of cases, especially if the source language is the foreign one and is in the focus of attention, the lexicographer, unless he omits it at all (and only the biggest dictionaries can afford to quote proverbs), will either give a verbatim translation of the proverb, or explain its meaning, or both: for example, in a German-English dictionary for the speakers of English, the Germ. proverb will either be verbatim translated, "who says A, must say B", or explained, "one should accept the consequences", or both. To use a real proverb of the target language as such an explanation is of use only if it is itself absolutely clear (preferably less metaphorical than that of the source language) and really well known. For example, the meaning of the French proverb *Qui premier arrive au moulin, premier doit moudre*, transl. "who comes first to the mill should grind first",[126] can be explained by Engl. "first come, first served" which is itself a good equivalent.[127]

Let us mention in this connection that such verbatim translations of different expressions are sometimes highly useful if the dictionary is intended to serve some pedagogical or analytically-descriptive purposes. Garvin[128] quotes as an example Kutenai *natanik'nana* "watch" which is used in this "accultured meaning" only and which can be translated verbatim as "little sun". Such verbatim translation should not, however, grow into etymological excurses, if the dictionary is not a historical one.

Idiomatic expressions which are indicated among the examples should be treated by an explanatory equivalent, for example French *revenir à ses moutons*, Eng. *come back to the main topic*. Sometimes it may happen that there will

[126] The French proverb seems to go back to a *sententia* of Erasmus; there are descendants of it in different languages, including an English version which is rather obsolete; cf. A. Arthaber, *Dizionario comparativo di proverbi e modi proverbiali*, Milano 1929, p. 5563.

[127] Cf. Malíková LSB 122 (strict principle of equivalence); Borovkov LS 1, 1957, 143ff. (not only the equivalent).

[128] *Anais* 7; cf. Martin PL 158.

be an equivalent idiomatic expression in the target language clear enough to be indicated as the really translational equivalent; but in the majority of cases, it will not be necessary to give a verbatim translation ("to come back to one's sheep"), unless the idiomatic expression is very unclear and the pedagogical character of the dictionary very much stressed.

These are only some points in which examples can be useful. In reality, any semantic phenomenon, whether in the field of designation, connotation, or the range of application can be clarified by means of examples.

GRAMMATICAL INFORMATION

7.10 Examples are also used for grammatical purposes.[129] We have heard (§ 6.5.2) that the lemma should contain the necessary grammatical indications about the entry-word and that similar indications should follow the equivalents. Besides these so-to-say identifying indications, the dictionary may supply the reader with various other grammatical information about either the entry-word, or the equivalent, or both. This information will be concerned with the way in which the entry-word (or the equivalent) is combined with other words in the sentence; in languages with richly developed morphology, this information will be much concerned with the required forms (e.g. "with dative") and with combinations with grammatical operators (required prepositions, etc.); in languages with poor morphology, the combinatory possibilities will be the center of attention.

The character and amount of the grammatical information is correlated with the intention of the dictionary in an obvious way: a dictionary for the comprehension of the source language can afford (if it is strictly limited in its intentions) to concentrate only upon those grammatical indications by means of which the multiple meaning of the entry-word is disambiguated; the intention to describe the source languages brings with it the necessity of indicating all such grammatical properties of the entry-word, irrespective of whether or not they disambiguate its meaning; and the dictionary which intends to help to generate texts in the target language must give rich instructions on how to use the equivalent.[130]

These indications can have the form of direct quotation of the necessary element;

e.g.:   [Fr.] *regarder*, [Eng.] *look at*
         [Fr.] *chercher*, [Eng.] *look for*.

---

[129] We shall not try draw a sharp boundary between lexicality and grammaticality. The subsequent statements can be used with.

[130] General rules which are stated in the grammatical appendix can be used again.

Or the grammatical indications can be given by a formula;

e.g.: [Lat.] *petere* (1) aliquid ab aliquo, [Eng.] *to ask, to request*

(2) + acc. [Eng.] *to make for, to travel to*

Or the grammatical indications can be given by an example,

e.g.: [Lat.] *petere*, [Eng.] (1) *to ask, to request* (p. pecuniam a faeneratore)
(2) *to make for, to travel to* (p. Romam).

It is not necessary to develop here all the possible combinations and permutations which can be obtained from these types. It is also possible and sometimes advisable to employ them all. A smaller dictionary can use one or the other type in different cases, according to what seems to be more practical; a bigger dictionary can combine them, if need be, and give, for example, both a general formula and an example (or even more than one).

The formula has the advantage that it is more general so that the single concrete cases can easily be subsumed.[131] The example, on the other hand, has the advantage that it is more specific and therefore can be more "telling". Frequently the examples (unless they are direct quotations from texts[132]) are given in a form which implies a certain generality, i.e. in the form of the shortest possible context of the exemplified word which is supposed to be in the canonical form: for instance, Lat. *petere*, examples: *pecuniam a faeneratore*; *Romam*. But sometimes it would be difficult to quote the example in such a short general form; in such a case, the example can have a less general form. Cf. for instance (see above) *cares have clouded his brow*, Fr. *Les chagrins ont assombri son front*; a more general form of the example or even a formulaic expression of the underlying pattern world probably be more difficult to understand than his sentence. But this does not mean that sentences should

[131] The form of the formula is largely determined by the tradition of the language. In the European languages, for example, it is usual to use the indefinite pronouns for the purpose. Still, Martin (PL 158) prefers formulae with a "light-weight algebra" of the type "A shows X to B" to the more traditional type, "somebody shows something to somebody (else)". The preference is largely a matter of the lexicographer's choice; but the user's probable taste should be also taken into consideration. That it is possible to abbreviate or modify the pronouns is a matter of course. They have the advantage that they are correlated to many relevant categories of the respective language. E.g., in the above example, the user would have to get somewhere the information that A, B refer to persons, X to things; or one would have to assume that the user will recognize that inasfar as the verb *to show* usually has, in this sense, a "human subject", A which substitutes for it must represent a person, and consequently also B, whereas X being taken form a different series of letters will represent a thing, *a contrario*. The pronouns have these categories of English implied.

[132] Quotations from texts may have such specificities of their own that they need glosses or other explanations in their turn. This happens above all in big philological dictionaries and is quite legitimate within the type. Cf. Malkiel PL 15.

be freely quoted as examples if it please the lexicographer. Quite apart from the consideration of space, it should be understood that a sentence is always strongly over-specific; much of its content is irrelevant to the matter at hand; for instance in our case, it is quite irrelevant whose brows have been clouded and when the process took place. By this overspecificity, the sentence, or a long, sentence-like example, suggest somehow a restricted validity of what is exemplified. The lexicographer should, therefore, try to exemplify generally valid phenomena by short contexts showing, if possible, only the collocation itself (in free combinations), or the set combinations; this should be done in all cases when it is possible, unless the dictionary approaches the type of a concordance.[133]

ABSTRACTIVE POWER

7.11 Concerning the power, or the validity of indications, it can be said in general terms that all the indications in the entry of a bilingual dictionary are as abstractive as those in the monolingual one; only concrete quotations from real texts are absolutely factual. All these indications will also be used in an abstractive way:[134] to interpret new sentences, or to generate them, or both, and all this in a foreign language at that. The restriction of the validity of the single indications is therefore of the highest importance, because it shows the user the limits within which he can apply or modify the respective indication without committing a mistake, i.e. without infringing upon the rules of the language. We have seen how these restrictions are operated by means of the equivalents and their glosses etc. One of the most difficult problems in this respect is posed by the examples. For example, if we exemplify the English-French (partial) equivalence *realize* = *réaliser* with Fr. *projet*, does this mean that this and only this word is a possible context of *réaliser*, in this sense? Certainly not, since the context *réaliser un plan* is possible. What validity, then, does the example have? Though there is no unified practice, the usual situation is that an example like *projet* is taken as representing also its closest synonyms (*plan*); or of each group of such close synonyms, one example is indicated. Good dictionaries try, however, to suggest by different devices that there are more synonyms or more such groups of synonyms, cf., for instance,

---

[133] Cf. Kratochvíl-Novotná-Štovíčková-Zgusta, Archiv orientální 30, 1962, 275ff.; exemplification in a Czech-Chinese dictionary intended for the generation of Chinese texts problems of generality and of conflicting structure of the two languages.

[134] Let us not forget that even a factual quotation of an actually existing context will, in the majority of cases, serve as the basis of analogical interpretations or constructions.

[Eng.] *inspire*, [Fr.] (1) *inspirer, aspirer* (de l'air dans les poumons)

(2) *inspirer* (un poète, un prophète, etc. une oeuvre)

(3) (into) *inspirer* (un sentiment, etc., à quelqu'un).[135]

Let us now compare (a) a specifying gloss with (b) an example:

(a) [Fr.] *travail*, [Eng.] (profession) *employment, job*

(b) [Eng.] *inspire*, [Fr.] *inspirer* (un poete, un prophete, etc.; une oeuvre).

We see that in this type of restriction, the lexicographer commits himself much more by the gloss than by the example: in the gloss, he states precisely the range of the equivalence: everything that can be called a profession and only what can be called a profession can be subsumed. The example is only a representative of one for many. On the other hand, the example has the advantage that it can convey both the grammatical and the semantic information; the mere indication *petere Romam* gives double indication: that the complement is in the accusative and that it is the name of a city.

On the other side of the scale, it can happen that something is restricted to only one possibility; e.g., a word can be combined with another word only. Phenomena of this type are extremely hard to recognize; they should, however, be indicated in a bilingual dictionary, especially if it is of the generative or descriptive type.[136]

OTHER INFORMATION

7.12 Apart from all these indications, the entry of a bilingual dictionary may give different other information more or less loosely connected with the basic task, i.e. the coordination of the lexical units.

We have mentioned above (§ 7.3) that some dictionaries give different rather encyclopedic information on the milieu in which the foreign language is spoken. This is usually the case in ethnographically or historically interesting situations; but there are also dictionaries which, while not being restricted to the technical terminology of a branch of science, have a slightly encyclopedic approach to scientific expressions (not necessarily only the terms).

To add some information on the etymology of the entry-word is useful only in dictionaries with considerable scholarly interest.[137] Some information on

---

[135] Reduced from Ch. Peliot, *Dictionnaire anglais-français*, Paris 1934, p. 537. Note the *etc.* that follows nearly each group of examples.

[136] Cf. Kratochvíl-Novotná-Štovíčková-Zgusta, op. cit. p. 277ff. on their use of the colon which warns the reader that what follows cannot be changed or modified by the usual analogy, but can be used only as it is.

[137] Yet cf. Malone PL 112.

the lexicalized and the verbatim meaning of different morphemic and word combinations (which can be regarded as sui generis historical, too, is, however, useful also in some description dictionaries; see above, § 7.9.

SEQUENCE OF ENTRIES

7.13 The sequence of entry-words as given by the alphabet of the source language will be the basis of arrangement of the bilingual dictionary, as is the case of the monolingual one. But it is necessary to remember that the source language is foreign to the user (or, if the dictionary is prepared for the speaker to the user (or, if the dictionary is prepared for the speaker of the source language, that speakers of the target language will occasionally seek information in it also). It is, therefore, even more necessary than in the monolingual dictionary to list the more difficult irregular of suppletive forms in their place in the alphabetical sequence, with a reference to the canonical form.[138] Sequences of particles which sometimes, in different languages, are difficult to break into the single parts, should also not be forgotten.[139] The user should be taken into consideration in every erspect; for instance, it is very useful to indicate the usual alphabetical sequence of letters as used in the source language if it is different from that of the language of the expected user.

[138] Cf. Majtinskaja LS 1, 1957, 171.
[139] Cf. Martin PL 155.

CHAPTER VIII

PLANNING AND ORGANIZATION OF LEXICOGRAPHIC WORK

In this last chapter, we wish to discuss cursorily some problems in the planning of lexicographic projects, and some aspects of the organization of work. All these topics are only adumbrated here; a more detailed discussion of them will be found in our *Introduction to Lexicography* (forthcoming).

THE LEXICOGRAPHER'S PERSONAL DECISION

8.1 At the very beginning of the discussion of planning, we shall mention the purely personal aspect of it, viz. the personal decision to devote one's time to lexicography. Each prospective adept of the discipline should know that it is a decision of great consequence for him. Only the excerptors and informants can eventually devote but a smaller part of their time to their tasks. The lexicographer who intends to prepare a dictionary of a small linguistic community which has little or no literary tradition may suppose that one or two field trips will suffice to collect the oral sources and that the editing of the dictionary will also not take a long time; this supposition is sometimes correct, but ist is no exception if the necessary time proves to be much longer than originally planned. And the lexicographer who plans for example a small and purely commercial bilingual dictionary (i.e. one with exclusively practical tasks) of two well-known and well-described, stabilized languages may hope to compile it in one or two years' time, or so. But the normal situation is that the lexicographer, both the member of the staff and the chief of it, should be fully aware that the realization of a lexicographic project takes many years, frequently some decades, and in the case of really big dictionaries, practically a good part of one's life; and more than that, he should also be aware of the circumstance that during those years, all or nearly all his time and mental capacity will be taken up by lexicography; so much will he be absorbed (sometimes against his own original decision) in the endless sequence of various little riddles presented by nearly each card and every entry not to speak about the endless practical problems connected with organization, money, the staff of excerptors and informants, etc., which arise every day. This circumstance contains the germ of possible frustration both for the lexicographer who has started a project supposing that he will be free for other investigations in a few years' time and is then disappointed by further procrastination, and for the young man who becomes member of a lexicographic staff because of the lack of another oppurtunity and because he (wrongly) presumes that this work will leave his mind free and fresh for his own researches in his free time. If it is necessary to combine lexicographic work with other researches simultaneously within one career, it is advantageous if the latter are concerned with problems that are of a rather philological character, or that need many investigations of different utterances, or contexts; i.e., of one activity will be useful to the other. If the themes of such investigations are well chosen, and if neither the lexicographer whose time is thus divided nor his superiors have exorbitant expectations of the amount of output of individual research, such a division of time frequently proves a success.

THE SEQUENCE OF THE NECESSARY DICTIONARIES

8.2 The decision as to what dictionary to plan depends largely upon the situation of the respective language itself, and upon the state of its lexicographic treatment. What interests us most here is the sequence of work to be done in the case of a language whose standard national form is not yet (fully) developed and which is spoken by a society whose pattern is changing under the influence of a more modern one. The situation may vary from one case to another, but the broad lines of the strategy could be sketched as follows.

If necessary, probably the first step is a very small dictionary which is concerned primarily with orthographic rules and their application in particular cases of single lexical units.

The next step, then, in the opinion of the present author, is a bilingual dictionary whose target language is the vernacular in question and whose source language is the language through whose medium the respective society comes most frequently and most extensively into contact with modern civilization. In short, the conceivable majority of such dictionaries will be, in our day, English-..., and French-...; the Russian- ... series is well worked out by now (for the languages of the Soviet Union), but there could imaginably besome Chinese- ... dictionaries of this type (for the national minorities of China).

The compilation of a monolingual dictionary of the respective language can then follow, after a considerable number of years.

There may be doubts as to whether the sequence of the bilingual and of the monolingual dictionary should not be reversed. In the situation which we have in mind here, the bilingual dictionary is more advantageous. First, it brings a greater number of people into contact with the cultural patterns represented in the foreign language in question, and thus is increases the number of people for whose activities the development of the standard national form is necessary. Second, such a bilingual dictionary helps more effectively to renove the onomasiological gaps. Certainly, a monolingual dictionary can also try to introduce the necessary terminological neologisms, but it is difficult to find them there, just because they are not generally known. On the contrary, an engineer, or a teacher etc. who knows the technical terms of his field of interest very well in, say, English or French, and tries to write on such a subject in his own language, will easily find the necessary expressions in the bilingual dictionary. Thus the bilingual dictionary is a more effective tool for this purpose than the monolingual one. It should also not be forgotten, that it is difficult and frequently impossible to couch the definitions of lexical meaning, necessary in a monolingual dictionary, in a language whose standard national form is not yet fully stabilized or even lacks many an expression.[1]

In this connection, we may make the following remark. It is quite possible that small series of such bilingual dictionaries will be compiled in adjacent areas at the same time (broadly spaking). In such a situation, much time and money can be spared if the different lexicographers join forces to work out a list of, say, English or French entry-words which will be used by all of them, or if one lexicographer (or lexicographic team) works out a list which is then used also in the other projects. Such a common list of entries can be easily specified for the necessities of the particular target languages.

The preceding remarks should, however, be understood, only in limited application to the situation described; the beginning of the development of the standard national language in a society whose contact with Europe and America is only recent. It should be also understood that such bilingual dictionaries can be only small and of a rather temporary, or even tentative character. Once the standard national language is reasonably stabilized and becomes capable of the task (i.e. can be used in the lexicographic definitions, etc.), a monolingual dictionary of it is a first-rank necessity; really good bilingual dictionaries can the follow.

The program sketched in the preceding paragraphs can observably be completed within half a century, but rarely requires less than at least twenty years.

The problems of languages which develop a modern standard national form in a situation which is characterized by a strong diglossia are not always less

---

[1] Cf. on this subject Gedney PL 230 and Householder PL 279 (the first dictionary should be as general as possible). Isačenko LSB 40f. suggests the following sequence: (1) rules of orthography, (2) a smaller monolingual dictionary, (3) a standard-descriptive dictionary for general use, (4) bilingual dictionaries.

complicated. One can say generally that bilingual dictionaries as conceived and discussed above are not always necessary in this situation. But particular cases are so different that neither a discussion which would be both general and short, nor even generally applicable advice seem possible.

TIME ESTIMATES IN PLANNING

8.3 Lexicography is a costly activity — at least if measured on the scales usual in the humanistic sciences. It is a rather infrequent phenomenon that the lexicographic activities are turned into a self-supporting undertaking (by the mere sale of the resulting dictionaries), though such cases have been known (e.g. the Stephanus family in the XVIth century, and Dr. Clarence Barnhart at present). The usual situation is that funds must be found to finance the project. Contracts with different publishing houses are a convenient source of finances. But though there are many cases of a highly enlightened approach (after all, Dr. Samuel Johnson himself, having been refused by his original sponsor, worked under contract with a group of publishers), it is usually only those dictionaries that promise some financial gain by their sale which are compiled on this basis. Sale success and scientific value are certainly not mutually exclusive; but purely scientific projects are, in the majority of cases, directly or indirectly financed by such institutions as Academies, Universities, Language Boards, Scientific Foundations, etc. Very frequently, the circumstance that a dictionary has been compiled under the auspices of a renowned institution of high prestige adds significantly to its own authority. In any case, when negotiating financial support and when submitting his plans, the lexicographer should be very careful in his estimate of both the necessary time and money.

I certainly do not know all lexicographic projects past and present; but of those I know not a single one was finished in the time and for the money originally planned. The reasons for this need not be discussed here; but let us remark only quite generally that — apart from the universal fragility of human nature — one group of reasons is related to the difficulties of collective team-work and another to the still frequently cherished but fundamentally mistaken idea that lexicography is an activity both simple and mechanical; there is, however, yet another group of much more important causes of delay related with the circumstance that nearly each context has something particular that defies generalization and that (unless we are dealing with a dead language all of whose texts are known) there are always new contexts generated and new semantic effects produced. In any case, Casares[2] analyzes four big

---

[2] P. 272.

dictionaries, namely the *OED*, the *Dutch Woordenboek der Nederlandsche Taal*, the *Swedish Ordbok över Svenska Spraket*, and the Danish *Ordbog over det Danske Sprog*. The comparison of the original time planned for these dictionaries with the time actually spent shows the following results:

OED: planned — 13 y., really spent — 39 y., delay rate 400%;

the Dutch dictionary: planned — 25 y., really spent — 65 y., delay rate 360%;

the Swedish dictionary: planned — 12 y., really spent — 65 y., delay rate 640%;

the Danish dictionary: planned — 12 y., really spent — 49 y., delay rate 408%.

It is easier to form time estimates for smaller projects, because it is more possible to survey the whole necessary work and its problems. Such a time estimate should be based on samples of work: how much time is needed to excerpt a certain quantity of different texts and how much time will, therefore, be needed for the whole excerption supposing a certain number of excerptors, etc. Such tests (and the following time calculations) should be done in all domains of the future work. The fragility of the testing by anticipated samples of future work and of the resulting calculations is obvious, because nobody can sample, for example, the construction of the entry before the material is collected, etc. I would estimate the usual rate of delay against the original plans as 100—150%, with honourable exceptions. In my experience, a more precise time estimate is possible only when the work on the project is somewhere toward the middle of completion, because only then the factors (also the subjective ones, such as the abilites of the members of the staff, etc.) are known.[3]

I discuss all this not in order to discourage the future lexicographer, but in order to warn him to be very prudent in his negotiations with the financing institutions. If there has been too much optimism in the original time estimate and if the financing institution is not very magnanimous, it may prove a nerve-racking business to try to get more money just when the work is verging to the final stages and the lexicographer needs concentration and no interruptions.

[3] Cf. Gleason, *A file for a technical dictionary* (in: Georgetown monograph series on languages and linguistics, 14, 1961), p. 115 (a thorough discussion of precise sampling and calculations). Cf. also the more general discussion of G. Spies, *Leistung, Leistungsvergleich und Arbeitsproduktivität bei lexikographischen Projekten* (in: Spektrum, Mitteilungsblatt für die Mitarbeiter der Deutschen Akademie der Wissenschaften zu Berlin, 14, 1968, 306ff.).

ORGANIZATIONAL AND OPERATIVE DETAILS

8.4 In our day, lexicographic projects carried out by one man can result, apart from exceptional cases, only in smaller dictionaries. The usual situation is that there is a staff of workers, the most important members of which are the editors, or the sub-editors grouped around one or two (chief) editor(s). About the organization of such a staff we shall make only a few remarks (in addition to what has been stated (see above). The main work of the editors is the construction of entries. This work (as all other lexicographic tasks) should be governed if not by explicit rules, then at least by agreed-upon principles. For this purpose, it is necessary to arrange the flow of work in such a way that each (sub)editor is constantly kept informed about the results of his colleagues, at least in samples. It is quite effective if samples of entries as constructed by one (sub)editor are read by his colleagues and if they are compared with the contexts and other material on which the entry is based. A common discussion should then take place in which the conflicting or at least competing possibilities for constructing the entry are analyzed as frankly as possible. This system can be operated on the rotating principle, so that samples of each (sub)editor's work come repeatedly under discussion. The value of this procedure is not only in the circumstance that many a material, concrete error is detected in this way, but above all in that it increases the effectiveness of the editoral staff. The members of the staff are educated to mutual understanding and to the knowledge of their colleagues' attitudes and occasional preferences. But above all, the desired effect of these rotated readings and discussions is the mutual adjustment of the editors to problems and decisions on questions which are not covered by rules or explicitly stated principles.

To take the simplest possible example: There may be an editorial principle that a comma separates two equivalents which are closer synonyms than those which are separated by a semicolon. This is a rule accepted by many dictionaries and very useful in its application. In the majority of cases, the decision as to which of the two marks to apply will be self-evident. Still, there will be a good number of doubtful cases. There is no intrinsic harm in this if one danger is avoided, viz. that one of the (sub)editors will strongly prefer the comma and another the semicolon. To my knowledge, there is no diagnostic and classificatory procedure which would guarantee that two members of the staff working separately on different entries will necessarily and automatically have an identical approach, based on explicit and generally applicable rules, to pairs like *red, purple* :: *green, turquoise*. Should the two pairs be treated uniformly, and if yes, by comma or semicolon? Or are they different? Or does perhaps the different context of the respective entries themselves require a different treatment of the pairs? Given a certain experience, it is possible to answer, in concrete cases, these and similar questions with an approximative precision; but it would be difficult to imagine a rule, i.e. an instruction explicit and detailed enough to make decisions unequivocally uniform even if applied by different people without a previous mutual adjustment of their points of view. The mutual adjustment effected by rotated readings of the worked-out entries and by the dicussions of the motives and reasons which lead to one or another solution should help all the (sub)editors to build a common and shared bulk of experience and therefore also to develop a certain uniformity in their independent decisions.[4] To this purpose, it is also necessary that all the (sub)editors have an intimate knowledge of all the aims, purposes, intentions, etc. of the prepared dictionary, and of its character, scope, etc., so that the particular concrete decisions are always made on the background of the general policy and as its implementation. These rotated readings and discussions can be stopped when their purpose is reached.

We see that the real practice of the lexicographer requires more than the four "steps" discussed above (§ 6.2), viz. (1) the collection of material, (2) the selection of entries, (3) their construction, and (4) their arrangement. The most important modification of this scheme is that in "real life", the third step, the construction of entries, is almost completely done a second time, and steps two and four are minutely controlled at this occasion; which may, alas, cause some partial repetitions of step one.

Practically speaking: the first draft of the manuscript resulting from the four "steps" (the form of which is irrelevant) must be re-read and controlled in considerable detail.[5] If there are one or two chief editor(s) among more suboditors, the logical solution is that the latter prepare the drafts and the former make the second reading. If there are only two or three (usually not more) editors all working on a par, they can rotate and exchange drafts among themselves. In any case, the second reading, or, as some terminologies call it,

---

[4] Kahane-Kahane PL 256 speak about the "mutual education to tolerance", among the editors. This notion is related to the one discussed above, but different. It is based on the observation that idiolects, even those of the lexicographers, differ. For instance, even several Czech co-authors of the present book voiced some dissent with some of the Czech examples used in the text above, though these examples and their treatment are based on the best existing Czech dictionaries and are correct within the idiolect of the main author and other co-authors. The same phenomenon could be observed among the co-authors who had to deal with the Chinese material. The notion of the "mutual education to tolerance" should cover the ability to transcend one's own idiolect (which is taken here in a very broad sense, inclusive the understanding of the passive lexicon). This is very difficult in a language like Chinese, but also not easy in a language like Czech.

[5] This does not imply that it is necessary to finish, say, the letter Z and only the start the second reading. One can begin earlier, but only when work is well progressed (for instance, when one half or more of the entries is constructed) so that it may be safely assumed that really all problems have appeared by that time.

the editing, can be done much more quickly; nevertheless, it should not be a mere reading, but a real control with the use of excerpts, with occasional new questioning of the informants, with comparison of parallel entries, with consultation of other dictionaries, etc.

The second reading must necessarily bring some changes into the draft; they should, however, be only material corrections or modifications of particular entries. Changes within the entries are the most frequent result of the second reading. It may also happen that here and there a whole entry is recast; this can be considered quite legitimate, though unpleasant. It is, however, a major disaster if the second reading shows that it is necessary to change some of the basic principles of the dictionary, such as the decision as to which grammatical categories will preferably be used in the equivalents of a bilingual dictionary, the scope of exemplification, etx. Such changes of policies at this stage should be allowed only in extremely important cases; but they nearly always show that the preparatory deliberations were not sufficient. Even things that must be respected, such as an unexpected but official change in orthography, are not only dilatory in their effect but frequently confusing; for instance, even such a simple thing as a slightly modified orthography, the change of which seems to cause only some mechanical work in the manuscript, may cause some disturbance in the alphabetical order, and this in turn may entail the necessity to re-build the eventual nests. In short, changes concerning single entries are quite legitimate in the second reading, but changes entailing re-reading and re-working of the whole manuscript should be avoided as real calamities, unless time and money play no role in the situation. In the final polishing up of the printer's copy, no substantial changes should be made and all eventual changes should be reserved for the second edition.[6]

Other practical necessities such as the necessity to polish up the whole apparatus of signs, marks, abbreviations, labels, etc. (as they are interspersed through the whole manuscript), to control the cross-references, to control the unity presentation from the beginning to the end of the alphabet (if not held under control, the length of the entries keeps increasing during the elaboration, if it takes some years), etc., or the possibility of putting some particular tasks (for instance, technical terms of different scientific branches and their consultation with pertinent specialists,[7] or orthography, etc.) to the charge of particular (sub)editors, and, finally, the writing and proof-reading of the printer's copy, are things of only minor theoretical importance, though they

[6] Cf. Harrell PL 59f.

[7] The cooperation of these specialists can be very extensive. They can be asked even to work out lists of the necessary terms, to submit definitions or equivalents, etc. The final responsibility must, however, be retained by the lexicographer, because the specialists necessarily deal with their tasks from their own point of view and cannot know the total policies of the project with which they are cooperating. Cf. Barnhart PL 173.

may represent years of hard labour themselves; for the speedy and smooth progress of the work, it is important to have them well organized and well related into a harmonizing system.[8] Such a system usually needs the appointment of one man, i.e. the chief editor (or one of the chief editors), whose right and duty is to decide matters in which no agreement has been reached, such as cases of contested selection of entry-words, etc. A matter of practical character but of great importance is the decision concerning the types in which the dictionary will be printed; this problem should be given attention from the very beginning of work and should be finally decided as soon as the lexicographer begins to construct entries. It would seem that there is no problem in this decision, that the entry-word is simply printed in bold types, the rest of the lemma in smaller italics, the definitions or the examples in normal italics, etc. In reality, it is not an easy task to make all these decisions; they should be made after a thorough consultation with the prospective printer.

THE USE OF AUTOMATIC DATA-PROCESSING MACHINES

8.5 One of the most important decisions the lexicographer will make is whether or not to use automatic data-processing machines.

We shall not discuss here the technicalities of the application of these machines, nor the problems connected with the preparation of material for them, such as the handling of the text on the punch-cards, or its conversion into a code suitable for the computer, or the construction of the program for the machine, etc. All this requires a special study of its own,[9] and usually also cooperation with a real specialist in the field.

---

[8] For a detailed description of a work instruction, cf. Harrell PL 57ff. (Arabic material).

[9] A thorough and concrete description of the application of the "machines" in lexicography is F. de Tollenaere, *Nieuwe wegen de lexicologie*, Amsterdam 1963 and *Die Automatisierung in der Lexikologie* (in: Beiträge zur Sprachkunde und Informationsverarbeitung 1, 1963, 33ff.). A general survey of the field is offered in: *Les machines dans la linguistique* (Colloque international sur la mécanisation et l'automation des recherches linguistiques), ed E. Mater — J. Štindlová, Prague — The Hague 1968. More general but very instructive are the proceedings of the *Colloque international sur la mécanisation des recherches lexicologiques; réalisations récentes et nouveaux équipements*, published in *Cahiers de lexicologie*, vol. 3, 1961. Still more general but indispensable are P. L. Garvin (ed.), *Natural language and the computer*, New York 1963, D. Hymes/ed./, *The use of computers in anthropology*/ in: Studies in general anthropology, vol. II/, The Hague 1965. Practical analyses of real tasks and of their solutions can be found in P. L. Garvin/ed./, *Computation in linguistics*, Bloomington 1966. Cf. also Wahrig, *Wörterbucharbeit*, p. 59f. (a rather optimistic appraisal of the possibilities offered by the computer. The progress in the whole field is so rapid, above all on the technical side, that it is necessary to keep an eye constantly on the developments. From the purely lexicographic point of view, probably the most effective and simple way is to

From the point of view lexicography, one can make the following remarks.

The use of the machines is advantageous above all if (a) great quantities of data are to be handled, and (b) if their handling can be governed by a program every single step of which consists of an unambiguous yes-or-no answer or choice, or of a chain of such answers.

The obvious consequence of this is that lexical data are the more reducible to handling by machines the more we are dealing with the form and with things that are in a one-to-one correlation with the observable properties of the form. Therefore, it is expecially big indices and concordances that can be compiled with the help of the machine which can be programmed to recognize (with negligible exceptions) to which canonical form a word found in the context belongs, and to order the quotations by some formal principle. The first project of this type (and within my knowledge generally the first lexicographic project which used the machines) was Father R. Busa's concordance to the works of St. Thomas Aquinas.

On the same or comparable level of formality are also different reversed dictionaries (such as Juilland's French or Mater's German dictionaries or frequency vocabularies etc., all of which it would now be unreasonable to compile without the machine.

A great collection of contexts can also be advantageously handled by the application of the machine. This application has the additional advantage that the lexicographer can make easy cross-chekings in the whole material. If, for instance, he decides to check whether all neuters of the third declension, or all nomina agentis, or all archaisms, etc., are presented in the same way throughout the whole draft of the dictionary, he can get a list of all the pertinent items very quickly from the machine, instead of making a long search in the files. This is possible, however, only if the necessary information is really in the machine. In other words, if instructed, the machine will very quickly compile a list of all words labelled as, say, archaisms, and only of words thus labelled. Consequently, when the material is being fed into the machine, the lexicographer has to know very precisely what he will require from the machine in future and has to label the data according to his future wishes.

The advantages of such a handling of the material by the machine are so great that one can quite legitimately suppose that vast archives of lexical material will in future be handled only by the machines. It is also quite possible that large academic dictionaries will not be published any more. The point is that even the academic dictionaries which consist of ten, twenty, or any number of volumes do not and cannot present the whole material contained

follow the *Cahiers de lexicologie*, especially the reports on new projects and techniques published there. Cf., for example, H. Josselson, *Automatization of Lexicography*, Cahiers 9, 1966, 73 ff.; J. Kohout, Jazykovědné aktuality 2, 1965, 2/3, 39 ff.

in the archive of the contexts, i.e. in the slips with the quotations (the exceptions to this are again some of the thesauri of the dead languages; but not even
the *Thesaurus Linguae Latinae* presents all the quotations in which a word
occurs). The result of this circumstance is that a really deep study of a lexical
unit cannot be founded merely on the material presented in the academic
dictionary, but that a search in the archive is necessary. But if this is so, then
why publish a twenty-volume reduction of the material if a one, two, or
four-volume reduction could suffice for the first information, which must
eventually be followed by the archive search, in any case? This consideration
seems to be the more valid in that the machines make such a search quick
and easy. It seems that the first project which heads in this direction is
P. Imbs' *Trésor de la language francaise* at Nancy.[10] It is no idle exercise of
fantasy to imagine the big computerized lexicographic centers of the future
where every change in the lexicon is registered and richly documented (so
richly that even the argumentum e silentio will have a strong persuasive
power) and which will serve as the source for all studies of the lexicon and all
compilations of dictionaries of the respective languages.

If the machine can be instructed to recognize, e.g., the case forms of Lat.
gentem and *gentibus* as both belonging to a lexical unit whose canonical form
is gens, there is no reason why it could not be instructed to recognise that
Lat. *genus*, Greek *génos*, Sanskrit *janas* "kin" (and all the forms of these
lexical units) all belong to Indo-European *g'enos*, though this form is only
reconstructed. The necessary proviso is the same as always; the conditions
under which and the comparative steps by which the choices of the false
possibilities are eliminated and the correct conclusion reached must be stated
in an unequivocal, unambiguous, and exhaustive way. Projects of different
comparative dictionaries can be or are operated on this principle; the more
regular the correspondences of the languages involved, the better the prospects
of good results.

On the other hand, the central part of the lexicographer's work, i.e. the
construction of the entry with the definitions in a monolingual and with the
equivalents in a bilingual dictionary cannot be done by the machine: the
abstractive activity of a lexicographer who is able to cope with the elusive
properties of meaning, with its generality and contextual variation etc.,

---

[10] Chapman, *Lexicography* 16, states that "there is high authority for the view that the day
of the comprehensive general dictionary is over". This view, expressed before the advent of the
machine, coincides remarkably with facts like the decision (dating also from pre-machine times)
to compile not one general *Thesaurus Linguae Graecase*, but several thesauri of the particular
literary genera. The advent of the machine seems to have vigorously fostered this development. —
The fact that the archive of contexts is always richer than even the biggest dictionary is correctly
stressed by Havlová LSB 188, who also discusses the "secondary usefulness" of such an archive
as a source for the history of language.

cannot be reduced to an unambiguous program suitable for a machine. Researches in this direction are going on, not only with respect to lexicography, but also generally in the whole field of mechanical linguistic analysis, and specifically in the domains of machine translation and information retrieval. Some promising success can be registered; for instance, the machine can frequently discern from the disambiguating context which of the homonyms is present in a concrete passage, or which sense of a polysemous word is applied. But the finesse and abstractive power necessary for the core of lexicographic work is not yet reached.

It would seem that progress in this direction can be expected only if the continuum of the lexical meaning is analyzed into its constituent elements; which circumstance adds further importance to the componential analysis and other comparable studies of meaning discussed above (§ 1.7.3.8). It seems, too, that a successful solution of this task would render also possible easier and quicker translation of bilingual dictionaries into a third language.

In any case, it may safely be expected that the technical terms will be the first to yield to such treatment.[11]

When making up his mind as to whether he should use the machines, the lexicographer should also take into consideration the following points. First, the use of the machines is itself rather costly. Second, experience observably shows that application of the machines to material which is not limited by itself frequently somehow pushes the project to a far greater amassing of material than originally planned or than what would probably be collected but for the machine; this eventual effect may render the whole subsequent work more cumbrous (if sometimes richer in the resulting detail), if hypertrophy is allowed.

Third, it seems to be advantageous if the material collected and handled with the aid of the machines is used to more purposes: indexes and concordances; basis for the construction of entries in a dictionary; material for lexicological investigations and grammatical, above all syntactical, studies; and research in machine translation.[12] In this way, the costs are split and the huge material amassed is thoroughly exploited.

These considerations regarding the application of the machines are not of immediate importance to many a lexicographer who will not use them, either because of his own preference, or because of the cultural and economical milieu in which he is living, or because the nature of his project does not allow

---

[11] Malkiel PL 14 expects that the need for restricted dictionaries "of technical terms may soon altogether recede as a result of the invention of the electronic translating machines. This may be especially the case of big terminological dictionaries of rapidly developing scientific branches.

[12] Different variants of the scheme sketched here are the policy of different centers. One of the oldest pioneer conters whose activities are well documented and easily accessible, is the center of B. Quemda at Besançon; see the reports in the *Cahiers* and in the *Bulletin d'information*.

it. It could also be stated that a really massive use of these machines can be expected in the future: at present, the computer (at least in linguistics, including lexicography) is itself still more the object than the instrument of investigation. But it would be wrong to expect the lexicographer's situation to be basically changed by such a massive application of data-processing machines: the lexicographer has been called a harmless drudge by Dr Johnson, and he will not advance to a harmless electrician. The masses of material will be even greater though easier to handle, the authors will be as truculent as ever in their applications of words, and the single particularities of actual contexts will be as recalcitrant to generalization as they are now: drudge he is and drudge he will remain.

CONSOLATION OF LEXICOGRAPHY

8.6 At the beginning of this book, we quoted some voices complaining about the difficulties of lexicography. Their number could easily be increased, and a catalogue of the complaints raised would show that the lamentations concern vastly different grievances ranging from the size of the task to general and systematic underpayment. But lexicography has also its charms and rewards. As antidote against the complaints, let us quote the beautiful and, as I believe, basically true praise of lexicography by J. R. Hulbert:[13]

"I know of no more enjoyable intellectual activity than working on a dictionary. Unlike most research, lexicography rarely sends one in fruitless quests; one does not devote days, months, or even years to testing an hypo thesis only to decide that it is not tenable, or to attempting to collect evidence to prove a theory only to have to conclude that sufficient facts are no longer in existence to clinch it. It does not make one's life anxious, nor build up hopes only to have them collapse. Every day one is confronted by new problems, usually small but absorbingly interesting; at the end of the day one feels healthily tired, but content in the thought that one has accomplished something and advanced the whole work towards its completion."

And with this idyllic, optimistic note we shall bring the book to its overdue end.

---

[13] *Dictionaries* p. 42f. Besides other lexicographic merits, Professor Hulbert was one of the co-editors of the *Dictionary of American English*.

ABBREVIATIONS

Berg, *Report*	s. page 9, footnote 1
Cahiers	*Cahiers de lexicologie*, s. page 12
Chapman, *Lexicography*	s. page 10
Concise Oxford D.	*The Concise Oxford Dictionary of Current English*, ed. by H. W. Fowler and F. G. Fowler, 4th edition, ed. by E. McIntosh, Oxford 1951
Doroszewski	s. page 11
Garvin, *Anais*	s. page 11
Gleason, *Introduction*	H. A. Gleason, Jr., *An Introduction to Descriptive Linguistics*, revised edition, New York 1961.
Harrap	*Harrap's Standard French and English Dictionary*, ed. by J. E. Mansion, London 1939, new edition 1961
Hornby	A. S. Hornby — E. V. Gatenby — H. Wakefield, *The Advanced Learner's Dictionary of Current English*, second edition, London 1963
Hulbert, *Dictionaries*	s. page 11
LS	*Leksikografičeskij sbornik*, s. page 11
LSB	*Lexikografický sborník* (Bratislava), s. page 11
Mathiot	s. page 12
Migliorini, *Vocabolario*	s. page 11
Nida, *Translating*	E. Nida, *Towards a Science of Translating*, Leiden 1964
OED	*The Oxford English Dictionary*, Oxford 1934 ff.
PL	*Problems in Lexicography*, s. page 11
Ščerba, *Izvestija*	s. page 10
SS	*Slovo a slovesnost*
Wahrig, *Wörterbucharbeit*	s. page 12
Webster	*Webster's Third International English Dictionary*, ed. P. M. Gove
Weinreich, *Universals*	*Universals of Language*, ed. J. Greenberg, Cambridge 1963, 144 ff.

ADDENDA TO THE BIBLIOGRAPHY

TO THE CHAPTER III (§ 3.3 SET COMBINATIONS; p. 142)

H. Wissemann, *Das Wortgruppenlexem und seine lexikographische Erfassung*, Indogermanische Forschungen 66, 1961, 255 ff.

TO THE CHAPTER V (THE TYPES OF DICTIONARIES, p. 197)

K. Hjort, *Lexicon, Wörterbuch, Enzyklopädie, Konversationslexikon. Versuch einer Begriffs-erklärung*, Muttersprache 77, 1967, 353 ff.
369 ff.

TO THE CHAPTER VI (§ 6.3.1 EXCERPTION, p. 225)

B. Migliorini — A. Duro, *Norme per la schedatura lessicografica*, Firenze, Acc. crusca 1964 (non vidi).

§ 6.5.3.1 The Lexicogragraphic Definition (p. 252)

L. C. Eksteen, *Die leksikale definisie. 'n Leksikografiese ondersoek*. Diss. Pretoria 1965 (non vidi).

§ 6.6 Arrangement of Entries (p. 282)

L. G. Heller, *Lexicographic etymology, practice versus theory*, American speech 40, 1965, 113 ff.

§ 6.6.1 Alphabetical Sequence (p. 283)

K. Baldinger, *Alphabetisch oder begrifflich gegliedertes Wörterbuch*, Zeitschrift für romanische Philologie 76, 1960, 521 ff.

R. Hallig — W. von Wartburg, *Begriffssystem als Grundlage für Lexikographie*, Berlin 1952 2nd ed. 1963.

TO THE CHAPTER VIII (§ 8.5, p. 353)

J. Bahr, *Zur Neubearbeitung des Deutschen Wörterbuchs. (Von der Exzerption zur der Elektion.)*, Zeitschrift für deutsche Wortforschung 18, 1962, 141 ff. (photographed passages and contexts used in excerption).

L. Dezsö — F. Papp, *Mechanizacija leksikografičeskich rabot i obratnyje slovari*, Computational linguistics 3, 1964, 212 ff.

S. M. Lamb — L. Gould, *Concordances from computers*, Berkeley 1964 (non vidi).

F. de Tollenaere, *Lexikographie mit Hilfe des elektrischen Informationswandlers*, Zeitschrift für deutsche Sprache 21, 1965, 1ff.

H. H. Josselson, *Lexicography and the computer*, To honor R. Jakobson II, 1046ff.

H. H. Josselson, *Automatization and lexicography*, Cahiers de lexicologie 9, 1966, 73ff.

J. Bahr, *Technische Verfahren in der Lexicographie*, Zeitschrift für deutsche Sprache 22, 1966, 96ff.

E. Tellenbach — M. Blumrich, *Lochkarten als lexikographisches Hilfsmittel*, Zeitschr. f. d. Sprache 22, 1966, 140ff.